"Tan and DeFrank-Cole's edited volume is an essential read for anyone interested in gender and leadership. Its chapters range from women's stories of their career journeys, to presentations of important studies, to new explanations of why there are too few female leaders."

Alice H. Eagly, *Northwestern University, USA*

"*Women's Leadership Journeys* is a treasure trove for women at every level seeking to give scope to their talents and reach their full potential. The honest insights the contributors share about their rich and varied paths to extraordinary success teach a fundamental truth: that resilient women who are mindful of their strengths and unafraid to articulate them—and willing to take risks—can transform organizations, institutions and our common culture."

Sally Helgesen, *independent practitioner and author of*
How Women Rise, The Female Vision, *and* The Female Advantage

"Despite a half century of equal opportunity legislation and initiatives, women's representation in leadership positions remains anything but equal. This book offers a wide range of important insights about why such underrepresentation is a serious problem, and how we can more effectively address it."

Deborah L. Rhode, *Stanford University, USA*

WOMEN'S LEADERSHIP JOURNEYS

This volume brings together research from leading scholars with stories from women leaders in diverse sectors to provide insights from their leadership journeys. The book begins with personal stories of women's leadership journeys by chief executive officers, a former U.S. ambassador, a college president, and others. The stories enable readers to make sense of their own leadership journeys by learning about the varied paths to leadership and taking note of key elements such as role transitions, defining moments, identity development, and growth mindsets. Next, scholars discuss novel research that can guide women in navigating their journeys to leadership, including on followership, competition, representation of women in politics, and the role of biology in leadership. This must-have volume offers cutting-edge perspectives and a guide for women to navigate their own journeys to impactful leadership.

Sherylle J. Tan is Director of Internships and KLI Research at the Kravis Leadership Institute at Claremont McKenna College, USA. Her research focuses on women and leadership and evaluation of leadership education programs.

Lisa DeFrank-Cole is Associate Professor and Director of Leadership Studies at West Virginia University, USA. Her research interests include the combined topics of women and leadership.

Leadership: Research and Practice Series
A James MacGregor Burns Academy of Leadership Collaboration

Series Editors

Georgia Sorenson, Ph.D., Møller Leadership Scholar and Møller By-Fellow, Churchill College, University of Cambridge, Founder of the James MacGregor Academy of Leadership at the University of Maryland, and cofounder of the International Leadership Association.

Ronald E. Riggio, Ph.D., Henry R. Kravis Professor of Leadership and Organizational Psychology and former Director of the Kravis Leadership Institute at Claremont McKenna College.

The Future of Leadership
Leveraging Leadership in an Age of Hyper-Change
Michael Genovese

Applied Leadership Development
Al Bolea and Leanne Atwater

Teaching Leadership
An Integrative Approach
Barbara C. Crosby

The Global Hillary
Women's Political Leadership in Cultural Contexts
Dinesh Sharma (Ed.)

College Student Leadership Development
Valerie I. Sessa

Women's Leadership Journeys
Stories, Research, and Novel Perspectives
Sherylle J. Tan and Lisa DeFrank-Cole (Eds.)

For more information about this series, please visit: www.routledge.com/psychology/series/LEADERSHIP

WOMEN'S LEADERSHIP JOURNEYS

Stories, Research, and Novel Perspectives

Edited by
Sherylle J. Tan and
Lisa DeFrank-Cole

Routledge
Taylor & Francis Group

NEW YORK AND LONDON

First published 2019
by Routledge
711 Third Avenue, New York, NY 10017

and by Routledge
2 Park Square, Milton Park, Abingdon, Oxon, OX14 4RN

Routledge is an imprint of the Taylor & Francis Group, an informa business

Library of Congress Cataloging-in-Publication Data
Names: Tan, Sherylle J., editor. | DeFrank-Cole, Lisa, editor.
Title: Women's leadership journeys : stories, research, and novel
    perspectives / edited by Sherylle J. Tan and Lisa DeFrank-Cole.
Description: 1 Edition. | New York : Routledge, [2019] | Series:
    Leadership: Research and practice series | Includes bibliographical
    references and index.
Identifiers: LCCN 2018010330 | ISBN 9780815382010 (hardback :
    alk. paper) | ISBN 9780815382034 (pbk. : alk. paper) | ISBN
    9781351209359 (ebook)
Subjects: LCSH: Leadership in women. | Women executives.
Classification: LCC HQ1233 .W646 2019 | DDC 303.3/4082—dc23
LC record available at https://lccn.loc.gov/2018010330

ISBN: 978-0-8153-8201-0 (hbk)
ISBN: 978-0-8153-8203-4 (pbk)
ISBN: 978-1-351-20935-9 (ebk)

Typeset in Goudy
by Apex CoVantage, LLC

CONTENTS

PART III
Looking at Women's Leadership Journeys Ahead:
Cutting-Edge Perspectives   **193**

ABOUT THE EDITORS

Dr. Sherylle J. Tan is a developmental psychologist and Director of Internships and KLI Research at the Kravis Leadership Institute (KLI) at Claremont McKenna College (CMC), a small liberal arts college in Southern California. Dr. Tan's current research focuses on undergraduate leadership education and program evaluation of leadership development and social innovation programs. Specifically, the research on undergraduate leadership education seeks to establish an ongoing assessment and predictive value of the long-term impact of leadership development and education in higher education through a quasi-experimental longitudinal study. Much of Dr. Tan's research and publications focused on applying developmental theory and methods to understanding the issues of leadership education and development, women and leadership, work and family, and child development.

Prior to her role at the Kravis Leadership Institute, Dr. Tan was Associate Director of the Berger Institute for Work, Family, and Children at Claremont McKenna College. Her research then examined the impact of paid family leave on health outcomes of caregivers and new parents and assessed whether it can help to alleviate the stresses and demands of combining work and family care responsibilities; the influence of workplace factors on maternal employment and mothers' decision to return to work; and the relation of workplace factors on maternity leave and postpartum depression.

Most recently, Dr. Tan is series coeditor of a Sage case-study collection on women and leadership with Lisa DeFrank-Cole. She coedited, with Ron Riggio, *Leader Interpersonal and Influence Skills: The Soft Skills of Leadership* (2014). With Amy Marcus-Newhall and Diane Halpern, Dr. Tan coedited *The Changing Realities of Work and Family: A Multidisciplinary Approach* (2008). Dr. Tan has been an active member of the International Leadership Association (ILA) since 2008 and has served on the Executive Leadership Team for the ILA Women and Leadership Affinity Group (WLAG) from its inception. She was elected chair for 2016. She continues to serve as an emerita member of the WLAG Executive Leadership Team.

Additionally, Dr. Tan has over 15 years of experience as an evaluator and evaluation consultant for nonprofit agencies providing services for children and families in Southern California. Dr. Tan completed her bachelor of arts degree in psychology from the University of California, Irvine, and master of arts and Ph.D. in psychology with an emphasis in applied developmental psychology from Claremont Graduate University. She has received a certificate in leadership coaching through LeAD Labs at Claremont Graduate University and is certified with the Connective Leadership Institute. In addition to her scholarly and professional work, Dr. Tan is a registered yoga teacher and teaches vinyasa and restorative yoga at Pitzer College and The Yoga Unit in Claremont, CA.

Sherylle J. Tan

Dr. Lisa DeFrank-Cole is Associate Professor and Director of Leadership Studies at West Virginia University (WVU), where she has worked since 2007. Prior to teaching at WVU, she worked in state government, serving as Executive Director of the West Virginia PROMISE Scholarship and as Assistant for Policy and Research for Governor Bob Wise. Earlier in her career, she worked at Carnegie Mellon University and the University of Michigan.

DeFrank-Cole received a bachelor of science degree in landscape architecture and a master of arts degree in higher education administration from WVU. She earned her doctorate in higher education administration from the University of Pittsburgh. In 2017, she completed a six-month course entitled the Leadership and Negotiation Academy for Women at Carnegie Mellon University.

She was awarded a Fulbright Specialist Grant to the Kingdom of Bahrain in 2012, where she taught a course on the Principles of Leadership to female students from Bahrain and the Kingdom of Saudi Arabia. She has coauthored several articles and served as co-series-editor, with Sherylle Tan, of a Sage case-study collection on women and leadership. Her work has been published in the *Journal of Leadership Studies*, *Leadership and the Humanities*, the *Journal of Leadership Education*, *Advancing Women in Leadership Journal*, *the Journal of Leadership, Accountability and Ethics*, and *Public Administration Review*, among other outlets.

A longtime proponent of women and leadership, she has been researching, writing, and teaching about this subject since the early 2000s. Taking her research into practice, she was a founding member of the WVU Women's Leadership Initiative and has served on the steering committee since 2012. From 2011–2016, she was a state representative to the ACE (American Council of Education) Women's Network in West Virginia. She has also led leadership development workshops for women who work in higher education in Saudi Arabia. In 2017, WVU awarded her the Mary Catherine Buswell Prize for excellence in the field as it relates to the advancement of women.

She has been an active member of the International Leadership Association (ILA) since 2008. DeFrank-Cole was elected to serve as the 2015 chair of the Women and Leadership Affinity Group (WLAG) in the ILA. She continues to serve on the Executive Leadership Team of the WLAG. Through this organization, she has also contributed to the planning of two conferences about women and leadership in California and New York.

DeFrank-Cole teaches undergraduate courses in the Leadership Studies program at WVU, where she also designed and taught an elective course on Women and Leadership. In addition to leaders, she teaches about followers and the necessary and important partnerships between the two entities. Lastly, she is the co-creator, with Brent Bishop, of the "leader-follower cycle," a model developed to show the importance of exemplary followership and the role it plays in the leadership development process.

Lisa DeFrank-Cole

CONTRIBUTORS

Barbara Barrett, international business woman, pilot, astronaut, diplomat, and philanthropist, served on more than one hundred corporate and non-profit boards in her career. She is chairman of The Aerospace Corporation and owner of Triple Creek Guest Ranch. Through four decades, Barrett has advised Commerce, State and Defense Secretaries and the U.S. Trade Representative. President George W. Bush appointed her U.S. ambassador to Finland in 2008. Barrett earned her pilot's license and instrument rating, and in 2009 she qualified for space flight to the International Space Station. Barrett earned her bachelor of science, master's, and juris doctorate at Arizona State University.

Brent Bishop is a graduate of West Virginia University's Benjamin M. Statler College of Engineering. In 2016, he earned a bachelor of science degree in chemical engineering with minors in mathematics and leadership studies and is currently pursuing a Ph.D. in chemical engineering. Bishop has become an advocate for the study of followership in leadership studies programs. He has also worked to bring his leadership and followership knowledge to the engineering field. As part of this effort, Bishop now provides talks/discussion to engineering students on gender biases in STEM, a topic of conversation not often discussed in the engineering curriculum.

Andrew T. Bolger serves as Campus Minister at College of the Ozarks. His responsibilities support the mission of the college by facilitating leadership development, ethical maturation, character formation, coordinating and designing the service and international mission trip program, organizing and teaching within the chapel program, and instructing within the Biblical and Theological Studies, Sociology and Family Studies, and Philosophy and Religion departments. Most recently, he assumed the role of Director of the Institutional Quality Initiative. Andrew completed his B.A. from John Brown University, a M.Div. from Samford University, and recently, his Ph.D. from Azusa Pacific University.

Jeni L. Burnette is an associate professor of psychology at North Carolina State University. She received her undergraduate degree at the University of North Carolina and completed her Ph.D. in psychology at Virginia Commonwealth University. Jeni's research applies basic social psychological theories to understanding fundamental social issues such as obesity and stigma. She primarily focuses on how mindsets matter for self-regulation and goal achievement across domains ranging from education to health to increasing the science, technology, engineering, and math (STEM) pipeline. Her most recent research aims to understand how to best implement growth mindset interventions.

Athena R. Castro has been the executive director of the Caltech Y, an independent 501c3 organization formally affiliated with the California Institute of Technology (Caltech) since 2000. Prior to joining the Caltech Y, Athena worked in the Minority Student Affairs Office and with the Assistant Vice President for Student Affairs at Caltech, focusing on diversity, outreach, and community service programs. She earned a B.A. in English literature at Scripps College, an M.Ed. at Azusa Pacific University, and a Ph.D. in higher education at Azusa Pacific University.

Jolyn Dahlvig is a part-time instructor of higher education at the University of Louisville, as well as Azusa Pacific University (CA), Geneva College (PA), and Whitworth University (WA). Dahlvig studies the impact of evangelical culture on women's leadership development as well as the identity development processes associated with college students and leadership formation. Dahlvig holds a Ph.D. in higher education from Azusa Pacific University and her MAIS in college student services administration, gender studies, and adult education from Oregon State University. Jolyn lives with her partner, two emerging adult children, a dog and a cat in Spokane, WA.

Connie K. Duckworth Social entrepreneur Connie K. Duckworth serves pro bono as Chairman and CEO of ARZU, the nonprofit organization she founded in 2004, to empower women weavers in Afghanistan. Ms. Duckworth is a retired partner and managing director of Goldman Sachs Group, Inc., where she was named the first woman sales and trading partner in the firm's history. The recipient of numerous awards for leadership, social impact, and innovation, she holds an M.B.A. from the Wharton School and a B.A. from the University of Texas at Austin. She has been married for over 30 years and is the mother of four children.

Elaine Hunchuck DeFrank recently retired from Penn State Fayette, The Eberly Campus, where she was oral historian at the Coal and Coke Heritage Center. From 1992 through 2016, DeFrank interviewed 327 people about their experiences in the coal, coke, and supportive industries. She earned an associate's degree in letters, arts, and sciences from Penn State Fayette at age 69. She was married and raised four children before pursuing her own college education. Entering the workforce later in life, she was able to bring personal experiences as a coal miner's daughter to her position at the Heritage Center.

Jeffrey A. Flory is Assistant Professor of Economics at Claremont McKenna College and founder of the Science of Diversity and Inclusion Initiative, a "living laboratory" of innovators, diversity researchers, and practitioners that designs, tests, and scales new models to accelerate diversity and inclusion in companies and organizations. Professor Flory uses experiments to examine pressing questions on gender differences, diversity in the workplace, inequalities across gender/age/race, and how different incentives affect workplace behaviors. His work helps practitioners achieve their objectives through evidence-based research. He received a B.A. in history from Reed College and his Ph.D. from the University of Maryland.

Sandy L. Hough is Associate Dean of Residence Life and Student Care at Biola University in La Mirada, California; she oversees Residence Life, Student Care, Housing, Student Health Center, and the Learning Center. She received her M.Ed. (emphasis in college student affairs) from Azusa Pacific University and is currently pursuing her Ed.D. in higher education leadership. Sandy's scholarly interests are in the areas of women in leadership, student development, and student success. With 20 years in Christian higher education, she has worked within student life, enrollment management, and academic services.

Crystal L. Hoyt is Professor of Leadership Studies and Psychology at the University of Richmond. Her research interests include female and minority leaders, stereotyping and discrimination, stigma, and cognitive biases. She explores the role of beliefs in the experiences and perceptions of women and minorities in leadership or STEM fields. She examines factors that may buffer individuals from the deleterious effects of stereotypes and discrimination. Her research appears in journals such as *Psychological Science*, *Journal of Experimental and Social Psychology*, *Personality and Social Psychology Bulletin*, and *The Leadership Quarterly*. She has published over 50 articles and book chapters and coedited three books.

Barbara Kellerman, James MacGregor Burns Lecturer in Public Leadership at the Harvard Kennedy School and Founding Executive Director of the Center for Public Leadership, cofounded the International Leadership Association and authored and edited books including *Hard Times: Leadership in America*; *The End of Leadership*; *Bad Leadership*; *Followership*; and *Women and Leadership*. Kellerman has appeared on media outlets and contributed to the *New York Times*, *Washington Post*, *Boston Globe*, and *Los Angeles Times*. Kellerman speaks globally and was named "Top 50 Business Thinkers" (*Forbes.com*) and "World's Top 30 Management Professionals" (ranked 13th by Global Gurus). Her most recent book is *Professionalizing Leadership*. She blogs at barbarakellerman.com.

Karen A. Longman, who holds a Ph.D. from the University of Michigan, is Professor and Program Director for Azusa Pacific University's Ph.D. program in Higher Education. Karen is also a senior fellow with the Council for Christian Colleges & Universities (CCCU), and over the past two decades she has directed bi-annual offerings of the CCCU's Women's Leadership Development Institutes, the Women's Advanced Leadership Institutes, and the Multi-Ethnic Leadership Development Institutes. Karen coedits a peer-reviewed journal, *Christian Higher Education: An International Journal of Research, Theory and Practice*, and edited four books, including *Diversity Matters: Race, Ethnicity, and the Future of Christian Higher Education*.

Susan R. Madsen is Orin R. Woodbury Professor of Leadership and Ethics in the Woodbury School of Business at Utah Valley University. She is considered one of the top global thought leaders on women and leadership and a globally recognized speaker. She authored or edited six books and published hundreds of articles, chapters, and reports. As lead series coeditor for the International Leadership Association's "Women and Leadership" book series, she coedited the first three volumes. Her book, *The Handbook of Gender and Leadership*, is known as a seminal work worldwide. Dr. Madsen serves on boards and committees and has received numerous awards and recognitions.

Joan Marques reinvented herself from a successful radio and television producer and host in Suriname, South America, to a groundbreaking academic entrepreneur in California. She is Dean and Professor of Management at Woodbury University School of Business. Dr. Marques is cofounder of The Business Renaissance Institute and The Academy for Spirituality and Professional Excellence and founding editor of three peer-reviewed journals. Joan has received teaching, research, and outreach awards. She has written more than 150 articles and more than 20 books, including *Ethical Leadership, Progress with a Moral Compass*; *Leadership, Finding Balance Between Acceptance and Ambition*; and *Leadership and Mindful Behavior: Action, Wakefulness, and Business*.

Cindy R. Pace, Ed.D. is a global leadership scholar practitioner with 20 years of professional experience working in health care, biopharmaceuticals, and financial services. Cindy has held various management and leadership roles in clinical research, organizational change, executive development, and diversity and inclusion. She is a lecturer and adjunct professor of organizational leadership. Her research and coaching practice centers on advancing women in business leadership. Cindy received her doctorate in education in organizational learning and leadership from Teachers College-Columbia University, master's in business education from New York University and B.S. in biology from Morris Brown College.

Claudia Raigoza is a product manager for a Fortune 500 technology company in Silicon Valley. Her interest in leadership theory and application was ignited while working for the Kravis Leadership Institute (KLI) at Claremont McKenna College and has grown exponentially with each passing professional and personal experience. Claudia received a B.A. in government and Spanish with a Sequence in Leadership Studies from Claremont McKenna College in 2014 and currently serves as a Kravis Fellow at KLI. She remains an avid student of leadership with a keen interest in research on women and leadership, corporate leadership, social enterprise, and transformational leadership.

Heather Inez Ricks Scott is Director and Assistant Professor of Leadership Studies at Kennesaw State University. She holds a bachelor's degree in Theatre from Agnes Scott College, a master's of education from The University of Georgia, and a doctorate in educational leadership from Mercer University. Dr. Scott's research interests include women and leadership, succession planning, and online teaching pedagogy. She has presented on her research at regional, national, and international conferences and published journal articles and book chapters on women and leadership. She was awarded the University College Faculty Development Award for her research and work in women and leadership.

S. Lynn Shollen is Associate Professor of Leadership Studies and chair of the Department of Leadership and American Studies at Christopher Newport University. Her research interests include identity work and the faculty to administrator transition, identity and perceptions of leadership, leadership identities construction, and teaching about women and leadership. She has published articles and chapters, coauthored the book *Faculty Success Through Mentoring: A Guide for Mentors, Mentees, and Leaders*, and leads workshops on the topic of effective faculty mentoring. Dr. Shollen served as 2017 chair of the International Leadership Association's Women and Leadership Affinity Group and serves on its Executive Leadership Team.

Carolyn J. Stefanco is the 11th president of The College of Saint Rose in New York. Stefanco joined Saint Rose after serving as vice president for academic affairs at Agnes Scott College; as founding dean of the College of Humanities and Social Sciences at California State University, Stanislaus; and after a long career as professor of history at California Polytechnic State University. She has been a board member, committee member, and officer and held other leadership roles in higher education organizations. Her research focuses on the history of women, women and leadership, and global leadership. She speaks and writes about these and other educational issues.

Carrie Stockton serves as Dean of Student Success at Biola University and has worked at the university since 2001. In her role as dean, she provides oversight of Academic Advising (including study abroad), Career Development, First Year Seminar, and Online/Graduate Success. Stockton obtained her B.A. in business/economics from Wheaton College, M.A. in organizational leadership from Biola University and is currently finishing her Ph.D. in higher education from Azusa Pacific University. Her research interests include women in leadership, postsecondary student success, and social justice in higher education. Her dissertation research focuses on male advocacy and mentorship of women in leadership.

Vanessa C. Tyson is associate professor of politics at Scripps College. Dr. Tyson wrote *Twists of Fate: Multiracial Coalitions and Minority Representation in the US House of Representatives*. As an expert on U.S. Congress, policy formulation, race, gender, and social justice, Tyson has been featured in *U.S. News and World Report*, *Sacramento Bee*, *NPR*, *The Huffington Post*, and *The Bryan Callen Show*. She has won numerous awards for teaching excellence. Dr. Tyson has a bachelor's degree from Princeton University in politics with a certificate in African American studies and an M.A. and Ph.D. from the University of Chicago in political science.

SERIES EDITORS' FOREWORD

This is a collection for our time—new empirical findings on women and leadership, deep scholarship, and personal stories challenging old assumptions. In short, this book has it all.

An important question runs through this book: Why does the research show that women view professional advancement as equally attainable but significantly less desirable than men?

The authors tackle this key question and others on three levels: macro (societal), meso (group or organizational), and micro (individual). Using an eclectic array of theoretical perspectives, the reader is richer for their creative and diverse approach: feminist theory, critical mass theory, role congruity theory, leader identity development, identity threat theory, implicit leadership theory, system justification theory, and followership theory.

While assiduously using a women's self-referential approach (including unique challenges of women of color), they do allow a gendered analysis of risk aversion, self-efficacy, competition, and childrearing.

Finally, the scholars do a deep dive and review the impact of motherhood and lactation on leadership, discuss the "Opt-Out Revolution," and even broach the original sin in the U.S.—the "Motherless State"—a country conceived by male Founding Fathers.

The volume is unique in offering the wisdom of five women leaders who discuss the challenges and rewards of pursuing leadership in business, education, and science. It includes a fascinating sui generis three-generation account of how women's leadership is fostered in one author's family over time.

Why is this book so timely? Many of us continue to be in shock from the Electoral College defeat of the first major-party woman presidential candidate in the U.S. to a misogynistic opponent. And in the wake of this election, the powerful #MeToo women's movement emerged.

Our aim in this series is the integration of theory and practice and this book, with current social science findings and an honest accounting by practitioners, is a fine example of this vision. As scholars and activists we need answers and a roadmap, and this collection is a godsend.

Georgia Sorenson
Ronald E. Riggio

ACKNOWLEDGMENTS

The topic and title of this book emanates from the 24th annual Kravis-de Roulet Conference. First and foremost, we want to thank our chapter authors for their excellent contributions to the book and to the presenters of the Kravis-de Roulet Conference. We thank Tiffany Nolasco, Vanessa Romo, Hayley Giffin, and Pema Donyo for their assistance in the production of the final manuscript. Thank you to the Kravis-de Roulet Conference committee, who first brought these ideas together: Tina Daniels (co-chair), Meredith Brenalvirez (your presence is deeply missed), Tamara Duggan-Herd, Sarah Smith Orr, Beth Pagel Serebransky, Leigh Teece, and Sara Thompson; and the Kravis Leadership Institute staff, especially Nancy Flores and Angelica Ferreira, and the KLI students who made the conference a success.

Kravis-de Roulet Conference

The Kravis-de Roulet Leadership conferences, which began in 1990, are annual leadership conferences funded jointly by an endowment from Henry R. Kravis and the de Roulet family. This perpetual funding, along with additional support from the Kravis Leadership Institute and Claremont McKenna College, enables us to attract the finest leadership scholars and practitioners as conference presenters and participants. The 24th annual Kravis-de Roulet Leadership Conference, *Women's Leadership Journeys Revealed: Attributes, Styles, and Impact*, was held in Claremont, California, on February 20, 2016.

Kravis Leadership Institute

The Kravis Leadership Institute at Claremont McKenna College (CMC) is a premier academic center for the promotion and understanding of responsible, innovative leadership. KLI provides unique opportunities for CMC students to develop as outstanding real world leaders in the public, private, and social sectors.

WVU Leadership Studies Program

The West Virginia University Leadership Studies program produces engaged citizens that understand and appreciate diverse leadership perspectives. The program provides opportunities for experiential leadership engagement outside the classroom and encourages students to study abroad to enrich their undergraduate careers.

1

INTRODUCTION

Sherylle J. Tan and Lisa DeFrank-Cole

Women possess all the qualities required for effective and impactful leadership in the twenty-first century (Eagly & Carli, 2007). Women leaders have shown themselves to be persuasive, strong motivators, problem solvers, and mentors (Eagly, Johannesen-Schmidt, & van Enge, 2003). Yet, the journey to leadership for many women is not a simple, linear road. There are various twists and turns, starts and stops, and assorted roadmaps that women must navigate through toward leadership (Hewlett, 2007; Mainiero & Sullivan, 2005).

In 2007, Alice Eagly and Linda Carli proposed the metaphor of the labyrinth, a negotiable yet challenging set of routes and "circuitous paths" that women must take to attain top leadership positions. Eagly and Carli believed that the presence of women in elite leadership positions called for a new metaphor to replace "the glass ceiling" to appropriately reflect the obstacles and diversions that women face as they navigate their path to leadership. Introduced in 1986 by two journalists from the *Wall Street Journal*, Carol Hymowitz and Timothy Schellhardt, the glass ceiling references the transparent layer that allows a woman to see the top job but not the invisible barriers that hinder her advancement to it. While women navigate the rise to leadership, they are inundated with obstacles that they had not seen or anticipated on their way up and hit the ceiling unable to ascend to those senior leadership positions. Those hard-to-see barriers, such as discrimination and prejudice, have been the focus of a substantial body of research dedicated to women and leadership over the past three decades (see Barreto, Ryan, & Schmitt, 2009; Bruckmuller, Ryan, Haslam, & Peters, 2013; Eagly & Carli, 2007).

The glass ceiling is believed to be an outdated metaphor given that women have begun to move into top leadership positions. Women are encouraged to take on larger roles in leadership, as popularized by books including those by

Sheryl Sandberg and Deborah Spar, and we now see women as chief executive officers, business owners, and members of Congress. While some women have broken through the glass ceiling, men continue to "outnumber women in nearly every sector of leadership" (DeFrank-Cole & Tan, 2017, p. 43), despite the fact that women make up half of the American population and are earning the majority of degrees at every level of higher education (Johnson, 2016). For example, women hold about 5.2% of S&P 500 chief executive officer positions (Catalyst, 2017), and while a record number of women (104 in 2017) are serving in the House and Senate, women make up little more than 19% of the U.S. Congress (Center for American Women and Politics, 2016). Furthermore, in the political sphere, we saw in 2016 the first woman nominated by a major political party for the office of the U.S. presidency, but she was not elected.

Whether the glass ceiling has been cracked or broken remains up for debate; however we do know that this underrepresentation of women in leadership does not appear to be an issue of qualification or ability to lead. In fact, there are plenty of qualified women to serve in leadership roles. There is a great deal of research to show that women are capable of being effective leaders and exhibit the traits and skills necessary for complex contemporary organizations and society (Eagly & Carli, 2007; Eagly, Johannesen-Schmidt, & van Engen, 2003; Eagly, Karau, & Makhijani, 1995). A meta-analysis found that women's leadership styles tend to be more transformational and women tend to engage in more contingent reward behaviors than men, styles that are both associated with effective leadership (Eagly, Johannesen-Schmidt, & van Engen, 2003), and other research has supported the effectiveness of women's leadership when rated by others in a variety of contexts (Paustian-Underdahl, Walker, & Woehr, 2014).

The scarcity of women leaders has been attributed to gender role stereotypes people hold along with discrimination and prejudice women often face in the workplace (Eagly & Carli, 2007). While many improvements have been made, the workplace in many ways remains an artifact of the twentieth century. Gender stereotypes, while more subtle than in the past, continue to be a prominent issue for women due to the cultural and historical views of leadership being a masculine trait (Koenig, Eagly, Mitchell, & Ristikari, 2011). These subtle cultural beliefs that inadvertently favor men, referred to by Ibarra, Ely, and Kolb (2013) as second-generation forms of gender bias, impede women's journeys to leadership and hinder their leader identity development. Second-generation bias reinforces the status quo by preventing women from being seen as leaders and role models to other women, thus placing them at a disadvantage from being considered for leadership positions (Ibarra, Ely, & Kolb, 2013).

The impact of these biases and stereotypes plays out in a variety of ways and has implications on women's perception of their own leadership abilities and how they perceive themselves. In a study where women were exposed to leader stereotypes, women performed more poorly and showed lower self-efficacy than those who were not primed with the stereotypes (Hoyt & Blascovich, 2010). Similarly, later research by Simon and Hoyt (2012) found that women who viewed gender-stereotypic commercials preferred a follower role in a leadership task that ensued. The findings also indicated that there was indeed a positive effect on increasing women's leadership roles after viewing media images of women in counter-stereotypical roles highlighting the importance of women as role models for leadership.

The influence of exposure to women as leaders can shape women's beliefs about leadership and its attainability. Research by Dasgupta and Asgari (2004) emphasized the importance of *women viewing women* in leadership positions, specifically finding that the experience of learning about women leaders coupled with seeing women as leaders helped women to adjust and change their gender-stereotypic views of leadership. They found that the exposure to female leaders helped women to interpret their leadership goals as realistic targets for themselves and for other women. One way to enhance women's leadership, in addition to seeing women in leadership roles, is to understand how other women have broken barriers and navigated their way to leadership. Because women's career and leadership trajectories are not linear (Wittenberg-Cox & Maitland, 2008), the journeys women take to leadership are often individual and thus important to understand and reflect upon. This volume not only provides research from scholars to support and develop women on their roads to leadership but also includes stories from women leaders.

Storytelling is an important method for learning and gaining insight into the paths of leadership. Storytelling allows us to make meaning of the world in which we live. It allows us to connect to those around us whose experiences resonate with us.

> Storytelling is a uniquely human experience that enables us to convey, through the language of words, aspects of ourselves and others, and the worlds, real or imagined, that we inhabit. Stories enable us to come to know these worlds and our place in them given that we are all, to some degree, constituted by stories.
>
> *(Alterio & McDrury, 2002, p. 1994)*

Regarding leadership, trust is built through communication (Auvinen, Aaltio, & Blomqvist, 2013) and stories have "emerged as a potential approach in terms of coaching and leadership development" (p. 497). Therefore, using stories as a method to demonstrate women's connections with leadership is a beneficial and legitimate strategy to expose women to female leaders and to support their leadership development. Thus, the chapters in this book provide stories, as well as research essays, to encourage women on their journeys to leadership.

This anthology stems from the long-standing and highly successful Kravis-de-Roulet conference series held in Claremont, CA, and sponsored by the Kravis Leadership Institute at Claremont McKenna College, which highlights cutting-edge research topics in leadership. In 2016, the conference focused on women and leadership and provided insights from women in the field who have made an impact through their leadership journeys. In addition to the speakers from the conference, a richness to this volume is produced by the inclusion of chapters from four past chairs of the Women and Leadership Affinity Group (WLAG) in the International Leadership Association (ILA). The WLAG is the largest interest group in the ILA, with over 1,000 members. These women, combined with renowned scholars and practitioners (including male researchers), provide a compilation of chapters where the authors discuss leadership through the lens of a diverse and well-informed group.

This edited volume explores women's leadership journeys and the remarkable influence women leaders are having on the world. The intent is to join research from leading scholars with stories from women leaders in diverse sectors to provide readers with a guide to navigate their own journeys to leadership. The collection does this through three sections: Women's Leadership Journeys: Stories From Women Leaders, Navigating the Leadership Journey, and Looking at Women's Journeys Ahead: Cutting-Edge Perspectives.

Women's Leadership Journeys: Stories From Women Leaders

In the first section, the chapter authors tell personal stories of their leadership journeys. The variety of stories is what makes this segment of the book so interesting and compelling. As Nancy Adler (2011) tells us, "(p)erhaps one of the most powerful early influences on future leadership success is embedded in the personal stories and behavior" of others (p. 160). You will learn from those who did not hold formal *positions* of leadership and from those who did. Several of the positions highlighted are chief executive officers, members of boards, a former U.S. ambassador, professors, a social entrepreneur, and a female college president. Women use their influence in many ways, and it is important to recognize the diversity of these examples, some of which may not be discussed frequently in the leadership literature. Reading women's stories of leadership will empower others to look at their lives and see examples in their own experiences. Having a broad view of leadership, one not based solely on holding a position of leadership, will demonstrate multiple ways of influencing that were not originally considered when defining the term in masculine ways. "One anomaly is that there are few women in leadership roles, in part the result of our having defined leadership solely in terms of position" (Astin & Leland, 1991, p. 3). This broader view of leadership is especially important to highlight the various ways in which women influence others and should be valued for their roles. The chapter authors in this section share their stories about leadership to enable readers to make sense of their own journeys by connecting to those whose stories resonate with them and to learn about the varied paths to leadership that exist.

To share a less-publicized perspective in chapter 2, DeFrank-Cole and DeFrank discuss the impact of family on one's leadership journey, specifically in a matrilineal context. Also present are the intersections of leadership with gender, class, ethnicity, and education. This chapter calls attention to women who may not have held formal positions but definitely demonstrated leadership attributes and influence. As Barbara Kellerman (2003) states: "a growing body of evidence demonstrates that although women have not generally held formal positions of authority, this is not tantamount to saying they did not exercise power or exert influence" (p. 54). Thus, this chapter highlights women who embodied this description and how they have influenced others. The authors stress the importance of their stories not for merit or for recognition but for the concept of ordinary, commonplace leadership that takes place outside and inside the context of traditional careers.

As a woman who has served in some of the highest-level leadership positions, successful business executive and diplomat Barbara Barrett shares her insight in chapter 3. Writing from the perspective of a senior leader for the majority of her life, she gives a variety of lessons and supports them with practical examples. Since she has had many diverse experiences, which began with enormous family responsibility at an early age, Barrett provides examples as someone who has "seen it all." After her father died, she was the sole source of income for six children and her mother in southwestern Pennsylvania. She persevered, pursued an undergraduate and law degree in Arizona, and continues to believe that education is one of the keys to her success. She has served as ambassador to Finland and the CEO of several corporations and professes "life is what we make of it."

Heather Inez Ricks Scott brings original research to light with her knowledge of women who served as board chairpersons in chapter 4. She examines how resistance and support impact women during the journey to the role of trustee board chair. The findings from this qualitative study offer a firsthand perspective and view of the participants' leadership journeys. Sitting at just less than 20%, the small number of women who serve as chairperson points to the lack of representation at the highest levels in academe. When women have been earning baccalaureate degrees in higher numbers than men since the 1980s (U.S. Department of Education, 1990), this disproportionate number of women in the boardroom gives reason for concern. The experiences of the women featured in this work offer a variety of perspectives on obtaining executive level roles of leadership in higher education. An analysis of the respective leadership journeys provides insightful themes into the ascension patterns of the leaders.

Carolyn J. Stefanco is the 11th president of the College of Saint Rose in Albany, New York. Building on the previous chapter about boards of trustees at academic institutions, in chapter 5, we hear from a person who reports directly to the chair of such a board. As someone who wants to encourage more women to become college presidents, Stefanco gives a firsthand account of what it is like to apply for and obtain such a high-profile position. She states that resilience is a critically important skill not only during the application process but also when holding the job. She gives advice about persistence and how skills learned during the application period are also directly relevant to the public personae one will take on when becoming *Madame President*.

In chapter 6, Connie K. Duckworth, a social entrepreneur, gives us insight from someone who has worked on Wall Street as the first female sales and trading partner at Goldman Sachs Group Inc. After retiring as partner from this high-level career, she turned her sights to philanthropy and to community engagement. She founded ARZU, which means "hope" in Dari, in 2004, and helps Afghan women weavers break the cycle of poverty. In her role as CEO, she is focused on providing a sustainable and profitable model of economic development. Through her leadership lessons, she gives pragmatic advice on how to live life as if it were not a dress rehearsal. From taking risks to seeking feedback and learning how to plan for the near and far terms, Duckworth gives an inspirational message of optimism.

Navigating the Journey

In the first section, we presented stories from women leaders and their journeys to leadership. In the second section, we focus on how women navigate their journeys to leadership. We know that the leadership and career trajectories of women are not linear and that they are heavily influenced by a multitude of factors that impact their decisions and pathways to leadership (Hewlett, 2007; Mainiero & Sullivan, 2005). In navigating their journeys, many women often encounter barriers that have kept them from leadership positions. Much of the earlier research on women and leadership has primarily focused on identifying those barriers. As previously mentioned, discrimination and prejudice are two obstacles that have been largely researched and found to keep women from senior leadership. Understanding the literature on the barriers to leadership has helped inform women and scholars. This literature has allowed scholars and practitioners to develop women's leadership in ways that address the challenges and hurdles they face during their leadership journeys. In Part II, rather than taking us back to barriers for women in leadership, scholars discuss research that can guide women in their own journeys to impactful leadership. By looking at the role of relationships and motivation to lead in career transitions into entrepreneurship; exploring how diverse, midlevel women progress to achieve their leadership aspirations; finding the courage to push through comfort zones and make bold moves; identifying defining moments in self-perceptions of leadership; understanding leadership identity and building a team for mentorship and support; and buffering against leadership identity threat through efficacy and mindsets, women can use this research to navigate their leadership journeys in ways that best fit their needs.

First, Tan and Raigoza identify the complex reasons why women make career transitions and become entrepreneurs. Focusing on women's relationships and their motivations to lead, there is a tendency for them to leave corporate jobs and start their own businesses. Chapter 7 investigates the impulse of women to find work-life balance, while also maintaining their needs for a challenging career. With work-family conflict playing a larger role in the life of working women than working men, they attribute the desire for balance to the prevalence of nonlinear career paths. This discussion includes the role of domestic responsibilities such as caring for children and the elderly, lack of advancement within corporate organizations, and high levels of motivation to lead as considerations that women make as they transition into the world of entrepreneurship. No matter what career path they take, women will continue to support their leadership journeys in ways that may not be conventional or predictable. Because women are relational and motivated to lead, they navigate leadership by making career decisions that support their need for balance along with their need for challenge.

Pace explores how diverse women, in midlevel corporate management, learn and progress toward their aspirations of top leadership positions. Specifically, chapter 8 covers women's perceptions and reflections along their leadership journey, including learning experiences and strategies that were instrumental in their career progression. The chapter provides a background on women in management and leadership, including findings from a qualitative case study with insights and recommendations. The featured research identified four ways diverse women managers learn and progress toward their leadership aspirations and goals: (1) aspiring to become top corporate leaders who lead with impact and influence, add value, motivate others, and influence business strategy; (2) proactively identifying and seizing opportunities in their midst; (3) managing challenging situations and relationships; and (4) accessing diverse company-sponsored experiences. The findings were explored with the context of career progression strategies that these high-potential women adopted. This information has implications on theory building and leadership development for diverse women that contributes to the literature and organizational practice.

In chapter 9, Marques cites courage as being essential to women's leadership journeys. As human beings, we are risk-averse by nature. As women, we have a tendency to stay in our comfort zones as long as we can, even when those comfort zones are not pleasant, productive, or rewarding at all. And when we try to step out of them, there will always be people who tell us why we should stay where we are. Oftentimes, these others want us to stay where we are, either because they are envious of our courage or the progress we might make or because they are fearful about what might happen to us. It may also be that they just want us to hang around because they do not dare to make a bold move. It requires courage to move on when things no longer work out. And that moment comes for every one of us. The chapter author presents COURAGE as an acronym: Choice, Open-Mindedness, Usefulness, Reality-Check, Attitude, Genius, and Education. Each of these concepts is discussed as it applies to fulfilling one's leadership journey in a rapidly changing and continuously challenging world.

Longman and colleagues, in chapter 10, look at the contributors to women's leadership identity development, described by Ibarra, Ely, and Kolb (2013) as an "often fragile process of coming to see oneself, and to be seen by others, as a leader" (p. 62). In this qualitative study, women who attended a four-day Women's Leadership Development Institute indicated that their participation in the institute was a "defining moment" in shaping their leadership self-perceptions and subsequent trajectory. The chapter authors sought to understand "what works" in the formation of women's leadership identity development as a means of informing further research and programming to support women's leadership development. Given that limited research has explored the long-term influence of women's leadership development programs, this qualitative study identifies four dimensions (affirmation, awareness, agency, affiliation) of the institute experience that participants identified as having contributed significantly to their enhanced sense of leadership identity. Further, six impactful components of leadership development programs to advance the leader identity development process are discussed.

In chapter 11, Shollen discusses women's leader identity development as a social-relational process. Women's career progression and development of their leadership practice are enhanced by mentoring, sponsorship, and other forms of support, but women also need to establish and draw upon various types of relationships in order to grow their identity as a leader. Shollen asserts that developing a leader identity cannot be done alone; it takes a team of people and various relationships that provide both support and challenge along the way. Women in particular need to be proactive in building a team that meets their leader identity development needs. This chapter provides practical insights and strategies grounded in a scholarly foundation that can enhance women's ability to build and optimize the impact of their own leader identity development team.

Hoyt and Burnette discuss an approach to buffer against identity stereotype threat for women in leadership positions. Women are often at a distinct disadvantage when serving in leadership roles, especially when leadership legitimacy begins with others perceiving one as a leader. Women are often keenly aware of the pervasive gender stereotypes and are cognizant that others may perceive and treat them accordingly. These stereotype-based expectations of inferiority can be threatening and psychologically burdensome. In chapter 12, Hoyt and Burnette discuss the powerful role of belief systems in shaping how we perceive and act toward leaders as well as how those belief systems influence our leadership behaviors and self-perceptions. Specifically, leadership efficacy and growth mindsets can buffer against the negative responses to identity threats. This integrated approach can inform interventions designed to encourage belief systems that attenuate deleterious threat effects.

Looking at Women's Journeys Ahead: Cutting-Edge Perspectives

At recent leadership conferences over the past two years, we have heard repeated calls for research in new areas that will "move the needle" forward for women and leadership. If we keep replicating studies that have already been done, we will keep learning what we already know. We have a good understanding of such things as the many barriers that prevent women from attaining senior leadership positions such as discrimination, prejudice, and the impact of societal gender norms. Despite having this knowledge, we have seen scant progress in the number of women holding the most senior-level leadership positions. What is it that we do not yet know? This section is an exploration into what may be lying ahead as we work toward a more favorable representation of women in leadership. We definitely need more theories of leadership that incorporate the ways in which women lead. We need to have more interdisciplinary research and we need to know how to take this knowledge into practice. The chapters in this section provide a glimpse into the areas of research that are novel—cutting edge—and may provide additional resources for women to move forward on their pathways to leadership. New research looking at followership as a means to empower women, competition in the workplace, the role of biology in leadership, and the representation of women elected to political positions, along with a call to action, completes this volume to help women through their journeys.

Using *followership* as the foundation on which to empower women, DeFrank-Cole and Bishop present a think piece about the partnerships between leaders and followers for chapter 13. Whether it be through their degree of engagement or through their use of dependent or independent thinking, followers have a substantial role to play in the accomplishment of goals in any organization. If influence without authority is familiar terrain for many women, how can being an "exemplary follower" help women move forward? Advocating seeing more women in leadership roles, the chapter authors hypothesize that one possible way ahead is to teach women the partnering skills necessary to use their influence to affect change in their roles as followers. This is where women can flourish. Women are said to work collaboratively, in teams with a nurturing sense, according to Eagly (Eagly, 2007; Eagly & Johnson, 1990). How can we use these strengths to better understand and to solve problems? It comes first by acknowledging that 80–90% of work that gets done is done by followers (Kelley, 1992). Bishop and DeFrank-Cole created the leader-follower cycle, a model that identifies a pathway where women may become exemplary followers and then, with the help of a sponsor, take on a leadership position. If women utilize the influence they already have to accomplish goals, they will not only feel more empowered but perhaps may be seen as more adept at stepping into leadership roles.

Barbara Kellerman, noted author and scholar from Harvard University, takes the discussion of women and leadership in a new direction with her work in chapter 14. She begins with a brief overview of the gender gap in leadership—which continues nearly unabated, even two decades after the issue first surfaced in politics and the professions. She goes on to enumerate the conventional explanations for why the gap, explanations that increasingly are being revealed as miserably inadequate. The recent research on, for example, the gap in ambition between women and men suggests that something remains excluded from the collective conversation, certainly as it pertains to women and leadership. Kellerman hypothesizes that the lack of representation by women in leadership positions may be biological. There are biological differences between women and men, pertaining particularly to pregnancy, lactation, and parenting, differences that are not irrelevant to women and leadership. To a considerable extent these issues are responsible for the problem, which suggests that to a considerable extent they must inevitably be part of any solution. With this cutting-edge perspective, Kellerman is again causing us to think differently in how to create policies that will remove the barriers and enable more women to take on leadership roles.

Jeffrey A. Flory tells us that unequal representation by women in key areas of leadership persists despite recent advances and large amounts of resources dedicated to correcting imbalances. While discrimination, stereotypes, and human capital differences are all likely to play a role, a new line of research has uncovered another critical factor that is likely to be a major driver of these gender imbalances: men and women can react very differently to competition. The field of experimental economics has shown that, among men and women of the same skill level, men have a tendency to be attracted to situations in which they compete, while women often avoid these situations. This may help explain the relative dearth of women in top positions in public life and in high-profile careers in the private or government sectors, since such positions are typically achieved through competition against others. Chapter 15 discusses several of the major findings emanating from the latest work in this area and explores some of the practical policies and approaches to correcting gender imbalances suggested by this research.

After reading chapters from both women and men who shed light on the cutting-edge perspectives, the author of chapter 16 presents insights about women in the public-service sector. Tyson shares her keen observations from women, especially those from multiracial coalitions, serving in elected positions. Her chapter offers contextual analysis regarding political representation by and for women in the United States, with specific attention paid to the 2016

U.S. presidential election and the defeat of former Secretary of State Hillary Clinton. From there, the chapter focuses on two dynamics that directly impact the contours of women's representation. First, utilizing contemporary events and historical knowledge, the social and political cleavages that impede feminist consciousness among women as a collective are identified. Second, suggestions and alternatives for successfully bolstering a greater sense of feminist consciousness are offered.

Completing the book is a summary by Madsen and Dahlvig. The authors bring together some concluding thoughts on the prior chapters of the book focused on women's leadership journeys and navigating the leadership journey. They emphasize the point that the work of understanding women's leadership needs to continue if we want to see more women join the leadership ranks in all sectors, including government, business, and education. Although many scholars do highlight the global progress that has been made in recent decades in terms of the number of women in top positions (Adler, 2015), Joshi, Neely, Emrich, Griffiths, and George (2015) called this progress "both promising and problematic" (p. 1459). One McKinsey Global Institute (2015) report states that "gender inequality is a pressing global issue with huge ramifications not just for the lives and livelihoods of girls and women, but more generally, for human development, labor markets, productivity, GDP growth, and inequality" (p. ii). Hence, even with some progress, there is still much more work that needs to be done, including along the journeys of women's leadership development in communities and countries across the globe. Research, theorizing, policy changes, and leadership development are all recommended in the authors' call to action.

References

Adler, N. J. (2011). I am my mother's daughter: Early developmental influences on leadership. In S. E. Murphy & R. J. Reichard (Eds.), *Early development and leadership: Building the next generation of leaders.* New York: Routledge.

Adler, N. J. (2015). Women leaders: Shaping history in the 21st century. In F. W. Ngunjiri & S. R. Madsen (Eds.), *Women as global leaders* (pp. 21–50). Charlotte, NC: Information Age Publishing.

Astin, H. S., & Leland, C. A. (1991). *Women of influence, women of vision: A cross-generational study of leaders and social change.* San Francisco, CA: Jossey-Bass.

Auvinen, T., Aaltio, I., & Blomqvist, K. (2013). Constructing leadership by storytelling: The meaning of trust and narratives. *Leadership & Organization Development Journal, 34*(6), 496–514.

Barreto, M., Ryan, M. K., & Schmitt, M. T. (2009). *The glass ceiling in the 21st century.* Washington, DC: American Psychological Association.

Bruckmuller, S., Ryan, M. K., Haslam, S. A., & Peters, K. (2013). Ceilings, cliffs, and labyrinths: Exploring metaphors for workplace gender discrimination. In M. K. Ryan & N. R. Branscombe (Eds.), *The Sage handbook of gender and psychology* (pp. 450–465). Thousand Oaks, CA: Sage Publications.

Catalyst. (2016, July). *Women CEOs of the S&P 500*. New York: Catalyst. Retrieved from www.catalyst.org/knowledge/women-ceos-sp-500

Catalyst. (2016, October). *Women earn more degrees than men*. New York: Catalyst. Retrieved from www.catalyst.org/knowledge/women-workforce-united-states; Snyder, T. D., & Dillow, S. A. (2012). *Digest of education statistics 2011 (NCES 2012–001)*. Washington, DC: National Center for Education Statistics, Institute of Education Sciences, U.S. Department of Education.

Center for American Women and Politics. (2016). *Women in U.S. Congress 2015*. Retrieved from www.cawp.rutgers.edu/women-us-congress-2015

Dasgupta, N., & Asgari, S. (2004). Seeing is believing: Exposure to counterstereotypic women leaders and its effect on the malleability of automatic gender stereotyping. *Journal of Experimental Social Psychology, 40*, 642–658.

DeFrank-Cole, L., & Tan, S. (Eds.). (2017). Reimagining leadership for millennial women: Perspectives across generations. [Special Symposium Issue]. *Journal of Leadership Studies, 10*(4), 43–46.

Eagly, A. (2007). Female leadership advantage and disadvantage: Resolving the contradictions. *Psychology of Women Quarterly, 31*, 1–12.

Eagly, A. H., & Carli, L. L. (2007). *Through the labyrinth: The truth about how women become leaders*. Boston: Harvard Business School Press. Eagly, A. H., Johannesen-Schmidt, M. C., & van Engen, M. L. (2003). Transformational, transactional, and laissez-faire leadership styles: A meta-analysis comparing women and men. *Psychological Bulletin, 129*, 569–591.

Eagly, A. H., & Johnson, B. T. (1990). Gender and leadership style: A meta-analysis. *Psychological Bulletin, 108*(2), 233–256.

Eagly, A. H., Karau, S. J., & Makhijani, M. G. (1995). Gender and the effectiveness of leaders: A meta-analysis. *Psychological Bulletin, 117*, 125–145.

Hewlett, S. (2007). *Off-ramps and on-ramps: Keeping talented women on the road to success*. Boston, MA: Harvard Business School Press.

Hoyt, C., & Blascovich, J. (2010). The role of self-efficacy and stereotype activation on cardiovascular, behavioral and self-report responses in the leadership domain. *Leadership Quarterly, 21*, 89–103.

Hymowitz, C., & Schellhardt, T. C. (1986, March 24). The glass ceiling: Why women can't seem to break the invisible barrier that blocks them from top jobs. *Wall Street Journal*.

Ibarra, H., Ely, R. J., & Kolb, D. M. (2013, September). Women rising: The unseen barriers. *Harvard Business Review*. Retrieved from https://hbr.org/2013/09/women-rising-the-unseen-barriers?referral=03758&cm_vc=rr_item_page.top_right

Johnson, H. L. (2016). *Pipelines, pathways, and institutional leadership: An update on the status of women in higher education*. Washington, DC: American Council on Education.

Joshi, A., Neely, B., Emrich, C., Griffiths, D., & George, G. (2015). Gender research in AMJ: An overview of five decades of empirical research and calls to action. *Academy of Management Journal, 58*(5), 1459–1475.

Kellerman, B. (2003). You've come a long way, baby—and you've got miles to go. In D. Rhode (Ed.), *The difference "difference" makes: Women and leadership*. Stanford: Stanford University Press.

Koenig, A., Eagly, A., Mitchell, T., & Ristikari, T. (2011). Are leader stereotypes masculine? A meta-analysis of three research paradigms. *Psychological Bulletin, 137*(4), 616–642.

Madsen, S. R., Ngunjiri, F. W., Longman, K. A., & Cherrey, C. (Eds.). (2015). *Women and leadership around the world*. Charlotte, NC: Information Age Publishing.

Mainiero, L. A., & Sullivan, S. E. (2005). Kaleidoscope careers: An alternate explanation for the opt-out revolution. *Academy of Management Executive, 19*(1), 106–123.

McDrury, J., & Alterio, M. (2004). *Learning through storytelling in higher education: Using reflection and experience to improve learning*. London: Taylor & Francis e-Library.

McKinsey Global Institute. (2015, September). *The power of parity: How advancing women's equality can add $12 trillion to global growth*. Retrieved from www.mckinsey.com/global-themes/employment-and-growth/how-advancing-womens-equality-can-add-12-trillion-to-global-growth

Paustian-Underdahl, S. C., Walker, L. S., & Woehr, D. J. (2014). Gender and perceptions of leadership effectiveness: A meta-analysis of contextual moderators. *Journal of Applied Psychology, 99*(6), 1129–1145.

Simon, S., & Hoyt, C. L. (2012). Exploring the effects of media images on women's leadership self-perceptions and aspirations. *Group Processes & Intergroup Relations, 16*(2), 232–245.

U.S. Department of Education, Office of Educational Research and Improvement NCES 91–660, National Center for Education Statistics. Digest of Education Statistics. (1990). *Degrees conferred by sex and race*. Retrieved from https://nces.ed.gov/pubs91/91660.pdf

Wittenberg-Cox, A., & Maitland, A. (2008). *Why women mean business: Understanding the emergence of our next economic revolution*. San Francisco, CA: Jossey-Bass.

PART I

Women's Leadership Journeys

Stories From Women Leaders

2

EXPANDING POSSIBILITIES

Matrilineal Stories of Leadership

Lisa DeFrank-Cole and Elaine Hunchuck DeFrank

> But the effect of her being on those around her was incalculably diffusive: for the growing good of the world is partly dependent on unhistoric acts; and that things are not so ill with you and me as they might have been is half owing to the number who lived faithfully a hidden life, and rest in unvisited tombs.
>
> —Mary Anne Evans, aka George Eliot (p. 896)

Leadership, historically speaking, was about families. "For the leadership elite in the ancient world, the fundamental imperative was clear: the long-term preservation and enhancement of one's extended family" (Markham, 2012, p. 1140). In the modern era, leadership is often about maximizing profits in organizations (Markham, 2012), and families are less often discussed. We learn from our families and may be able to identify the genesis of our own leadership attributes by studying them. As will be discussed, leadership occurs in many places and situations, including families, and not just in corporations or in formal settings.

People who hold prominent leadership positions are often discussed and researched, (Parry, 2006), and those people are traditionally men (Catalyst, 2016). Frequently, however, women do not hold the highest-level leadership positions and therefore may not be written about as role models or even seen as examples. Truly, those who hold positions may not even be the leaders. "(T)he person who has an impact upon followers is the leader, and that it is the nature of this leadership impact that we should investigate" (Parry, 2006, p. 25).

In this chapter, we look at leadership as a process of influence rather than a position to be held, which enables women to be seen as agents of change whether they occupied paid positions or not. There is definitely a need for more research on women leaders and their identities (Gilligan, 1996; Ngunjiri, 2015; Sanchez-Hucles, 2010). In addition, Storberg-Walker and Madsen (2017) in The Women and Leadership Theory Think Tank Report 2015 encourage research in several areas, including these: "Using research to legitimize alternative leadership roles; Research on women, not just compared to men; Research on women at the margins; How women lead at the intersections; How women get ready for leadership; and Facilitators of leadership for women" (p. 7–8). Therefore, this chapter addresses some of the gaps and research priorities in the area of women and leadership. At its core, this narrative offers a story of ordinary women—and of their *regularness*. For they, too, have had a hand in developing the world we live in and have contributed to the leadership dialogue through lived, everyday experiences—not through power, position, or financial privilege.

This interpretation of leadership may be considered feminist and builds on the work of Reynolds (2014) in linking feminism with servant leadership. It focuses on "women's practice of leadership" (Reynolds, 2014, p. 38) and "new possibilities for constructing leadership that had been previously ignored" (Reynolds, 2014, p. 39). The researchers agree with Suyemoto and Ballou (2007) that "Leadership *is* informed by gender, race, ethnicity, class, and other social systemic phenomena" (p. 48). Fine (2007) tells us that making a positive contribution and acting collaboratively, with open communication and honesty in relationships, constitutes a style of women's leadership. It is at these intersections that we craft this chapter.

The authors are looking at two women who were not in typical leadership *positions*—but definitely demonstrated leadership attributes—and relating them to a current woman who does hold an academic leadership position. Questions we wanted to answer are these: What can we learn from women who did not have a professional career or who were not paid for their work but did influence others and effected change? Specifically, the researchers of this chapter are investigating the impact of a mother, daughter, and granddaughter—all raised in low socioeconomic status families—and how leadership knowledge was gained and imparted, especially in the era in which each one has lived.

The eldest in this triad (mother) is deceased, and this study was undertaken by the daughter and granddaughter. Others have indicated that learning leadership from one's mother is not new (Adler, 2008; Ngunjiri, 2015), but we have found it is not deeply explored. What knowledge was passed down (and up) to allow a present-day focus on the importance of women's leadership and equality? The authors are shining a light on the importance of unpaid work and nonwork identities as they relate to leadership and cultivating an appreciation of these contributions. The findings point to the use of servant leadership by each of those studied.

In this chapter, the youngest (granddaughter) is Lisa DeFrank-Cole and the older (daughter) is Elaine Hunchuck DeFrank. The eldest (mother) was Mary Vrabel Hunchuck, who passed away in 1994 and did not serve as a researcher for this manuscript. However, transcripts of an oral interview from 1977 were used to glean perspectives in Mary's voice.

The Initial Idea

As an associate professor of leadership studies and as a member of the Women and Leadership Affinity Group (WLAG) in the International Leadership Association (ILA), I, Lisa, spent a lot of time thinking about leadership as it relates to women. But where did it come from—this interest in women and leadership?

As I entered middle age, and my mother, Elaine, was about to turn 80, I began reflecting on how I ended up teaching leadership studies and why I was so interested in this subject. I discovered a newer method of qualitative research known as collaborative autoethnography and began learning more about it. I felt compelled to talk with my mother about her lived experiences and about those of her mother—my maternal grandmother, Mary. There had to be elements in their lives that have impacted my life and my interest in leadership. So began the journey that is outlined in this chapter.

We are inspired by the quote from Eleanor Roosevelt that says (p. 101): "*You must do the thing you think you cannot do.*" It signifies to us that even if one does not think of herself as a leader, she can become one by utilizing her strengths and learning leadership skills through community service. This is in agreement with much of the leadership experiences that we have encountered. To organize our thoughts in this narrative, we begin by identifying how intersectionality and servant leadership were our frameworks. We discuss how we collected our stories and proceed into our individual journeys of leadership. We end by demonstrating how the attributes of servant leadership apply in each of our lives.

Intersecting with Servant Leadership

We have learned from the work of Kimberlé Crenshaw (1991) about intersectionality and how we belong to multiple groups simultaneously. From Patricia Hill Collins (1991) and her concept of black feminist thought, we've learned that those who are marginalized and those whose voices are suppressed also have a lot to contribute to the scholarly literature. We also note that Suyemoto and Ballou (2007) taught us that there is value in learning from those with diverse backgrounds, especially those who were not considered when initial theories of leadership were being developed. It became apparent that our work was at an intersection of leadership with gender, class, ethnicity, marginalization, and education. Therefore, intersectionality frames how we make sense of our experiences. Hernandez, Ngunjiri, and Chang (2015) discuss how the inter-section of multiple social identities, either socially or culturally constructed, can become oppressive for women. Though we could use one of many theories or concepts to study leadership in our tri-generational context, we chose to focus on servant leadership, as it best represents what we wish to convey. Spe-cifically, it captures a positive and hopeful nature that we conceive of mentally as well as practiced physically.

Each of us in this study has demonstrated servant leadership, even though we didn't realize it at the time. Robert Greenleaf, who coined the term servant leadership in 1970, defines it this way: "It begins with the natural feeling that one wants to serve, to serve *first*" (Greenleaf, 1991, p. 13). With our consistent mindset of wanting to do for others and having less interest in power and privi-lege, we embody the principles as described by Greenleaf.

As we looked back to the story that inspired Greenleaf (1977) to create the concept of servant leadership, we were intrigued to reread the segment that highlighted the servant in *Journey to the East*.

> The idea of the servant as leader came out of reading Hermann Hesse's Journey to the East. . . . The central figure is Leo, who accompanies the party as the servant who does their menial chores, but who also sustains them with his spirit and his song. He is a person of extraordinary pres-ence. All goes well until Leo disappears . . . [later] he discovers that Leo, whom he had known first as servant, was in fact the titular head of the Order, its guiding spirit, a great and noble leader.
>
> (Greenleaf, 1977, p. 7)

We liken the experiences in our own lives with those in the story by Hesse. We have found that, much like the stories that inspired Greenleaf to conceive of his theory, we have used our stories to create a link with servant leadership. Green-leaf (1991) notes that meeting the needs of the community is a hallmark of servant leadership. Thus, we share our personal examples of community service in this narrative to demonstrate how each woman in this study can be identified as a servant leader. The use of personal stories made collaborative autoethnog-raphy a good fit for this research.

Documenting Our Stories

Ongoing discussions or conversations of past and current events were recorded over a nine-month period of time in 2016. This iterative process of discuss-ing and documenting between Lisa and Elaine enabled each of us to reminisce about the influences of our mothers. Recalling the memories to understand when and where leadership attributes manifested themselves and how family played a role in this development was critical. Collaborative autoethnography best describes how we worked together to document our stories. Ellis (2004) defined autoethnography "as research, writing, story and method that connect the autobiographical and personal to the cultural, social, and political" (p. xix). In attempting to study women's leadership in one family, this qualitative method enabled the authors to be subjective in their approach when researching themselves. We worked together (collaboratively) and looked at ourselves (auto) in trying to understand leadership by women (ethnography). The approach of using family stories to convey leadership was also an enjoyable process.

Each author reflected on her own life and documented several activities or events that could be defined as leadership using the Northouse (2013) definition: "Leadership is a process whereby an individual influences a group of individuals to achieve a common goal" (p. 5). The activities and stories were revised, contemplated, and discussed with each other. During the discussions, we each looked for common themes of leadership learned from her mother. In addition, we listened to a recorded oral interview and read the written transcripts of the interview where Mary was the one being questioned. Because the eldest in the triad being investigated had passed away more than 20 years prior to the study, the interview and transcripts provided rich data about her and were in her own words. Lastly, artifacts including videos, pictures, quilts, and other memorabilia were collected and reviewed for possible information that could lead to additional information about leadership. Especially regarding the eldest, these artifacts were her legacy of the types of activities she engaged in while not being involved in paid work outside the home.

Lisa's Leadership Journey

BossyPants. The title of that inspired book by Tina Fey could describe me when I was young (and maybe even not-so-young). From the time I was a child, I was interested in being "*the boss,*" and this was before the term was co-opted to empower little girls to develop their leadership skills. I was precocious—I couldn't wait to go to school. I was the recipient of endless love and attention by virtue of being the youngest girl in a combined (maternal and paternal) family totaling 37 first cousins. When my parents were away, I was at the bottom of the hierarchy in terms of leadership. As the youngest of four children, my two older brothers and sister were in charge. I asked my mother whom I could *be the boss of* since all of my siblings were *my boss* in their absence. My mom responded with: "*Pierre. You can be the boss of your grandmother's poodle, Pierre.*" Ok, then— that was something, and I was happy to have a role!

Coming from a large, extended family made up of recent immigrants from Slovakia and Italy, I had a limited view of leadership roles for women. I saw women in the kitchen preparing and serving food. I saw men come into the kitchen and eat, then relax in the living room or on the back porch while the women hand-washed and dried the dishes. I understood that men earned the money through their jobs outside the home, so they had the need for relaxation when they were not at work. My mother's work, however, was never done. She never got to relax from her unpaid job within the home.

As a child in elementary school, I was a dutiful student and enjoyed helping teachers with anything they asked of me. During this time, my father lost his job when I was 9 years old, and it was a particularly difficult time in the family. Due to my father's unemployment and subsequent lower-paying position, I received free lunches at school through the National School Lunch Program. My fourth-grade teacher empowered me to be responsible for myself and for the other students needing lunch tickets. He asked that I hand out the tickets to all the students who required one, including myself. I remember being embarrassed by this handout of food and asked my mother about it at the time. We had plenty to eat in our home, and I was never hungry. What my mother tried to explain was that our overall family income was low, even though we had enough food, and that is why I received free lunches at school. This small leadership role gave a less-than-confident little girl an opportunity to practice responsibility and trustworthiness. I never forgot the teacher who gave me this experience—nor did I forget the dignity with which he treated me.

The combination of old-world family values and immigrant-family Catholicism shaped my views of women as I grew. I love my family and always enjoyed time together (even when cooking and washing dishes), but I was never quite comfortable with the limited leadership roles for women. Seeing my mother as second to my father in the family pecking order didn't make me happy. Why didn't women in my family get to make the important decisions, especially those involving money?

I recall my grandmother's stature after her husband, my maternal grandfather, passed away. She was the head of her own household; she made decisions about how to spend her money and her time as a widow. She was well-respected by many people, and I didn't quite understand why. When she went to church on Sundays, she always wore a dress/suit and a scarf or hat on her head. She was dignified. She emitted a wisdom and confidence that came with her age and many experiences. People would go up to her and give her a compliment, and I remember her telling us "*if one more person tells me I look beautiful, I'm going to start believing them!*"

As I became a teenager, I began to understand more about why my grandmother enjoyed the fondness and respect of others in her golden years. She had earned it in an era before I was born. Over time I heard more stories of the good deeds my grandmother had done for others. Family friends from Ohio came back to their former home place and visited with my grandmother, who was their neighbor years before. They shared in open conversation how Mary had cooked for their family multiple times, sewed for their mother when she was infirm, and empathized when there were struggles in their small, community store. It was not just this family from Ohio but many others who recalled my grandmother's sage advice or assistance. I was struck by their gratitude. This instilled in me that good deeds did not go unappreciated—even years later. I wanted to emulate the service that my grandmother did and have meaningful relationships with people in my own life.

My mother always advocated for her children to obtain a college education. Though she was not able to pursue her degree directly after high school, she encouraged us to do just that. She pushed us to get good grades and one day achieve the dream that she had not realized. So that's what we did. I was able to attend university with the assistance of need-based aid, such as Pell Grants and the Pennsylvania Higher Education Assistance Agency Grants, in addition to some small scholarships and a lot of loans. I also worked every year that I was in college, another benefit of the federal work-study program. On weekends, I would often babysit to earn extra cash. We did not have means, and my financial aid package made it possible to attend college.

In the mid- to late 1980s, I witnessed my mom take Holy Communion to the sick and elderly from the church in a new program she created for the homebound. Lessons on leadership began to take root when I observed that, even without a paying job, one could accomplish goals. Mom did what she was good at and enjoyed—and within the confines of the organization that was dear to her—the church.

In college during the late 1980s and early 1990s, I also became a Eucharistic Minister and lector in my university parish. I led retreats for our Catholic student Newman group and enjoyed the familiarity of the church. I also started to branch out more in college and joined a coed service organization. I enjoyed community service, and there was an overlap in many members of my church group and the service fraternity, of which I was elected president.

One particular service project that I enjoyed and learned an enormous amount from took place during the week of Thanksgiving break in the early 1990s. As president of a service club, I assisted in the planning and execution of a student-led trip to build a community center for a tri-racial isolate group in rural Barbour County, West Virginia. In addition to the coordination of college student volunteers, transportation, and the actual physical labor, I had an opportunity to work with inmates from a nearby prison, Pruntytown Correctional Center. Driving a state van, I picked up a few inmates and drove them to our work site, where they helped build the community center, and then drove them back to prison at the end of the day. My mother was quite concerned, but the prison staff and community center organizers approved this arrangement, so I was fine with the plans. I imagined what it would have been like for me to be in prison and how I would be eager to help do work in the community after being incarcerated. I hoped people would treat me with dignity and respect—so that is what I gave to them. It was an important lesson in empathy, one I've never forgotten. It reminded me of the many times my mother and grandmother had shown empathy to those in need and the impact it had on them. I look back at this point in my life as when I began to see myself in leadership *roles* and not just as a follower or observer. Leaders being able to imagine themselves in another person's shoes is a quality I appreciate and try to mimic. I loved being the leader of a group in which I was so heavily invested—one with service as its mission.

After graduating with a master's degree but before pursuing a doctorate, I was married. The man I married loved me and encouraged me—much like my family had done. But he was entirely different. He was not the grandchild of recent immigrants, nor was he Catholic, but he was the smartest man I had ever met. I could be anything I wanted to be, and he enthusiastically supported me. He also inspired me to learn more about feminism, which I had dismissed out of hand prior to meeting him. But once I started learning more and questioning the role of women in the world, especially in the realm of leadership, I could think of little else. The lens through which I see most things now is gendered and often colored by social class and equality.

It is ironic, then, at the very time in my life when I was becoming a feminist, I wanted to enjoy my cultural family traditions at our wedding. Having attended more weddings than I could count, I always had a good time singing, dancing, and participating in the Slovak rituals, none of which my husband had ever seen. Wedding guests put cash in a satin apron, worn by my sister, the maid of honor, in order to have a dance with me at the reception. After the dance, revelers could take a shot of whisky and have a piece of cake. I tossed my bouquet to one of the *lucky* single women in attendance, signaling it was her turn to be married next. And I wore a garter on my leg that my husband removed in front of the entire group of guests and tossed it to an unmarried man in attendance. It was a time of growth and a time of tradition for me—and I guess life still is. How conflicting it can be! This taught me about being authentic and true to myself in my personal and professional life. It may be archaic, and these customs were certainly not progressive for women, but they were meaningful, especially to the women in my family. Learning to balance the old with the new—keeping some older ways of doing things and blending them with fresh ideas—provides perspective. This is important for leaders so they are not stuck in the past but not too quick to adopt the latest fads. Looking back, my husband and I laugh and think what a good sociological experiment a researcher could do at a wedding having similar traditions to ours.

In my doctoral program, I sought out women leaders in higher education and their stories. I learned that not all women leaders were feminists, a point I found staggering. Before I even knew there were college classes offered on the subject of leadership, I was interested in the topic and was drawn to do research in this area when writing my doctoral dissertation. I spent the requisite time doing a literature review and became even more fascinated with what I read—and what I wasn't reading. There seemed to be a gap in the literature—at that time in particular in the late 1990s and early 2000s—around the pairing of topics including women and leadership. I was especially drawn to Sally Helgesen's books entitled *The Female Advantage* and *The Web of Inclusion*. Also, Carol Gilligan's work, *In a Different Voice*, resonated with me. They got to the point of women and leadership and broadened my understanding.

This was a challenging time for me, as I was the first one in my family to pursue a doctoral degree. As a first-generation, low-income college student, I was nervous about completion and wondered if I was just an imposter. It had not been that long before that I had received free lunches in school, and it was disconcerting to find myself at the other end of the education spectrum earning a doctorate degree.

After completing my dissertation, I worked in state government before eventually taking on a faculty role at a large research university. Being called "honey" and "sweetie" by some of my older male colleagues in state government didn't sit well with me. With an earned doctorate and as director of major, statewide program, I never referred to myself with the title *doctor* so as not to intimidate others. I found that being charming was equally, and sometimes even more, effective than giving people just the facts. Dressing in a feminine way with skirts and heels seemed to garner more respect for me, but I didn't fully understand why that was the case.

I welcomed the opportunity to work on a college campus after being in state government for six years. Coming back to the literature in the area of women and leadership, I was thrilled to find so much more being written and discussed in the second decade of the twenty-first century. The work by Alice Eagly was refreshing, and understanding gender and social norms for women in the context of leadership was enlightening. I better understood why, when I was acting in accordance with my perceived gender norms, that I thought I was being more well-received in state government. I still wondered how I would fit into the world as a woman with strong ethnic/cultural ties and as an educated leader.

It was during this time that mom found enjoyment in preserving the history of the women and men who worked in our region, because she witnessed the coal industry in her own life. The lives of coal barons and entrepreneurs had been well-documented, but the hard-scrabble lives of the laborers and their families garnered less attention. I admired her interest in documenting the immigrants' experiences in our region—and in particular the work of women, who are so often forgotten.

As I recently began to reflect on the activities my mother engaged in—I did a double-take and realized that I am a lot like her. While I couldn't see it when I was younger, she pushed the boundaries by telling the stories of the marginalized, especially women. She was committed to the recognition and growth of people, especially those who had not been acknowledged before. She expanded her possibilities—and she taught me to do the same thing. I now carry the mantle of studying and promoting women and leadership. I feel as though I am compelled to live the life that neither my mother nor my grandmother could live. I have the opportunity to achieve many different goals because of when and where I was born, because I have a doctorate degree and because of the continual love and support of my family. It's not a burden of obligation, but rather an honor, to take what I have been given and do the best with it. I respect the sacrifices my relatives have made for themselves and for me. I pay homage to them by teaching others and working for equality for women and especially women leaders. And to some degree, the writing of this chapter is part of "paying it forward," since I could never fully pay them back.

Elaine's Leadership Journey

I walked a mile to and from elementary school for the first eight years of my education in the 1940s. My sisters and brothers often walked together with me. In addition to students in my grade level, we also had younger children in our class, as there were two grades in the same room. We had a modest library in our classroom, most of the books stacked neatly in repurposed wooden boxes. While my teacher taught the second-graders, I was chosen to read a book aloud to my classmates from the library. I read well and expressed emotion in the stories that I told. This was my first recollection of assisting others.

As I grew up the seventh child in a family of nine children, my father, Matthew, worked as a coal miner, and my mother, Mary, worked in our home. This was the era when "coal was king," when the company owned the mines where the men worked, owned the stores where the miners shopped, and owned the homes in the small communities where miners and their families lived, though by the time I was born, my parents had the opportunity to purchase a "patch-house" rather than rent one in the late 1930s. The term "patch," as it relates to a coal community in Southwestern Pennsylvania, comes from the German word "*pacht*" which means *to lease*. The German word became Anglicized, and many began referring to their coal community as a "patch." These houses were built specifically for mining families to lease (and later to purchase), and there were three different styles to choose from. Ours was a bungalow style—it was small for our family of 11 people, but we made many happy memories there. Rather than having grass all around our home, we planted several large vegetable gardens in the back and side yards to supplement our purchased food. We also preserved many jars of vegetables to be used throughout the winter months.

During my primary grades, I took religious instruction classes, or catechism, after regular school hours in our public school. It was not uncommon at that time for the *public* school and the church to have such an arrangement. As I got older, I went with the Sisters of the Blessed Trinity to visit the homebound. We also visited the Fayette County Home, where I passed out magazines to the men living in the homeless shelter. I later taught catechism at the sisters' cenacle in Uniontown to children unable to attend regular classes at our school.

When I was in eighth grade, the American Automobile Association (AAA) sponsored a program for students to become crossing guards, or road patrols, as we called them. An older student was appointed to watch the other children as they walked along the road for nearly a mile from their homes to Newcomer School and back. A patrol boy or girl wore a white cloth strap across his or her chest and around his or her waist with a silver badge stamped with AAA. My older brother, Donald, was a road patrol boy and was tasked with watching the students. They were supposed to walk alongside the road, as there were automobiles and coal trucks traveling the roadways, and safety was an issue for all students since there were no sidewalks. Another student, Charlie, reported Don for walking *on* the road instead of alongside it, so our teacher replaced my brother with Charlie. When I saw Charlie walking *on* the road and not alongside it, I reported *him* to our teacher, and then I became the patrol girl!

To show appreciation to the students, at the end of the term, the patrol girls and boys were given a bus trip to Pittsburgh, where we saw a Pirate's baseball game. We also visited the Buhl Planetarium, now part of the Carnegie Science Center, and had dinner in the University of Pittsburgh cafeteria. Despite coming to the position via a tattletale route, I took it seriously. It gave me a sense of pride to serve in this role, but I didn't think of it as leadership; it was more of a feeling of contributing to the safety of students. And certainly no one I knew referred to what I was doing as leadership.

I was a freshman at Georges High School in fall 1950, and at that time there was no cafeteria in our building. During the period before lunch I rode with my English teacher to a nearby restaurant to purchase lunches for the faculty members. I purchased meals with their money and delivered them to the teachers who requested one. While I didn't hold a formal job position, teachers asked me to assist them, and I enjoyed the trust that they put in me. I later learned to drive in that same teacher's car, and I was happy he was willing to teach me. Students did not have the opportunity to take driver's education classes at my school in the 1950s.

As a class officer, historian, I sold tickets for dances and worked the concession stands for football games and took the money to a nearby bank the next day. During my high school years, I was the announcer for the assemblies and fashion shows and other programs in our school auditorium. I was named to the National Honor Society, which recognizes students for their excellence in scholarship, leadership, service, and character.

After high school, I was a factory worker in Uniontown. I was married at age 21, and my primary role was wife and mother. I took care of all aspects surrounding the children, paid the bills, and cooked meals from scratch. There was little time for my own interests, as my four children came first. In addition, I also cared for my aging parents, who lived nearby. To earn extra money, I did sewing alterations in my home and for a boutique shop in Uniontown. Because

I enjoyed sewing, I learned to quilt, and that became a shared hobby for my mother and me. My only social outlet was the church.

Circa 1988, I became one of the first female Eucharistic Ministers to serve on the altar at Saint Therese Roman Catholic Church in Uniontown. Due to changes outlined by the Second Vatican Council, or Vatican II (1962–65) in the Roman Catholic Church, women were allowed to serve in more visible roles. Clearly, change takes time, and it took about 20 years before women in Uniontown, PA, experienced these roles in our church. I joined the Catholic Cursillo movement, where I was encouraged to use my strengths and creativity to develop a service project within the church. Due to this involvement, I created a program of outreach to the elderly and asked volunteers to take Holy Communion to the homebound. The volunteers were also asked to do small chores, such as grocery shopping, for the elderly. It was very successful, and I was happy to coordinate volunteers to serve those in need. Again, this is an example of service to others without thoughts of leadership.

I began as a volunteer in 1991 and then became the first oral historian for the Coal and Coke Heritage Center at Penn State Fayette. I had always loved history, and this gave me an outlet in which to speak to many of the men and women who had toiled in this very difficult, dirty, and often deadly industry. Because I was a coal miner's daughter, I collected the stories of coal miners, coke workers, and women involved in the industry during the 100-year period 1870–1970.

After a few years of working at Penn State and in my late 50s, I began taking a computer class, and my mom volunteered to pay for it since she couldn't afford to send me to college when I was 18. She didn't get to see me complete my education, since she passed away on September 28, 1994, at age 89. After 10 years of dedication, I received an associate's degree in Letters, Arts, and Sciences in 2005. Having the highest grade-point-average, I was invited to give the commencement address to my fellow students. I was 69 years old when I completed it, and I am proud to be a college graduate.

As a result of the work of multiple professors, several books were published with the help of the staff at the Coal and Coke Heritage Center at Penn State Fayette. I was a coeditor of two of them: *Common Lives of Uncommon Strength: Women of the Coal and Coke Era 1880 to 1970*, by Dr. Evelyn Hovanec, and *Another Time Another World*, by Dr. John Enman. I contributed to a documentary on coal and coke titled *Silver Cinders*, and it was made available on DVD.

After collecting 327 oral histories of people from the coal and coke industries, I wanted to pay tribute to the individuals who worked so hard to provide for their families, especially in my own neighborhood. I secured donations from local residents in Amend, a community of about 50 families, and had a memorial stone with bronze plaque dedicated to the Amend coal miners and Newcomer coke workers. Amend is where I grew up and still live today, and Newcomer is a neighboring community, about one mile away, where I attended elementary school. The memorial is located on the same grounds as the Amend military honor roll in my small community.

Though I never really conceptualized myself as a leader, I lived my life by serving others. Not until my daughter pointed out to me that what I have done could be categorized as leadership did I even consider it. I believe that my contributions of developing programs for the church, collecting oral histories, and speaking and writing about the work of women and men in my region point to leadership activities.

Memories of Mary and Her Leadership Journey

Born in 1906 in Elm Grove, near Connellsville, PA, Mary was taken back to her parents' homeland in Velbac, near Presov, Slovakia, as an infant. She returned to the United States of America at the age of 3 years, with Slovak being her first language. Since she attended school to only the fourth grade, she did not have much formal education. By the age of 14 she worked as a live-in domestic for a wealthy family in Uniontown. She stayed with the family during the week and returned home on weekends via public transportation. She married at age 16—three weeks before her seventeenth birthday.

Mary would often assist neighbors during times of illness and death. For example, after the midwife left her patient, she was there to comfort a neighbor, her dear friend, who was dying after giving birth to her fourth child. Though mother and baby died, the older children grew up next door and attended school together with Mary's children. Elaine was a longtime friend of the youngest, Nick. Honoring her dear friend, Mary, together with several other women, cooked all the food for his wedding as a gift to the groom and the new bride. He retired to Florida and still keeps in touch and speaks fondly of Mary's assistance.

Not only did Mary do all forms of household chores in her home, including cooking on a coal stove, washing clothes on a washboard, and sewing/quilting, she also assisted with bathing. She did not have a shower in her home, and at that time men did not have showers at the coal mines. As an act of love and service, Mary washed the coal dust from her husband's back when he returned from his shift in the mine. When her oldest son went to work in the coal mine in his late teenage years, she helped him, too. In her own words, Mary describes this act in a transcript from May 1977.

> And I forgot to tell you about the man's bath before the bathrooms came in at the mines. The men would have to come home. We would put a big tub in the middle of the floor and make sure we had lots of [hot] water. And they would kneel down by the tub and we'd have to wash their back. Of course, they washed their face and hands and belly. But when it come to their back we had to wash their back.

> *(Hunchuck, 1977)*

It bears clarification that the hot water provided for the bath was heated on a coal stove. Life at that time was not easy, and no job was beneath Mary. To assist her husband and her eldest son, she scrubbed their backs. She also worked to keep the unending veneer of coal dust on everything in our home at bay and to keep her family and house clean. She provided order in her home. It could not have been easy for her to maintain a household with nine children and two adults, but she did it by keeping regular routines of cooking, cleaning, and praying.

Mary and her husband, Matthew, were both active in their small community known as Amend. People of mixed ethnicities were living there, and one could hear neighbors speaking in foreign languages, as there were many immigrants from Europe who were working in the mines. Mary knew the Slovak language before she spoke English, and she would often translate English to Slovak for the women who did not speak or could not understand the language of their new country.

During the local political elections in the spring and fall, Mary walked through Amend passing out cards with information about a slate of candidates. Having been born before women had the right to vote, she was eager to participate in the electoral process. Not only did it give her a feeling of being a patriotic American, but it also gave her a feeling of participation within her community. With many neighbors having limited access to transportation, she would secure rides for local women to get to the polls and vote. One of the local politicians paid Mary $20 to help campaign in this way, and with that money she purchased herself a pair of shoes.

Mary was also interested in education, though her formal schooling ended when she was quite young. During the Second World War, she took first aid classes from the local Red Cross. These classes enabled her to learn how to bandage someone's wound or to help the infirm. She would use these skills to primarily help her family and neighbors when the need would arise.

In the late 1970s, during the long-term illness and disability of Mary's husband due to a stroke, she sat nearby and tore apart an old quilt she had started 20 years before. To pass the time, Elaine assisted her mom in this quilt remaking process. It was the double wedding ring pattern, which was especially significant since Mary and Matthew were married for more than 55 years. Because she used two different types of fabric when originally making the quilt, the muslin shrunk after washing it and the seams did not lay flat. So she tore apart the patches, and they remade the entire quilt top. In the left corner of the quilt they sewed Mary and Matthew's names and the date of their marriage. On the right side of the quilt were sewn the names and birth dates of their nine children.

After Matthew passed away on June 2, 1980, Mary's sister invited her to come and visit awhile in Pittsburgh, PA. She encouraged Mary to enter the quilt in the Golden Age Hobby Show in downtown Pittsburgh. A few days later they went back to view all the quilts that were displayed and judged. Mary didn't see her quilt anywhere along the wall and thought it was not competitive with all the other beautiful quilts. She was amazed to see her quilt hanging from the balcony with a blue ribbon on it, signifying first place. She cried out "We won, Matt!"

About the time Elaine began volunteering at Penn State Fayette, she encouraged her mother to get more involved with the campus, too. There were always activities happening, and it was a way to include Mary and keep her engaged in the community after becoming a widow. The early to mid-1980s were a difficult time for her as she lost her husband and subsequently three of her adult children. She learned to live on her own, carried her grief, and developed new interests.

Robert Eberly, a local entrepreneur and civic minded philanthropist, initiated an idea in the early 1990s to produce a play in Uniontown about the immigrant experience within the coal and coke industry. Because Eberly knew the industry well from his ownership of several related businesses, he was exposed to the hard work and effort of the laborers and wanted to highlight their lived experiences. He convened a group of stakeholders, including professors at Penn State Fayette, to create a stage play entitled *Streets of Gold*.

Since Penn State Fayette had faculty members teaching about the local industries, an English professor who was teaching a humanities class was part of the stakeholder's group. Being a distant cousin, she called Mary for information about an early twentieth-century mining family. Since our family lived the immigrant experience and worked in the coal mines, the cousin knew that Mary could provide additional details. Elaine drove Mary to the meeting (Mary never learned to drive) and met several key players. The stakeholders contracted with playwright, author, and screenwriter Tom DeTitta, from West Virginia, to write the stage play about the European immigrant experience. Frank Lewin, a music professor at Yale School of Music and at Columbia University School of the Arts, wrote the musical score, and mom served as a primary source for this play.

Mary provided many details including what clothing was worn, what food was eaten, and even what songs were sung at a traditional Slovak wedding. Already in her 80s, she had a keen memory and enjoyed being called upon to share her knowledge. She relished hosting Frank Lewin at her home and cooking traditional food for him. Frank, a Jewish man who was born in Germany and whose family escaped from the ravages of World War II, loved Mary's traditional meal. She also sang some folk songs for him so he could write the musical score for the wedding scene. He was deeply interested in our family, and it was a pleasure to work with him.

Though Mary never held a formal position of leadership, nor did she have much education, she absolutely made an impact in her lifetime. She raised nine children, maintained a home and family, and campaigned for political elections, and later in life recalled important historical aspects to inform a stage play. Looking back at her life it is clear that Mary worked with others to achieve a common goal—and that is a definition of leadership.

Reflections on Our Stories

I, Lisa, especially wanted to write this chapter together with my mom, Elaine, to honor her and the contributions to her family and community. I realize from doing this project that I don't want to forget what she has done and needed her input quickly in this project, as her yesterdays are more plentiful than her tomorrows will be. I want to ensure that we accurately convey what she has done with her lived experiences and with my grandmother's. She made the most of her time and talents and, unfortunately, many people who do this are never recognized. Marginalized people, those not in the limelight, have much to offer but are rarely seen, much like the quote by George Eliot indicates at the beginning of this chapter.

This is *not* the type of story that one reads in the newspaper or online—how one family has pulled itself up by its "bootstraps" and accomplished amazing things—power and position. Ours is more commonplace—one I believe is worth telling because of its ordinariness. Many, many *regular* people throughout history have made significant impacts on this world, though few are recognized for doing so. Patricia Hill Collins was one of the first to recognize the importance of the contributions of marginalized people, and this article builds on her ideas. This is just one such story in the context of leadership and the American Dream. What was possible for each of us was largely influenced by the era in which we lived, though each of us made the most of what we had to work with.

Women were not educated in the same numbers in the early part of the twentieth century as they were by the end of it (Snyder, 1993). The compulsory education laws of the twentieth century may have enabled the eldest of us, Mary, to attain more than a fourth-grade education had they been enforced. Student loans and the availability of more financial aid may have allowed Elaine to have an opportunity at attending college in the 1950s. Unfortunately, neither of the two oldest in this chapter had the same opportunity for education as the youngest one did. The possibilities were the greatest during my life. Universal public education and later a financial aid package bundled together with family encouragement certainly expanded all opportunities for the youngest. This is one reason why writing this chapter is so important to us—so that others know that we stand on the shoulders of giants and that others assisted us in becoming who we are today. We also hope that other women will do the same kind of investigations in their own families.

Living as Servant Leaders

Each of us in this tri-generational study has had many servant leadership experiences in her life. Though at the time we were performing such acts, we could not conceive of ourselves as servant leaders. There are three important reasons for this: (1) servant leadership did not exist as a theory or concept prior to 1970 (Greenleaf, 1977); (2) we did not initially perceive ourselves to be leaders when we serving; and (3) without the youngest in this study being a professor of leadership and learning about this theory, the description never would have been applied to any of us.

It is clear that the oldest in this study did a lot of service but had the least recognition as a leader. She most-emulated the role of "Leo" in the story that inspired Greenleaf to develop the concept of servant leadership in Hesse's book *Journey to the East*. Mary actually was a servant in a home when she was 14 and began developing skills of competence, awareness, and empathy, which are cited by Spears (2007, p. 6) as attributes of servant leaders. When she "disappeared," the family wanted to have her back in the home, since she made an impact on them. She became the matriarch of our immigrant family and by all accounts had presence and spirit. Based on recollection, we are sure that the oldest of us did not identify herself as a leader.

As an example of servant leadership for Elaine, we note her becoming one of the first female Eucharistic Ministers and lectors in her church. The purpose of these roles were the distribution of the bread and wine or reading scripture to those who attended the service. Later, by preserving the oral histories of women in the coal and coke era, she shed light on the marginalized. Leadership attributes that Spears in 2007 (p. 6) cited of stewardship, commitment to the growth of people, and healing were learned by being in this role. She also stood out being a woman on the altar in the Roman Catholic Church—thus being a role model for younger women, who then thought that they could serve in these positions in the future.

Lastly, Lisa learned quite a lot early on through her service fraternity and, in particular, one service project involving inmates. While the main focus was the coordination of volunteers for a service organization to assist in building a community center, she also transported men from a nearby prison to help with the project. Many lessons on leadership emerged from this experience including conceptualization, listening, persuasion, foresight, and community building, all of which were noted by Spears (2007, p. 6) as attributes of servant leaders. Combining the leadership lessons with the experience of serving others established a firm foundation for servant leadership for each of us.

All of the skills or lessons on leadership that were described here define a servant leader. According to Larry Spears, the former CEO of the Greenleaf Center, 10 attributes have been ascribed to servant leaders: "(1) listening; (2)

empathy; (3) healing; (4) awareness; (5) persuasion; (6) conceptualization; (7) foresight; (8) stewardship; (9) commitment to the growth of people; and (10) building community" (Spears, 1998, p. 6). We have identified ways in which each of us has embodied several of these based on lived experience. Each of us may, however, have embodied or do embody more than the few attributes listed here. More important is the ideal that Greenleaf himself outlined in wanting to serve above other considerations.

***

Our story is written with the concept of narrative momentum, as Ballard and Ballard (2011) call it. This is the passing down of family stories so that the next generation will have them. However, as I, Lisa, am composing this piece of the conclusion for the chapter, I realize that I do not have children of my own with whom to share it. Perhaps the academy is my extended family, the students are my surrogate children, and conferences are my family reunions.

In my quest to understand where my interest in leadership has come from, I have learned, from both my mother and my grandmother, about the importance of service to others. No matter how bad times may seem, there is always room to give of oneself to help someone who may need an extra hand. It provides hope. Serving others and improving one's community was a way of life for them, and I have learned that it is for me as well. Though I may not serve in the same ways that they have, I work in a field—education—that by its very nature is a profession of service to others. I also attempt to empower women as leaders in both my scholarship and in my volunteerism. My feminist values are indeed in alignment with my practice of servant leadership, in its nonhierarchical and participative approach.

Wherever one is located—whether that is characterized geographically or generationally, she can make a difference and lead. We have learned from this study that community service was a key component in each of our lives as it relates to leadership and influencing others. We did not think of ourselves as "leaders," but we considered ourselves "doers." When we saw something that needed to be done, we would act on it and do it—without the expectation of reward or recognition. We believe this is an authentic and desirable form of leadership—and fits the definition of a servant leader.

References

Adler, N. J. (2008). I am my mother's daughter: Early developmental influences on leadership. *European Journal of International Management*, *2*(1), 6–21.

Ballard, R. L., & Ballard, S. J. (2011). From narrative inheritance to narrative momentum: Past, present, and future stories in an international adoptive family. *Journal of Family Communication*, *11*, 69–84.

Catalyst. (2016, June 6). *Women CEOs of the S&P 500*. Retrieved from www.catalyst.org/knowledge/women-ceos-sp-500

Collins, P. H. (1991). *Black feminist thought: Knowledge, consciousness, and the politics of empowerment*. New York, NY: Routledge.

Crenshaw, K. (1991). Mapping the margins: Intersectionality, identity politics, and violence against women of color. *Stanford Law Review, 43*(124), 1241–1299.

Eliot, G. (1947). *Middlemarch: A study of provincial life*. London, UK: Oxford University Press.

Ellis, C. (2004). *The ethnographic I: A methodological novel about autoethnography*. Walnut Creek, CA: AltaMira Press.

Fine, M. G. (2007). Women, collaboration, and social change: An ethics-based model of leadership. In J. Chin, B. Lott, J. Rice, & J. Sanchez-Hucles (Eds.), *Women and leadership: Transforming visions and diverse voices* (pp. 177–191). Malden, MA: Blackwell Publishing.

Gilligan, C. (1996). *In a different voice* (Rev. ed.). Cambridge: Harvard University Press.

Greenleaf, R. K. (1977). *Servant leadership: A journey into the nature of legitimate power and greatness*. New York: Paulist Press.

Greenleaf, R. K. (1991). *Servant leadership: A journey into the nature of legitimate power and greatness*. New York: Paulist Press. Hernandez, K. C., Ngunjiri, F. W., & Chang, H. (2015). Exploiting the margins in higher education: A collaborative autoethnography of three foreign born female faculty of color. *International Journal of Qualitative Studies in Education, 28*(5), 533–551. doi:10.1080/09518398.2014.933910

Hunchuck, M. A. (1977, May 12). *Interview by Jerome M. DeFrank*, transcript.

Markham, S. E. (2012). The evolution of organizations and leadership from the ancient world to modernity: A multilevel approach to organizational science and leadership (OSL). *The Leadership Quarterly, 23*(6), 1134–1151. doi:doi.org/10.1016/j.leaqua.2012.10.011

Ngunjiri, F. W. (2015). Women as community leaders: A portrait of authentic, collaborative, and transformational leadership. In S. Madsen, F. Ngunjiri, K. Longman, & C. Cherrey (Eds.), *Women and leadership around the world* (pp. 187–204). Charlotte: Informational Age Publishing, Inc.

Northouse, P. (2013). *Leadership: Theory and practice* (6th ed.). Thousand Oaks, CA: Sage Publications.

Parry, K. W. (2006). Qualitative method for leadership research: Now there's a novel idea! *Regulatory Compliance Journal-the Journal of the Australasian Compliance Institute, 1*(1), 24–25.

Reynolds, K. (2014). Servant-leadership: A feminist perspective. *The International Journal of Servant Leadership, 10*(1), 35–63.

Roosevelt, E. (2010). Goals, achievements, & success: Wisdom from paragons of success. In E. Partnow (Ed.), *The little book of the spirit* (p. 101). New York: Fall River Press.

Sanchez-Hucles, J. V., & Davis, D. D. (2010). Women and women of color in leadership: Complexity, identity, and intersectionality. *American Psychologist, 65*(3), 171–181. doi:10.1037/a0017459

Snyder, T. D. (Ed.). (1993). *120 years of American education: A statistical portrait*. National Center for Education Statistics. Washington, DC: U.S. Department of Education, Office of Research and Improvement. Retrieved from https://nces.ed.gov/pubs93/93442.pdf

Spears, L. C. (1998). Tracing the growing impact of servant leadership. In L. Spears (Ed.), *Insights on leadership: Service, stewardship, spirit, and servant-leadership*. New York, NY: John Wiley & Sons.

Storberg-Walker, J., & Madsen, S. R. (2017). *The women and leadership theory think tank report 2015*. Retrieved from www.uvu.edu/uwlp/docs/wlthinktankreport2015.pdf

Suyemoto, K. L., & Ballou, M. B. (2007). Conducted monotones to coacted harmonies: A feminist (re)conceptualization of leadership addressing race, class and gender. In J. Chin, B. Lott, J. Rice, & J. Sanchez-Hucles (Eds.), *Women and leadership: Transforming visions and diverse voices* (pp. 35–54). Malden, MA: Blackwell Publishing.

3

LIFE IS WHAT WE MAKE IT

Barbara Barrett

In preparation for space flight, an early screening is a psychological analysis. Despite my trepidations, this phase seemed to be more game than test. One exercise in particular conveyed a message. The psychologist asked me to name the ten people who had been most influential in my life. The first three names were automatic and easy. The fourth, fifth, and sixth came quickly to mind. The seventh and eighth were a little less obvious. To save time, for the ninth and tenth, I somewhat arbitrarily wrote two names without belaboring the question.

With only a glance at my list, the psychiatrist quickly pronounced that I was wrong. I was stunned. How could he possibly know who was influential in my life? He knew very little about me and knew nothing of the people whose names were on my list. Still, he confidently declared that I failed to list the top ten people who influenced my life.

Why? Simply put, I failed to include myself. He delivered a potent message: no matter how influential others have been in our lives, we each set our own course.

"Life is what we make of it," summarizes the responsibility each of us has for making good decisions that lead to the life we want. This chapter discusses lessons in leadership and strategies for success derived from my career and leadership journey with a focus on leadership in the C-suite and on corporate boards. For those who aspire to contribute on corporate boards or in C-suite roles, a few leadership lessons follow.

Leadership Lesson #1: Get the Best Education That Is Accessible to You

Learn about a lot of things; learn in depth something that is important to you. Law, finance, strategy, and the business of business can be reliable preparations for corporate leadership purposes. Whatever your academic preparation, learn more. As a corporate board or C-suite candidate, you are expected to understand the company's strategy and financial statements thoroughly.

Education transformed my life and predicted my life's opportunities. Defying a misguided stereotype, I was a math major. Then, I completed a master's degree focusing on international business and then a law degree.

My training as a pilot opened doors for me to take a leadership role as the deputy administrator, the number two person, at the United States Federal Aviation Administration (FAA). The FAA's portfolio is large. It manages air traffic control across the U.S. and advises beyond our borders. The FAA also licenses and inspects aircraft for airworthiness, pilots for flight training and capability, and airports for security and safety and much more.

Later, my community education was enhanced when I participated in an Arizona program called Valley Leadership. Both the formal education credentials and informal programs enhanced my preparation for future roles and opened doors to unexpected opportunities. For example, I joined the International Women's Forum, which introduced me to many extraordinary women like America's first woman astronaut, Sally Ride, Canadian Prime Minister Kim Campbell, British humorist Katharine Whitehorn, and many others. Through my space training and other defense and corporate work, I became chairman of the board of the Aerospace Corporation and vice-chairman of the Jet Propulsion Laboratory governance committee under Caltech's board.

The best education often derives from hands-on experience. Service on not-for-profit and academic boards can build collegiality, technique, confidence, and skills that lead to corporate board invitations. Personally, I served on a variety of not-for-profit boards earlier, including the local chapter of the American Red Cross, Big Brothers Big Sisters, Ballet Arizona, United Way, and many other academic, cultural, service, and philanthropic boards. Today, I enjoy working with exceptional institutions like California Institute of Technology, Jet Propulsion Laboratory, Arizona State University, RAND Corporation, Carnegie Mellon University, and the South Dakota School of Mines and Technology.

Leadership Lesson #2: Get Involved

Sometimes a little advice can have a big impact. Once, Justice Sandra Day O'Connor gave me just two words of advice, "Get involved." An avalanche of involvement resulted and led to unexpected career progression, from negotiating international aviation agreements for the U.S. government to working at the UN and as CEO of the American Management Association. Justice O'Connor swore me in to a number of my federal roles, including to the job as U.S. ambassador to Finland. Involvement as a volunteer built skills, understanding, and relationships that last a lifetime. Volunteer work and extracurricular activity distinguishes graduates in the job market and allows social networks to develop (Kaufman & Gabler, 2004; Stuart, Lido, Morgan, Solomon, & May, 2011). A similar effect applies during and after university life; additional activities help distinguish careers and build networks.

Even today, Justice O'Connor's advice influences my activities as a regent of the Smithsonian Institution—the world's largest network of museums, galleries, and worldwide research centers.

I had a friend who, at the age of 86, decided he should cut back on his community activities. He asked if I would agree to take his seat on the governing board of a venerable academic institution in Arizona, the Thunderbird School of Global Management. Involvement on Thunderbird's board led to requests to speak on campus, a couple terms as chairman of the board, and eventually to service as the interim president of the graduate school. Thunderbird educates international leaders. The school follows a mantra that "Borders frequented by trade seldom need soldiers." Thunderbird was founded by a retired World War II Army Air Corps lieutenant general who had seen the tragedy of war and thought that more commerce between countries would obviate wars. He built Thunderbird School of Global Management on a surplus World War II pilot training airfield in Arizona to train young people to learn languages, cultures, and business practices of other lands. Over 75 years later, Thunderbird continues to train aspiring business, government, and nonprofit leaders in global management skills.

Corporate philanthropy is little understood but pivotal to many communities in which the companies operate and beyond. Today, corporations usually operate significant foundations to manage their corporate philanthropy. In 2015, corporate giving increased by 4% over the previous year, to $18.46 billion (The Giving Institute, 2016). As a child I personally benefited from the philanthropy of the founder of the Hershey Chocolate Company, who, over a century ago, donated most of his Hershey stock to a trust to benefit an orphanage he founded in Hershey, PA. Today, about 2,000 boys and girls from broken homes or troubled circumstances go to school and live at the Milton Hershey School as a result of his largesse. My brothers went to the Milton Hershey School after my father died, so my appreciation for this century-old philanthropy runs deep.

Today, I consider it a privilege to serve as chairman of The Aerospace Corporation, a near-billion-dollar company that plays a significant role in ensuring the success of satellite launches for civil and military government customers. The Aerospace Corporation just established a scholarship for STEM (science, technology, engineering, and math) support. Through the years, Justice O'Connor's advice to "get involved" to make the world better has guided much of what I try to do.

Leadership Lesson #3: Build Meaningful Relationships

Personal and business relationships add value and meaning to life; they may even define our lives. We build relationships in many ways, such as working on a project team, collaborating to win a program, or by pursuing a common goal. What may seem like a simple family, community, or business project may be a strategically important engagement because participatory projects often become a foundation for long-term beneficial relationships, usually unintentionally. Cooperative goals and interaction contribute to an effective use of a business network (Tjosvold & Weicker, 1993). Collaborating, cooperating, or teaming up offers fulfillment in many ways and builds a reputation for making good things happen through worthy projects.

The distinction is formidable between building friendships by working together on a project versus less positive interactions. Even when a child undertakes a project like putting together a party to watch a sporting event or organizing a hike or bike ride, that child is building skills in planning, communication, and logistics. The more participatory the project is, the more likely that relationships and skills will benefit long-term strategies for corporate C-suite or board involvement.

Working on projects helped me build relationships that unexpectedly played a decisive role in becoming U.S. ambassador to Finland. President George W. Bush nominated me to serve as ambassador, and at the time, the Senate was controlled by Democrats, so few nominations were receiving confirmation hearings and fewer still were being confirmed by the full Senate. My proven ability to work with both sides was pivotal to my confirmation. Notably, after I taught as a Fellow at Harvard's Institute of Politics, I was asked to serve on the Kennedy School's Institute of Politics Senior Advisory Board. United States Senator Ted Kennedy was a member of that Board. He and I worked together in those meetings on projects with students at the Kennedy School. Senator Kennedy and I were of opposite political parties, but we worked together to enhance student experiences. In the end, although there were nominees who had been waiting for over a year for confirmation, I was confirmed quickly and without controversy.

My confirmation was expedited, as President Bush nominated me around St. Patrick's Day (March 17, 2008), and I was confirmed on April 29 of the same year. I was sworn in on April 30, then received mandatory training and was at my post in Helsinki on May 12. To go from nomination in mid-March to sitting at the desk in Helsinki in less than two months is lightning fast by the standards of the time. I attribute the Senate's quick and favorable action to my bipartisan work through the years on meaningful projects, especially at Harvard with influential Senate icon Senator Kennedy.

Leadership Lesson #4: Work Well With Others

Today, most leadership roles require good working relationships; collegial bodies are especially dependent upon a cooperative and trusting atmosphere. Each member must bring value to the table. Although each board member has a duty to speak up and explore contrary points of view, the board member who cannot find something to support or is unable to offer better alternatives will soon be marginalized. Groupthink at the board level can be fatal to an organization, yet, a corporate board is a poor fit for an obstructionist or incorrigible contrarian. Instead, each board member has a duty to participate in animated discussion of pros and cons to fashion better decisions by the board.

As ambassador, my role included responsibility to demonstrate American leadership. Although Finland is small in population its international leadership and geostrategic location make it pivotal to U.S. foreign policy. East meets West in Finland. Through the twentieth century, Soviet and Russian leaders shopped and vacationed in Helsinki. Finland has the longest border with Russia of any European nation. Finland simply has got to get along with its titanic neighbor. The Finnish culture is dramatically different from the Russian culture in many ways. Still, they have learned to work together. The Finland/Russia relationship may be a metaphor for the necessity of getting along in a lopsided relationship where principles are not generally shared but when civility and cooperation are essential to survival or success.

A one-time advisor to General Douglas MacArthur offered advice during a particularly dicey time in the general's career. He said, "Now General, you are going to have to ration your enemies." His point was that making enemies may be unavoidable, but you cannot make too many enemies without losing effectiveness. His was good advice.

Leaders work well with others and build relationships even with those whose interests or culture differs from their own.

Leadership Lesson #5: Take the Lead

Leaders lead. Leaders control some enterprise, whether business, academic, charitable, professional, or scientific. Leaders have a plan, goal, or vision and inspire others to subscribe to it. Leaders engage a team and define a path to achieving that plan, goal, or vision. Leaders rarely lead in just one situation. Leaders rise to the top in other elements of their lives and in multiple environments.

Almost without exception, board members and C-suite executives have resumes laden with significant leadership roles. Good board members understand and have compassion for the challenges that face the executive leadership team. Nominating committees often look for board members who have led entities in comparable business or industry environments and understand the distinct roles of governance and management. My background included corporate, academic, and governmental leadership, but the international experience of leading a diplomatic mission proved particularly interesting to board recruiters.

As ambassador, I looked for occasions when Finland and the United States could work together on issues, including anything from humanitarian aid to commercial relationships. Business relationships often pave the way for diplomacy of other sorts. Global businesses recognize the importance of maintaining peaceful relations, and business partners are more likely to promote productive global relationships (Goodman, 2006). Finland is not a member of NATO; instead, Finland partners with NATO and regularly participates in NATO exercises. When Finnish defensive aircraft are equipped to refuel from NATO tankers, for instance, operational challenges are minimized.

During my time as ambassador, terrorism threatened many nations and cost countless innocent lives in the U.S. and worldwide. When I arrived at my post in Helsinki, a relationship existed between Finland and Afghanistan including both provincial reconstruction efforts and other limited support. Our embassy sought opportunities for Finland to strengthen civil society in Afghanistan. Finns helped women in Afghanistan. Prior to my service in Finland, I had met with Afghanistan's President Karzai, who emphasized the need for forestry. Decades of war had denuded the once-lush Afghan hills. Wood was needed for firewood, furnishings, and building materials, but at that time wood was imported from Pakistan. Throughout time, Finns have known cold-tolerant forestry, and Afghans were desperate for cold-tolerant trees. Finns could help rebuilding forests with saplings that tolerate the cold Afghan winters.

During the time I was ambassador, Russia invaded Georgia. The Finns worked aggressively but quietly behind the scenes to end the bloodshed. Finland chaired the Organization for Security and Cooperation in Europe (OSCE) at the time. In keeping with U.S. interests, Finland was one of the key players for negotiating cessation of Russia's hostilities in Georgia and enabling humanitarian aid there. In this case, Finland was a leader through its role in the OSCE and through respect it had earned in other situations.

Taking the lead may be self-initiated or externally mandated, but C-suite dwellers and corporate board candidates will almost universally have demonstrated their leadership skills in some significant pursuits.

Leadership Lesson #6: Map Your Journey

Your life will follow its unique map, tracking how one thing leads to another. Similar to Kaplan and Norton's (2000) corporate strategy maps, which guide corporations toward desired goals, visual mapping can effectively guide individual progress toward personal aspirations. Mapping how one thing led to another and who and what facilitated attainment of goals in the past can help plan a route to future aspirations.

A cherished friend, Dr. Laurie Leshin, is president of Worcester Polytechnic Institute in Massachusetts. Her map would look like this: Her chemistry B.S.

from Arizona State University led to a California Institute of Technology Ph.D. in geochemistry. Then she became the Dee and John Whiteman Distinguished Professor of Geological Sciences at Arizona State University, where she directed the Center for Meteorite Studies and led development of the first-of-its-kind interdisciplinary School of Earth and Space Exploration. In her work involving space science, especially encouraging girls to study science, she shared her passion with astronaut Sally Ride. Sally Ride and others supported Dr. Leshin for leadership in space-related scientific and research associations and commissions. Soon, Dr. Leshin was invited to work in leadership positions at NASA's Goddard Space Flight Center and NASA headquarters in Washington, DC. Then she was asked to be dean of the School of Science at Rensselaer Polytechnic Institute in New York and served on the advisory board of the Smithsonian National Air and Space Museum in Washington, while continuing her work on the Mars Rover Curiosity. From dean of science she became Worcester Polytechnic Institute's first woman president. One thing leads to another, as Dr. Leshin's map proves; each step is preparatory for another.

A career map demonstrates the influence of education, a particular program, or a written commentary presented to a key audience. One thing leads to another. The course of my career was largely coincidental, but career mapping demonstrates pivot points in my past and can clarify touchstones for future aspirations. It has been said that "If you don't know where you're going, any map will do." But a roadmap of life goals enhances the likelihood of getting to desired goals.

Leadership Lesson #7: Know How to Define Success

When leading an organization, leaders are well served by identifying what the goal is and how to achieve the success they or their superiors seek. It is often helpful to learn from the experience of others in similar enterprises.

The Horatio Alger Association summarized *The Ten Traits That Make Nonprofits Great* in a booklet (Foss, 2014). Here are their ten traits:

1. Have an important mission with a great leader
2. Focus on a few things
3. Explain what you do and show results
4. Develop diverse funding sources
5. Continuously review the organization
6. Have board members who want to participate and give generously
7. Know who needs to know the organization
8. Know where the organization is going
9. Know how to ask and say "thanks"
10. Commit to excellence

Leadership Lesson #8: Add Adventure to Life

Adventure and curiosity keep life interesting.

In Finland, I explored urban and rural settings throughout the country. To stay physically active, I bicycled across Finland and back again, and to keep my pilot license current, I flew to every operational airport that I could reach. Finland operated American-made F/A-18 Hornets as its air force fighter. The chief of staff of the Finnish Air Force challenged me to an F/A-18 dogfight in the skies over Northern Finland, of course with instructor pilots. Finland's use of American-manufactured fighters spoke to the closeness of our defense collaboration.

After work and on weekends, I bicycled across Finland and the entire coastal perimeter of the country. I sailed on Finland's famous ice breakers. I mushed dogs. I drove snowmobiles, and I rode helicopters, a reindeer sleigh and all manner of boats and ships. I rounded up reindeer. I tried to learn as much about the Finnish people and their diverse cultures as I could.

After Finland, I had the privilege of training for a flight to the International Space Station. As with all astronaut trainees, the process begins with medical clearances, then physical, classroom, simulator, and off-nominal situations training. I looked for situations where I could learn more and where I could fuel my curiosity.

Life Is What We Make It

As a member or candidate for corporate board or C-suite positions it is important to have basic skills and personal courtesies. Successful candidates should know how to run an effective meeting. Careful preparation and time management are rewarded. An effective chair demonstrates respect for the time of the participants, moves the agenda with alacrity, engages all attendees, summarizes actions, employs rules of order when appropriate, and focuses on accomplishing the goals of the meeting.

Often the best leadership lessons come from role models of good practices. In college, I interned for then-Arizona State Senate Majority Leader Sandra Day O'Connor. Although she is best known as the first woman justice on the U.S. Supreme Court, she is also one of the few Supreme Court justices ever to have had experience in all three branches of government. Justice O'Connor's peerless career included experience as an attorney in the Arizona Attorney General's Office in the executive branch, several terms in the Arizona State Senate, where she was the first woman in the U.S. to be majority leader of any state legislative house or senate, and finally in the judiciary. She was first appointed to the bench of a court of first impression; then she was elevated to the appellate court; and finally she was appointed to the U.S. Supreme Court, where she served for almost 25 years.

Justice Sandra Day O'Connor motivated everyone in her ambit. Seemingly effortlessly, she kept an extraordinary tempo. While she excelled at the demanding senate leadership job, she simultaneously raised three sons and hosted backyard fiestas at her home for her legislative colleagues from both political parties. She chaired the local museum board and was active in myriad elements of civic life in her community. She played tennis and golf formidably, including a hole-in-one on her home course. Moreover, while traditionally senate majority leaders do not accept committee chairmanships, O'Connor chaired one of the busiest committees in the senate. Most impressively, she simultaneously combed all state laws to gender-neutralize Arizona statutes. Sandra O'Connor had high expectations of herself and those with whom she worked. She convinced us the correctness of her standard for meetings: if a meeting is well prepared and well run, the business of the meeting should not take more than an hour.

Whether planning for space travel, a corporate board, or C-suite role, life will be fulfilling if you emulate leaders you admire, build meaningful relationships, and get involved. After all, your life will be what you make of it.

References

Foss, B. (2014). Ten traits that make nonprofits great. *Horatio Alger Association*. Retrieved from www.horatioalger.org/wp-content/uploads/2015/11/2014-Horatio-Alger-Ten-Traits-Book.pdf

The Giving Institute. (2016, June 23). "Giving USA 2016" infographic. *Giving USA*. Retrieved from https://givingusa.org/see-the-numbers-giving-usa-2016-infographic/

Goodman, M. (2006). The role of business in public diplomacy. *Journal of Business Strategy, 27*(3), 5–7. doi:10.1108/02756660610663763

Kaplan, R., & Norton, D. (2000, September 1). Having trouble with your strategy? Then map it. *Harvard Business Review*. Retrieved from https://hbr.org/2000/09/having-trouble-with-your-strategy-then-map-it

Kaufman, J., & Gabler, J. (2004). Cultural capital and the extracurricular activities of girls and boys in the college attainment process. *Poetics, 32*(2), 145–168. doi:10.1016/j.poetic.2004.02.001

Stuart, M., Lido, C., Morgan, J., Solomon, L., & May, S. (2011). The impact of engagement with extracurricular activities on the student experience and graduate outcomes for widening participation populations. *Active Learning in Higher Education, 12*(3), 203–215. doi:10.1177/1469787411415081

Tjosvold, D., & Weicker, D. (1993). Cooperative and competitive networking by entrepreneurs: A critical incident study. *Journal of Small Business Management, 31*(1), 11–21.

4

THE RIGHT KIND OF GIRL

Resistance Faced and Support Offered to Women on the Journey to Board Chair

Heather Inez Ricks Scott

The inequity in the representation of women at the highest levels of higher education administration calls for the continued examination of challenges faced by women who strive to attain high-stakes policy-making roles. Equally important in solving the continued mystery of inequity is identifying venues of support for women as they traverse upon their leadership journey. This chapter examines how resistance and support impact women during their journey to the role of trustee board chair. Emanating from a research study focused on female trustee board chairs at private colleges and universities, the findings from this qualitative study offer a firsthand perspective and view of the participants' leadership journeys. The experiences of the women featured in this work offer a variety of perspectives on obtaining executive level leadership roles in higher education. An analysis of the respective leadership journeys provides insightful themes into the ascension patterns of the leaders. In some instances, these themes may serve as guidance to women desiring similar leadership roles.

The Problem

Inequity in leadership opportunities between men and women leaders in the field of higher education administration, particularly the role of trustee board chair, is evident from a cursory review of data. Recent data from the Association of Governing Boards (AGB) continues to reflect an uneven representation of women serving as governing board chair at both private and public institutions of higher learning. The most recent board composition study conducted in 2010 by AGB reports a decline in the number of women serving on governing boards in comparison to their previous two studies. Specifically, the data reflect that more men continue to serve in the role of board chair. Women served as chair at a rate of 19% at independent institutions and 17.4% at public institutions. These numbers reflect a lack of representation of women at the highest levels of governance. Most importantly, this data paints the picture of systemic inequities that create significant challenges for women on their leadership journeys.

Research revolving around the concept of critical mass theory suggests that for a difference to be made in leadership, women need to be represented at a number that moves beyond tokenism (Erkut, Kramer, & Konrad, 2008). Their work further indicates that when at least three women serve on corporate boards, the opportunities for those women to have an impact is increased.

At institutions of higher learning, those that have the ability to make an impact are at the highest levels of policy-making roles, such as those serving as trustee board members and chairs. Policies made at these levels of governance set the tone and stage for an institution's mission and work. If the population of an institution is not represented on a governing board, there may be missed opportunities to address and meet the needs of a school's constituents. This divergence between representation and mission is a critical area to address to maintain an institution's health and success. The AGB further ascertains that there is a positive correlation between the number of female board members at an institution and females who serve as presidents, provosts, and faculty members at those institutions.

Overview of the Study

Exploring the executive level experiences of women in the role of board chair adds to the body of knowledge regarding leadership and gender at the policy-making level. The plethora of definitions regarding leadership and leadership styles contributes to the complexity of investigating this issue. Researchers have sought to identify issues regarding gender and leadership from various perspectives, ranging in viewpoints from feminist ideology to business models. These various disciplines have employed qualitative and quantitative approaches to seek answers to the questions surrounding women and leadership roles.

The findings presented in this chapter will focus on experiences of challenge and support that a sample of female board chairs encountered during their leadership journeys. Additionally, this work explores the preconceived notions, stereotypes, and expectations associated with gender and leadership. The study that was utilized to explore this phenomenon was qualitative in nature, using a phenomenological analysis approach. This methodology describes the meaning of the lived experiences for several individuals about a concept or phenomenon (Creswell, 2007). The researcher identified independent institutions in a southeastern state with female governing board chairs. Individuals from these institutions were invited to participate in the study. All invited participants accepted the invitation, resulting in a sample of five women.

The guiding theoretical framework for this study was feminist theory. This theory seeks to analyze the conditions that shape women's lives and to explore cultural understandings of what it means to be a woman in modern times (Jackson & Jones, 1998). Feminists refuse to accept that inequalities between women and men are natural and inevitable and insist that they should be questioned (Jackson & Jones, 1998). A feminist research approach explains the diverse problematic situations that women face and the institutions that frame those situations (Creswell, 2007). Furthermore, the importance of studying power relationships and the impact of social positions is highlighted.

Additional insight is offered into possible causes of inequity by reviewing literature in the areas of critical mass theory, societal expectations on perceptions of women in leadership, and microaggressions. Critical mass theory has been utilized to address issues of inequity in a variety of sectors—ranging from politics, to education, to business. In the critical mass theory work, it is suggested that women are more effective in their ability to bring about change when serving on boards where there are three or more women represented.

Literature regarding the role and presence of women in the corporate sector often references critical mass theory. Erkut, Kramer, and Konrad (2008) cite in their study on critical mass on corporate boards why three or more women enhance governance. The researchers cite the failures of companies such as Enron and WorldCom as contributors to the call for increased accountability and improvements to governance. As a result, many companies are demanding more competent board directors. Erkut, Kramer, and Konrad assert that the traditional pool of directors is no longer adequate to meet the need for independent, outside board members required by the Sarbanes-Oxley Act of 2002 and other reform guidelines. These reforms and others have caused nominating committees and search firms to enlarge the scope of their searches to include previously excluded candidates, including women. Regardless of this expansion, some of the largest companies still do not have women board directors. The 2005 Catalyst Census of Women Board Directors of the *Fortune* 500 indicated that women held only 14.7% of all *Fortune* 500 board seats. Among the *Fortune* 500 companies, 53 had no women on their boards, 182 had one woman, 189 had two, and 76 had three or more women. The research of Erkut, Kramer, and Konrad illustrates not only the presence of women in the boardroom matters but the number of women present has an impact.

Leadership Journey Profiles

The experiences of the women featured in this chapter are as varied as the women themselves. The group of participants included five women who ranged in age from their early 60s to early 70s. Two of the participants are African American, and three are Caucasian. These demographic details provide insight into the backgrounds of the participants and were indicated by the participants as impactful elements of their leadership journey.

Chairperson One: Being the third alumna to serve in the role of chairperson at her alma mater, Chairperson One grew up in the middle to upper class and has enjoyed an extensive career as a human resources executive. In the sharing of her story she recounted strong familial ties to the school and a childhood goal to become a graduate of the institution.

Chairperson Two: While she did not have familial or alumni status at the institution she served, Chairperson Two served due to her passion for service in the community. She grew up with an educator mother and spoke of the occurrence of her father's death in her early childhood years.

Chairperson Three: Chairperson Three had strong familial connections to the institution where she served as chair. She is an attorney by trade and owns a prominent luxury car dealership. She grew up with a middle to upper class upbringing with an attorney father and educator mother.

Chairperson Four: Chairperson Four is retired and served at her alma mater as board chair. She has had a long and varied relationship with the institution. Her service to the college ranged from volunteer alumnae roles to high-level administrative roles.

Chairperson Five: An attorney by trade, Chairperson Five served as a law school administrator for the bulk of her professional career. Her father was employed as a law school professor, and she grew up in a middle- to upper-class household. She has had a long-standing relationship with her alma mater as a trustee and board chair.

Leadership Journey to Board Chair

One's leadership journey can be impacted by a variety of factors; the journey for a woman serving as a college or university board chair is no different. In the exploration of these women's journeys external and internal factors have had significant impacts. While journeys have starts and stops that impact an individual's trajectory, there are pivotal moments that mark the leadership journey experience. A common impact shared among the women was that of their educational experiences. There was particular impact for the women who served as chairs at their respective alma maters. Chairperson One and Four felt positively about their time at their college. Chairperson One believed that the support and nurturing that she experienced helped her to grow:

> [College One] shaped me in a lot of ways for a lot of things. I was a terrible student my first two years. I was awful. I flunked biology, and didn't do well on some of my subjects, because I didn't study, and I just partied and partied, and I was a young student who had fun. I had a lot of fun.

And, then I got serious my junior and senior years, very serious. If I had been in any other college, they would have flunked me out. . . . [College One] faculty . . . was nurturing, and I was supported. They allowed me to explore myself, and my blackness, and you know this was the late '60s, and I grew up there. I grew up to be woman there.

Chairperson Four expressed her admiration for her alma mater:

I attended [College Four], not necessarily for all the right reasons. I had a boyfriend at Vanderbilt, and my parents wouldn't let me go to Vanderbilt, so they told me I could go to Agnes Scott in Atlanta or stay where [College Four] is located. With all the wisdom of an 18-year-old, I chose to stay in [College Four city], thinking when he came home I would be here. We broke up six weeks after school started, and by then I had fallen in love with [College Four], and though I didn't come here for the right reasons, it was the right school for me.

In contrast to Chairperson One and Four, Chairperson Five identified her displeasure with her alma mater both as a student and an alumna. This displeasure motivated her to voice her concerns, and as a result she was invited to become a trustee. Chairperson Five described her days at College Five:

The goal was to get as much as you could and we had classes six days a week, and your freshman year courses were three hours a week, three quarters a year, nine quarter hours, which would be equivalent to six semester hours. Freshman year was 18 hours, so a very different kind of mindset from what the pace is now. I hated it, I absolutely hated [College Five]. It was the worst experience of my life. It was like going from the real world to a convent . . . people told you what to think . . . it was hideous.

While the alumna chairpersons identified their educational experiences at their respective institutions as being pivotal to their involvement as alumnae, trustees, and ultimately chairs, the chairpersons also shared impactful educational experiences in their journey to the chair role. Chairperson Three offered her experience in law school as one of a few women as an illustration of the impact that gender has played in her leadership journey. This recollection is helpful in providing insight into the era of Chairperson Three's educational experience, an era during which women were just beginning to find equality in educational opportunities. She recounts the following:

I graduated from law school in 1977, but when I first entered in 1973, my class was the first large class of women attending law school at [Law School Three], and I suspect the same for around the country. They admitted about 10 of us, and it was the first large class of women to attend law school back in the early 70's.

Chairperson Five referenced a similar experience:

> in my day if you were female you could be a school teacher, airline hostess, bank teller, a nurse, or you could get married. That was roughly what was out there. There was no one I wanted to marry, I certainly was not going to be an airline hostess, I did not have the credentials to be a nurse or a teacher. Someone suggested being a bank teller, and I did not think that was something I am going to be very good at. So I decided to take the LSAT because my father was a law professor. And he said why don't you do this because maybe you will get into law school, and I did very well on the LSAT and I applied to three law schools, Duke, Emory, and Vanderbilt. Vanderbilt called me up almost immediately and said we would love to have you and we will pay for you to come to law school. Emory did the same thing, but I did not want to go to Emory because that is where my dad was. So my dad called a friend at Duke and said she's got a great offer from Vanderbilt, is Duke going to be willing to admit and/or give her a scholarship. And they said we are going to admit her but we will not give her a scholarship because we don't give scholarships to women. Our expectation is that a woman will not use their degree. So I went to Vanderbilt, that was the best offer I had on the table. At Vanderbilt you had this orientation, one of the young men came over to me the first day we were in orientation and said, "You know if you weren't here some man that has to support a family could be here."

Role, Expectations, and Perceptions of Female Chairpersons

Lessons Learned Along the Journey

A common experience noted by each woman on her respective leadership journey was the impact of gender upon expectations for success or failure. While the barriers and obstacles that some of the chairpersons faced varied, a consistent theme that surfaced throughout the interviews with the participants will be the focus of this chapter. The chairpersons referenced incidents whereby they had experienced or observed individuals, both male and female, exhibiting behaviors that questioned the role of gender and the role of the chairperson.

Smith (2015) asserts that there is a perception of women having "soft personas" which may be seen as an inability to have a strong character to be a leader. Chairperson One speaks to this experience as she recalls her interactions at a national meeting of governing boards. She describes her experience with this perception through her conversation regarding women and the chairperson role:

> I think women generally have a tougher role here in the sense that other women can be "catty." I've worked in quite a few female organizations, so I know about that. And, you also have to prove yourself to whatever degree, you commit. Now, at [College One] and on [College One]'s Board, that's not an issue. Because it's a female college, there is an expectation to having a female board chair, and so having one is a good thing. The guys get in, and they know it's their job to help this person be successful. But . . . I was a co-facilitator for a program that AGB had with United Negro College Fund (UNCF) for board chairs and college presidents, and there were not any female board chairs in that room; in fact, there were no (female) board chairs in the room for that particular group of which we facilitated this educational program for board chairs and presidents. I listened to the chatter among some of the people, and it was clear that there is still this male/female thing going on all the time. It hasn't changed, much. You'd think so, but not enough to keep that chatter down to a lower level.

Chairperson Three expresses her observations and encounters with barriers and obstacles as it relates to gender:

> The basic barriers that I had on boards, sometimes as a woman, when you would make a statement, particularly if it was not a repetitive statement that someone had just said, but an original thought, it was oftentimes ignored. Oftentimes it would be dismissed, and you would have to really fight to get the point out there. I found myself fighting to get my ideas to the table, and what typically happens is your suggestion is that we do "so and so" to fix this. An hour-long discussion would go on until somebody would come back to a point that you made and they would take credit for your idea! And then you start questioning yourself as if, "did I even say that?" And when you realize that you really did say it, you wonder how you can get credit for that. So, that is the number one barrier for female leadership, because men are not mean and vindictive, they are just accustomed to the "little lady" doing all the work and giving them ideas and the credit for it. I'm not saying that men don't come up with original ideas, but when it comes to dealing with a woman they are not accustomed to that woman getting her own due. You are there for their benefit, and so the same thing happens within the board that happens in offices every day around this country. Women are coming up with brilliant ideas, but we don't always get credit for coming up with it, and men will take those ideas unto themselves.

Bongiorno, Bain, and David (2013) further assert through their examination of role congruity theory that prejudice toward women who are agentic is a challenge that female leaders face when in leadership roles. Their work focuses on prejudice based on the prescriptive component of the stereotype that women should be less agentic. They further posit that this form of prejudice puts female leaders in the difficult position of displaying the agentic behavior required of leaders that is in conflict with the nonagentic behavior expected of women. Chairperson Three's own experience with the challenge of being credited for her contributions adds to the reality of the difficulty that women face when asserting agency. It was noted by Bongiorno, Bain, and David that women who spoke assertively achieved less influence and were liked less by men.

Chairperson Four's responses vary in regard to this theme, she indicated that her institution did not have female board chairs until the late 1980s; however, she also indicated that because the institution is a women's college, women do not face barriers at the institution:

> We had our first female board chair in the 1980s, and she was an alum. She was followed by another woman, who was not an alum, but who had long, close family ties with the college, very philanthropic ties with the college. This is a women's college, we don't have barriers for women here. We open doors for women here and the men on the board are all committed to that, which just makes my position a joy.

While Chairperson Four lauds College Four for opening doors for women, she does reference experiences that have increased her comfort level of working in male-dominated arenas:

> I think one of the things that best prepared me was being the vice president [VP] for advancement. And it would have prepared me whether at [College Four] or for anywhere else, because as VP for advancement, you work closely with the college's committees of development and finance. And I don't know whether that's true at other colleges, but those are largely male-dominated at [College Four], and so you work very closely with men. I worked very closely with the president of the college as his primary development officer, and I was able to observe, firsthand, his interaction with the board. Though I didn't pursue the position of board chair, I felt comfortable assuming it because I had worked with so many men, specifically, the college president. I had worked with a lot of community leaders and trustees and called on a lot of businesses in the city of [College Four]. I attended a lot of professional meetings, called on a lot of foundations which were and still are dominated largely by men.

While Chairperson Four found a supportive environment at College Four, researchers like Eagly (2009) contend that women are held to a different standard of leadership achievement than their male counterparts to achieve roles of leadership.

Chairperson Five identified that men's perceptions about the role of women in leadership often impacted the outcome of where women were placed in leadership positions. She indicated that in her opinion one of the biggest factors regarding individuals who did not support her as chair was that she did not meet the expectations that individuals had regarding perceptions of female leaders, saying:

> I think they are related in the sense that, I think had I been a male exhibiting the same levels of impatience and sort of let's get it on the table sort of thing. I think it would have been more acceptable for women than the men. The people who, with one exception, were less thrilled with me being chair of the board were other women (fellow alumnae). We did not have any women on the board who were not alums. That has changed but at the point we did not. It was probably generational as is anything, my class, the class of '64 . . . The early '60s were still pretty much the picture of the '50s. Everybody still wore their ideal shoes . . . and I had just never marched well to that drummer. So, I think, when I became chair I think some of the folks were thinking, we are going to send her out there to try to raise money for the college. People who tend to have the money tend to be older and they've gotten their kids through college and all of that stuff and these people expect to see someone who is going to dress appropriately, high-heeled shoes, whereas I wore the shoes with the chunky heels that are comfortable. My ideas of doing your hair is washing it, stepping out of the shower . . . I can understand that my appearance bothered a couple of them. And again, I am pretty forward and that bothered people. And I know there were some people bothered by the fact, that I was pushing at the bylaws, for a long time the bylaws were that 51% of the board had to be members of the Presbyterian church, and I felt that time had come and gone for it to be changed, but the board was still struggling with that. I managed to get the bylaws changed enough to exclude the former presidents of the alumnae association from that calculation, because we can't control that. Many saw that as rejecting the values of the college, and I think the fact that I was a woman.

Chairperson Five's experience once again supports the findings associated with women and agentic behavior as well as role congruity theory. These findings continue to support the clash between characteristics stereotypically associated with women and those stereotypically associated with leaders. As a result, some women aspiring to roles of leadership find themselves balancing between acting as their authentic selves as leaders and ascribing to the expectations associated with behavior for a female leader.

Chairperson Five indicates that there were few women represented on the board of College Five at one point; here, she reflects on her experience regarding gender and roles:

> Until the last three years that I was on the board during that first era . . . there were very few women on the board; when I joined the board we had the women who were the presidents of the alumnae association who were essentially the only women, with the exception of those who had a lot of money . . . when I joined the board we had (a trustee) who was an active Presbyterian woman, minister's wife, and her husband was on the faculty at Columbia theological, then another trustee who is an alumni who was a member of the faculty at a college, so we had those two women, the alumni president, and me. So you had six women, so of course now, it's majority women, a significant amount of women, it shifted to majority women about ten years ago, so I go back on the board. The chairperson's view was that women should have leadership roles within the board, within the college. It is, I would say, classically corporate in the sense of what constitutes leadership and there's a certain, "We the men will bestow upon you, the women, roles we have designated as important but they are not critical." And I say that [because] in the finance decisions, the committee on trustees was chaired by a woman . . . and that's a very important committee, but finance, budget, audit, the committee around the economics of the institution are all chaired by men. I actually began to chair buildings and grounds, I had been on it for a while, when I came back it was chaired by a man, and that is where the significant spending was at the time. So, when you looked at the financial aspects, it was controlled by the men. When you looked at what I would characterize as the softer aspects from a corporate perspective, academic affairs, student affairs, those were the ones chaired by the women.

Interactions Between Male and Female Trustees

The dynamics of interactions between males and females were often cited as a barrier or obstacle encountered by the female chairpersons during on their leadership journey. Chairperson One shared the following:

> I think some of it is about leadership, some of it is about I would say inclusiveness, because women, I think, are more inclusive. Some of it is about making tough decisions. . . . You could ask the same question about "Why there are not more women at the top of this or the top of that?" and you

know the answers are probably deeper and more systemic than either of us could articulate.

It has been said that there are fundamental differences in the leadership styles of men and women (Eagly & Chin, 2010). Chairperson Two concurs with this sentiment, noting the following in her experiences:

> Actually, a lot of females succeed in being go-to people. In a lot of institutions, women who have a willingness to take on responsibility, take it a little bit more to heart than maybe a male in the same role. I think that a lot of times that women immerse themselves into things a little further than a male does.

Chairperson Three expressed some of her experiences in her interactions with men, indicating that men in her experience have different interactions and expectations based on gender:

> Right now, I'm doing a very good job, but I'm telling you the biggest barrier is men, because they don't want you to be in charge of this thing. They just want you to be a figurehead and to speak correctly and to do all of the improvements. They will meet and talk on the phone and gang up on you. And you get to the point where you say this is not a battle I choose to fight. I can step down from that headache. Learning which battles are worth the fight, that is an extremely important lesson.

The Ideal Woman

An appraisal of empirical research in the area of gender and leadership illustrates slight differences in leadership effectiveness and style, with women exceeding men in the use of democratic, relational, and transformational leadership styles (Hoyt, 2006; Kezar, 2006). In most instances the women identified experiences when others had imposed their ideas about the roles, expectations, and perceptions of female chairpersons upon them. The source of these ideals regarding women and their behavior was at times very surprising.

A particularly telling account was that of a chairperson who revealed that her female peers had been the least receptive of her as a chair because she did not fit their ideals regarding women. As she described it everything from her demeanor to her physical appearance was subject to be questioned. She had the distinct feeling that had she possessed the same personality traits, but as a male, she would have been welcomed and not objected to. She also indicated that when she assumed the role of chair, individuals shared with her that they expected her to be more "hands on" and "touch-feely" in her leadership style.

Another chairperson referred to what she called the "little lady" mentality. Indicating that some of the men that she had worked with had expectations that women would do all of the work and allow the men to take credit for it. She also referenced her experience of women putting ideas on the table and not being listened to until a man repeated the same idea.

Additionally, a chairperson spoke about the ideas that the past chair at her institution had about women's role on the board as trustees. While he felt there was a place for women on the board, he indicated that women should be relegated to certain tasks and specific roles, in particular roles that were deemed lesser.

Appropriate Behavior

The demographics of a group often impact group dynamics and communication (Phillips & Apfelbaum, 2012). The case was no different in the experience of female board chairs. The chairpersons indicated that gender at times played a role in negative or strained interactions between male and female trustees.

One chairperson indicated that she was comfortable in situations that called for communications with men because she had worked in a male-dominated environment. She did, however, indicate that most of the men she had worked with were very cooperative and supportive. Another chairperson shared an account of interaction between males and females that was more volatile than the experience mentioned previously. She indicated that she had interacted with men who simply did not want a woman in charge. In her experience they just wanted the women to serve as "figure heads" who would speak correctly and do all of the needed improvements.

In comparison to these two experiences an additional chairperson indicated that she found men and women to be more cognizant of gender roles and expectations during their interactions. She stated that women trustees at her institution often expressed their dismay if the women were not interacting with the men trustees in a way that was deemed "appropriate" for women. In her experience the preference for women was not to be seen as too aggressive or pushy, although this behavior was considered appropriate for the men, and in most cases expected.

The Journey Ahead

In regard to addressing the question of why there is gender inequality in relation to how many men versus how many women are in the board chair role, there is not a definitive answer. The experiences of these women mirror those historical and systematic inequities that are noted in the literature. There has been a historical unequal representation of women in the academy (Bontrager, 2008;

Glazer-Raymo, 1999; Schwartz & Akins, 2004). Women continue to be under-represented in leadership positions, with evidence suggesting that they typically confront the invisible barrier of a "glass ceiling," while men are more likely to benefit from a "glass escalator" (Ryan & Haslam, 2005). This historical inequity can be seen in colloquial language and phrases such as "the old boys club." The notion that there is an old boys club yet no reference of a girls club speaks to the disadvantage that women have historically sustained when it comes to reaping the benefits of networking and mentoring (Smith, 2015). The work of Smith further indicates that the increased tendency of men to mentor and guide other men leads to a leadership gatekeeping phenomenon that has been sustained over time and regards this as a lack of an opportunity for the empowerment of women. Smith's work further ascertains that the unequal opportunities for women to obtain support has contributed to the "glass ceiling" effect and has allowed for men to have an advantage that limits the leadership capacity of women and fosters institutional prejudices that favor men's methods of decision making and leadership style as the norm.

As stated in the theoretical framework of feminist theory, it is important to note that the experiences should be looked at individually. While this lens of inquiry focuses on giving a "voice" to the often voiceless, researchers who employ feminist theory are reminded that there is not one voice that represents the experience of all women (Creswell, 2007). One experience cannot represent that of an entire population; however, the insight provided by the journeys of the individuals featured in this chapter illuminates the issues that women may encounter on their respective leadership journeys.

While women continue to be underrepresented in the role of chairperson in comparison to their male counterparts, the women featured here have success-fully attained the role of chairperson. The experiences of these women vary, yet commonalities can be found among their experiences. Based upon the tremen-dous insight offered by the chairs and the resources provided in the literature, there are numerous recommendations that can be offered to the woman seeking a role on a board and potentially serving as chair. As the literature indicates, a sup-port network and system is critical. To attain success in established organizations and systems, women must be intentional about supporting each other through mentorship, simply stated—find a mentor, be a mentor. Studies have indicated that one barrier to women mentoring other women is a dearth of women who were available to serve as mentors, yet Brown (2005) found in a study that a majority of college presidents had received mentoring. This may illustrate the importance of mentoring to women who seek executive level roles of leadership.

Mentoring is also taken one step further and coupled with networking as an essential tool, according to the work of Collins, Chrisler, and Quina (1998). This work recognizes that when senior faculty network and mentor junior fac-ulty, a symbiotic relationship is created. This is seen as a beneficial practice to women being prepared as leaders.

Embracing one's talents and leadership skills can be important in achieving goals of attaining high-level leadership roles. The importance of acknowledging and accepting the value of being a transformational leader is paramount in attaining leadership roles. As indicated by Northouse (2009) and research on transformational leadership theory, it is also critical for leaders to possess or work toward cultivating certain leadership styles and skills if they desire to be perceived as leaders. Throughout the stories of women presented in this chapter, distinct leadership talents and skills can be seen. All describe the possession of particular skill sets and experiences that contributed to their ability to ascend to the chair role. These experiences provide insight into the journey of the women to the chair role and present a paradigm of ascension patterns for others to follow.

References

Association of Governing Boards of Universities and Colleges. (2010). *Policies, practices, and composition of governing boards of independent colleges and universities.* Retrieved from agb.org/sites/default/files/legacy/u3/2010IndependentBoardCompositionSurvey Summary.pdf

Bongiorno, R., Bain, P. G., & David, B. (2013). If you're going to be a leader, at least act like it! Prejudice towards women who are tentative in leader roles. *British Journal of Social Psychology*, 53(2), 217–234. doi:10.1111/bsjo.12032

Bontrager, K. A. (2008). *A profile of trustees: Characteristics, roles and responsibilities of trustees in Ohio's two year college system* (Doctoral dissertation, Ohio University).

Brown, T. M. (2005). Mentorship and the female college president. *Sex Roles*, 52(9–10), 659–666. doi:10.1007/s11199-005-3733-7

Catalyst. (2005). *Catalyst census of women board directors of the fortune 500: Ten years later: limited progress, challenges persist.* Retrieved from www.catalyst.org/system/files/ 2005_Census_Women_Board_Directors_10thAnniversary.pdf

Collins, L. H., Chrisler, J. C., & Quina, K. (1998). *Career strategies for women in academe: Arming Athena.* Thousand Oaks, CA: Sage Publications.

Creswell, J. W. (2007). *Qualitative inquiry & research design: Choosing among five approaches.* Thousand Oaks, CA: Sage Publications.

Eagly, A. H. (2009). Female leadership advantage and disadvantage: Resolving the contradictions. *Discovering Leadership*, 277–296. doi:10.1007/978-1-137-24203-7_20

Eagly, A. H., & Chin, J. L. (2010). Diversity and leadership in a changing world. *American Psychologist*, 65(3), 216–224. doi:10.1037/a0018957

Erkut, S., Kramer, V. W., & Konrad, A. M. (2008). Critical mass: Does the number of women on a corporate board make a difference? In S. Vinnicombe, V. Singh, R. Burke, D. Bilimoria, & M. Huse (Eds.), *Women on corporate boards of directors: International research and practice* (pp. 350–366). Northampton, MA: Edward Elgar Publishing, Inc.

Glazer-Raymo, J. (1999). *Shattering the myths: Women in academe.* Baltimore, MD: Johns Hopkins University Press.

Hoyt, C. (2010). Women, men, and leadership: Exploring the gender gap at the top. *Social and Personality Psychology Compass*, 4(7), 484–498. doi:10.1111/j.1751-9004.2010.00274.x

Jackson, S., & Jones, J. (1998). *Contemporary feminist theories.* Edinburgh, UK: Edinburgh University Press.

Kezar, A. J. (2006). Rethinking public higher education governing boards performance: Results of a national study of governing boards in the United States. *The Journal of Higher Education, 77*(6), 968–1008. doi:10.1353/jhe.2006.0051

Northouse, P. G. (2009). *Leadership: Theory and practice.* London: Sage Publications.

Phillips, K. W., & Apfelbaum, E. P. (2012). Looking back, moving forward: A review of group and team-based research. In *Delusions of homogeneity? Reinterpreting the effects of group diversity* (pp. 185–207). Bingley, West Yorkshire: Emerald Group Publishing. doi:10.1108/S1534–0856(2012)0000015011

Ryan, M. K., & Haslam, S. A. (2005). The glass cliff: Evidence that women are over-represented in precarious leadership positions. *British Journal of Management, 16*(2), 81–90. doi:10.1111/j.1467–8551.2005.00433.x

Schwartz, M., & Akins, L. (2004). *Policies, practices, and composition of governing boards of independent colleges and universities.* Washington, DC: Association of Governing Boards.

Smith, A. E. (2015). On the edge of a glass cliff: Women in leadership in public organizations. *Public Administration Quarterly, 39,* 484–517.

5

SEARCHING FOR A PRESIDENCY

Lessons for Women in American Higher Education

Carolyn J. Stefanco

When my always-positive leadership coach asked me if I was sure I wanted to continue the search for a presidency, I realized my experiences were taking an incredible toll. Stories like mine—an almost three-year journey with more than 30 conversations with search consultants, 19 applications, 13 first-stage, airport interviews, and seven experiences as a finalist before I accepted a presidency—are not the ones you often hear about. Yet they must be told if we are serious about helping other women reach the top positions in American higher education.

First, however, I had to overcome my discomfort as a scholar with writing about myself. Knowing from the time I was an undergraduate women's studies certificate student that the personal is political certainly helped (Morgan, 1970). I was also motivated by my lifelong commitment to women's advancement and my involvement over the past two years with the American Council on Education's (ACE) "Moving the Needle" project, which seeks to create parity for women in higher education leadership by 2030 (American Council on Education, Moving the Needle). Positive responses from women who heard me discuss presidential search experiences on panels for the ACE National and Regional Women's Leadership Forums and the International Leadership Association Global Conferences encouraged me as well, as did the opportunity to consider a joint research project on this topic with a colleague who also writes about leadership.

The second hurdle I had to overcome in telling my story was being willing to admit my failings. This was a startling realization, because, as a long-serving tenured faculty member in the past, I had taught my students about the willingness to fail. In fact, I routinely assigned to my history research seminars a first-person account by my father-in-law, a brilliant writer who made a living from his craft, about the importance of failure (Gordon, 1974). I also published an article on failure with a group of coauthors who struggled to understand why our federally-funded project from a wide variety of disciplinary perspectives became so difficult to bring to completion (Vanasupa, McCormick, Stefanco, Herter, & McDonald, 2012). My interest in failure had also led me to research resilience, or how one triumphs over it. I read popular articles and books by psychologists such as Martin E.P. Seligman and Meg Jay about resilience, and by those who have overcome personal tragedies, such as *Option B* by Sheryl Sandberg and Adam Grant (Jay, 2017; Sandberg & Grant, 2017; Seligman, 2011). Colleagues who counsel students also recommended scholarly works by authors such as Michael Hartley (2012). Of course I was aware of the numerous efforts underway in higher education to teach undergraduates how to overcome setbacks, such as "Failing Well" at Smith College, and the professional development opportunities that are promoted to support the creation of such programs (Bennett, 2017; Innovative Educators, 2017). Yet despite being familiar with these many aspects of the subjects of failure and resilience, I continued to resist documenting my story.

What finally compelled me to start writing was my desire to correct the historical record. One too many times I have listened to women talk about being "tapped on the shoulder," asked to "please come and talk to us," and "finding themselves as the new president or chancellor without ever having applied for the job." In one case, the new president who was recruited in this manner had never applied for a presidency before. I applaud these women's great fortune, but it is not the norm (Gagliardi, Espinosa, Turk, & Taylor, 2017; Stefanco, 2014). The existence of professional development programs for those seeking presidencies, along with wisdom gleaned from coaches and consultants about the difficulties of the search process, make clear that seeking a presidency is not easy (Stefanco, 2014). While sitting and former presidents and those who study them write about the lessons learned from *being* a president, their experiences in obtaining their positions are rarely mentioned (Madsen, 2008; Pierce, 2012; Turner, 2007; Wolverton, Bower, & Hyle, 2009).

A Steep Learning Curve

Searching for a presidency taught me a lot about myself and about higher education and prepared me, in ways I would not understand until recently, for the vicissitudes of being a president. Like a lot of women, people of color, and those who are the first in their families to attend college, I had never imagined myself as a president at some future date. Rising through the ranks of the faculty, assuming administrative positions because of a desire to create greater equity and inclusion, being encouraged to pursue professional development, and, most significantly, working closely with a supportive president, all helped me to realize that I could do the job. I also missed being in close contact with students in my positions as dean and vice president, and I longed for the social interaction I witnessed between presidents and undergraduates. With my president's nomination and the recommendation of another sitting president, I applied and was selected for a yearlong program offered by the Council of Independent Colleges (CIC), a professional organization of 650 small and midsized independent (private) nonprofit colleges and universities. Called Presidential Vocation and Institutional Mission, it is designed to help prospective presidents and their spouses and partners, if they have them and choose to participate, to determine if the presidency is their calling and to consider the type of institution where they might best serve.

Like many of the other prospective presidents in my small cohort, I began the process of applying for presidencies as soon as the program started. Although I had spent more than half my career at public institutions of higher education and I did apply and interview for a few presidencies at state universities, most of the searches I entered were at CIC independent colleges and universities.

In the first year and one half of searching, I contacted search consultants on my own after reading notices for positions in *The Chronicle of Higher Education*, and I responded to the emails that those in vice presidential positions frequently receive from search consultants about presidential opportunities. Email correspondence often led to phone conversations, and I stated my intention to apply for the position. To prepare to do so, I paid a consultant a small fee to review my curriculum vitae and give me advice about both content and style. I also asked my husband, who was an active participant with me in the Presidential Vocation and Institutional Mission program, to help me edit my letters of application. I knew that each had to be crafted to respond to the specific qualifications stated in the presidential prospectus. Given my inexperience with the process, however, many of the letters I first submitted sounded similar to each other, and, in retrospect, they were probably too general.

Nevertheless, out of nine applications over about 18 months, I was invited to four first-stage interviews. These are often called "airport interviews" because they are held at airport or nearby large hotels, where candidate confidentiality can more easily be assured. Those applicants who make this first "cut" are invited to fly to these meetings, with expenses reimbursed at a later date by the search company. The interview consists of a 60- to 90-minute meeting with the search committee, and each candidate is asked the same set of nine to 12 questions, with an opportunity provided at the end for the candidate to ask questions of the search committee. In some cases the search consultant, or a search consultant assistant, sits in the room during the interview. This can be unnerving, particularly if one does not expect it, but it does enable search consultants to share more information with candidates about their strengths and weaknesses. I knew that one of these airport interviews had not gone well, but, despite my nervousness, I was hopeful about the other three. Within a few days of each interview, I had heard from each of the search consultants. In only one search was I being invited to be a finalist.

Many presidential searches are public at the finalist stage, meaning that typically three candidates are invited in succession to multiple-day on-campus interviews, where they interact with the search committee and meet with many other constituencies, including trustees, faculty, senior administrators, staff, students, and members of the community. With the finalists' permission, often curricula vitae and sometimes even letters of application are shared on institutions' websites or in emails to campus employees. In my first finalist interview, however, the mid-Atlantic institution had been involved in a protracted search for its new president, and I was told that I would be given tours of the campus and of the city, but I would only meet with the search committee. My identity would not become public. As I would later learn is often the case, as a finalist I was sent much more detailed information about the college in order to prepare. It took an incredible amount of time to study the institution's history, mission, culture, academic programs, finances, student body, policies, physical plant, strategic plans, and fundraising successes. Although the search consultant told me that there were two finalists, and the other woman was ultimately selected, I had learned a lot about higher education. While I would not assume the presidency of this college, the in-depth knowledge I had gained by being a finalist provided a reference point in thinking about my own institution and its challenges. The insights gained were also useful as I continued my search.

Lessons Learned

Later that year I thought I had found a presidency. The southern college seemed to be a great fit. It was in the same *U.S. News and World Report* category as the institution where I was employed as a vice president, and it was similarly ranked. My strengths tracked exceptionally well with the position prospectus, and people who had successfully served in leadership positions there were happy to talk to me about the institutional culture and to serve as references. After speaking to the search consultant and submitting my curriculum vitae and letter of application, I was invited to a first-stage airport interview. It went exceedingly well, and, shortly thereafter, I was asked to become a finalist. Again, this would be a confidential search until the announcement of a new president was made. So that meant that I was being invited to a large city near the institution to meet for a longer period of time with the search committee. To prepare for this stage, the search consultant sent detailed information about the institution. This was now familiar to me. Not only did I study this material, I pursued other sources to better understand the college's challenges and aspirations and its place in the region. The lengthy conversation with the search committee was wide-ranging and extremely positive, and, a few days later, the search consultant called to assure me that I was their top candidate. I was surprised, however, when she told me that the search committee wanted to meet with me again at the location I had recently visited. I was sent more material and asked to prepare my thoughts on additional topics. I bought more airline tickets and, again, rearranged my work and home life to accommodate the date selected by the search committee. This meeting was as great as the others, and, feeling reassured by the search committee and the search consultant, I returned home to wait for the offer. I should have started to doubt what seemed like an all but certain outcome when I did not hear from the search consultant over the next few days. (In all my search experiences, no news never bodes well.) Nevertheless, I was shocked when the consultant called to tell me that the institution had selected another candidate and he had accepted the offer. When the official announcement naming the new president appeared from the institution several weeks later, my hurt turned to anger. The man chosen did not meet *many* of the stated criteria for the position! I learned months later that the board chair, who also chaired the search committee, had "fallen in love" with the selected candidate, and nothing and no one would persuade him that this man should not be the institution's next president. In case this candidate rejected the offer, I had to be kept in the search as the back-up choice. While disheartening, these situations do occur. My experience with the southern college taught me about the unpredictability of searches and helped me to more fully understand the adage that, no matter how friendly, encouraging, and affirming they appear to be, search consultants work for the institution. Once again, it had come down to two candidates, and for the second time I was not chosen to become the president.

With experience, my presentation skills had improved, however. I had also picked up tips from other presidential candidates and from sitting presidents through the oral histories I conducted for a conference presentation and later book chapter on women's searches for presidencies (Stefanco, 2014). Participating in the ACE's Advancing to the Presidency workshop helped, too, as did all the suggestions and support I received from mentors and those who agreed to serve as references for me. What made the biggest difference, however, was hiring a coach. Quite by accident I ended up sitting next to a provost who had recently been announced as a new president at a dinner hosted by the *New York Times* at an ACE meeting, and I asked her how she had been successful. She told me her coach helped enormously, and she shared his name with me. Hiring a leadership coach was a big decision because of the cost. Initially, I signed a year contract at $1,000 a month. This gave me a weekly hour-long phone call and email communication about my searches. My coach also spent time reading about the institutions where I was an applicant, reviewing the search position descriptions, and helping me to improve my letters of application. I learned that I should be having higher education leaders nominate me for positions rather than applying myself. Most significantly, I came to see that, rather than trying so hard to appear presidential, I needed to draw on my real gifts—in my case as an historian—to be the only president I could be—ME. In the second 18 months of applying for presidencies, I was nominated for many positions, and, after speaking to the search consultants, I sent letters to 10 colleges and universities. I went on nine airport interviews, and I became a finalist six times. In some ways I was much more successful, but still the offer of a presidency would elude me for some time.

Public Searches

Only after I had been a finalist in searches that were public in their last stage did I appreciate the enormous personal costs of my presidential aspirations. My husband was "invited" to join me for the multiple-day experience of an on-campus interview on four occasions. Added to my own excitement and stress, along with the herculean expenditure of energy required to be "on" for 12 or more hours a day, was my concern about my husband. It was tricky being a male spouse of a woman presidential candidate, since men are not often put in a public role as supporters of their wives. We both wondered about what search committees and people on campus would expect of him. Although he made some funny jokes about swapping recipes, he had no interest in being a traditional presidential "wife." Of course, he also had to spend time learning about the institutions to prepare for the interviews, and he had to take time off from work to go with me on them. While only I was asked to take personality tests and to have every aspect of my life subjected to background checks, because we are a married couple, his financial records were being investigated as well. Of course, he had also agreed to move with me to states in which he never wanted to live, including one in the Upper Midwest, where he would have very limited opportunities to work in his profession. The hardest, however, was when, after a protracted search, I was not selected and he felt—in some ways more strongly than I did—the hurt that often accompanies rejection. After two of these experiences, he was not sure he wanted to go through it again.

For me, the hardest aspect of public searches was the impact on my professional relationships. In searches where the names of the three finalists were shared, everyone where I worked knew I was away at an on-campus interview, and, within a few weeks, they all learned I had not been selected. To some I was a traitor to the institution. Others felt sorry for me, which I liked even less. Some also saw me as a leader who no longer mattered, because I was on my way out. My president's unwavering support helped to blunt some of the criticism. She went out of her way to remind everyone about the institution's commitment to women's advancement and implored them to honor that for women employees as well as students. Outside my institution, I wondered if those who were serving as my references were getting tired of speaking to search consultants and search committee members on my behalf. I also thought quite a bit about how colleagues at other institutions perceived me when they heard that I had failed, again, to get the presidential offer. When I was not selected after the second public final phase of a search, even my coach wondered aloud if the price to continue to look for a presidency was too high.

Persistence

What helped to keep me going was a brief women's restroom conversation during a National Association of Independent Colleges and Universities (NAICU) conference break in Washington. Although we were only acquaintances, when the new woman president asked me how I was doing while we washed our hands, I told her I was really discouraged. After being a finalist multiple times and not being selected, I explained that I was not sure I could continue the grueling process. She looked me in the eye and told me, "Do not give up." Her words were powerful and continue to resonate many years later, for two reasons. First, because, unlike many other college and university presidents, she shared the truth about her own search experiences and recounted in quick succession all the times over many years she had applied for presidencies, participated in airport interviews, and became a finalist in public searches, only to fail to get the position. Second, because, although I did not reveal this to her, I was the second choice in the closed search where she had finally been selected as president two years before at a mid-Atlantic college.

I would experience the humiliation of another protracted, public search at a university in a Great Plains state where I was a finalist, which, unfortunately, to this day one can still read about on the internet. I also invested a great deal of time and energy into an unusual closed search at a "perfect" university, where I loved the institution and the region and my husband could keep working. Rather than submit the traditional application materials, for example, the search firm representing this institution requested that short essays be written in response to specific questions. After a great "airport interview," I was invited to two more finalist stage interviews with the search committee. Thankfully, this was another confidential search that did not require my husband's participation, because it, too, ended with the presidency going to another woman candidate.

Toward the end of my third year of looking, my husband and I prepared for two more public, on-campus, finalist interviews. The institutions were both wonderful but quite different, and both offered great opportunities to make a difference. After the long journey of many, many rejections, we were amazed when I was offered both presidencies within a day of each other. Persistence had paid off, and now I had to quickly decide between them. It is here that the reading, reflection, and conversation with leaders and participants in the CIC's Presidential Vocation and Institutional Mission program really paid off. The position I selected seemed to be the best fit for me.

Coming to Terms With the Presidential Search Process

It was late in the academic year when my presidency was announced, and I was busy preparing to leave my vice presidential position and to move 1,000 miles, where I would take up my new responsibilities on July 1, 2014. I took the time, however, to apply right before the final deadline for the Harvard Seminar for New Presidents. I was fortunate to have my new institution's support and to be selected for the institute, which took place only a few weeks after I began my presidency. The Harvard Graduate School of Education, which sponsors the institute, took great pride in the fact that the 2014 cohort of new presidents reached near parity for women for the first time, with 23 female participants out of a total of 50. The article posted by the Graduate School of Education noted that, along with studying the topics of "leadership, fundraising, planning, strategizing, and the life of the presidency," the institute "is also designed to help presidents build relationships with colleagues" (Anderson & Weber, 2014). While we were given a lot of information to prepare for our time at Harvard, when I arrived in Cambridge, I was surprised to find that many of my new presidential colleagues and I had competed for the same positions. The man who was selected as president of the southern college was there, for example, as was the woman who got the job at the college in the Upper Midwest. I assumed that the woman who became president of the "perfect" university did not know that I had been a finalist for her position, since the search was confidential until the announcement. Of course, I knew. Even though we had all been successful, albeit at different institutions, it felt awkward at best.

I do not remember our instructors taking steps to normalize this situation, which undoubtedly had occurred many times before. Although we were encouraged to build bonds of mutual support with each other that would last beyond our time at Harvard, we did not acknowledge in our small groups or in one on one conversations with each other that only a few months earlier we had been competitors for the same positions. At least in my case, the feelings of pride and joy in being selected by my institution were still mixed with feelings of sadness and embarrassment about the other searches where I had not been chosen.

As I became more active in professional associations, such as CIC and NAICU, and continued to attend other conferences, such as the annual meeting of the ACE, I got used to finding myself with presidents with whom I had competed for presidencies. On one occasion I was seated next to a president at a banquet dinner where we both knew I had come in second for her position, since it had been a public search at the finalist stage. I have since shared the stage with women presidents on panel presentations and have served on committees with women presidents where we had been in the running for the same presidencies. The passage of time has certainly made these encounters easier, and, I hope, like all presidents, we come to believe we were meant to lead the particular institutions that chose us and that we chose. For presidential candidates who follow higher education pathways to top college and university leadership positions, however, it is important to recognize that you are likely to know other applicants in your searches. If not, you will certainly get to know them through professional development opportunities and participation in higher education associations, and you will work with them as presidents.

It is worth noting that almost all the finalists I competed with were women because the search committees had only invited women to the final round of interviews. What helps to explain this, perhaps, is the fact that along with being a woman, my background as an historian of women and as a lifelong proponent for women's advancement helped me to reach the last stage of presidential searches at women's colleges, where presidents are more likely to be women. I was also a finalist at coeducational institutions that began as women's colleges and have a strong history of commitment to women's leadership and at colleges and universities where the former president had been a man and was associated with a controversy. In some instances, there were personal failings, and in others, there were institutional issues, such as tremendous financial challenges. In these situations, it seems that in recent years, boards of trustees have been more likely to turn to women leaders. This means that women have been given more opportunities to break through the "glass ceiling," to be selected to lead institutions, and to overcome the biases that still help to make the presidency of colleges and universities overwhelmingly male (Gagliardi et al., 2017). Yet being chosen to lead challenged institutions with grave financial or other problems is sometimes a recipe for failure. This is why scholars and popular writers refer to these opportunities for women as "glass cliffs" (Caprino, 2015; Ryan & Haslam, 2007).

If my experiences are instructive, they seem to indicate that I was less likely to advance in searches where a man was ultimately chosen as the president. In addition, I never received an offer when there were male candidates at the finalist stage. At both institutions where I was chosen as president, all six of the finalists were women. What does this suggest about our ability to create parity for women as college and university presidents? First, we should recognize that in some searches, the desire to create diverse pools will lead search committees to invite candidates to interview whom they are unlikely to recommend as presidents. My own research and many conversations with women provosts and presidents over the years indicate that there have been many occasions where women concluded that they were never seen as serious candidates. Second, we must work proactively to make all those involved in presidential searches—and especially trustees who hire the president at independent colleges and universities—more aware of the biases that limit opportunities for women and people of color. Ideally, we will enlist search consultants and sitting presidents—both women and men—in this effort. Third, if aspiring women presidents are more likely to be successful at a minority of institutions that are seeking a woman for the top job, we need to prepare female candidates for this reality.

Over my career, women faculty, staff, and administrators have been the most generous with their time in helping me to develop professionally and to realize my ambitions. Perhaps that is why it was so startling to find myself repeatedly in the position of competing with women for presidencies.

Most significantly, we need to educate women presidential candidates about the realities of the search process. For most of us who become presidents, the journey is longer and harder than we anticipated. As I hope my own experiences have demonstrated, it often takes years to improve one's skills and become a successful candidate. Along the way, however, those who persevere will learn a great deal about higher education through their preparation for applications and interviews at a multitude of institutions. They will also learn greater resilience, especially when they fail to get offers in public searches. It is my greatest hope that women candidates for presidencies will know that when they are not selected, this is just a part of the process. It happened to me, over and over again. "Do not give up." We need you to become the leaders of American colleges and universities.

References

American Council on Education. (n.d). *Moving the needle: Advancing women in higher education leadership*. Retrieved from www.acenet.edu/leadership/programs/Pages/Moving-the-Needle.aspx

Anderson, J., & Weber, M. (2014, August 18). The growing number of women college presidents. *Harvard Graduate School of Education News & Events*. Retrieved from www.gse.harvard.edu/news/14/08/growing-number-women-college-presidents

Bennett, J. (2017, June 24). On campus, failure is on the syllabus. *The New York Times*. Retrieved from www.nytimes.com/2017/06/24/fashion/fear-of-failure.html

Caprino, K. (2015, October 20). The "glass cliff" phenomenon that senior female leaders face today and how to avoid it. *Forbes*. Retrieved from www.forbes.com/sites/kathycaprino/2015/10/20/the-glass-cliff-phenomenon-that-senior-female-leaders-face-today-and-how-to-avoid-it/#ede548c79c65

Gagliardi, J. S., Espinosa, L. L., Turk, J. M., & Taylor, M. (2017). *American college president study 2017*. Retrieved from www.acenet.edu/news-room/Pages/American-College-President-Study.aspx

Gordon, A. (1974). On the far side of failure. In A. Gordon (Ed.), *A touch of wonder, a book to help people stay in love with life* (pp. 69–73). Old Tappan, NJ: Fleming H. Revell Company.

Hartley, M. T. (2012). Assessing and promoting resilience: An additional tool to address the increasing number of college students with psychological problems. *Journal of College Counseling, 15*(1), 37–51.

Innovative Educators. (2017). *Educating faculty, staff & students online—Growth mindset matters: Incorporating grit, resilience & self-efficacy in your FYE program*. Retrieved from www.innovativeeducators.org/products/growth-mindset-matters-incorporating-grit-resilience-self-efficacy-in-your-fye-program-917

Jay, M. (2017). *Supernormal, the untold story of adversity and resilience*. New York, NY: Twelve, Hachette Book Group.

Madsen, S. R. (2008). *On becoming a woman leader: Learning from the experiences of university presidents*. San Francisco, CA: Jossey-Bass.

Morgan, R. (1970). *Sisterhood is powerful, an anthology of writings from the Women's Liberation Movement*. New York, NY: Vintage Books.

Pierce, S. R. (2012). *On being presidential, a guide for college and university leaders*. San Francisco, CA: Jossey-Bass.

Ryan, M., & Haslam, S. A. (2007). The glass cliff: Exploring the dynamics surrounding the appointment of women to precarious leadership positions. *The Academy of Management Review, 32*(2), 549–572.

Sandberg, S., & Grant, A. (2017). *Option B: Facing adversity, building resilience, and finding joy*. New York, NY: Alfred A. Knopf.

Seligman, M. E. P. (2011). Building resilience: What business can learn from a pioneering army program for fostering post-traumatic growth. *Harvard Business Review, 89*(4), 100–106, 138.

Stefanco, C. J. (2014). Interviews with women presidents, all of whom were granted anonymity for preparing women to be president: Advancing women to the top leadership roles in higher education. In A. Vongalis-Macrow (Ed.), *Career moves: Mentoring for women advancing their career and leadership in academia* (pp. 109–119). Rotterdam, The Netherlands: Sense Publishers.

Turner, C. S. V. (2007). Pathways to the presidency: Biographical sketches of women of color firsts. *Harvard Educational Review, 77*(1), 1–38.

Vanasupa, L., McCormick, K., Stefanco, C., Herter, R., & McDonald, M. (2012). Challenges in transdisciplinary, integrated projects: Reflections on the case of faculty members' failure to collaborate. *Innovative Higher Education, 37*(3), 171–184.

Wolverton, M., Bower, B. L., & Hyle, A. E. (2009). *Women at the top, what women university and college presidents say about effective leadership*. Sterling, VA: Stylus Publishing.

6

FROM WALL STREET TO SOCIAL ENTREPRENEURSHIP

Connie K. Duckworth

Leadership is optimistic and aspirational. Leadership is also a participatory sport. We are well-equipped to play if we choose to do so. Leadership acumen is like any other muscle. You are born with some foundation, and you will develop that over time the more you engage it, strengthen it, and stretch it. There are core qualities for leaders that I believe are essential: honesty, work ethic, initiative, empathy, innate desire to help those around you succeed, and a willingness to take risks. I would like to share my own personal journey with you to discuss some skills I acquired along the way.

First of all, I am an optimist at heart. How else would I willingly go and enjoy business school when I was often the only woman in the classroom? Or spend a career on Wall Street where I was always the only woman in the room? Or become a social entrepreneur in Afghanistan, where you actually do not want to be a woman? Well, luck and timing—those two exogenous key factors—clearly played a role.

Size Your Downside Risk

Women have greater risk aversion than men, and female leaders in particular take less risk than male leaders in decision making (Croson & Gneezy, 2009; Eckel & Grossman, 2008; Ertac & Gurdal, 2012). But every decision you make involves some risk, large or small. You make decisions on a daily basis with imperfect information, and you will never have the luxury of having all the facts. There are at least two sides to every story. Judgment about how to evaluate risk can be learned on the job. At the end of the day, people listen and follow a leader because they trust you, they respect you, and they like you.

I joined the bond department of Goldman Sachs in 1981. That was during the time of a peak interest rate, high volatility, and rapid innovation. Over the next 20 years, for all practical purposes, the capital markets were invented, which opened up unprecedented opportunity and growth. It goes without saying that today we are in the midst of an even more exciting revolution with an even more exciting pace of change. You are now fluent in the new universal language of technology, and both the opportunities and demands for good leaders are greater than ever. Ladies and gentlemen, carpe diem.

I actually joined Goldman in the Los Angeles office in institutional sales. My prior employer thought that I would be fired the first time I made a mistake. This warning registered with me in two ways: first, I put my head down and worked hard to become technically competent and good with clients; and second, I developed a perspective that if this did not work out, I could always flip burgers at McDonald's or—better—In-N-Out. That is how I couched my downside. So why not give it a try? This ability to size my own downside risk was actually very liberating.

Test Your Leadership Ability

When I looked up four years later, I was doing a lot of business and turning small clients into big clients. It was this level of productivity that brought me to the attention of the partners that would influence my career trajectory. A couple of years later, I was the largest producer in the office. They came and presented a proposition to become a "player-coach." Translated, this meant I had the opportunity to give up all my large clients, take over unprofitable ones, and have the chance to run a small desk of eight to 10 people. This was not a change that I was willing to take on, so, naturally, I declined. Just as naturally, I was informed that I did not have sufficient information with which to reach this decision and it would be in my best interest to make this change.

They were actually right. The unknown, the risky choice paid off. This small-scale leadership position was the first baby step that gave me a chance to explore, test, and learn what kind of leader I could be. When I think back to some of the hare-brained things I asked my staff to do, I think, "Whoa, you do learn as you go." Acquiring this skill set actually made me the best candidate to take over the office two years later when my boss retired. The irony is that those guys that got all my big accounts ended up reporting to me.

While I was the logical choice, I was not necessarily the obvious one. I was the riskier choice. There had never been a woman desk head; there had never been a woman office head. However, the partners once again saw something in me that made them willing to take a risk, as they did two years later when I was named a partner in the firm in 1990. The same supportive message accompanied each one of these steps in my career path: "Don't eff it up." Goldman Sachs has since promoted many women to a partner position; however, females are still underrepresented in many financial leadership roles. While women represent 43.6% of management, business, and financial operations occupations, the higher up you look the fewer women you find (Catalyst, 2016). Women occupy just 17.6% of the executive officers in finance and insurance companies within the U.S. *Fortune* 500 (Catalyst, 2014).

Promoting Diversity through Policy

In addition to my day job, I also had a night job. I was asked to lead a new, firm-wide diversity undertaking. Now this was the fox in the henhouse. For the next five years, irrespective of what I was doing on the revenue-producing side, I established the firm's policies related to gender inclusion and family-friendly benefits. This included policies regarding mandatory sensitivity training for all partners and managers (largely men), flextime, and job sharing, before the advent of cell phones, Blackberry, and the internet, which was a bit of a trick. Telecommuting did not exist back then.

I also worked on establishing maternity and adoption leave policies. I availed myself not once, but four times, of the maternity policy, because I was the perpetually pregnant partner. Having four kids in six years, I must have been asked a thousand times, "Well, when are you coming back?" Because the assumption was that I would not. I count on my fingers, "Gee, I am due April 1st, so April, May, June, July, so I will be back August 1st." We know that workplace support has shown to have an impact on whether women are likely to return to work part-time after maternity leave (Houston & Marks, 2003).

We established Wall Street's first day care center. To me, that was one of the visuals that set up the conversation for the more strategic issues relating to advancement at the firm for men or women: how assignments were made and who got access to senior-level people relevant for career growth. Today, gender inclusion and family-friendly policies have been institutionalized and expanded to the point where nobody really recalls when there were not women on the partnership list or when there were not lactation rooms. Family-friendly policies help the organization as well as the employees. Employees with access to family-responsive policies also exhibit greater organizational commitment and express lower intention to leave their jobs (Grover & Crooker, 1995). As I think back on my career, this is the work I am actually most proud of.

Leadership Lessons

Surround Yourself With the Best

Over time, through experience, I have learned to flex my leadership muscle, and I want to share some observations. First, much of leadership is common sense and empathy. Since human capital is your most important asset, leaders hire the very best people. In a perfect world, you want to surround yourself with everyone smarter than you and harder working than you. That is what gives you leverage. There is a difference between managing and leading. As someone said, "You manage things and you lead people." Your job is to position those around you to be highly effective and to clear obstacles away so that they can reach their greatest potential. You have to remember that people are human, so there will always be mistakes and missteps. Nevertheless, you want to create a culture where people are willing to take risk and willing to fess up as soon as practical because it is much easier to get the ship righted earlier rather than later.

Lean on Your Strengths

The other thing I have learned is that everyone has strengths and weaknesses. As a general rule, we should all lean to our strengths, because that is where we can expect our best outcomes. Self-awareness as a leader leads to increased perception of leader effectiveness by others and increases leader self-efficacy and belief that one can be a leader (Butler, Kwantes, & Boglarsky, 2014). It is important to be cognizant and realistic about what you can do to be better; then you can make the effort to bolster those weaknesses over time.

Seek Honest Feedback

I have learned that you can teach specific skills, and on the margin, a leader can help people smooth over rough edges. But a leopard does not change its spots. The core qualities you see in others really are, for the most part, what you get. Those central, innate qualities—honesty and initiative—really cannot be acquired or adopted. Either people have these or they do not. As a leader, you also want some truth tellers in your inner circle. One of the hardest things to get as a leader is honest feedback. Yet, that is some of the most valuable information you can have. Leaders develop a kind of peripheral vision. It is like a third eye in yoga; it is the ability to see, hear, and recognize subtleties and to pick up on vibrations in your team or organization. Leaders also can think in a nonlinear way. They have an ability to see patterns and connect dots.

The Now, the Near, and the Far

Leaders execute on three planes simultaneously: the now, the near, and the far. Each of these requires a slightly different kind of thinking. In the now, you have to know enough about the details to recognize if execution is going well. For the near, you are anticipating the next three or four moves. However, a leader is most valuable when your focus in on what is beyond the horizon, and that is the far.

Now, I will reference my work in Afghanistan. In the now, my business, ARZU, which means "hope" in Dari, employs destitute but highly skilled women weavers who make hand-knotted rugs for the U.S. market for high-end residential and socially responsible corporations. In the near, we are focused on proving out a sustainable model of economic development, where sustainability means profitability. In the far, we are modeling behavioral economics that is replicable and scalable—linking good-paying jobs to certain behaviors that in turn will shift the cultural norm over time. ARZU, on one hand, is about making rugs and employing women; on the other hand, it is about gender equality and social justice.

***

Consider that nonprofit leadership involves taking a strategic, high-level perspective and focusing on commitment to the organizational mission (Bish & Becker, 2016; Cheverton, 2007). Business serves as a fantastic training ground for doing whatever you want to do over the course of a lifetime. I am often asked if it is better to start a career in the private sector or at a nonprofit. I always advise, "Go into business first." This allows you to acquire a toolkit that is transferable to any arena and that you can deploy for life. It is a skill set sorely needed in both the government and nonprofit sectors.

There are an overwhelming number of enormous, seemingly intractable problems in the world. If you can successfully navigate the private sector, then you can apply the perspective of the now, the near, and the far as it applies to these social problems. You develop the ability to break problems down into small, executable pieces rather than always hovering at 30,000 feet and trying to guess from that vantage point. As the generation of digital natives enters the workforce, you are armed with an entirely new arsenal that is ripe to be aimed at the world's problems. You can do even more good by developing and refining your leadership skills. Strong leaders focused on fixing the world are the game changers. They will promote a tsunami of social change. That is your job.

In the words of Mikki Taylor, the editor of *Essence* magazine: "Many women live like it is a dress rehearsal. Ladies, the curtain is up and you are on."

References

Bish, A., & Becker, K. (2016). Exploring expectations of nonprofit management capabilities. *Nonprofit & Voluntary Sector Quarterly, 45*(3), 437–457. doi:10.1177/0899764015583313

Butler, A. M., Kwantes, C. T., & Boglarsky, C. A. (2014). The effects of self-awareness on perceptions of leadership effectiveness in the hospitality industry: A cross-cultural investigation. *International Journal of Intercultural Relations, 40*(5), 4087–4098. doi:10.1016/j.ijintrel.2013.12.007

Catalyst. (2014, March 3). *Quick take: Women in financial services*. New York, NY: Author.

Catalyst. (2016, August 11). *Quick take: Women in the workforce: United States.* New York: Author. Retrieved from www.catalyst.org/knowledge/women-workforce-united-states

Cheverton, J. (2007). Holding our own: Value and performance in nonprofit organisations. *Australian Journal of Social Issues, 42*(3), 427–436.

Croson, R., & Gneezy, U. (2009). Gender differences in preferences. *Journal of Economic Literature, 47*(2), 448–474.

Eckel, C., & Grossman, P. (2008). Men, women, and risk aversion: Experimental evidence. *Handbook of Experimental Economics Results, 1*(1), 1061–1073.

Ertac, S., & Gurdal, M. Y. (2012). Deciding to decide: Gender, leadership and risk-taking in groups. *Journal of Economic Behavior & Organization, 83*(1), 24–30. doi:10.1016/j.jebo.2011.06.009

Grover, S., & Crooker, K. (1995). Who appreciates family-responsive human resource policies: The impact of family-friendly on the organizational attachment of parents and non-parents. *Personnel Psychology, 48*(2), 271–288.

Houston, D. M., & Marks, G. (2003). The role of planning and workplace support in returning to work after maternity leave. *British Journal of Industrial Relations, 41*(2), 197–214. doi:10.1111/1467-8543.00269

PART II

Navigating the Journey

7

ENTREPRENEURIAL TRANSITIONS

Meeting the Need for Balance and Challenge in Navigating the Leadership Journey

Sherylle J. Tan and Claudia Raigoza[1]

The feminist movement of the late twentieth century created a nation in which women now comprise 60% of college undergraduates, half of medical and law school students, and half of the U.S. workforce (Collins, 2009). Women are candidates for high political office, astronauts, brain surgeons, and movie directors. As a result, women are said to have broken the "glass ceiling"—no longer completely blocked by impermeable obstacles to leadership. Instead, they now maneuver through the "labyrinth" by tapping into their skills and talents as they advance in their careers (Eagly & Carli, 2006). Despite these advances, we continue to see a discrepancy between men and women in leadership positions. Women compose more than half of our population, but only 19.1% of Congress (Center for American Women and Politics, 2016), 19.9% of *Fortune* 500 board seats, and a mere 4.6% of *Fortune* 500 Chief Executive Officers (Catalyst, 2016). In other words, in the most powerful leadership positions in the United States, women are still grossly underrepresented.

Early in the twenty-first century, the media pointed to a phenomenon in which educated women are said to be leaving the workforce at high rates (Belkin, 2003). Research on women leaving the workforce has suggested that women experience many "pulls" and "pushes" that result in some women exiting the workforce—though not altogether as the media would have the public believe (Hewlett, Luce, Shiller, & Southwell, 2005). Interestingly, many of these same family pulls and workplace pushes are what send women into entrepreneurship, with the number of female business owners growing yearly. While the reasons that women enter into entrepreneurship are similar to the reasons women leave the workforce, there are more complex reasons as to why women make their respective career transitions.

A myriad of causes combine to leave women hovering only slightly above the glass ceiling. The gender inequity in leadership is seen in the workplace evidenced by the underrepresentation of women in top leadership positions. Much of the discrimination and stereotyping that occurs today is less overt and often very subtle. Other than those obvious barriers, basic social structures, such as family responsibilities, also contribute to the obstacles women face. Moreover, as women reach various milestones in their life regarding work and family, their perception and execution of leadership changes. Thus, the attainment of leadership for women does not appear to be a static concept throughout one's life but is rather a dynamic entity that responds to changes in environment and context. In this chapter, we will examine the relationship between two rising trends in the literature: the rise of women entrepreneurs and the rising number of women leaving the workplace (i.e., the "opt-out revolution") (Jome, Donahue, & Siegel, 2006; Belkin, 2003).

Family Care Responsibilities

One of the most dramatic changes affecting the North American family system during the latter half of the twentieth century was the huge increase in the proportion of women working outside the home (Aldrich, 2003). In 1960, 90% of adult men were in the labor force, compared to only 30% of adult women (Bianchi & Casper, 2000). By 1998, men's participation rate had declined to 78%, while women's participation rate had increased to 60%. As a result, dual-income households became more prevalent: in 1998, both spouses were working in 60% of all married couples (Aldrich, 2003). One might expect the growing number of employed women and their increasing contribution to household income to lead to more sharing of household tasks with husbands and children. However, according to researchers, women continue to carry the bulk of the responsibility, and the division of household labor remains traditional (Kan, Sullivan, & Gershuny, 2011; McKinsey and Company & Lean In, 2015). Because of this imbalance, work-family conflict is greater among women because they still assume a majority of household responsibilities (Shelton, 2006).

The family has changed and with it the leadership role of women. In a society where the workforce is aging and women continue to assume the majority of the domestic responsibilities, women have to care for not only children but also aging parents. Neal and Hammer (2007) refer to women in this situation as the "sandwiched generation." More and more women are becoming a part of this situation due to several demographic trends—delayed childbearing, general aging of the population and workforce, rising health care costs, and an increase in the number of women in the workforce. Neal and Hammer (2012) found that not only do women front the majority of the physical responsibility of elder care but also the emotional burden. They found that husbands in general reported less family-to-work conflict than wives, and these wives had significantly more absences per month due to care responsibilities at home for children and the elderly—5.4 absences, on average, compared to the husband's 2.6 absences, on average. It should be noted, however, that women also reported a higher level of *positive* spillover of family-to-work, which means women are seen to be more susceptible to the influences of family in general (Neal & Hammer, 2012).

One aspect of this "sandwiched generation"—balancing a job and *family*—has always been in conflict. Many adjustments within the workplace have been made to try to alleviate some of the conflict. Organizations have developed work-life initiatives to support both men and women in meeting their family responsibilities; however, women tend to be the most frequent users of work-life programs (Vandello, Hettinger, Bosson, & Siddiqi, 2013; Wise & Bond, 2003). However, the responsibility for continued organizational support around work-place policy and initiatives for women still rests largely on the organizations themselves (Schmidt & Duenas, 2002). Unfortunately, the use of work-family policies does not always support positive outcomes nor improve the work-family conflict that women experience (Kossek, Su, & Wu, 2017). In fact, the use of policies is not always supported by organizations and creates a stigma against those juggling work-family responsibilities (Kossek et al., 2017; Williams, Blair-Loy, & Berdahl, 2013). The result is mothers who are stressed, depressed, and consumed by guilt when they must sacrifice even the slightest amount of time with their children for their job, which creates an even greater pull from their family and domestic responsibilities.

Achieving Balance Through Entrepreneurial Leadership

In 2003, Lisa Belkin drew attention to what is called the "Opt-Out Revolution" in her article published in the *New York Times Magazine*. The "Opt-Out Revolution" claims that highly educated women are ending their careers to rear their children. Some statistics show that there is a slight trend of women ceasing to work completely in order to care for their children: the number of children with stay-at-home mothers increased 13% in the past decade (Vanderkam, 2005). However, further research has negated the existence of any such "revolution" and has instead pointed toward the complex career patterns of women (Antecol, 2010; Mainiero & Sullivan, 2005). This is primarily due to the fact that women's careers are not totally "linear," like those of most men. Linear careers have long been considered the traditional model and are described as "taking place within the context of stable, organizational structures," with individuals progressing up the firm's hierarchy seeking to obtain greater extrinsic rewards (Rosenbaum, 1979). In contrast, women's career progressions are often characterized by many starts and stops due to the complexities of women's work and nonwork lives that directly influence their career decisions and paths. Some women no longer find corporate ladder-climbing rewarding or experience obstacles, and this pushes them to find alternative career and leadership paths that allow them to balance and integrate family and work responsibilities.

One such pathway is self-employment or entrepreneurship, which means that although women are leaving large corporations, they are not ending their careers or leadership prospects altogether, as the media portrayal of the opt-out revolution proposes. In support of this notion, Cabrera (2007) found that 47% of the women surveyed in their study had stopped working at some point in their career, but 70% of women eventually returned to the workforce, debunking the myth that women opt out and do not return to the workforce. A career is defined as "an individual's work-related and other relevant experiences, both inside and outside of organizations, that form a unique pattern over the individual's life span" (Sullivan & Baruch, 2009, p. 1543). This definition is most adequate for our purposes because it encompasses movement between jobs and industries, as well as successful outcomes. Women's career development differs from men's in that women experience more interruptions in their careers, often due to family responsibilities and relationships (Albrecht, 2003). Entrepreneurship and self-employment are thus just another important part of women's career paths.

Because women have a higher motivation to balance work and family than their male counterparts (Noor, 2004), self-employment is perceived to be a career option that is more conducive to balancing these work and family role responsibilities and has greater opportunities for leadership (Cromie, 1987). Entrepreneurial leaders have ambition and motivation to start a new organization. They place emphasis on business growth, culture development, establishing credibility, and concern with the survival of the organization (Conger & Riggio, 2007). Because of these greater opportunities, the number of women entrepreneurs has been on the rise for the past two decades (Jome et al., 2006). According to the U.S. Census Bureau (2012), women owned 9.9 million nonfarm U.S. businesses. This accounted for 35.7% of businesses in the United States overall, up from 28.7% in 2007.

With the staggering increase of female entrepreneurs, it is important to carefully note and understand the "pulls" and "pushes" that lead them to this alternative career. A primary "pull" factor has to do with family responsibilities and meeting the needs of their family due to both parenting and elder care responsibilities, and even spousal job relocation (Hewlett, 2007; Stone & Lovejoy, 2004). Women's career decisions are strongly influenced by how these decisions will affect significant people in their lives (Powell & Mainiero, 1992). Women often see entrepreneurship as an opportunity to accommodate the needs of their work and family responsibilities and desires (Patterson & Marvin, 2009). Particular attention has been paid to the impact of children. Carr (1996) notes that women's employment decisions are often tied to family considerations. She found that having children, particularly young children, has a differentially strong, positive impact on women's tendency to be self-employed.

She considered this finding to be consistent with her central hypothesis that some women pursue self-employment for flexibility of working hours in order to accommodate family-related obligations (Carr, 1996). Similarly, Caputo and Dolinsky (1998) used national survey data from the National Longitudinal Survey of Labor Market Experience to determine why women choose self-employment as a career. The study found that the presence of young children in the household significantly increased the likelihood of a woman being self-employed because of the flexibility it allows.

External factors, such as increased globalization and rapid technological advancements, have also changed the way individuals approach careers. Many individuals are now creating work for themselves, using the internet as an inexpensive tool to connect with partners and suppliers and to find their products (Carraher, 2005). Furthermore, corporate "pushes" or barriers to women have helped thrust women out of the workforce and into business for themselves. The workplace, while many improvements have been made, is still an artifact of the twentieth century in many ways. The gender stereotypes and biases are "more subtle" than in the past, but they certainly do exist. While a small percentage of women feel passed over for promotions or denied a raise at work because of their gender, many of the biases and organizational structures that exist have failed to allow women to reach their full potential of leadership, as evidenced by the underrepresentation of women at those levels of leadership (Saad, 2015).

Most often, women enter entrepreneurship due to barriers that are linked to unconscious biases, such as frustration with hitting the "glass ceiling," dissatisfaction with slow career advancement, unmet career expectations, corporate downsizing, lack of independence and autonomy, inflexible work schedule, achieving business success, and pay gaps (Buttner, 1993; Jome et al., 2006; Saad, 2015; Still & Timms, 2000). Notably, some of these reasons are gender exclusive to women. Extensive research on the gender differences between male and female entrepreneurs has been conducted, and notable differences do exist. Lyness and Thompson (2000) found in a comparative study of 69 male and female executives that women reported greater barriers to career advancement, citing lack of general management experience, exclusion from informal networks, stereotypes about women's roles and abilities, and failure of top leaders to assume accountability for women's advancement. Researchers also found that managers who had been promoted were less likely to resign than nonpromoted managers, and promoted women were less likely to resign than promoted men (Lyness & Judiesch, 2001). All of these findings point to one conclusion: lack of advancement may be the foremost reason as to why women leave corporations (Mainiero & Sullivan, 2005).

Gender stereotypes are so dominating for women because leadership has been culturally and historically viewed as masculine (Koenig et al., 2011). While the discrimination that stems from stereotypes are less explicit today, unseen barriers continue to exist and are pervasive from the second-generation forms of gender biases—"cultural beliefs about gender, as well as workplace structures, practices, and patterns of interaction that inadvertently favor men" (Ibarra & Petriglieri, 2016, p. 1). These subtle second-generation gender biases, while lacking discriminatory intent, create a more challenging process for women to become leaders and hinder the development of women's leader identity (Ibarra, Ely, & Kolb, 2013). This second-generation gender bias impedes women from taking on top leadership roles, creating a lack of role models for women. This encourages a work environment, structure, and practice that creates a sense of being less connected to male colleagues, putting women at a disadvantage in considerations for key leadership positions and pushing them to seek alternative leadership and career opportunities (Ibarra et al., 2013). The obstacles that keep women from rising to the ranks of leadership in organizations lead many women to seek out entrepreneurial activities to put to use their knowledge, skills, and abilities in ways that better reflect their level of experience and ambitions.

The Impact of Life-Stages

When comparing the career patterns of men and women, it is important to note that an individual's career is influenced by many contextual factors, such as national culture, the economy, and the political environment, as well as by many professional factors, such as relationships with others (Sullivan & Baruch, 2009). This attention to context is even more relevant to women, given the trajectory of their careers. Women face complex decisions and barriers from professional, personal, and societal expectations that impact the choices they make in their careers (Powell & Mainiero, 1992). Women's careers have been described as "relational" by many researchers to-date, meaning that their career decisions are normally part of a larger, intricate web of interconnected issues, people, and aspects (Mainiero & Sullivan, 2005; Stone & Lovejoy, 2004; Still & Timms, 2000). This relational pattern has given way for the development of new models to better understand the career patterns of women—particularly, the "kaleidoscope career model."

The kaleidoscope career model (KCM) proposed by Mainiero and Sullivan (2005) may provide a more comprehensive understanding of the transitions that women make during the course of their careers. The KCM describes how career patterns for both men and women shift as their needs and interests change over time. Like a kaleidoscope that produces changing patterns when the tube is rotated and glass chips fall into new arrangements, women shift the pattern of their careers by rotating different aspects of their lives to arrange their roles and relationships in new ways (Mainiero & Sullivan, 2005). These changes may occur in response to internal changes, such as maturity, or in response to environmental changes, such as change in employment or family status. Individuals evaluate the choices and options available to determine the best fit among work demands, constraints, and opportunities, as well as relationships, personal values, and interests. As one decision is made, it affects the outcome of the kaleidoscope career pattern.

The KCM model describes three factors or values that influence career decisions: authenticity, balance, and challenge. *Authenticity* reflects the need for fulfilling work, giving back to community, and meaningful/appreciated work contributions. It has to do with being true to oneself and looking for work that is compatible with personal values. *Balance* refers to finding ways to integrate work and nonwork lives, including flexibility and decreased hours. *Challenge* is the need to experience career advancement that contributes to feelings of self-worth. These three parameters, known as the "ABC's" of the KCM, are simultaneously active over an individual's life span. The strength of a parameter is what shapes a career decision or transition, depending on what is going on in that individual's life at that particular time. Over the course of the life span, as a person searches for the best fit that matches the character and context of his or her life, the kaleidoscope's parameters shift in response, with one parameter moving to the foreground and intensifying as that parameter takes priority at that time. The other two parameters lessen in intensity and recede to the background but are still present and active. All aspects are necessary to create the current pattern of an individual's career. In the early stages of their careers, women are usually more concerned with goal achievement and challenge, so authenticity and balance are less important. In midcareer, women must cope with issues of balance between family-demands and career, and so challenge and authenticity take a secondary role. In late career, women focus on questions of authenticity, and their needs for balance and challenge become subdued.

The KCM is based on the results of five different studies (interviews, focus groups, and three surveys) of more than 3,000 U.S. professional workers. The analysis of the women's responses to the first survey helped Mainiero and Sullivan understand the nature and character of women's careers. Keeping in line with past findings, women were found to follow a relational pattern when making decisions, whereas men tended to examine career decisions from the perspective of goal orientation and independent action, acting first for the benefit of careers. As women move through the life-stages, they must make sacrifices for the greater good of themselves and any affected persons. Furthermore, the women indicated that they were more likely to have "non-traditional careers," characterized by various career interruptions that required attention to nonwork needs, than "traditional linear careers," as described by the men (Mainiero & Sullivan, 2005).

Women's Career and Leadership Decisions

The career decisions and transitions that women make during the course of their lives vary and are influenced by the context of women's life-stages. With the increasing number of women becoming entrepreneurs and seeking leadership opportunities through nontraditional career paths, it is critical to identify and understand the important influence of life-stages in the career and leadership decisions that women make. The decisions women make in their careers are not made independent of relationships or responsibilities, but rather, women's leadership motivations and decisions are contextual and complex, heavily dependent on whether they are in the early, middle, or late stage of their careers.

With a sample of 163 women recruited through various women's business associations we reviewed the reasons women seek out entrepreneurial careers, examined the predictors of KCM, and discussed how these career transitions and decisions map onto the KCM. These women were surveyed online. Women were asked about their entrepreneurial orientation and career transitions; specifically, they were asked questions regarding business, entrepreneurial orientation, career transitions, previous employment, family responsibilities, and leadership. Women were also asked questions based on the three values of the KCM: authenticity, balance, and challenge (Sullivan, Forret, Carraher, & Mainiero, 2009). In addition, they were surveyed on their motivation to lead (MTL), using the three-factor model developed by Chan and Drasgow (2001), and work-family conflict, based on Carlson, Kacmar, and Williams' (2000) six dimensions of work-family conflict.

These women ranged in age from 25–76 years (mean age = 51, SD = 11.73), with more than half who were parents (60%), and the majority were married (67.5%). The preponderance of participants were white (74.2%) and well-educated, with 69.5% reporting attaining a bachelor's degree or higher. Of the 163 women who completed the online survey, 95 were female entrepreneurs, with a mean age of 54 years (SD = 10.14). Almost all of these female entrepreneurs (97.9%) had worked outside the home prior to their current entrepreneurial venture, 81.9% had previous business experience, and 34.4% had a parent who was an entrepreneur. On average, they were in business for 13.7 years, ranging from less than 1 year to 45 years (SD = 11.28). The majority of the women entrepreneurs (77.4%) had made at least one career transition or pivot during their career cycle.

The Need for Balance

Balance, especially the achievement of work-family balance, has often been an important value and motivator for women who take on career transitions (Zimmerman & Clark, 2016). Entrepreneurship is often a path of transition or reentry within a career that women pursue due to the flexibility and potential to provide the work-family balance that they seek (McKie, Biese, & Jyrkinen, 2013). Balance played an important factor in seeking entrepreneurship, and even though these women entrepreneurs tended to have older children, the majority of women entrepreneurs (56.8%) were more likely to define success as being able to balance work and family. As expected, we found that balance was valued most by women with young children.

An examination of the literature on conflict between work and family roles suggests that work-family conflict exists when time devoted to one role makes it difficult to fulfill the requirements of another (Greenhaus & Beutell, 1985). In other words, tending to the responsibilities of a high leadership position at work conflicts with at-home responsibilities and is a source of stress for many women. Gornick and Marcia (2009) summarize this dilemma:

> in terms of tradeoffs between the interests of women, men, and children. Children can have more time with their parents, some observers suggest, only if women scale back their employment commitments and achievements. Or women can join men in the public spheres of employment and civic life, but only if the care and rearing of children is outsourced to non-family members.
>
> *(p. 4)*

The construct of work-family conflict is much more complex and multidimensional. For one, the conflict individuals experience is examined from dual directions; work interference with family and family interference with work. Secondly, there are various forms of work-family conflict: time-based conflict, strain-based conflict, and behavior-based conflict (Carlson et al., 2000). Typically, work interference with family is more prevalent than family interference with work conflict. However, family interference with work conflict was actually found to be stronger for women than for men (Byron, 2005).

The need for balance is heightened by work-family conflict, especially among women with younger children. We found that three dimensions of work-family conflict (after controlling for age) significantly predicted women's ratings of KCM balance as a career value (explained by 25% of the variance). Among the entrepreneurs, women who experienced conflict from family interfering with work, specifically time-based and behavior-based conflict, were the ones who wanted more balance. When the time that a woman devotes to her family responsibilities and the behaviors that are necessary to her family role interferes with her role at work, this conflict creates a desire and value for increased flexibility and ways to better integrate work and life. This was especially important to women with young children. Interestingly, women who experienced less conflict from behavior-based conflict from work interfering with family also had the need for balance. Despite having less conflict between behaviors expected from them in their professional and family lives, these women continued to seek balance. What we can conclude is that even when work-family conflict is low, women still desire the opportunity to seek integration of work and life.

The Need for Challenge

Entrepreneurship provides a forum for women to fulfill their desires for leadership and balance. Some women have left corporations to create firms that reflect their values while providing themselves and other women with challenging work and the flexibility to balance work and family (Buttner & Moore, 1997; Moore, 2002). The motivators of men and women entering entrepreneurship also differ. In a study between male and female MBA graduates, married women with dependents ranked career flexibility, family policies, family obligations, and spouse/co-career issues as very important at statistically significant higher rates than married men with dependents (DeMartino & Barbato, 2003). Male entrepreneurs differ from female entrepreneurs in that they are primarily motivated by wealth creation and career advancement. Research has shown that money is not a measure of success for women, and this is because they are often free from the obligation of being the primary breadwinner for the family. However, for women who were unmarried, they did indicate that money was a primary motivator (Still & Timms, 2000). Interestingly, marriage and children do not have much effect on the goals of male entrepreneurs (DeMartino & Barbato, 2003).

According to KCM, challenge provides women feelings of self-worth while providing the opportunity for increased responsibility and control (Mainiero & Sullivan, 2005). While challenge is typically a focal point early in one's career (Cabrera, 2007; Mainiero & Sullivan, 2005), the need for challenge was also an important driver for entrepreneurial women as they made career transitions. Women often break away from corporations as an alternative to facing the glass ceiling (Catalyst, 1998; Lanier, 2008). Entrepreneurship offers women the opportunity for success, leadership, challenge, and career development that they would not have received if they remained stagnant in organizations (Lanier, 2008). Entrepreneurship also allows women to advance their careers and leadership in ways that align with their values and need for challenge (Knorr, 2011). While the pulls and pushes motivate women to seek alternative career paths, underlying motivations to lead also include changes in priorities and needs and the hope of finding meaning, fulfillment, and balance (Knorr, 2011).

Interestingly, for both men and women, the enjoyment of being one's own boss is the single most commonly cited reason for becoming self-employed (Boden, 1999). This finding speaks to the leadership ambition of women and their desire for challenge in their career lives. Motivation to lead has been defined as an "individual difference construct that affects a leader's or leader-to-be's decisions to assume leadership training, roles, and responsibilities and that affects his or her intensity of effort at leading and persistence as a leader" (Chan & Drasgow, 2001, p. 482). According to Chan and Drasgow (2001), there are three underlying cognitive reasons that motivate an individual to lead: affective, social-normative, and calculative. Some lead because they have the desire to lead and do so for the pleasure and satisfaction; this exhibits an *affective* motivation to lead. *Social-normative* motivation to lead describes an individual who leads out of responsibility or a sense of duty. Lastly, there are others who aspire to lead in order to enjoy the concrete benefits related to the position. These individuals with a *calculative* motivation to lead carefully weigh the costs of leading and take on the leadership position if there is a clear benefit (Chan & Drasgow, 2001).

Women entrepreneurs continued to value challenges in their professional careers and sought them out by seeking an alternative path to leadership. In fact, we found that women's level of motivation to lead predicted their need for a challenge in their career and leadership decisions. Specifically, two factors of motivation to lead—affective and calculative—significantly predicted women's ratings of challenge as a career value (explained by 12% of the variance). Women who had high levels of affective and calculative motivation to lead valued and sought out challenge in their career decisions and transitions. The desire to lead explains women's motives to seek challenge and therefore transition into entrepreneurial ventures. Furthermore, women who calculate the risks and costs to leadership value challenge by taking on an alternative career path when there is a clear potential benefit.

***

According to Mainiero and Sullivan (2006) women will pursue careers for various reasons, depending on their career life-stage. Overall, our research finds that balance appears to be a recurring theme that women value at any stage of their career life-stage, while challenge is influenced by women's motivation to lead. As traditional gender roles and career paths evolve, women have found new ways to do it all. The KCM provides context to the study of women's career trajectories and decisions and puts gender in the foreground. Because women are the child bearers and because they are relational, it is important to understand their career patterns in tandem with their familial responsibilities throughout their life-stages, as this also affects their decision-making processes. Thinking in this contextual way will give researchers greater insight as to future career options and will also help organizations and society meet the needs of the growing female workforce population.

While the literature has focused on the reasons women seek alternative career trajectories such as entrepreneurship, few examples focus on the career life-stages and values that impact their career decisions. For women entrepreneurs, balance and challenge are strong values that are influenced by work-family conflict and their motivation to lead. Balance continues to be an important value for women that shapes their career and leadership decisions—no matter where they are in their life-stage. As the needs of family have changed, so has the composition of the "family" unit. In addition to children, many women nowadays find themselves caring for an elderly parent, which explains the extended importance of balance. Women seeking balance in organizations will often find that this need limits their leadership opportunities and choose to navigate their leadership journey by taking on an alternative career path. Entrepreneurship is a path that provides women the opportunities to meet this need as well as continue to fuel their leadership journey in positive ways.

Some women navigate leadership by taking on their own businesses. Leadership moves beyond position but includes the need for challenge as it stimulates and motivates. Many entrepreneurial women are motivated to lead and want to lead when the workforce creates barriers to leadership. These women pursue self-employment to provide the challenge they need to lead and work. Women do not opt out of corporations because of their lack of ambition; many do so because of the ambitions to which they aspire. Entrepreneurial women navigate through their leadership journeys by seeking entrepreneurial ventures that provide them the challenge they seek through added responsibility and control, enhancing their leadership skills and abilities.

Our research did not find strong associations with the need for authenticity, the third value in the KCM. This value is typically most important toward the later life-stage of one's career. Given that only a small proportion of the women in our study were late in their careers, this was not surprising. As women experience many starts and stops throughout their career trajectory, it is expected that through time their career and leadership decisions will be influenced by their need to find meaning and being genuine to themselves. Authenticity may take on different forms for women that are not reflected in their career journeys, such as taking on artistic or leisurely pursuits (Mainiero & Sullivan, 2005).

Because we know women continue their career and leadership pursuits rather than opt out altogether, organizations need to consider how they can retain talented women. Mainiero and Sullivan (2005) suggest that organizations adopt kaleidoscope-oriented job policies, such as time banks of paid parental leave, reduced-hours, job sharing opportunities, and options for career interruptions, to retain excellent workers struggling with work-family conflict. If the organizations fail to meet the values and needs of women and their ambitions to lead, they may lose valuable employees, or in the case of entrepreneurial women, gain competitors. Whether it is through entrepreneurship or traditional corporate positions, the growing population of women as leaders is surely to remain on the rise as they continue permeating the business world.

Women will continue to support their leadership journeys—no matter what career paths they take. Women are not leaving the workforce as described by the "Opt-Out Revolution"; rather, they are shaping and navigating their leadership journeys in unconventional and nonlinear ways that cannot be easily compared to the career trajectories of men. The paths women take are as individual as the women themselves. Women must consider various factors, as their decisions are much more relational and influenced by their life-stages.

Note

1 The contributions of Stephanie Haft and Taryn Akiyama during stages of this research project are acknowledged with thanks.

References

Albrecht, G. H. (2003). How friendly are family friendly policies? *Business Ethics Quarterly*, 13(2), 177–192.

Aldrich, H. (2003). The pervasive effects of family on entrepreneurship: Toward a family embeddedness perspective. *Journal of Business Venturing*, 18(5), 573–596.

Antecol, H. (2010). The opt-out revolution: A descriptive analysis. *Institute for the Study of Labor*, 5089.

Baskt, D. (2012, January 30). Pregnant, and pushed out of a job. *New York Times*. Retrieved from www.nytimes.com/2012/01/31/opinion/pregnant-and-pushed-out-of-a-job.html

Belkin, L. (2003). The opt-out revolution. *The New York Times Magazine*. Retrieved from www.nytimes.com/2003/10/26/magazine/the-opt-out-revolution.html

Bianchi, S. M., & Casper, L. M. (2000). Maternal employment and time with children: Dramatic change or surprising continuity? *Demography*, 37(4), 401–414.

Boden, R. J. (1999). Flexible working hours, family responsibilities, and female self-employment: Gender differences in self-employment selection. *American Journal of Economics and Sociology*, 58(1), 71–83.

Buttner, E. H. (1993). Female entrepreneurs: How far have they come? *Business Horizon*, 2(36), 59–65.

Buttner, E. H., & Moore, D. P. (1997). Women's organizational exodus to entrepreneurship: Self-reported motivations and correlates with success. *Journal of Small Business Management*, 35(1), 34–47.

Byron, K. (2005). A meta-analytic review of work-family conflict and its antecedents. *Journal of Vocational Behavior*, 67, 169–198.

Cabrera, E. F. (2007). Opting out and opting in: Understanding the complexities of women's career transitions. *Career Development International*, 12(3), 218–237.

Caputo, R. K., & Dolinsky, A. (1998). Women's choice to pursue self-employment: The role of financial human capital of household members. *Journal of Small Business Management*, 36(3), 8–17.

Carlson, D. S., Kacmar, K. M., & Williams, L. J. (2000) Construction and initial validation of a multidimensional measure of work-family conflict. *Journal of Vocational Behavior*, 56, 249–276.

Carr, D. (1996). Two paths to self-employment? Women's and men's self-employment in the United States, 1980. *Work and Occupations*, 23(1), 26–53.

Carraher, S. (2005). An examination of entrepreneurial orientation: A validation study in 66 countries in Africa, Asia, Europe, and North America. *International Journal of Family Business*, 2(1), 95–100.

Catalyst. (1998). *Women entrepreneurs: Why companies lose female talent and what they can so about it.* New York, NY: Catalyst.

Catalyst. (2016). *Quick take: Women in the workforce: United States.* New York: Catalyst. Retrieved from www.catalyst.org/knowledge/women-workforce-united-states

Center for American Women and Politics. (2016). *Women in U.S. Congress 2015*. Retrieved from www.cawp.rutgers.edu/women-us-congress-2015

Chan, K., & Drasgow, F. (2001). Toward a theory of individual differences and leadership: Understanding the motivation to lead. *Journal of Applied Psychology, 86*(3), 481–498.

Collins, G. (2009). *When everything changed: The amazing journey of America women from 1960 to present.* New York, NY: Bay Back Books.

Conger, J. A., & Riggio, R. E. (2007). *The practice of leadership: Developing the next generation of leaders.* San Francisco, CA: Jossey-Bass.

Cromie, S. (1987). Motivations of aspiring male and female entrepreneurs. *Journal of Occupational Behavior, 8*(3), 251–261.

DeMartino, R., & Barbato, R. (2003). Differences between women and men MBA Entrepreneurs: Exploring family flexibility and wealth creation as career motivators. *Journal of Business Venturing, 18*(6), 815–832.

Eagly, A. H., & Carli, L. E. (2006). *Through the labyrinth: The truth about how women become leaders.* Boston, MA: Harvard Business School.

Gornick, J. C., & Meyers, M. K. (2009). *Gender equality: Transforming divisions of labor.* London, UK: Verso.

Greenhaus, J. H., & Beutell, N. J. (1985). Sources of conflict between work and family roles. *The Academy of Management Review, 10*(1), 76–88.

Hewlett, S. A. (2007). *Off-ramps and on-ramps: Keeping talented women on the road to success.* Boston, MA: Harvard Business School Press.

Hewlett, S. A., Luce, C. B., Shiller, P., & Southwell, S. (2005). The hidden brain drain: Off-ramps and on-ramps in women's careers. *Harvard Business Review Research Report.* Boston, MA: Harvard Business School Publishing Corporation.

Ibarra, H., Ely, R. J., & Kolb, D. M. (2013, September). Women rising: The unseen barriers. *Harvard Business Review.* Retrieved from https://hbr.org/2013/09/women-rising-the-unseen-barriers?referral=03758&cm_vc=rr_item_page.top_right

Ibarra, H., & Petriglieri, J. (2016, March). Impossible selves: Image strategies and identity threat in professional women's career transitions. *INSEAD Working Paper No. 2016/12/OBH.* Retrieved from http://dx.doi.org/10.2139/ssrn.2742061

Jome, L. M., Donahue, M. P., & Siegel, L. A. (2006). Working in the uncharted technology frontier: Characteristics of women web entrepreneurs. *Journal of Business and Psychology, 21*(1), 127–147.

Kan, M. Y., Sullivan, O., & Gershuny, J. (2011). Gender convergence in domestic work: Discerning the effects of interactional and institutional barriers from large-scale data. *Sociology, 45*(2), 234–251.

Knorr, H. (2011). From top management to entrepreneurship: Women's next move? *International Journal of Manpower, 32*(1), 99–116.

Kossek, E. E., Su, R., & Wu, L. (2017). "Opting out" or "pushed out"? Integrating perspectives on women's career equality for gender inclusion and interventions. *Journal of Management, 43*(1), 228–254.

Lanier, P. A. (2008). *Women and minorities in management forum.* Retrieved from www.referenceforbusiness.com/management/Tr-Z/Women-and-Minorities-in-Management.html

Lyness, K. S., & Judiesch, M. K. (2001). Are female managers quitters? The relationships of gender, promotions, and family leaves of absence to voluntary turnover. *Journal of Applied Psychology, 86*(6), 1167–1178.

Lyness, K. S., & Thompson, D. E. (2000). Climbing the corporate ladder: Do female and male executives follow the same route? *Journal of Applied Psychology, 85*(1), 86–101.

Mainiero, L. A., & Sullivan, S. E. (2005). Kaleidoscope careers: An alternate explanation for the opt-out revolution. *Academy of Management Executive, 19*(1), 106–123.

McKie, L., Biese, I., & Jyrkinen, M. (2013). The best time is now! The temporal and spatial dynamics of women opting out to self-employment. *Gender, Work, & Organization, 20*(2), 184–196.

McKinsey and Company & Lean In. (2015). *Women in the workplace.* Retrieved from https://womenintheworkplace.com/

Moore, D. P. (2002). *Careerpreneurs: Lessons from leading women entrepreneurs on building a career without boundaries.* Palo Alto, CA: Davies-Black Publications.

Neal, M. B., & Hammer, L. B. (2007). *Working couples caring for children and aging parents: Effects on work and well-being.* Mahwah, NJ: Psychology Press.

Noor, N. (2004). Work-family conflict, work and family-role salience, and women's well-being. *Journal of Social Psychology, 144*(4), 389–405.

Patterson, N., & Marvin, S. (2009). Women entrepreneurs: Jumping the corporate ship and gaining new wings. *International Small Business Journal, 27*(2), 173–192.

Powell, G. N., & Mainiero, L. A. (1992). Cross-currents in the river of time: Conceptualizing the complexities of women's careers. *Journal of Management, 18*(2), 215–237.

Rosenbaum, J. (1979). Tournament mobility: Career patterns in a corporation. *Administrative Science Quarterly, 24*, 220–241.

Saad, L. (2015, September). Working women still lag men in opinion of workplace equity. *Gallup.* Retrieved from www.gallup.com/poll/185213/working-women-lag-men-opinion-workplace-equity.aspx

Schmidt, D. E., & Duenas, G. (2002). Incentives to encourage worker-friendly organizations. *Public Personnel Management, 31*(3), 293–308.

Shelton, L. M. (2006). Female entrepreneurs, work—family conflict, and venture performance: New insights into the work—family interface. *Journal of Small Business Management, 44*(2), 285–297.

Still, L. V., & Timms, W. (2000). "I want to make a difference": Women small business owners: Their businesses, dreams, lifestyles, and measure of success. *Proceedings of International Conference of Small Bus.* Retrieved from www.sbaer.uca.edu/Research/2000/ICSB/index.html Article 77

Stone, P., & Lovejoy, M. (2004). Fast-track women and the "choice" to stay home. *The ANNALS of the American Academy of Political and Social Sciences, 596*(1), 62–83.

Sullivan, S. E., & Baruch, H. (2009). Advances in career theory and research: A critical review and agenda for future exploration. *Journal of Management, 35*(6), 1542–1571.

Sullivan, S. E., Forret, M. L., Carraher, S. M., & Mainiero, L. A. (2009). Using the kaleidoscope career model to examine generational differences in work attitudes. *Career Development International, 14*(3), 284–302.

Sullivan, S. E., & Mainiero, L. A. (2008). Using the kaleidoscope career model to understand the changing patterns of women's careers: Designing human resource development programs that attract and retain women. *Advances in Developing Human Resources, 10*(1), 32–49.

U.S. Census Bureau. (2012). *Statistics for All U.S. firms by industry, gender, ethnicity, and race for the U.S., states, metro areas, counties, and places.* Retrieved from https://factfinder.census.gov/faces/tableservices/jsf/pages/productview.xhtml?pid=SBO_2012_00CSA01&prodType=table

Vandello, J. A., Hettinger, V. E., Bosson, J. K., & Siddiqi, J. (2013). When equal really isn't equal: The masculine dilemma of seeking work flexibility. *Journal of Social Issues, 69*(2), 303–321.

Vanderkam, L. (2005, December). A new mommy track. *USA Today*. Retrieved from https://usatoday30.usatoday.com/news/opinion/editorials/2005-12-06-vanderkam-edit_x.htm

Williams, J. C., Blair-Loy, J. L., & Berdahl, J. L. (2013). Cultural schemas, social class, and the flexibility stigma. *Journal of Social Issues*, 69(2), 209–234.

Wise, S., & Bond, S. (2003). Work-life policy: Does it do exactly what it says on the tin? *Women in Management Review*, 18, 20–31.

Zimmerman, L. M., & Clark, M. A. (2016). Opting-out and opting in: A review and agenda for future research. *Career Development International*, 21(6), 603–633.

8

NAVIGATING LEADERSHIP

How Diverse Women Learn and Progress Toward Their Leadership Aspirations and Goals

Cindy R. Pace

Overview: Women and Diverse Women of Color in Leadership

The upsurge of women entering the workplace has been one of the biggest economic revolutions of our time (Sherwin, 2014). Over the past decade, women have been entering the professional and managerial ranks in U.S. companies, public institutions, and organizations at about the same rate as men (Ahmad & Iverson, 2013). At the senior management level, women are being promoted or appointed to increasingly high-level C-suite positions such as CEO (Credit Suisse, 2014; Grant Thornton, 2013; International Labour Organisation [ILO], 2015). Workplace scholars' and practitioners' research has shown there is a benefit to diversity within corporate leadership as well as the talent pipeline (Corporate Leadership Council [CLC], 2002, 2013; Credit Suisse, 2012; Kilian, Hukai, & McCarty, 2005). In addition, having gender and ethnic/racial diversity is positively associated with more customers, increased sales revenue, greater relative profits, and greater market share (Credit Suisse, 2012; Desvaux, Devillard, & Sancier-Sultan, 2010; Government Accountability Office [GAO], 2013, 2017; Herring, 2009). The Catalyst research report, *The Bottom Line: Corporate Performance and Women's Representation on Boards* (2007), linked profitability to women in leadership. The study found that companies with more women board members, on average, significantly outperformed those with fewer women by 53% on return on equity, 42% on return on sales, and 66% of return on invested capital.

McKinsey's research report, *Diversity Matters*, revealed that racial and ethnic diversity had a stronger impact on financial performance than gender (Hunt, Layton, & Prince, 2014, 2015). By 2050, ethnically and racially diverse women will comprise the majority of all women in the U.S. Diverse women will make up 53% of the nation's female population, an increase from 36.3% (Ahmad & Iverson, 2013). Thus, this population is predicted to become a large part of the workforce in the United States, making them vital to the economic success of the nation. To ensure that U.S. companies can fill the high-impact jobs of the future, organizations need to understand how to leverage the skills, knowledge, and talents of a changing workforce (Ahmad & Iverson, 2013).

Diversity also brings challenges. Kilian (2009) argued that without senior executives and managers actively engaging in diverse talent management, any progress that has been made in developing a diverse pipeline to corporate leadership can quickly diminish. Even though the financial services industry is a major source of employment in the United States, management and executive leadership lacks diversity (GAO, 2013, 2017). The industry continues to be dominated by white men, which makes inclusion of underrepresented groups such as women and diverse women of color extremely challenging (Bagati, 2008). The leadership gap is even wider for diverse women, who remain in the first to middle management levels much longer than nonminority women and all men (GAO, 2013, 2017). According to the McKinsey and Lean In *Women in the Workplace* report, women of color make up 12% of first-level managers, compared with 45% for their white male peers. At the C-suite level, women of color make up just 3% of the workforce, compared with 71% for white men (McKinsey and Lean In, 2016). High-potential identification of managers has been deemed important in developing a company's leadership pipeline. However, the percentage of diverse women in management is low in high-potential talent pools and still does not easily mitigate the issue of slow progression and ascension into senior executive positions (Edmondson-Bell, 2013; Giscombe, 2011; Sanchez-Hucles & Davis, 2010). In order to increase diversity at senior executive levels and unlock the full potential of this talent pool, more must be known about how high-potential diverse women midlevel managers who aspire to attain senior leadership roles successfully develop and progress to the top.

A review of the literature indicates a paucity of research that provides perspective on the leadership aspirations and career development of diverse women. The majority of existing research on women's career development references the career experiences of white women, who are dominant in many study samples. Given these points, the research study highlighted in this chapter sought to: (1) expand the knowledge and insights gained from the few pivotal studies on diverse women in management and leadership; (2) gain an understanding of the leadership aspirations and developmental experiences of diverse women in midlevel management, where little research exists; and (3) shed light on factors that influence their development and progression into leadership roles while working in financial services organizations, where they are often underrepresented and disadvantaged (Pace, 2017).

Therefore, this chapter will discuss how diverse women in midlevel corporate management at a global employee benefits and insurance firm learned to lead and progress toward their aspirations and goals. Specifically, the chapter covers diverse women's perceptions and reflections along their leadership journey, including their highest aspirational leadership goals and the learning experiences and strategies that were instrumental in their pursuit of top leadership.

Framework for Navigating Leadership

The following framework provides a simple organizing structure for understanding how diverse women navigate their leadership journeys in their effort to progress toward their highest leadership aspirations and goals. The framework seen in Figure 8.1 was derived from a select review of the literature, study research questions, and key findings. As a foundation of understanding diverse women, the framework leverages the self-efficacy work of Fassinger and colleagues from the National Study on Women's Achievement (NWSA; Fassinger, 2002, 2005; Gomez et al., 2001; Prosser, Chopra, & Fassinger, 1998; Richie et al., 1997). Similar to Fassinger's "Career Model," the core of this framework is composed of self-identity constructs—ethnicity, race, and gender—and belief in self-attributes—leadership self-efficacy, self-determination, perseverance, values, and sense of purpose. After establishing the center of the framework, other elements were added to further explain the model. The first question sought to uncover how diverse women describe their highest leadership aspirations and goals, known as their desired aspirations; hence the category was appropriately titled "Leadership Aspirations and Goals." The second research question sought to understand what specific actions diverse women take to obtaining their highest leadership aspirations and goal. Therefore, the category is titled "Enacted Aspirations." The third research question intended to uncover how diverse women learn to lead. Specifically, what were the instrumental experiences to date they felt best prepared to progress toward their aspirational leadership roles and goals? Hence, the categorization is "Instrumental Learning Experiences." The fourth and final research question attempted to reveal the organizational factors diverse women felt supported or hindered their learning and progression toward their leadership aspirations and goals. Thus, "Organizational Resources and Support" was an appropriate title. Each of the four areas of the framework is discussed in the following section.

Leadership Aspirations and Goals

Aspirations are defined as motivational drivers that trigger effort, actions, and persistence to attain a leadership role in an organization (Tharenou, 2005; Tharenou & Terry, 1998). In addition, Litzky and Greenhaus (2007) defined

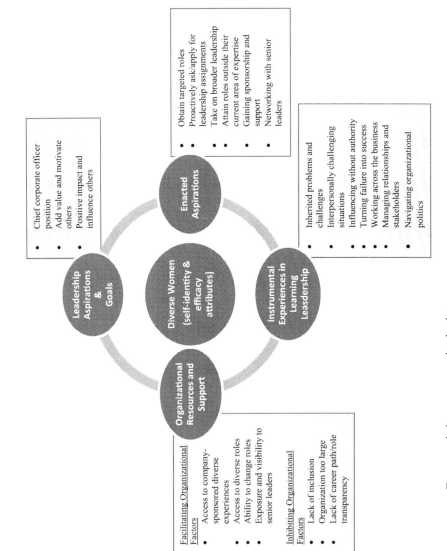

- Chief corporate officer position
- Add value and motivate others
- Positive impact and influence others

- Obtain targeted roles
- Proactively ask/apply for leadership assignments
- Take on broader leadership assignments
- Attain roles outside their current area of expertise
- Gaining sponsorship and support
- Networking with senior leaders

- Inherited problems and challenges
- Interpersonally challenging situations
- Influencing without authority
- Turning failure into success
- Working across the business
- Managing relationships and stakeholders
- Navigating organizational politics

Leadership Aspirations & Goals

Enacted Aspirations

Diverse Women (self-identity & efficacy attributes)

Instrumental Experiences in Learning Leasdership

Organizational Resources and Support

Facilitating Organizational Factors
- Access to company-sponsored diverse experiences
- Access to diverse roles
- Ability to change roles
- Exposure and visibility to senior leaders

Inhibiting Organizational Factors
- Lack of inclusion
- Organization too large
- Lack of career path/role transparency

FIGURE 8.1 Framework for navigating leadership

leadership/senior management aspirations as an individual's desire and intention to move into a senior management position in an organization. They defined two facets of aspiration as desired and enacted. Desired aspiration is the drive to achieve a leadership position, while enacted aspirations are the actions (mastery, experiences, positions) taken to achieve leadership roles. Tharenou (2005) found that women and men both have desired and enacted aspirations, defined as plans of action one undertakes to achieve the ultimate goal of attaining a position in senior management. Boatwright and Egidio (2003) argued that "women must intrinsically possess an interest in aspiring for leadership roles before they can take full advantage of emerging opportunities" (p. 654). It is important to note that Hoobler, Lemmon, and Wayne (2011) found a correlation between developmental opportunities and women's managerial aspirations. It seems when women reported receiving challenging work assignments, training and development, and career encouragement from their managers, they also reported higher managerial aspirations. Therefore, as one's leadership capabilities grow and expand, high-profile, challenging assignments, organizational sponsorship, and endorsements are more likely to be offered (Ely, Ibarra, & Kolb, 2011).

Enacted aspirations as described are plans of action that one undertakes to achieve the ultimate goal of attaining a position in senior management and leadership (Litzky & Greenhaus, 2007). The stronger the drive, the more extensively an individual engages in behaviors/actions that achieve the aspiration (Hall, 2004). Van Velsor and Hughes's (1990) groundbreaking research explored how women managers learn from experience, compared to men; the researchers noted that women more frequently reported recognizing and seizing opportunities, such as keeping eyes open for opportunities and getting budget profit and loss responsibility. In exploring aspirational goals that drove women's career strategies across ethnic identities, O'Neill, Shapiro, Inglos, and Beard-Blake (2013) found that women had a combination of contemporary goals, such as making a positive impact, intellectual challenge, role modeling, and conventional goals, including leadership positions, money, and success. Other studies have defined this as objective (financial) and subjective (work/life balance, sense of purpose, and significance) success (Ng, Eby, Sorenson, & Feldman, 2005). Similarly, Korn Ferry's (2015) research on leadership potential showed that high-potential leaders value the nature of leadership work, the opportunity to make a difference, having greater responsibility, and making a positive impact on their coworkers and organization.

Most recently, aspirational drivers also include a person's core values and interests that influence his or her career path, motivation, and engagement (Korn Ferry, 2015). According to Silzer and Church (2010), 90% of organizations now use an individual's career drive (aspirations) as one predictor to identify high potential. The Corporate Leadership Council (2005) defined a high-potential employee as someone with the ability, engagement, and aspiration to rise to and succeed in more senior, critical positions. McKinsey and Lean In (2016) conducted a survey with 34,000 employees from 39 companies to explore men's and women's experiences regarding gender, career, and work-life issues. Findings revealed that women of color are the most underrepresented group in the senior and upper ranks of companies, and their numbers drop steeply at the middle and senior levels. However, black/African American, Hispanic, and Asian women are more eager than white women to reach high-level positions. Of the women surveyed, 48% of women of color said they aspired to be a top executive, compared with 37% of white women (McKinsey and Lean In, 2016). Similarly, Center of Talent Innovation's (2015) study on black women in leadership revealed that black/African Americans have higher aspirations to obtain senior leadership roles than white women (Hewlett & Green, 2016). In 2015, Endeavor (alias), the employee benefits and insurance company where the women in the featured study were employed, conducted a customized women's leadership diagnostic (quantitative and qualitative survey) internally of 75 women leaders across the globe. Findings revealed that their high-potential women were highly ambitious, with aspirations of ascending into leadership. Yet they had low confidence in their ability to obtain senior leadership roles (Endeavor Women in Leadership Diagnostic, 2015).

Instrumental Experiences for Learning Leadership

According to the literature on women's learning in the workplace, including informal learning research in men and women, women usually learn informally through others and through self-directed means such as trial and error, observation, dialogue, and critical reflection (Marsick & Watkins, 1990, 2001; Van Velsor & Hughes, 1990). Wilson, Van Velsor, Chandrasekhar, and Criswell (2016) contended that leaders learn to expand their critical skills and competencies in challenging situations. The Center for Creative Leadership's multiple studies over a 30-year period have indicated that on-the-job leadership experiences are primary sources of learning and account for as much as 70% of a leader's development, thus emphasizing the importance of systematically measuring and understanding leadership experiences (McCall & Hollenbeck, 2002; McCall, Lombardo, & Morrison, 1988; Wilson et al., 2016). Wilson et al. (2016) argues that it is through key experiences that leaders learn, and their "ability and willingness to learn from experience is foundational for leading with impact" (p. 6).

Most recently, the Credit Suisse Gender (CSG) 3000 study analyzed more than 28,000 senior managers at over 3,000 companies to follow women's career paths to C-suite roles, such as CEO, CFO, and operations and strategy roles. As with previous research, the CSG 3000 study findings revealed that women who rose to CEO-level roles came from the so-called "management power line," rising gradually through line positions in business management and operational roles (business unit heads) and CFO and strategy roles (including investor relations). Therefore, line experience is necessary for women's advancement into the CEO post and other top leadership positions (ILO, 2015). However, women tended to be overrepresented in shared services and staff functions such as human resources, public relations and communications, and finance and administration and are therefore only able to go up the ladder to a certain point in the organizational hierarchy (Bagati, 2008; Credit Suisse, 2014; ILO, 2015). Even though women can advance in these roles, they are considered to have less influence or offer less opportunity to move into the most senior positions in a company.

Transitioning from a midlevel leader to a senior leader requires women to step outside their comfort zones to gain business experiences that are difficult and uncomfortable (Orr, 2013; PDI Ninth House, 2012). Burke (2001) found that specific work experiences, developmental job assignments, developmental work relationships, alternative work arrangements, and certain organizational initiatives have positive influences on women's career development. Lyness and Thompson (2000) reported that challenging job assignments, transition to new job responsibilities, and job mobility were specific developmental experiences that facilitated leadership development. Yet women have less access to challenging work assignments and are less likely to be given assignments that are high-risk to the company. High-risk job assignments, considered "glass cliffs" for women, generally carry large amounts of visibility and provide recognition for success that translates into future leadership opportunities. However, visibility is important for women who reported a proven track record of success (Lyness & Thompson, 2000) and consistently exceeding expectations.

Organizational Resources and Support

Human Capital Institute argues that organizations that are willing to move employees laterally and provide roles or assignments in departments other than the ones they are currently in are finding the strategy to be a unique and effective method of engaging their workforce, developing their competencies and careers, and ultimately retaining them longer than those who maintain the traditional, unidirectional "corporate ladder" approach (HCI, 2011). The Working Mother's Multicultural Women at Work 2016 report, which surveyed 1,370 women of color, recommended that organizations focus on advancement programs such as mentoring, sponsorship programs, and networking groups designed to reach women of color (Owens & DeHass, 2016). In addition, focus should be on middle managers to increase satisfaction and retention of multicultural women. A select review of the research literature revealed organizational factors that facilitate or impede the development and progression of diverse women into top leadership. For example, diverse women managers tend to lack access to influential networks. Therefore, having leaders in the organization who broker networking opportunities for diverse women could expand the depth and range of their developmental relationships as well as highlight the benefits of networking across the organization.

More importantly, sponsorship activities have been shown to be a differentiator in advancing diverse women leaders. On the other hand, women who continue to have careers in corporate management often encounter traditional masculine corporate cultures, which can be extremely difficult for women to learn, develop, and navigate (Bierema, 1999; Giscombe, 2011; Sabattini, 2008). White, male-dominated managerial hierarchies tend to be risk-averse cultures that are unwilling to step outside their norm to do things differently, which in turn inhibits the development and advancement of women and racially and ethnically diverse groups (Sanchez-Hucles & Davis, 2010). Porter and Daniel (2008) explained that women of color who are leaders experience an intense scrutiny because of their race/ethnicity and feel as though they have limited room to make mistakes. This seems particularly strong when a woman of color is the first and only woman of color to serve in a particular leadership role.

How Diverse Women Navigate Leadership

The purpose of the featured qualitative case study was to explore with 16 diverse women in corporate midlevel management their perceptions of how their learning experiences impacted their progression toward their leadership aspirations and goals. This section explores how diverse women navigate toward their leadership aspirations and goals, including the career strategies they employ to progress toward top leadership.

The participants were diverse American women whose racial/ethnic identity was of African, Asian, Latin/Hispanic, Native American, or Pacific Islander descent, and/or any combination of these races/ethnicities. They worked in the U.S. at a global employee benefits and insurance company at midlevel to upper midlevel management positions as assistant vice presidents and vice presidents. Their positions were below senior executive leadership, and they were employed within line/business roles or staff/enabling functions (e.g., strategy, finance, marketing, legal, procurement, research and development, or media/investor relations). Each had been employed for at least two years, with aspirations to move into executive management/senior leadership, and had received at least one promotion or expansion of roles and responsibilities within management at the present company. They had a career pattern with a history of career advancement in one organization or via different organizations and had been identified as key talent/future leader in their organization.

Based on findings from the featured study, Table 8.1 displays the four ways diverse women managers learn and progress toward their leadership aspirations and goals.

TABLE 8.1 How Diverse Navigate Leadership Aspirations and Goals

---

Diverse women managers learn and progress toward leadership aspirations and goals by:

---

1. Aspiring to become top corporate leaders who lead with impact and influence, add value, motivate others, and influence business strategy
2. Proactively identifying and seizing opportunities in their midst
3. Managing challenging situations and relationships
4. Accessing diverse company-sponsored experiences

Aspire to Become Top Corporate Leaders

An overwhelming majority of the diverse women managers in this study (94%) described becoming top corporate officers as their highest leadership aspiration. They described their leadership aspirations, specifically ascending to corporate officer roles, at two different levels of leadership with high status, power, and influence: chief corporate officer (C-suite)/executive vice president (EVP) and senior vice president (SVP)/vice president (VP). In this regard, aspiration served as an intrinsic motivator that drove the women to want to succeed at the highest levels of leadership. However, it is important to note that aspiration can go beyond the role itself and encompass the goals one wants to accomplish in the role. The diverse women managers described the goals they wanted to accomplish most while in their aspirational leadership role was to:

1. Lead With Positive Impact and Influence

More than half of the diverse women managers across the approaches (63%) articulated the ability to lead with positive impact and influence others as their primary goal as a leader. They also described taking actions with impact, such as fostering a positive culture, adding value, motivating others, like their direct reports, to have moon-shot aspirations, and having a broader scope and understanding of the business, which are discussed in the following sections.

2. Add Value and Motivate Others

Six of the 16 diverse women managers (31%) described adding value and motivating others as important aspects of attaining their leadership aspiration. They defined leadership as the ability to motivate others, make a difference, and add valuable contributions to their team and organization.

3. Influence Business Strategy

Four of the 16 diverse women managers (25%) described the importance of broadening their business scope to attain their leadership aspiration and goals.

They described broadening their business scope as a way to expand the perspective of what is happening in the company, influencing strategy, and gaining exposure to global business.

Identifying and Seizing Leadership Opportunities

Similar to Van Velsor and Hughes' research (1990), in this study, a strong majority of the diverse women managers, 14 of the 16 (88%), indicated identifying and seizing opportunities as the primary action they took to progress toward leadership roles. Identifying and seizing leadership opportunities was defined as purposeful actions taken to attain aspirations and advance into leadership roles which included raising a hand for assignments, learning new things, and changing roles.

When interviewed, the diverse women managers were asked to share the specific actions they took to progress into their aspirational leadership roles, known as their enacted aspirations. To ensure the collection of in-depth descriptions of their enacted aspirations, the diverse women managers were asked to provide detailed examples of the steps they took to fulfill their aspirations. They described four distinct actions: (1) obtaining targeted roles; (2) proactively applying for leadership assignments; (3) taking on broader roles; and (4) attaining roles outside their current area of expertise.

Managing Challenging Situations and Relationships

Diverse women managers were asked to think back on two defining moments in their managerial careers that stood out (instrumental) among the rest in preparing them to develop and progress into top leadership roles. They were asked to explain what happened and share lessons learned. An overwhelming majority of women in the study (94%) described managing challenging situations, relationships, and people as the most instrumental experiences in their development and progression into top leadership roles. Diverse women managers cited and described four distinct experiences that were instrumental in their learning: managing and building relationships, handling new/unfamiliar tasks and responsibilities, difficult staffing situations, and dealing with interpersonal issues.

Access to Diverse Company-Sponsored Experiences

Diverse women managers were asked to describe the facilitating organizational factors that had a positive impact on achieving their aspirations and progression into leadership roles. They were also asked to describe the inhibiting organizational factors that were barriers to achieving their aspirational roles. The vast majority of diverse women managers said being provided access to diverse experiences by their company had a positive impact on their aspirations and progression into top leadership roles. Access to diverse experiences is what the organization provides to diverse women, namely project assignments, new roles, and exposure and visibility to senior leaders. These opportunities can have a positive impact on diverse women's aspirations and progression into top leadership roles.

Specific Ways Diverse Women Navigate Progression Toward Top Leadership

In order to gain a more in-depth understanding of the research findings, the researcher further explored the impact of various career strategies these high potentials adopted with respect to their career progression. Based on participants' current role in the organization, their leadership aspirations/goals and developmental experiences, three distinct career progression strategies were identified: activation, influence, and motivation. Overall, these progression approaches were defined as dominant strategies participants used based on their description in one-on-one interviews. However, these career progression strategies presented in this chapter are based on snapshot perceptions reported during one-hour interviews and, thus, are not meant to characterize who each woman is or has been throughout her career advancement. Similar to the career strategies mentioned here from the literature, these career progression approaches are fluid; women can adopt any of these strategies based on their career aspiration and situational needs and can change or mix her approach over time.

These progression approaches were defined and organized based on the dominant career advancement strategies participants adopted and behaviors they described in interviews. Table 8.2, shows the career progression approaches used by diverse women in this study.

Activation

Women using "Activation" strategies reported leveraging self-promotion techniques including proactively asking for assignments, seeking advice and support regarding career moves, and raising their hand for on-the-job opportunities. Diverse women managers using this approach spoke as if they were self-assured, future-focused, and goal-oriented. They described themselves as independently focused on delivering strategic business goals and advancing toward more leadership responsibility. Women using "Activation" strategies were emerging mid-level leaders, occupying assistant vice president (AVP) roles in areas such as legal affairs, accounting/tax, investments, and change management. In their roles, they seemed to be proactive, collaborated when necessary, and were integral to executing strategic tasks. As technical experts and individual contributors, they described being adept at achieving individual tasks and executing strategy for leadership. They reported actively contributing to team performance and being loyal to their leadership and mentors. They took a more formal path to advancement by seeking sponsorship and mentorship from direct managers.

TABLE 8.2 Description of Career Progression Strategies.

Career Progression Strategies	Definition	Descriptors
Activation	• Core approach is focused on getting things done. Aspire to advance into broader leadership roles.	• Self-promotion defined by proactively asking for and/or raising their hands for on-the-job opportunities. • Hyper focused on advancing toward more leadership responsibility. • Adept and effective at achieving individual tasks, executing, and contributing to team performance. • Follow advice and guidance of leaders and mentors.
Influence	• Core approach is using influence and negotiation to make thing happen. Get things done through others via networks. Aspire to gain power and influence.	• Make things happen and get things done through others. • Put their personal stamp on their work. • Adept at developing, building, and leverage influential, powerful relationships across and outside the organization. • Aspire to gain power and influence.
Motivation	• Core approach is purpose-driven, inspiring action and engagement in others. Aspire to add value through their contributions.	• Inspire, motivate, and engage in others. • Adept at inclusion and cultivating stakeholders to make a positive impact in their organization. • Purpose-driven performers who foster change. • Seek to add value through their contributions and develop organizational talent.

Progression-wise, these emerging midlevel leaders broadened their leadership scope so they could advance within and beyond their current level. They tended to be more transactional in getting things done.

Since women using "Activation" strategies were midlevel leaders who had yet to advance into being a corporate officer at the vice president level, they were more focused on advancing into broader leadership responsibility, even though they aspired eventually to hold corporate officer roles. However, there might be a lack of clarity on the difference in corporate officer levels—vice president, senior vice president, and executive vice president. For example, in one case, there seemed to be a lack of understanding about the difference between VP and EVP. Therefore, their aspirations might change in nature as the women progress to higher levels. Women using "Activation" strategies at the AVP level seemed to want to have a broader business scope, more so than those using "Motivation" strategies.

In addition, women using "Activation" strategies reported using self-promotion strategies such as proactively asking for assignments and raising a hand for on-the-job opportunities. They reported being self-assured, future-focused, and goal-oriented. They identified and seized leadership opportunities by taking risks to move into roles inside and outside their area of expertise. Taking chances and putting themselves out there is one of the "Activation" strategies women described. It is important to note that women who use "Activation" strategies focus on seizing opportunities through others via relationships with mentors and sponsors in the organization.

The majority of women using "Activation" strategies managed challenging situations and relationships by managing stakeholders, navigating politics and handling difficult partnerships, and solving problems for others. They reported that these "Activation" strategies were the instrumental learning experiences that best prepared them for leadership. Other women who used "Activation" strategies reported learning from mistakes to influence and lead teams. They also faced challenging situations and relationships. Women using "Activation" strategies reported showing mastery in solving problems and dealing with challenges.

Women using "Activation" strategies also cited having access to diverse company-sponsored experiences such as advancement programs and the women's leadership development program. These programs had a positive impact on their aspirations and progression into leadership roles. Women using "Activation" strategies tend to take a more formal path to advancement by seeking development, sponsorship, and mentorship from direct managers.

Influence

Women using "Influence" strategies reported being adept at building and leveraging influential and powerful relationships across and outside the organization to get things done, gaining access to power, and influencing others. When women used influence, they reported using an approach characterized by power-oriented self-promotion. They reported being driven to succeed and advance into leadership on their own terms. They demonstrated their ability to make things happen for those they supported and led, which set them apart from others. They also reported putting a personal stamp on their work and that influence and action were the best tools for leadership. They occupied roles as chief of staff to executive leaders, business operations leaders, and strategists, which allowed them to operate in unconventional ways. In their roles, they tended to serve as negotiators, astute mediators at resolving conflict, relationship builders, and turnaround specialists. Women using "Influence" strategies demonstrated the ability to respect and understand different perspectives. They said that they had learned this through their experience.

Progression-wise, these seasoned midlevel leaders were on the cusp of advancing into divisional/business unit leadership, having gained some experiences in the area. Women using "Influence" strategies said they had cultivated relationships with many stakeholders and dealt with problems in adaptive and proactive ways. They were specific in describing the roles, since they worked directly for leaders at these levels and reported being savvy and confident in their ability to attain these roles. Women using "Influence" strategies were already vice presidents and seemed to have clarity about the differences in scope between an SVP, an EVP, and a C-suite. Women using "Influence" strategies see themselves obtaining their aspirations at their present company or elsewhere—for example, by holding a leadership position in the C-suite as a chief operating officer (COO) or chief administrative officer (CAO), but in a smaller company in an environment where they can have greater impact. Women using "Influence" strategies reported influence and action as the best tool for leadership. Only a few women using "Influence" strategies discussed inspiring greatness in others and making a positive impact. It is important to note women using "Influence" strategies usually spoke in these terms and were more self-focused.

The examples provided by women using "Influence" strategies could be interpreted as power-oriented, self-promotional, and driven to succeed and advance into leadership on their own terms. Women using "Influence" strategies reported influence and action as the tools for advancing in leadership. They reported seizing leadership opportunities and moving into roles with broader influence, opportunities for growth, and access to power. Women using "Influence" strategies tended to seek opportunities for growth. Also, women who reported using "Influence" strategies said they gain perspective on their abilities when they take on new opportunities. Women using "Influence" strategies reported managing challenging situations and relationships by serving as deal brokers, managing different constituencies, and keeping relationships though crisis. Women reported these previous "Influence" strategies were the instrumental learning experiences that best prepared them for leadership. Women who reported using "Influence" strategies who served as chief of staff to EVPs conveyed that an understanding that different relationships matter in business, knowing how to consolidate information, and managing through influence are important issues to know at the executive level.

Women using "Influence" strategies cited having access to diverse company-sponsored experiences such as company resources and opportunities, opportunities to move around, and working on a global scale. These experiences had a positive impact on their aspirations and progression into leadership roles.

Motivation

Women who reported using "Motivation" strategies were focused on adding value through their contributions and developing organizational talent. Women using this approach were similar in some ways as those using "Influence" strategies, but they reported being more purpose-driven and wishing to inspire greatness in others' potential and to make a positive impact to drive high performance and foster change. They occupied roles such as global operations leaders, sales leads, and lead actuary. Their examples suggested that they showed insight, engagement, and willingness to take risks for positive change to occur. Women using the "Motivation" approach discussed what they did in ways that seemed pragmatic and ethical; they said they sought to change corporate orthodoxy with new ideas. They reported working through others with a goal of achieving high performance. They aspired to adopt attributes of senior leaders in the way that they tried to inspire personal greatness in others' potential.

Progression-wise and similar to women using "Influence," these seasoned midlevel leaders were on the cusp of advancing to divisional/business unit leadership. They also reported on the mutual interdependence of relationships and cultivated stakeholders to make a positive impact on their organization.

Women using the "Motivation" strategy reported being ambitious in advancing to the highest levels of leadership but reported interest in the positive influence and impact they could make as leaders at the company. Even though they wanted to be influential leaders, some women using the "Motivation" approach placed less emphasis on titles but still discussed the type of leader they wanted to be. Women using "Motivation" strategies were, in comparison to others in this study, focused on adding value through their contributions and developing organizational talent. Two women who used the "Motivation" strategies wanted to focus on growing and developing talent, developing and motivating others, and to really make a difference and add value—being ethical, very influential, respected, not feared, and motivating to other people, not just being viewed as a business person or corporate figure. Women using "Motivation" strategies, on the contrary, seized opportunities as a way to assist others in their development. Women using "Motivation" strategies sought opportunities to evolve as leaders. Diverse women managers who reported using "Motivation" strategies managed challenging situations and relationships by making transparent decisions collectively, moving start-up projects forward, engaging teams, and establishing mutually beneficial relationships. These strategies were the instrumental learning experiences that best prepared them for leadership. Women who used "Motivation" strategies reported the importance of managing relationships and people. Similar to women who used "Influence" strategies, women who reported using "Motivation" strategies cited having access to diverse company-sponsored experiences such as moving around the company, traveling nationally and globally, and investing in internships.

***

Diverse women managers who aspire to hold top leadership roles are driven to succeed beyond status and financial reward. It is simply not enough to aspire to reach the highest levels of leadership; participants described a desired alignment with personal values and mission to make a difference and serve others (McClelland, 1985), as well as being driven by a sense of purpose—the ability to make a positive impact on others and the organization. Purpose-driven aspirations aligned with personal values can provide women with the focus and motivation to stay their course in the face of obstacles and career setbacks. Boatwright and Egidio (2003) argued that "women must intrinsically possess an interest in aspiring for leadership roles before they can take full advantage of emerging opportunities" (p. 654). While the diverse women managers in the study were driven by their personal values and a sense of purpose, they were also motivated to become senior corporate leaders with high status and power. However, beyond their desired aspirational roles, their primary goal once at the top was to lead with positive impact and influence. They wanted to foster a positive culture, bring out the best of diverse talent, and motivate and influence their direct reports to have high aspirations. Also, focusing on personal values and purpose can lead women to take action in areas that are critical to their success, such as building relationships (Ely et al., 2011). The diverse women managers who were savvy relationship builders also used the "Influence" progression approach and described receiving psychosocial support, career advice, and growth opportunities through the developmental relationships they fostered with senior leaders, former managers, and influential mentors in their network. Therefore, being driven by values and purpose is a key factor in aspiration because it moves one from the desire to hold a position to taking actions to attain one's leadership aspirations.

In order for diverse women to achieve their leadership aspirations, they need to believe in their ability to perform across a variety of situations (*self-efficacy*). Researchers have suggested that an important contributor to a leader's success is self-efficacy, which may better equip her to handle the demands of leadership (Bandura, 1997; Hoyt & Blascovich, 2007; Murphy, 1992). Self-efficacy has been shown to have a positive impact on women aspiring to leadership (Boatwright & Egidio, 2003; Hoyt & Blascovich, 2007; Killeen, López-Zafra, & Eagly, 2006; McCormick, Tanguma, & López-Forment, 2002, McCormick, 2003; Yeagley, Subich, & Tokar, 2010). Confidence and the belief that one can improve is built through action (Dweck, 2006; Kay & Shipman, 2014). Diverse women managers in this study demonstrated high self-efficacy that manifested in their taking action and calculated risks to move toward their aspirational roles. They proactively identified and seized leadership opportunities through actions like raising their hand and volunteering for a new assignment, taking a role beyond their area of expertise, and changing functions and business units. Self-efficacy also allowed the diverse women in the study to see themselves as leaders, thus supporting their ability to seize opportunities and promote their capabilities and interests.

Diverse women must be willing to pursue challenging experiences to develop their leadership skills and capability. The Center for Creative Leadership's report on grooming leaders revealed that emerging leaders learn to expand their critical skills and competencies in challenging situations (Wilson et al., 2016). Therefore, as one's leadership capabilities grow and expand, high-profile, challenging assignments, organizational sponsorship, and endorsements are more likely to be offered (Ely et al., 2011). Transitioning from midlevel leaders to senior leaders requires women to step outside their comfort zone to gain business experiences that are difficult and uncomfortable (Orr, 2013; PDI Ninth House, 2012). The majority of the diverse women in the study described managing challenging situations, relationships, and people as the most instrumental learning experiences that best prepared them for leadership. The challenging experiences they engaged in included learning to deal with high-risk situations, facing and resolving conflicts, handling critical decisions, interfacing with teams, and influencing without having authority. The diverse women managers in the study were also working in conditions where the organization was rapidly changing. During times of organizational change, challenging experiences can serve as important tools for diverse women to avoid becoming obsolete and stagnant in their advancement (Orr, 2013).

To advance diverse women into top leadership roles, the organization must provide a variety of developmental leadership experiences and support systems. Since the majority of leadership development happens on the job over formal training programs, organizations who provide advancement activities such as mentoring, sponsorship, and women's networking groups for diverse women are more effective and successful (Owens & DeHass, 2016). A strong majority of the diverse women managers in this study said having access to company-sponsored diverse experiences positively impacted achieving their aspirations and progressing into leadership roles. Examples of company-sponsored diverse experiences included special project assignments, new roles, leadership development programs, sponsorship and mentorship, and exposure and visibility to senior leaders. Contrary to arguments that formal training contributes less to overall development, researchers have contended that women's leadership programs, along with other leadership development initiatives, are essential for women to develop a stronger sense of self, which then increases their knowledge and skills and builds stronger relationships (Hopkins et al., 2006, 2008; Vinnicombe & Singh, 2003). The diverse women managers in this study who used "Activation" strategies took a more formal path to advancement because of their reliance on their managers and organization for leadership development opportunities. In this regard, a large majority of the participants cited their company's women's leadership development program had a positive impact on their aspirations and progress into leadership roles.

Recommendations

It is believed that women must be intrinsically motivated to aspire to leadership roles before taking action and seizing opportunities. The path to senior and executive leadership can be an arduous journey beset by challenges and trade-offs. While leadership aspirations can provide focus, it is recommended that diverse women anchor themselves in a meaningful purpose—fulfilling work aligned with their talents and core values as well as the organization's purpose. Purpose-driven aspirations can provide women with the direction and motivation to stay the course in the face of obstacles and career setbacks. By focusing on work that provides fulfillment and personal significance, women may strengthen the belief in their ability to perform across a variety of situations. Purpose-driven aspirations also give women insights into their capabilities and their value in organizations. This enables them to strategically chart a more authentic path to leadership. Therefore, it is recommended that diverse women who aspire to hold top leadership positions pursue their aspirations with purpose.

The cornerstone of leadership is learning from experience. Therefore, gaining access to critical experiences that develop one's leadership is imperative. Even though the organization has a role in providing critical experiences, diverse women can proactively begin to build a portfolio of critical experiences early in their careers. However, diverse women need awareness of the type of experiences that are most effective for their development and progression into top leadership. The developmental experiences that best prepare leaders, including women, are those that offer broader leadership responsibility, additional challenges, and greater business scope. In order to advance from first-level management to senior leadership, diverse women need access to high-risk situations, critical negotiations, start-up and new businesses, and external client relations. While women do well in finding challenging assignments, they lack the complex assignments necessary to ascend into business leadership, including experiences that focus on strategy, product development, business operations, and financial management. Therefore, it is recommended that diverse women begin to build a portfolio of critical experiences early in their careers that increases in complexity over time.

Given that the study was designed and conducted within a small yet specific population of participants, the data derived may not be representative of the majority of the population. It is also important to note that high-potential diverse women managers receive more organizational support and opportunities than the average employee. In addition, women at midlevel management are at a level where they are taking risks and challenging assignments to ascend into senior roles. However, it is unknown what happens before and after midlevel management along the leadership journey. It would be interesting to replicate this study with diverse women at different management levels: first level, middle level, and senior level. In addition, it would be important to expand to the study population to include diverse women across industries, including white women, who may have different leadership experiences and developmental needs that cannot be extrapolated from this study.

References

Ahmad, F., & Iverson, S. (2013, October). *The state of women of color in the United States: Too many barriers remain for this growing and increasing population.* Washington, DC: Center for American Progress.

Bagati, D. (2008). *Women of color in US securities firms—Women of color in professional services.* New York, NY: Catalyst.

Bandura, A. (1997). *Self-efficacy: The exercise of control.* New York, NY: W.H. Freeman.

Bierema, L. (1996). How executive women learn corporate culture. *Human Resource Development Quarterly, 7*(2), 145–164.

Boatwright, K. J., & Egidio, K. (2003). Psychological predictors of college women's leadership aspirations. *Journal of College Student Development, 44,* 653–669.

Burke, R. J. (2001). Managerial women's career experiences, satisfaction and wellbeing: A five country study. *Cross Cultural Management, 8,* 117–133.

Corporate Leadership Council (CLC). (2002). *The role of leadership in diversity efforts.* Washington, DC: Corporate Executive Board.

Corporate Leadership Council (CLC). (2005). *Realizing the full potential of rising talent (Volume I): A quantitative analysis of the identification and development of high-potential employees.* Washington, DC: Corporate Executive Board.

Corporate Leadership Council (CLC). (2013). *Creating competitive advantage through workforce diversity.* Washington, DC: Corporate Executive Board.

Credit Suisse Research Institute. (2012, August). *Gender diversity and corporate performance.* Zurich. Retrieved from https://publications.credit-suisse.com/ tasks/render/file/index.cfm?fileid=88EC32A9–83E8-EB92–9D5A40FF69E66808

Credit Suisse Research Institute. (2014, September). *The CS Gender 3000: Women in senior management.* Zurich. Retrieved from https://publications.credit-suisse.com/ tasks/render/file/index.cfm?fileid=8128F3C0–99BC-22E6–838E2A5B1E4366DF

Desvaux, G., Devillard, S., & Sancier-Sultan, S. (2010). *Women matter 2010: Women at the top of corporations: Making it happen.* New York, NY: McKinsey & Company.

Dweck, C. S. (2006). *Mindset: The new psychology of success.* New York, NY: Random House.

Edmondson Bell, E. L. J. (2013) Multicultural women in the pipeline: Finding hidden treasure. In C. D. McCauley, D. S. DeRue, P. R. Yost, & S. Taylor (Eds.), *Experience-driven leader development* (pp. 473–477). San Francisco, CA: John Wiley & Sons, Inc. doi:10.1002/9781118918838.ch71

Ely, R. J., Ibarra, H., & Kolb, D. M. (2011). Taking gender into account: Theory and design for women's leadership development programs. *Academy of Management Learning and Education, 10*(3), 474–493.

Fassinger, R. E. (2002, August). *Honoring women's diversity: A new, inclusive theory of career development.* Presented at 110th Annual Meeting of the American Psychological Association, Chicago, IL.

Fassinger, R. E. (2005). Theoretical issues in the study of women's career development: Building bridges in a brave new world. In W. B. Walsh, M. L. Savickas, & P. Hartung (Eds.), *Handbook of vocational psychology* (3rd ed.) (pp. 85–124). Mahwah, NJ: Lawrence Erlbaum.

Giscombe, K. (2011). *Navigating organizational cultures: A guide for diverse women and their managers.* New York, NY: Catalyst.

Gomez, M. J., Fassinger, R. E., Prosser, J., Cooke, K., Mejia, B., & Luna, J. (2001). Voces abriendo caminos (voices foraging paths): A qualitative study of the career development of notable Latinas. *Journal of Counseling Psychology, 48*(3), 286.

Government Accountability Report (GAO). (2013, April). Trends and practices in the financial services industry and agencies after the recent financial crisis. *GAO-13–238 Financial Services Industry*. Retrieved from www.gao.gov/ products/GAO-13–238

Government Accountability Report (GAO). (2017, November). Trends in management representation of minorities and women and diversity practices, 2007–2015. *GAO-18–64 Financial Services Industry*. Retrieved from www.gao.gov/products/GAO-18-64

Grant Thornton. (2013). Women in senior management: Setting the stage for growth. *Grant Thornton International Business Report (IBR)*. Retrieved from www.grantthornton.ie/db/Attachments/IBR2013_WIB_report_final.pdf

Hall, D. T. (2004). The protean career: A quarter-century journey. *Journal of Vocational Behavior, 65*(1), 1–13.

Herring, C. (2009). Does diversity pay? Race, gender, and the business case for diversity. *American Sociological Review, 74*(2), 208–224.

Hewlett, S. A., & Green, T. (2016). *Black women: Ready to lead*. New York, NY: Center for Talent Innovation.

Hoobler, J. M., Lemmon, G., & Wayne, S. J. (2011). Women's managerial aspirations: An organizational development perspective. *Journal of Management, 40*(3), 703–730. doi:10.1177/0149206311426911

Hopkins, M. M., O'Neil, D. A., & Bilimoria, D. (2006). Effective leadership and successful career advancement: Perspectives from women in health care. *Equal Opportunities International, 25*(4), 251–271.

Hopkins, M. M., O'Neil, D. A., Passarelli, A., & Bilimoria, D. (2008). Women's leadership development strategic practices for women and organizations. *Consulting Psychology Journal: Practice and Research, 60*(4), 348.

Hoyt, C. L., & Blascovich, J. (2007). Leadership efficacy and women leaders' response to stereotype threat. *Group Processes and Intergroup Relations, 3*(10), 596–616.

Human Capital Institute (HCI). (2011). *Connecting the dots: Comprehensive career development as catalyst for employee engagement*. Cincinnati, OH: Author.

Hunt, V., Layton, D., & Prince, S. (2014). *Diversity matters*. New York, NY: McKinsey & Company.

Hunt, V., Layton, D., & Prince, S. (2015). *Why diversity matters*. New York, NY: McKinsey & Company. Retrieved from www.mckinsey.com/insights/ organization/why_diversity_matters

International Labour Organisation. (ILO). (2015). *Women in business and management: Gaining momentum*. Global Report. Geneva, Switzerland: Author.

Joy, L, Carter, N. M., Wagener, H. M., &Narayanan, S. (2007). *The bottom line: Corporate performance and women's representation on boards*. New York, NY: Catalyst.

Kay, K., & Shipman, C. (2014). *The confidence code: The science and art of self-assurance—what women should know*. New York, NY: HarperBusiness/ HarperCollins.

Kilian, C. (2009, August). *Corporate leadership: Building diversity into the pipeline*. American Psychology Association. Retrieved from www.apa.org/pi/oema/ resources/communique/2009/08/diversity.aspx

Kilian, C. M., Hukai, D., & McCarty, C. E. (2005). Building diversity in the pipeline to corporate leadership. *Journal of Management Development, 24*, 155–168.

Killeen, L. A., López-Zafra, E., & Eagly, A. H. (2006). Envisioning oneself as a leader: Comparisons of women and men in Spain and the United States. *Psychology of Women Quarterly, 30*(3), 312–322.

Korn Ferry. (2015). *Korn Ferry Assessment of Leadership Potential research guide and technical manual: Version 15.1a*. Retrieved from http://static.kornferry.com/ media/sidebar_downloads/KFALP_Technical_Manual_final.pdf

Litzky, B., & Greenhaus, J. (2007). The relationship between gender and aspirations to senior management. *Career Development International, 12*(7), 637–659.

Lyness, K. S., & Thompson, D. E. (2000). Climbing the corporate ladder: Do female and male executives follow the same route? *The Journal of Applied Psychology, 85*(1), 86–101.

Marsick, V. J., & Watkins, K. E. (1990). *Informal and incidental learning*. London, UK: Routledge.

Marsick, V. J., & Watkins, K. E. (2001). Informal and incidental learning. *New Directions for Adult and Continuing Education, 2001*(89), 25–34.

McCall, M. W., & Hollenbeck, G. P. (2002). *The lessons of international experience: Developing global executives*. Cambridge, MA: Harvard Business School Press.

McCall, M. W., Lombardo, M. M., & Morrison, A. M. (1988). *Lessons of experience: How successful executives develop on the job*. New York, NY: Simon and Schuster.

McClelland, D. C. (1985). How motives, skills, and values determine what people do. *American Psychologist, 40*(7), 812.

McCormick, M. J. (2003). *Gender differences in beliefs about leadership capabilities: Exploring the glass ceiling phenomenon with self-efficacy theory*. Houston, TX: University of Houston.

McCormick, M. J., Tanguma, J., & López-Forment, A. S. (2002). Extending self-efficacy theory to leadership: A review and empirical test. *Journal of Leadership Education, 1*(2), 34–49.

McKinsey and Lean In. (2016, September). *Women in the Workplace Report*. Retrieved from https://womenintheworkplace.com/2016

Murphy, S. E. (1992). *The contribution of leadership experience and self-efficacy to group performance under evaluation apprehension* (Doctoral dissertation).

Ng, T. W. H., Eby, L. T., Sorensen, K. L., & Feldman, D. C. (2005). Predictors of objective and subjective career success: A meta-analysis. *Personnel Psychology, 58*, 367–408. doi:10.1111/j.1744–6570.2005.00515.x

O'Neil, R. M., Shapiro, M., Ingols, C., & Beard-Blake, S. (2013). Understanding women's career goals across ethnic identities. *Advancing Women in Leadership, 33*, 196–214.

Orr, J. E. (Ed.). (2013). *Korn ferry institute talent management best practice series: Women in leadership*. Los Angeles, CA: Korn Ferry Institute.

Owens, J., & DeHass, D. L. (2016). *Multicultural women at work: The Working Mother report*. New York, NY Working Mother Research Institute.

Pace, C. R. (2017). *Exploring leadership aspirations and learning of diverse women progressing toward top leadership* (Doctoral dissertation). Retrieved from ProQuest Dissertations and Theses database (UMI-10276495)

PDI Ninth House. (2012). *Can women executives break the glass ceiling?* Minneapolis, MN: Korn Ferry Institute.

Porter, N., & Daniel, J. (2008). Women and leadership. In *Developing transformational leaders: Theory to practice* (pp. 245–263). Oxford, UK: Blackwell Publishing Ltd. doi:10.1002/9780470692332.ch11

Prosser, J., Chopra, S., & Fassinger, R. E. (1998). *A qualitative study of the careers of prominent Asian American women*. Presented at the Annual Conference of the Association for Women in Psychology, Baltimore, MD.

Richie, B. S., Fassinger, R. E., Linn, S. G., Johnson, J., Prosser, J., & Robinson, S. (1997). Persistence, connection, and passion: A qualitative study of the career development of highly achieving African American-Black and White women. *Journal of Counseling Psychology, 44*(2), 133.

Sabattini, L. (2008, June). Unwritten rules: What you don't know can't hurt your career. *Catalyst*. Retrieved from www.catalyst.org/knowledge/unwritten-rules-what-you-dont-know-can-hurt-your-career

Sanchez-Hucles, J. V., & Davis, D. D. (2010). Women and women of color in leadership: Complexity, identity, and intersectionality. *American Psychologist, 65*, 171–181.

Sherwin, B. (2014, January 24). Why women are more effective leaders than men. *Business Insider*. Retrieved from www.businessinsider.com/study-women-are-better-leaders-2014-1

Silzer, R., & Church, A. H. (2010). Identifying and assessing high-potential talent: Current organizational practices. In R. Silzer & B. E. Dowell (Eds.), *Strategy-driven talent management: A leadership imperative* (pp. 213–279). San Francisco, CA: Jossey-Bass.

Tharenou, P. (2005). Does mentor support increase women's career advancement more than men's? The differential effects of career and psychosocial support. *Australian Journal of Management, 30*(1), 77–109.

Tharenou, P., & Terry, D. (1998). Reliability and validity of scores on scales to measure managerial aspirations. *Educational and Psychological Measurement, 58*(3), 475–492. doi:10.1177/0013164498058003008

Van Velsor, E., & Hughes, M. W. (1990). *Gender differences in the development of managers: How women managers learn from experience.* Greensboro, NC: Center for Creative Leadership.

Vinnicombe, S., & Singh, V. (2003). Women-only management training: An essential part of women's leadership development. *Journal of Change Management, 3*(4), 294–306.

Wilson, M. S., Van Velsor, E., Chandrasekhar, A., & Criswell, C. (2016). *Grooming top leaders' cultural perspectives from China, India, Singapore, and the United States.* Greensboro, NC: Center for Creative Leadership.

Yeagley, E., Subich, L., & Tokar, D. (2010). Modeling college women's perceptions of elite leadership positions with social cognitive career theory. *Journal of Vocational Behavior, 77*(1), 30–38. doi:10.1016/j.jvb.2010.02.003

9

COURAGE

Mapping the Leadership Journey

Joan Marques

Courage and Risk Aversion

Human beings, by default, are change-averse: we like to settle in circumstances that we know, because we fear the unknown. Sometimes, we stick to situations that are downright awful for that very reason: fear of the unknown. Comfort zones, whether pleasant or dreadful, have a powerful commonality: they are not easy to step out of. That may not even have so much to do with the comfort zone itself as it does with our change aversion. It requires courage to move on when things don't work out anymore. Yet, that moment comes—sooner or later—for every one of us: relationships end, jobs are lost, careers become outdated, you name it. In this chapter, I am inviting you to consider COURAGE—as a set of considerations that can help you see your life from a leadership perspective: through the ups and downs of new and old jobs, careers, relationships, opportunities, and challenges, with an expanded internal locus of control and decreased urge to blame your whereabouts on others.

Choice

Character is an important factor in the way you perceive your reality. Your character is the root on the tree of your life. But roots are fed by the soil in which the tree is planted, so in that regard you make your choices as well. This is not so much about when and where you are born but more about what you do after that: who you choose to hang out with as you go through life. Your character is not necessarily a fixed element inside you: you can always decide to change whatever you want about it. You can compare your character to the strategies of a company: you developed it because it worked for you once, and it was shaped by situations, people, and your qualities at a certain time. But that time is long gone, and if you take a critical look at yourself, you will find that the situation, people, and your qualities have changed since. Why would you hold on to characteristics that don't work for you in today's world? More importantly: why would you refuse to evaluate your character if it could help you in becoming happier? Companies often forget to evaluate their strategy when things do not go too well, and they blame their workforce, their products, their customers, their competitors, the economy, the government, maybe even the whole world, for their lack of performance. They have a fascinating arsenal of excuses ready when anyone would point out the successful performance of their competitors. You don't have to be like that. You can review the elements of your character that bring you down or get you in trouble repeatedly and do something about them.

The Courage in Choice

The fact that we always make our choices with insufficient data should be a huge point of pride to us. Since we are incapable of foreseeing all possible outcomes to the choices we make today, it is admirable that we make them anyway. After all, we cannot fathom all aspects that will enter the picture after we have made a choice, so we can only guess the consequences or outcomes of our choices. It is only after we have made our choices that we learn how they work out. This brings to mind a story told by Thich Nhat Hanh, a globally admired Vietnamese monk who lives in Plum Village, France. In the not-so-far past, Thich traveled around the world as an inspirational speaker. In September 2011, Thich gave a memorable talk in Pasadena, California, where he presented the parable of the second arrow. He warned that life often shoots arrows in our direction. These first arrows are painful indeed. But then we often do something worse: we shoot off a second arrow onto ourselves in the same spot, which makes the pain not twice but 10 times worse! Our second arrow is the negative mindset we choose to develop. We get angry, fearful, upset, disheartened, depressed. By giving in to this mentality, we poison ourselves and seal our fate in the cruelest way. As an example, Thich mentioned the case of a man who was diagnosed with cancer and was told that he only had six months to live. The man became so disheartened by the news that he died in a few weeks! As time went by, it turned out that there had been a mistake in the lab tests and that the man actually did not have cancer. Yet he shot himself with a second mental arrow and expedited his physical demise (Thich, 2011b).

We can see this attitudinal problem in many people around us, especially when they face the challenge of job loss and find themselves at a crossroads. Without realizing it, they choose—with their negative mindset—to guard themselves against any positive input. They wallow in their misery and weaken themselves to the point of no return. Any effort to pull them through fails, due to the solid wall of lethargy and pessimism they have surrounded themselves with.

Open-Mindedness

As indicated under "Choice," human beings are creatures of habit. We settle for dead-end jobs, abusive relationships, poor living circumstances, economic hardship, restrictive environments, and unrewarding chores, because it seems too hard to change. It takes courage to take the first few steps in a new direction, especially because there is no guarantee that you will succeed. You can come up with tons of reasons to justify why it is better to stay put than to change: what if you wouldn't find another job, partner, or place to stay? What if what you found turned out to be worse? What if you ended up being sorry for your boldness? What if you would have to go back and admit that you failed? What if . . .?

It is this list of "what if's" that plays such a huge role in lack of progress for many people. But here is something to consider: you will never know if you don't try, and oftentimes you will only realize how bad your previous situation was when you have stepped out of it. Whatever the reasons may be for family and friends to withhold you from changing, fear of your failure, dread of missing you, or perhaps old-fashioned jealousy: you can only defy their motivations if you try. And here is another great thing: once you have made a first step, every next one will be easier. In a larger scope: once you have exposed yourself to a major transition in your life, change will come easier to you.

An important factor is also that today's world does not reward lethargy. If you cling to a situation too long, especially if it is a dreadful one, you will only be tossed to the side and get disconnected from advancement entirely. Your workplace is no longer confined to the physical environment where you work. Your colleagues, customers, and competitors are everywhere in the world and are always wakeful and alert. This is not to make you fearful but rather to help you understand that it's time to release any mental programming that emphasized your limitations. The things you could not do yesterday are buried in yesterday. Today is another day: circumstances have changed, opportunities have changed, requirements have changed, and you have changed.

Dwelling in a situation that does not work for you today—even if it did before—should not be ignored. And please understand: I am not saying that you should leave your job, friends, or family as soon as something goes wrong, but if you struggle with a consistent and long-term nagging sense of dissatisfaction, sadness, depression, anger, or any other negative emotion, you should take a serious and hard look at your life and do something about it. None of us has eternal life. So why dwell in misery?

A wise and highly educated Tibetan monk in Dharamsala, India, named Geshe[1] Lhakdor once told me that many people in India (and elsewhere in the world) consider the hardship they encounter to be their karma. They sit back and wallow in self-pity, letting their trouble overwhelm them and claiming that they are living out the karma that they probably built up in this or a previous life. Geshe Lhakdor went on to tell me that the mistake all these people make is to dwell in a bad situation that was placed in their lap without trying to get out of it. He stressed that it is our human duty to do whatever we can to live a rewarding life, and when we enhance the quality of our own life, we actually enhance the quality of the lives of those around us as well, because when we are happy, those around us feel happier too. This is quickly explained: happy people want to make other people happy, while miserable people want to make others miserable.

Regardless of any shortcomings you may have, you can change, because everybody has limitations. The art of living is to convert our weaknesses into strengths where possible and to accept them as a non-determining issue at any time. Lhakdor shared with me the tale of a city where everyone was running for their life because a major tsunami was on its way. There were two people, however, who were unable to run: a blind man and a man without legs. They were sitting in the street, and the blind man was moping about his misfortune in life and his upcoming death due to his lack of eyesight. The man without legs had struggled with self-pity as well, but as time became of the essence, he realized that he had to be the stronger one, and this brought to him an ingenious idea. He told the blind man: "I see that you are built very athletic and strong, so if you take me on your shoulders, I can be your eyes, and together we will be much taller than all others!" That sounded like a plan worth trying to the blind man. Their collaboration worked better than if two fully capable people would have tried it, because they were so dependent on each other: because the blind man could not see, he did not second guess his partner's directions, and because the crippled man could not walk, he watched out twice as carefully where he sent his partner. Soon enough they became faster, and before you knew it, they were passing all others! Because they were also taller as a team, they could see much further than anyone, and eventually became the leading team of the entire city! Alone they were miserable, but together their limitations vanished, and they became stronger than all others.

The Courage in Open-Mindedness

Open-mindedness is a beautiful word, but practicing it is not very easy. There is so much we have adopted in our lives to this point. Our culture, religion, society, education, friends, ideologies: everything we have been exposed to has helped shape our mindset to what it is today. With that, there are some things we have a hard time accepting. We have learned to be cautious with some people, to be more open to others, to avoid certain situations, and to gravitate to others. Many of these behaviors we have adopted without thinking deeply why they are the way they are. We do not easily challenge ourselves to reconsider established mindsets. We cherish them as if they were our own, even though they have oftentimes been planted in us by others.

Ralph Waldo Emerson once wrote that most people would rather die than think. He was right. So many people do not question their established paradigms. They never entertain the idea of shifting them into a direction that may be more beneficial to them. They stubbornly hold on to old, sometimes downright outdated ideas, and then wonder why they cannot find anything they are passionate about or why they don't have as many opportunities as others.

Yet, even if you would try to tell those people that they may need to practice some more open-mindedness, the chance is small that anything will change. Closed-minded people prefer to stay closed-minded and therefore would rather die than think about the misery they wallow in due to their obsolete mindsets.

Usefulness

As a young woman of 24 with three young children, ages 5, 3 and 1, and a full-time job in the entertainment industry in South America, I did not have a lot of time for anything else. Yet when one of my sisters-in-law asked me to join her in a degree program in business-economics, I decided to embark on it—not that I had any purpose for such a degree at that time. Moreover, the chances that I would be able to finish this challenging educational journey, given my hectic living circumstances at the time, were slim at best.

Over the course of the four years after making that decision, I was tempted many times to give up and move on with my life. The program was a tremendous challenge and forced me to leave my children with my parents after day care or school until 9:30 at night before I could pick them up and start the 25-mile drive over sparsely lit roads to the small farm outside of town where we lived at the time. Four years later, and against all odds, I could proudly accept my degree as one of only seven graduates that finished this challenging program! The other students had been rerouted to other educational institutions. Perhaps the funniest part of the story was that the other six graduates were all single, childless, and working in the finance and economics industry, while I had no other intentions with this program than just earning a degree. That is, until 12 years later, when I found myself at the end of one life-stage and looking to start a new one 4,500 miles away from home. Education, my old passion, seemed like the most attractive path for me to go, and I could start as an undergraduate student . . . or pull that stuffy degree in business-economics from the shelf. Using that old degree saved me the time, money, and effort of four bachelor's-level years. The old effort of so many years ago now enabled me to embark on a new life full-blast, and I learned something important: nothing in life is wasted.

Here is the issue in one take: we human beings have limited ability to see into our future. That makes it difficult to stay positive about our current experiences. We get in a relationship, it gets sour, and we think we wasted precious years. We hold a job for seven years, then get laid off, and feel that we have lost precious time. In our bitterness and disappointment, we only focus on the loss and fail to consider the future advantage of our current distress.

There is a lesson to be learned in everything. Even when there is no physical advantage to be gained from our experiences, there is still a purpose to them. In his book *True North*, Bill George (2007) uses the term "crucibles" when he refers to leaders who have learned to lead with emotional awareness, a sense of fairness, and devotion to their morals and values. These are the ones who have been confronted with setbacks, varying from job losses and failed business endeavors to illness or even losses of dear ones. While those experiences remained dreadful for the leaders, they also awakened the sense of connectedness with others and reduced their tendency to become self-centered or to focus on excessive profits. Instead, these leaders started making different decisions, considering the well-being of employees, customers, suppliers, and members of the community in their performance plans. This is an example of a useful experience that had a long-term and nonmaterialistic advantage for the individuals involved. Yet the purpose was there, and the experience was not wasted.

The Courage in Usefulness

When we experience the usefulness of our actions in the weeks, months, or years after we engaged in them, we smile and have an "Aha!" experience. However, it still remains difficult to nourish the conviction that everything has a purpose. As soon as the next setback occurs, be it the loss of a job, the ending of a relationship, or the discontinuation of a lucrative contract, we will feel discouraged again and maybe even "hem and haw," like the two little people in Spencer Johnson's (1998) book *Who Moved My Cheese*: they were confronted with a sudden loss and started hemming and hawing about their misfortune. Finally, one decided that it was better to be brave and move on, so he did. The other stayed behind. The brave little man who moved on eventually ran into a much larger supply of cheese than he initially had, so his courage paid off.

Bravery may be risky and scary, but it gets rewarded. The usefulness of any mishap will reveal itself if we get up after a mental or emotional fall, dust ourselves off, briefly consider what just happened, and then move forward. It is as if the universe continuously has us on its radar. We may not feel that way all the time, but there are moments when it becomes very clear. Those are the moments when we realize that our hard work is paying off: perhaps not in the shape or form we had expected, but in a rewarding way nonetheless.

The successful people you meet today were not always this way. Some may have inherited their fortune from ancestors, but many have worked hard to attain their current status. What we see is the tip of an iceberg. There is much under the surface that is unfamiliar to us. We only witness the strength and the victory that these people are able to display today after many, many disappointments, setbacks, and reinventions. But life taught these successful people the usefulness of all their actions and experiences, and they have managed to put it to good use.

If, therefore, you face a loss today, take note of it, consider what lessons you can learn from it, even take a few days off to mourn the loss, because it is entirely allowed for us to feel a bit down and out when our comfort zone gets triggered. However, you owe it to yourself to shape up after those mourning days and move right along. This is what sets the winners in life apart from those who allow themselves to become losers: understanding, which enhances your faith in a great outcome of the things that happen today, regardless how they may look at this moment.

Reality-Check

We can all probably recall moments in our lives where we were envious of others' circumstances, only to find that experiencing those circumstances was not that great after all. And then we have probably also experienced the opposite: moments where the decision to go for the changed circumstances turned out to be a great one! This section is definitely not intended to discourage you from engaging in new ventures. It is meant to help you think things through and question your reasons when deciding on a change. The underlying message is to be responsible with the changes you make. Work on yourself to be moderate rather than anxious. Make sure your reasons for this change are solid and that you are not engaging in emotional "window-dressing"—displaying one reason, which you think will sound more acceptable, while actually doing it for one that may not be a very wise one. If, for example, you actually just want to move to this new place because you have met a pretty lady or handsome guy whom you have dated a few times, while you announce that you are going for a career opportunity, you may be in for a bad disappointment. This is not to say that you should not move if you met someone you love, but you should make sure you get to know the other party reasonably well and remain sober enough to explore all options and possibilities before making any leap. Again, whether your decision will turn out to be successful or not will ultimately depend on what you do afterward.

The grass may look greener on the other side, but things are often not what they seem. One of the grass-is-greener syndromes can be found among people who left their hometown or home country a long time ago, then went back for a vacation and got caught in the notion that they wanted to return to make a difference. Unfortunately, many of these people found out in hindsight that the place they left behind 20 or 30 years ago was not the same anymore. The place had changed, the people had changed, the culture had changed, and . . . they had changed. They had become accustomed to a different system and, shortly after their enthusiastic return, oftentimes became frustrated with the way matters were handled in their previous hometown. Within a year or two, 90% of these people usually left again.

Oftentimes the grass is not greener at all—it may just be a figment of our imagination. There is a striking story on the internet about a little boy who was living on a farm with his parents and would enjoy the view of a house with golden windows in the distance every morning before starting his chores. The golden windows were shining marvelously, and he imagined how wealthy and flamboyant the people living in that house must be. One day his father gave him the day off, and he finally had a chance to visit the house with the golden windows. He prepared a lunch bag and started walking. It took much longer than he had anticipated. He walked half the day, but finally, he was getting closer. But as he was nearing, he got more and more confused. The house before him had no golden windows. As he got even closer, he could see that the house before him needed an urgent renovation: the paint was almost gone, and the entire appearance was rather somber. What happened? Hesitatingly he knocked at the door, and another boy of about his age opened. The boy was very nice, and soon they were chatting at the front porch. As it was rapidly getting near evening, the boy knew he would have to go soon. He asked his new friend if he had seen the house with the golden windows? The friend said, "Oh yeah! Come and see!" They walked to the other side of the balcony, and indeed: in the distance was a house with golden windows, which he recognized as . . . his home! The setting sun was painting the windows in a glow of gold, just like the rising sun did in the morning to the home of his new friend! This is how the boy learned that everything should be seen in a certain context and that it may not look the same when you get closer . . .

The Courage in Reality-Check

Finding out that your reality differs from others is one thing. It is another thing to deal with it in a way that the least number of people gets offended. We can never fully escape disappointments, but we can reduce the intensity we feel when they happen. When we realize that everything arises and passes, we can prepare ourselves for greater acceptance of perceptual and situational differences.

There is an interesting story about this that I heard in India, about two brothers living and working on a farm with their father. Life was good, and everything went its merry way until one day the father died. The two sons did what they had to do and, after the funeral, decided to immediately clean up their beloved father's cabinet. They found a little box with two rings: one very expensive golden ring with diamonds, obviously a very exquisite piece of art, and a simple silver ring with no special features. The oldest brother, always a demanding and dissatisfied one, quickly claimed the expensive ring, telling his younger brother that their father would have probably wanted it this way, since he was the oldest son, and he would keep it as a family piece to be inherited later by his oldest son. The younger brother, always a calm and peaceful one, agreed and simply took the silver ring. Life continued its normal way, and one evening the young brother was sitting on the front porch, enjoying the evening. His eyes fell on the silver ring he was now always wearing. He wondered again why his father would have kept such a simple, insignificant looking ring. He pulled it off his finger and held it against the light. That's when he found out that something was engraved in the ring. As he got a better look, he could read the words, "This too shall pass." The young man smiled and understood instantly why his father had kept this simple ring so dearly. The message was strong and had the ability to bring its recipients back down to earth immediately. If one felt invincible due to a strike of luck, this statement could make the winner calm down and realize that everything is temporary. Similarly, if one felt down and out due to a series of mishaps, this statement could make the sufferer feel better, as (s)he would understand that the negative spiral would end in the near future.

Attitude

> Everything can be taken from a man but one thing: the last of human freedoms—to choose one's attitude in any given set of circumstances, to choose one's own way.
>
> —Viktor E. Frankl

Viktor Frankl (2006) experienced the power of attitude very personally. He was an Austrian neurologist and psychiatrist imprisoned in concentration camps in the 1940s due to his Jewish origins. Except for a sister, his entire family—his wife, Tilly, parents, and brother—was imprisoned along with him. At the time the Nazi anti-Semitic raid started, Frankl was a practicing neurologist in Vienna, Austria. He was married just one year when, in 1942, his family was deported to a Nazi ghetto in Austria, where his father died. From there, Frankl and his wife were transported to the infamous Auschwitz concentration camp, where they were separated. Frankl was later moved to other concentration camps, where he first worked as a slave laborer and later as a doctor among the inmates. By the time he was liberated, in 1945, he learned that his wife had died in the Bergen-Belsen concentration camp, his brother and mother in Auschwitz, and his only living family member left was his sister Stella, who had fled to Australia just in time before the family had been deported.

The hopelessness of living in a concentration camp, where every day can be your last, either due to severe malnutrition or illness or through the gas chamber, brought some critical insights to Frankl. In those dark years, he learned that one's attitude can make an immense difference in the course of one's life. The insights Frankl (*Viktor Frankl (1905–1997)*, 2013) acquired during his years in the concentration camps turned invaluable for the development of his treatment of patients later. His book, *Man's Search for Meaning*, which was published one year after his liberation, reflected on his experiences as an average prisoner and his interactions with other inmates in the camps and introduces his notions of meaning through a theory he developed and named "logotherapy." Frankl's basic premise in this all-time best-selling book is that there is meaning in everything we experience, even those things we dread, such as captivity, slave labor, suffering, or death. Through reflections on his concentration camp years, Frankl conveyed the stance that our mind is a powerful tool that can either break us long before our physique is exhausted or can help us withstand the grimmest of circumstances, long after others have succumbed.

Nelson Mandela is another example of a man who used his attitude to overcome adversity. In his case it was a 27-year-long imprisonment. Born in 1918 in a small African riverbank village called Mvezo in the Eastern Cape of South Africa, Rolihlahla—his real name—was sent for primary education to a Methodist mission school and secondary education to Clarkebury Boarding Institute (Feinstein, 2010). He subsequently enrolled at the University of Fort Hare, and later the University of South Africa, to work on his bachelor's degree. Meanwhile, he became involved in politics and joined the African National Congress (ANC). Earning his bachelor's in 1943, he picked up the study of law, got married, and started a family. His political involvement led him to prominence in the movement for equal rights but also placed a strain on his marriage, as his infidelities were widely known. As he managed his law office, his political involvement kept intensifying. Inspired by Mohandas Gandhi's views, he first practiced non-violent resistance but later submitted to a more violent approach. In 1956, as his first marriage was ending and the second was about to start, Mandela and a number of his political associates were arrested on the basis of accusation of high treason against the state.

In 1962, Mandela was transported to Robben Island, where he stayed for 18 years, manhandled by the prison guards and labeled as the lowest-class prisoner, which meant that he could only receive one letter and one visit every six months. Working in the blatant sun without sunglasses caused permanent damage to his eyesight, and he was regularly kept in solitary confinement (Frängsmyr, 1994). In the '70s, his influence grew in prison, as did his personal status as a prisoner, and he was allowed more visits. Twenty years into his imprisonment, Mandela, along with some other political prisoners, was moved to Pollsmoor Prison, where the circumstances were better but the confinement greater. In 1985 he was offered freedom by then-South-African president Peter Botha, if he would promise that he would cease his political movement. Mandela rejected the offer. He underwent prostate surgery while in prison and suffered from tuberculosis due to the poor conditions in his cell, which led him to be moved to Victor Verster Prison (now Drakenstein Correctional Centre), where conditions and treatment were better. Mandela had become 70 years of age by then, and global interest in his whereabouts was growing. In 1990, Mandela, then 72 years old, was finally released from prison and fully rehabilitated in society. He immediately started with negotiations to end apartheid in South Africa, won the Nobel Peace Prize in 1993, and ultimately became the first fully democratically, multi-racially elected President of South Africa, serving from 1994 to 1999. Mandela remains an icon of human perseverance and dignity in the world (All Things Considered, 2004).

Former U.S. President Bill Clinton once asked Mandela about his feelings on the day he was finally released from prison after 27 years of undeserved incarceration. "Didn't you hate them?" Clinton recalled asking Mandela privately, referring to Mandela's final steps as a prisoner walking to freedom. "Sure I did," Mandela responded, "I felt anger and hatred and fear. And I realized if I kept hating them, once I got in that car and got through the gate I would still be in prison. So I let it go because I wanted to be free" (Bradley, 2008).

Aside from his prolonged captivity, Mandela was confronted with several traumatic setbacks in his life: his second child (and first daughter), Makaziwe, died in 1947 at the age of nine months from meningitis; his oldest son, Thembi, died in a car accident in 1969 while Mandela was in prison and therefore not allowed to attend the funeral; and his second son, Makgatho, died of AIDS in 2005. In spite of it all, Mandela remained an icon of human strength and optimism throughout his life, and even after his death. His attitude enabled him to weather repeated ordeals that would have destroyed anyone with less perseverance and resilience. Mandela revealed another essential aspect to a positive attitude—the boost in morale it can provide others—in his statement, "And as we let our own light shine, we unconsciously give other people permission to do the same" (Thinkexist.com, 2013).

The Courage in Attitude

To maintain a positive or firm attitude in the face of adversity is not an easy task. It is so much easier to lay low and wait until the storm has passed, or follow the crowd, even if you do not agree with its cause. Many people do it already, when they stay in jobs that they dread day after day, year after year, but lack the will or stamina to target their real area of passion. Even if they know what they would really like to do in life, they erect a number of "justifications" why this would be impossible. These "justifications" vary from, "It would be impossible because there is no money to be earned with that," to "It would require a lot of money to set this up," and "At least I know where my paycheck comes from, and I don't feel like risking that for an insecure endeavor." Our attitude can determine whether we end up with a disappointed feeling about our lives and the many fascinating avenues we missed or with the elated awareness that we pursued our dreams and unleashed our potential. It takes a lot of backbone to dare this. So many people are afraid of the brick wall of failure to a degree that they avoid it entirely. By doing so, however, they forgo the chalice of sweet, internal gratification.

Genius

Sir Ken Robinson, an internationally renowned author and expert on creativity and education, has been very vocal about the way our educational system is set up: classified by age, and with total disregard for personal preferences or skills (AltNyttErFarlig, 2013). Robinson claims that schools kill creativity and, with that, the natural genius in each of us. In several of his presentations, available on YouTube, Ted.com and other online sources, you can hear and see him explaining the trend. In one particular presentation, he reveals a NASA developed study to measure thinking in engineers and scientists. The study was, however, done with 1,500 kindergarten children to measure their degrees of divergent thinking. Divergent thinking is the foundation for creative thinking, because it entails the ability to come up with different ways of looking at something. Of the 1,500 small children that were tested, 98% scored genius level. The children were tested again when they were between 8 and 10 years old. At that time, only 32% of the tested children scored genius level. When tested again between ages 13 and 15, only 10% of the same children scored genius level. The same test was also given to adults around 25 years of age, and only 2% of this group scored genius level.

Robinson admits that many things happen to people as they grow up that can inhibit their divergent thinking capacity, but the common factor for all of us growing up is education. Education is definitely not a bad thing, as we will further discuss in the next section. However, the way it is structured and implemented is oftentimes more limiting than liberating. In spite of these limiting factors, however, we can revive our inner genius, and the first step is to become aware of it. Once we dare to accept that we have genius ability, we can stop accepting everything as a given and start seeing the world through our own eyes. Take a walk daily, and enjoy the grass, the flowers, the clouds, the children, the scenery. . . . Look at things instead of just seeing them. Discover the miracle that is life. Thich Nhat Hanh (2002) states:

> People usually consider walking on water or in thin air a miracle. But I think the real miracle is not to walk either on water or in thin air, but to walk on earth. Every day we are engaged in a miracle which we don't even recognize: a blue sky, white clouds, green leaves, the black, curious eyes of a child—our own two eyes. All is a miracle.

The ability to actually see and enjoy all the things Thich mentioned is a true gift. It returns a long-lost blessing to us: the art of enjoying the simple things and finding happiness in appreciation. Awakening our inner genius doesn't only enable us to think divergently; it also provides us with the buoyancy that many around us lack. Genius manifests itself in many forms, as the following three examples may illustrate.

Muhammad Yunus studied economics and taught the subject in America until his home country, Bangladesh, gained independence in the early 1970s. He returned home and first held a government position, which he quickly exchanged for education. He became affiliated with Chittagong University and often wandered in the streets of Jobra, the village near his university (Grandin, 2006). He witnessed severe poverty and the grip that moneylenders had on the people, lending them just enough money to survive but prohibiting them from ever outgrowing the slum they were in. When Yunus' projects to help the poor through loans from local banks did not work, he realized that there were persistent, irrevocable mindsets within financial institutions that upheld the notion that poor people were not worthy of getting loans because they would not pay them back. Yunus realized that his only alternative to help the poor in the surrounding villages was to start a bank himself. This is how Grameen Bank was conceived, an institution that focuses on micro lending. It took years: Yunus' project started in 1976, but the bank only became a full-fledged entity in 1983. Grameen bank now has more than 2,000 branches and received, jointly with Yunus, the Nobel Peace Prize in 2006 (Biography.com, April 2014b). Unfortunately, Yunus has been ousted from the bank by Bangladeshi government authorities in 2011, a clear politically driven ploy, which has not diminished the world's admiration for Yunus by any means. Quite the contrary! Yunus still performs in many global entities as a major leader in the fight against poverty and is well-respected for his legacy as a divergent thinker who dared to challenge and change the status quo.

Wangari Maathai is another role model for divergent thinking. Born in Kenya, Maathai got an opportunity to study in the U.S. in 1960. She earned her bachelor's and master's degrees in biology. She subsequently studied in Germany and Nairobi and earned her doctorate in anatomy from the University of Nairobi (Frängsmyr, 2004). She got married, taught at the University of Nairobi, and had three children. As the 1970s were approaching their end, Wangari's marriage was, too. Her husband could not stand her passionate involvement in political activism, and a bitter divorce followed, in which he accused her of cruelty, madness, and adultery. As her political involvement grew, her educational affiliation waned, and she was eventually evicted from her university home. Soon thereafter, Maathai started the Green Belt Movement, an environmental nongovernmental organization focused on the planting of trees, environmental conservation, and women's rights. She experienced repeated opposition from the local government but ultimately found support from the Norwegian Forestry Society (The Green Belt Movement, 2013). The funding she received through this collaboration enabled her to encourage the women of Kenya to create nurseries and plant trees throughout the country and pay for their efforts. Maathai was a brave woman who got jailed several times during her life, but she did not let the threats and setbacks withhold her from fulfilling her mission. In 2003 she was appointed assistant minister in the Ministry for Environment and Natural Resources, and in 2004 she became the first African woman and the first environmentalist to win the Nobel Peace Prize. She died in 2011 from complications in the treatment of ovarian cancer.

Millard Fuller, another great role model for divergent thinking, was a self-made millionaire at 29 after earning degrees in economics and law and having started a family earlier. His hard work led to frequent absences from home, and his wife told him one day that she wanted a divorce (The Academy of Achievement, 2013). This sobered up Fuller, and he did what very few young millionaires would do: he gave away his wealth and focused his life on Christian service. With his wife and children, he moved from their home state Alabama to Koinona Farm in Georgia, where he became a partner and started small housing projects for low-income people. The Fuller family then moved to Mbandaka, a very poor city in Zaire, Africa, where they started a 100-house project to facilitate the neediest and most downtrodden. Upon return from Zaire in 1976, Fuller continued his building mania, starting with a project in the slums of San Antonio, Texas. This initiative became the foundation for Habitat for Humanity, a nonprofit organization that has since expanded its activities in many U.S. states as well as in other countries. One of the most prominent fans and supporters of Habitat for Humanity was former U.S. President Jimmy Carter, a native of Georgia himself. Since the early 2000s, Habitat has built more than 150,000 homes in more than 90 countries (Habitat for Humanity® International, 2013). Unfortunately, disputes with the board of directors led to Millard Fuller and his wife being fired in 2005 from the organization they founded and led for so many years. This setback did not stop Millard Fuller from his mission. He founded another nonprofit, The Fuller Center for Housing, and continued his work to get communities working together on housing projects for those in need. He did so until he passed away in 2009.

The Courage in Genius

The three individuals described in the previous section, Muhammad Yunus, Wangari Maathai, and Millard Fuller, have some essential qualities in common. Each of them saw a need in society and transcended the boundaries of conventional thinking. It took courage, and they were not always appreciated. In fact, they all experienced opposition from powerful adversaries, causing them to reroute their efforts in realizing their mission: Yunus was banished from Grameen Bank in 2011, Maathai was repeatedly jailed and threatened for her women's awareness efforts in the Green Belt Movement, and Fuller was fired from Habitat for Humanity in 2005. Their courage was demonstrated in the fact that they did not stop there but found alternative ways to support the causes they believed in. That is genius at work.

Education

We change through education: any form of education. It does not have to be the formal route of going through multiple levels of school and earning degrees that we can proudly hang on the wall. While these documents are still believed to support people in finding employment and moving up the corporate ladder, there is just as much to be said about undocumented, nondegree-awarding education. We can educate ourselves in many ways, now more so than ever before, because many of us have this mighty tool called the internet at our disposal, which enables us to look up practically anything we hear.

Education is a major change agent. It is through the books we read, the people we meet, the experiences we get exposed to, and the insights we develop that education plays such a critical role in our lives. It needs to be stated that it works differently for different people, as is the case with practically everything. Two people can earn the same degree but have entirely different levels of preparedness to enter the workforce. Similarly, some people may not even have any formal education yet perform impressively in the professions they choose to embark upon.

Some Manifestations of Education

The man who is sometimes referred to as the father of America's literature, Mark Twain, was mainly self-educated (The Mark Twain House & Museum, 2013). Born Samuel Clemens in 1835, right around the time Halley's Comet appeared closest to earth, he started his professional life at age 12 as a typesetter in his hometown, Hannibal, Missouri. He did this for about six years, meanwhile submitting short stories and sketches to a local newspaper, owned by his brother Orion. At 18, he moved to New York and found employment as a printer through the day while spending his evenings studying in the public libraries (Biography.com, April 2017a). He considered his access to information more expansive this way than through enrollment in a formal school. As he was on a voyage to New Orleans down the Mississippi, he became interested in the job of a steamboat pilot and threw himself into that profession. He studied the Mississippi for two years, after which he earned his steamboat pilot license. As the civil war broke out in the Southern states, Clemens followed his brother Orion, who was now secretary to the Nevada governor. There, he tried his hand at mining but failed at it and found employment as a journalist at a newspaper in Virginia City instead. This is where he first used his pen-name "Mark Twain." He subsequently moved to San Francisco, California, published his works in a New York paper, and found an opportunity to visit Europe and the Middle East. Everywhere he went, his pen went along. He continuously logged his experiences, resulting in a wide variety of published works over the course of his life (Hannibal.net, 2013).

Clemens made a lot of money with his publications, presentations, and his wife's inheritance but lost it all through bad investments and an excessively lavish lifestyle. He even had to declare bankruptcy in the early 1890s. Morally responsible as he was, he embarked on a yearlong tour of presentations to pay off all his debtors, even though he was not required to do so by law. He was not shielded from loss and despair in his life: three of his four children died before he did: his only son, Langdon, at 19 months, daughters Susy at 24, and Jean at 19. Clemens' travels taught him a great deal, and he had several changes of mind over the course of his life. A major one is his shift from an ardent imperialist to an anti-imperialist around 1890. As such, he even became the vice president of the American Anti-Imperialist League and wrote a short story titled "The War Prayer," which was published more than a decade after his death. In this short story, he criticizes the Christian habit of praying for the nation's soldiers at war and the unpronounced but silently conveyed plea for victory, which automatically entails death and destruction to the other party. Mark Twain, who is most known for his novels *Tom Sawyer* and *The Adventures of Huckleberry Finn*, received an honorary doctorate from Oxford University in 1907 and died in 1910 from a heart attack, one day after Halley's Comet made another appearance to our planet.

Education, regardless how gained, has one important by-product: different thinking. And through this enhanced capacity, the educated person learns to question things he previously accepted as a given. In Mark Twain's case the most noteworthy example was his shift from proposing imperialism to opposing it because he had come to understand the other side of the coin. His extensive travels to a wide variety of countries on multiple continents undoubtedly contributed to his transformation. In today's work environment it is an absolute plus to have had some exposure to other cultures before embarking on a career. Employers encourage this trend, because they are aware of the ever-increasing diversity in workplaces all over the world and the need this brings to embrace a broad scale of differences such as generational, ethnic, cultural, religious, experiential, and educational.

Another element that can determine the impact of one's education is the ability to engage in critical thinking as opposed to rote learning. Rote learning entails memorization with or without understanding of the learned material (*Rote Learning*, n.d.). It is often used in learning the alphabet, learning chemistry tables and multiplication tables, statutes in law, anatomy in medicine, foundational religious learning, and simple scientific formulae (Strauss, 2013). While it can be useful as a foundation to further development, rote learning does not lead to greater insights. In some cultures, such as Brazil, China, India, Greece, Pakistan, and Japan, rote learning is still heavily promoted. Students from these cultures perform exceptionally well on tests, but the question remains how much they really understand of the material. Critical thinking, on the other hand, entails the ability to reason and reflect on what has been learned. Abrami et al. (2008) define critical thinking as "the ability to engage in purposeful, self-regulatory judgment" (p. 1102). Consequently, a critical thinker will determine whether she considers the lessons to which she is exposed acceptable or not. A critical thinker attempts to find an application for the learned material in order to make sense of it.

A monumental reference to early critical thinking can be found in the Kalama Sutta, a lecture given about 2,500 years ago by Gautama Siddhartha, also known as "The Buddha." This happened when the Buddha visited the town Kesaputta and spoke with the local people called Kalamas, who were in distress about the many teachers visiting their town and glorifying their own doctrines while condemning others. The local people were wondering what to adopt and what to reject (Kinnes, 2002). The Buddha advised the Kalamas to refrain from merely clinging to written or verbal lectures, legends, scriptures, proverbs, assumptions, or any other form of knowledge transfer, merely because of what it represented. More specifically, the Buddha advised the Kalamas to examine anything that was taught to them critically before determining what to do with it. He thus alerted them to refrain from blindly accepting and believing things only because they are passed down for many generations, have become traditional practice, are just well known, are included in scriptures, are logically reasonable, are in line with one's philosophy, appeal to one's common sense, fit well within one's ideas, or come from a trustworthy speaker or respected teacher. The Buddha further encouraged the Kalamas to neither get caught by evil mindsets, hostility, and unwholesome teachings rejected by the wise nor adopt anything that turned out to be harmful to them or give rise to malicious sentiments such as greed, hate, or jealousy. Instead, he encouraged them to seek awareness through inner purity and only adopt those lessons and actions that turned out to be rewarding, enriching, praised by the wise, and contributing to their welfare and happiness.

The Courage in Education

Education is a time-consuming endeavor and often entails some elements of tediousness, which may result in giving up if one lacks determination. In educating ourselves, we have to be willing to make mistakes and be corrected. We also have to be willing to take risks, because there is no guarantee that our education will lead to a more prosperous future. There is just one guarantee: it will lead to better understanding and insight, and it's up to us what we want to do with that. Some people think that the very act of obtaining higher education means that their rise on the professional ladder will be a smooth one. When this doesn't happen, they get disheartened and blame their lack of progress on the institution where they gained their education. This is known as having an external locus of control: one blames all misfortunes on others and not on the self. "Individuals with a belief in external control interpret events to be the result of surrounding forces, such as luck, chance, or fate, whereas individuals with a belief in internal control perceive events as contingent on their behavior" (Specht, Egloff, & Schmukle, 2011, p. 132). Interestingly, these people don't mind taking all the credit when things move forward: then suddenly it is their own doing that got them to the point they achieved.

Educating ourselves takes courage, and what we do with the education we gained takes courage as well, as can be discerned from the Buddha's recommendations to the Kalamas. It's like a puzzle: we have to find the spot where we fit, and sometimes it may seem that we found it, but in hindsight we find that we don't fit as well as we would have liked to. While some people continue to force themselves in those increasingly uncomfortable spots, others courageously uproot themselves and continue their journey. Chances are that these on-movers find their sweet spot after all, while those who refused to explore their alternatives end up being dissatisfied and distressed.

Education also is a lifelong process. Perhaps the most interesting insight we gain from being educated is that there is such a vast amount of knowledge available that we will never be able to acquire. The human mind simply doesn't have the capacity to know everything. How little we know becomes obvious as we explore more. Education is therefore also a humbling process.

No Mud, No Lotus

Looking at the beautiful lotus flower, it is easy to feel awe for its serene beauty. While admiring this great gift of nature, it may not occur to us that it could only come into being through the collaboration of a variety of non-lotus elements, such as sun, rain, and mud. A lotus cannot grow on marble, no matter how much we would want that. It needs mud to grow, so if we care to look deeply into the lotus flower, we should see the mud. Therefore, the mud is not the enemy of the lotus. The same holds for our happiness and our suffering. Our happiness is like a lotus flower, and our suffering is like the mud that helps our happiness, our lotus flower, to manifest.

In our lifetime we will experience lots of muddy moments, most of them lasting much longer than we would want them to. When we go through the mud-puddles of our personal or professional life, we wonder "Why me?" "When will this end?" "What is this good for?" and more of those types of questions. We may start feeling senses of anger, despair, sadness, devastation, shame, inferiority, regret, and maybe even fall into a depression.

Thich Nhat Hanh, the monk who shares the story of mud and lotus in his speeches throughout the world, uses it to help us understand that the hard times in our lives serve a purpose. This was also highlighted in an earlier section, titled "Usefulness." In that section, the topic was mainly presented in light of the purpose of all our experiences, even if we consider them senseless at the moment (Thich, 1999).

To stick with the metaphor of mud and lotus, all of the people mentioned in this chapter used their mud to nourish the lotus flower that eventually emerged from their beliefs and passions. Subsequently, they did not keep their lotus flowers to themselves but shared them with their surroundings, whether small or large-scaled. Just like these people, we have a choice to look at the mud in our garden and either despise it or trust that it will lead to our own radiant lotus.

That radiant lotus does not have to be far from here. It depends on what we choose to focus on in our professional or personal life. Since we have mainly focused on professional life in this chapter, we can consider our "lotus" to be any achievement that we have long desired, such as a fine job, an advanced degree to position ourselves better in the market, or a promotion at our current workplace.

It may be good to consider that most lotuses (read: achievements) will come and go and that we will eventually get used to the things we have achieved. That much desired job will settle and you will start experiencing the politics in it or find out that some colleagues are rather difficult to work with. That degree may or may not lead to immediate placement in a better or higher position, and even if it does, you will get used to that as well and start looking for a next goal to achieve. That promotion may lead you into tasks and processes that you could not foresee when you had your previous job, and the stress may lead you to wonder why you ever desired this position. As you can tell, all of the external lotuses are fleeting sooner or later, and you suddenly feel as if you are once again in a mud puddle, wondering if there will ever be another lotus moment.

The only lotus that can last very long is the one you grow inside of yourself, the one that you achieve through the realization that nothing lasts and that there is a good reason for every transition and every stage. This mindset of inner peace is a precious one, which you can attain in several ways. Some people do it through long walks in silence, where they focus on their steps or enjoy the scenery of a beautiful place; others do it through prayers, and yet others through meditation. Meditation is a powerful instrument that can help you gain and regain internal peace, even when situations around you are in disarray.

Overall, however, courage turns out to be the overarching quality in reaching for heights we never attained before. Through our Choices, Open-mindedness, awareness of the Usefulness of everything, frequent Reality checks, a positive Attitude, nourishing our Genius, and continuing our Education (whether formally or informally), we can pave our own way to promising futures.

Note

1 "Geshe" implies an academic degree for Tibetan Buddhist monks and nuns

References

Abrami, P. C., Bernard, R. M., Borokhovski, E., Wade, A., Surkes, M. A., Tamim, R., & Zhang, D. (2008). Instructional interventions affecting critical thinking skills and dispositions: A review of educational research stage 1 meta-analysis. *Review of Educational Research*, 78(4), 1102–1134.

The Academy of Achievement. (2013). *Linda and Millard Fuller*. Retrieved from www.achievement.org/autodoc/page/ful0bio-1

All Things Considered (2004, April 29). *Mandela: An audio history*. National Public Radio. Retrieved from www.npr.org/2004/04/26/1851882/mandela-an-audio-history

AltNyttErFarlig. (2013). *Ken Robinson on genius, divergent thinking and creativity*. [Blog post]. Retrieved from http://altnytterfarlig.tumblr.com/post/15560990569/ken-robinson-on-genius-divergent-thinking-and

Biography.com. (April 2017a). *Mark Twain biography*. Retrieved from www.biography.com/people/mark-twain-9512564

Biography.com. (April 2014b). *Muhammad Yunus biography*. Retrieved from www.biography.com/people/muhammad-yunus-218222

Bradley, T. (2008, July 6). Bill Clinton invokes the "bad dreams" of a former P.O.W. *ABC News*. Retrieved from http://abcnews.go.com/blogs/politics/2008/07/bill-clinton-in/

Feinstein, F. (2010, October 16). Nelson Mandela's daughter: I don't know if my father loves me: Sometimes children are not really loved by their parents. *Daily Mail*. Retrieved from www.dailymail.co.uk/femail/article-1321130/Nelson-Mandelas-daughter-I-dont-know-father-loves-Sometimes-children-really-loved-parents.html

Frängsmyr, T. (1994). *Nelson Mandela—Biographical*. Retrieved from www.nobelprize.org/nobel_prizes/peace/laureates/1993/mandela-bio.html

Frängsmyr, T. (2004). *Wangari Maathai—Biographical*. Retrieved from www.nobelprize.org/nobel_prizes/peace/laureates/2004/maathai-bio.html

Frankl, V. E. (2006). *Man's search for meaning*. Boston, MA: Beacon Press.

George, W., & Sims, P. (2007). *True North: Discover your authentic leadership*. San Francisco, CA: Jossey Bass.

Grandin, K. (2006). *Muhammad Yunus—Biographical*. Retrieved from www.nobelprize.org/nobel_prizes/peace/laureates/2006/yunus-bio.html

The Green Belt Movement. (2013). *Wangari Maathai*. Retrieved from www.greenbeltmovement.org/wangari-maathai

Habitat for Humanity® International. (2013). *Millard Fuller: Habitat for Humanity co-founder*. Retrieved from www.habitat.org/how/millard.aspx

Hannibal.net. (2013). *Mark Twain biography*. The Hannibal Courier-Post and Gate-House Media, Inc. Retrieved from www.marktwainhannibal.com/twain/biography/

Johnson, S. (1998). *Who moved my cheese? An amazing way to deal with change in your work and in your life*. New York, NY: G. P. Putnam's Sons.

Kinnes, T. (2002). *The Kalamas go to see Buddha*. Retrieved from http://oaks.nvg.org/kalama.html

The Mark Twain House & Museum. (2013). *A life lived in a rapidly changing world: Samuel L. Clemens, 1835–1910*. Retrieved from www.marktwainhouse.org/man/biography_main.php

Rote Learning. (n.d.). In *The Free Dictionary*. Retrieved from www.thefreedictionary.com/rote+learning

Strauss, V. (2013, June 3). The problem with rote learning in one sentence. *Washington Post*. Retrieved from www.washingtonpost.com/blogs/answer-sheet/wp/2013/06/03/the-problem-with-rote-learning-in-one-sentence/

Thich, N. H. (1999). *The miracle of mindfulness: An introduction to the practice of meditation*. Boston, MA: Beacon Press.

Thich, N. H. (2002). *No death, no fear: Comforting wisdom for life*. New York, NY: Riverhead Books.

Thich, N. H. (Presenter). (2011a, March 29). Understanding our mind: No mud, no lotus (Audio Podcast). *Thich Nhat Hanh Dharma Talks*. Retrieved from http://tnhaudio.org/2011/04/21/understanding-our-mind-no-mud-no-lotus/

Thich, N. H. (Presenter). (2011b, September 3). Energies of Buddhism (Audio Podcast). *Thich Nhat Hanh Dharma Talks*. Retrieved from http://tnhaudio.org/2011/09/15/energies-of-buddhism/

Thinkexist.com. (2013). *Nelson Mandela quotes*. Retrieved from http://thinkexist.com/quotes/nelson_mandela/

Specht, J., Egloff, B., & Schmukle, S. C. (2011). The benefits of believing in chance or fate: External locus of control as a protective factor for coping with the death of a spouse. *Social Psychological and Personality Science*, *2*(2), 132–137.

Viktor Frankl (1905–1997). (2013, July 25). Retrieved from www.goodtherapy.org/famous-psychologists/viktor-frankl.html

10

DEFINING MOMENTS

Aspects of a Four-Day Women's Leadership Development Institute That Changed Participants' Self-Perceptions of Leadership Capacity

Karen A. Longman, Carrie Stockton, Andrew T. Bolger, Athena R. Castro, and Sandy L. Hough[1]

In her 2012 book titled *The End of Leadership*, Barbara Kellerman famously challenged the booming "leadership industry" (p. XV). Despite enormous investments to identify and prepare individuals for leadership, Kellerman charged that the industry seemed to have produced leaders who "by and large are performing poorly, worse in many ways than before" (p. XV). Yet simultaneous to offering this critique of the leadership field, Kellerman (2008, 2014) has also acknowledged the complexities today's leaders face and the need to respect the synergistic relationship between leader, followers, and context. Additionally, researchers have repeatedly documented the need for alternatives to the stereotypical models of male-normed leadership that may be inappropriate or inadequate to meet the complex array of issues facing today's organizations (Helgesen & Johnson, 2010; Kezar, 2014; Vinkenburg, van Engen, Eagly, & Johannesen-Schmidt, 2011). Specifically, the importance of having diverse perspectives around the leadership table (Catalyst, 2013; Smith, 2014; Williams, 2014; Woolley, Chabris, Pentland, Hashmi, & Malone, 2010) and greater representation by women in leadership roles (Eagly & Carli, 2007; Eagly, 2015; Gangone & Lennon, 2014; Gerzema & D'Antonio, 2013; Madsen, 2015; Sandberg, 2013; Turner, 2012) have received increased attention in the literature.

Numerous structural and attitudinal barriers have deterred women from advancing into senior-level leadership, as described by Ely and Rhode (2010) in a book chapter titled "Defining the Challenges." More expansively, Diehl and Dzubinski (2016) offered descriptions of 27 types of gender-based leadership barriers, organizing them "according to three levels of society in which they generally operate: *macro* (societal), *meso* (group or organizational), and *micro* (individual)" (p. 187). At the *macro* level, for example, barriers include gender stereotypes, cultural constraints on women's own choices, and gender unconsciousness and leadership perceptions. At the *meso* level, barriers include discrimination, exclusion from informal networks, a lack of mentoring and sponsorship, male gatekeeping, workplace harassment, and tokenism. At the *micro* level, identified barriers include communication style constraints, the psychological glass ceiling, and work-life conflict. Although considerable work has been done to design and implement constructive responses to specific barriers, Diehl and Dzubinski advocate that "the first step is to recognize that women encounter barriers at all three levels, and that macro and micro barriers impact women's ability to see themselves as leaders, as well as others' ability to consider them for leadership roles" (p. 199).

In addition to targeting attention on specific barriers that dampen women's leadership aspirations and advancement, some of the most promising work toward the goal of preparing a more diverse cadre of future senior-level leaders is found in a burgeoning body of literature related to *leader identity development* (e.g., Day & Harrison, 2007; Day, Harrison, & Halpin, 2009; DeRue & Ashford, 2010; Ibarra, Ely, & Kolb, 2013; Komives, Owen, Longerbeam, Mainella, & Osteen, 2005; Komives, Longerbeam, Mainella, Owen, & Osteen, 2009). According to DeRue and Ashford (2010), central to leader identity development are "the relational and social processes involved in coming to see oneself, and being seen by others, as a leader or a follower" (p. 627).

In contrast to an expansive body of literature that relates to strategies for leader development and/or leadership development (e.g., Day, 2001; Hopkins, O'Neil, Passarelli, & Bilimoria, 2008; Riggio, 2010), the focus on leader identity development emphasizes the process of *internalizing a leader identity* (DeRue & Ashford, 2010) and *receiving validation for one's self-view as a leader*, which bolsters self-confidence (Ely, Ibarra, & Kolb, 2011). Specifically related to women's leadership identity, Ibarra, Ely, and Kolb (2013) referred to this journey of self-discovery and confidence building as an "often fragile process" (p. 62), contributing to the underrepresentation of women in senior-level leadership roles.

This chapter provides an overview of the literature that relates to leadership identity development and reports the findings of a recent qualitative research study. Twenty-three women were interviewed as participants in a four-day Women's Leadership Development Institute (WLDI) who retrospectively (3–13 years after their participation) self-described the WLDI as having been a "*defining moment* in changing their self-perception about their leadership abilities or potential." Our research sought to better understand "what works" in the formation of women's leadership identity development as a means of informing future research and planning for women's leader identity development programming.

Defining Moments

The term "defining moments" was used to identify former WLDI participants who retrospectively stated that their four-day immersion into leadership development was a transformative experience—professionally and/or personally. This terminology seemed appropriate given the work of earlier scholars who have emphasized that leaders develop through seizing defining moments that prove to be building blocks on their leadership journey. For example, early work in the business arena by Badaracco (1997) described how certain decisions and actions (i.e., defining moments) often surface "something hidden. They can crystallize what was fluid and unformed. . . . [A] defining moment reveals something important about a person's basic values and about his or her abiding commitments in life" (p. 57).

Related specifically to leadership development, the results of qualitative research reported by Bennis and Thomas (2007) in *Leading for a Lifetime: Defining Moments Shape the Leaders of Today and Tomorrow* emphasized commonalities in the way that individual responses to crucible events shaped the lives of exemplary leaders under age 30 and over age 70. Numerous additional researchers have referred to defining moments as catalysts that stimulate leadership development (Avolio & Luthans, 2006; Badaracco, 1997; Denzin, 1989; Shamir & Eilam, 2005). Similar to variations in the nature of the "phenomenon" in phenomenological research (Van Manen, 1990), a *defining moment* might literally be only a moment in length (e.g., an automobile accident) or a much longer-lived experience (e.g., treatments for pancreatic cancer). Defining moments disorient leaders and consequently provide a leadership jolt (Avolio & Luthans, 2006), offering leaders psychological, emotional, and intellectual space to reevaluate their core ideas and values (Dahlvig & Longman, 2010, p. 243), leadership trajectory (Avolio & Luthans, 2006), and leadership identity (Pallus, Nasby, & Easton, 1991).

Although the term *defining moment* was not defined or explained, each of the participants self-reported that her four-day immersion in the WLDI had been a transformative event in terms of her leadership self-perceptions. Many also indicated that aspects of themselves had previously been fluid and unformed, consistent with Badaracco's (1997) description, yet increased self-awareness about their leadership potential and abilities had become more *internalized* (Shamir & Eilam, 2005). Specifically, these self-perceptions were reframed in ways that motivated them to reimagine their leadership trajectories (Avolio & Luthans, 2006; Ibarra, 2015). Such internal movement is significant and necessary within the progression of women's leadership development, as Ibarra (2015) has argued at length.

Women's Leader Identity Development

There is an emerging body of literature that explores the factors that contribute to the process of developing an internalized sense of leadership identity. Past research regarding leadership identity development theories includes the work of Komives (Komives, Owen, Longerbeam, Mainella, & Osteen, 2005), who created a *leadership identity development model* based on a grounded theory study involving 13 college students who had been nominated as "exemplars of relational leadership" (Komives, Longerbeam, Mainella, Owen, & Osteen, 2009, p. 594). They identified six stages in the process of leadership identity development: (1) deepening self-awareness, (2) exploration and engagement, (3) leader identified, (4) leadership differentiated, (5) generativity, and (6) integration/synthesis. Related work in the area of leadership identity development by Day (Day, 2001; Day & Harrison, 2007; Day & Lance, 2004) demonstrated the importance of cognitive complexity in leaders' sense of identity. Day and Harrison (2007) described leader identity as a "multidimensional construct" (p. 365) comprised of levels of identity (e.g., individual, collective) and types of identity (e.g., leader, spouse) that must be differentiated and integrated. The ability to embrace a leader identity was determined to be salient, particularly through demonstrated leadership competencies (Day, Harrison, & Halpin, 2009).

Ibarra, Wittman, Petriglieri, and Day (2014) more recently have organized emerging research related to leadership and identity into three areas of theoretical research: (1) role identity, (2) social identity, and (3) social construction, describing personal identity as a "linchpin across identity theories" (p. 290). Role-based theories have emphasized the acquisition of leadership skills and experiences as being highly influential in the development of a leader self-concept (Day & Harrison, 2007; Lord & Hall, 2005). Within social identity theories, social categories are emphasized at the group level; the concept of prototypicality associated with leaders is an essential dimension of these theories (Hogg, 2001; Hogg, van Knippenberg, & Rast, 2012). Prototypicality refers to a social categorization process that "perceptually segments the social world into ingroups and outgroups that are cognitively represented as prototypes" (Hogg, 2001, p. 187).

Increasingly in recent years, researchers have confirmed the applicability of social construction theories to leadership identity development. For example, Ibarra et al. (2014) have noted that the shaping of identity is "claimed and granted in social interaction" (Ibarra et al., p. 286); similarly, DeRue and Ashford (2010) observed the important roles of both "*claiming and granting*" (p. 672) as part of the leadership identity construction process in which individuals begins to see themselves as leaders. At the most basic level, *claiming* refers to actions associated with the assertion of a leader identity, and *granting* refers to actions associated with the bestowal of a leader identity onto another. Many forms of claiming a leader identity have been identified, ranging from public declarations of a leadership role to indirect claims such as setting a meeting agenda, dressing in a particular attire, or drawing attention to a personal relationship with other known leaders (Ashford & DeRue, 2012). According to Ashford and DeRue (2012), "a leader identity must be granted by others for it to be internalized, recognized, and endorsed by other individuals and the organization more broadly" (p. 148). Several recent studies have provided empirical support for this leadership identity construction theory (Guillén, Mayo, & Korotov, 2015; Marchiondo, Myers, & Kopelman, 2015; Miscenko, Guenter, & Day, 2017).

More recent scholarship by Ibarra (1999) and Ibarra et al. (2013, 2015), which has focused on leadership identity development in the corporate sector, sparked the curiosity that led to the study described in this chapter. Specifically, the phrase describing leader identity development as being an "often fragile process" (Ibarra, Ely, & Kolb, 2013, p. 62) resonated with the researchers as being accurate, based on related previous studies that had examined the motivators, barriers, and encouragers of women in faith-based higher education to move into leadership roles (Dahlvig & Longman, 2014, 2016; Longman & Lafreniere, 2012). According to Ibarra, Ely, and Kolb (2013), subtle forms of second-generation gender bias in organizations "disrupt the learning cycle at the heart of becoming a leader" (p. 62), negatively influencing the experiences of women considering or moving into leadership roles. In part, the challenges faced by women relate to the cognitive association of leadership and maleness, whether subconsciously or overtly (Eagly & Karau, 2002; Ritter & Yoder, 2004). For example, a meta-analysis of leader stereotypes by Koenig, Eagly, Mitchell, and Ristikari (2011) documented that leadership stereotypes continue to be largely male normed.

Similar to the claiming dimension of DeRue and Ashford's (2010) description of the leadership identity construction process, Ibarra (2015) has emphasized that the internalization of a leader identity is critically important. In fact, Ibarra has gone further to advocate that "becoming the person you aspire to be is the most powerful motivator of all" (p. 174). Yet *claiming* has an important counterpart in those who hold the power of *granting* a leader identity to others. Three elements or levels are at play in this dynamic process: individual internalization, relational recognition, and collective endorsement (DeRue & Ashford, 2010). Reflecting the cyclical nature of the identity development process, research by Kark and Van Dijk (2007) affirmed that social validation increases leadership confidence, which in turn leads to increased motivation to assume broader roles of leadership.

The Study

Clearly, more research is needed around various dimensions of what Ibarra, Ely, and Kolb (2013) referred to as the "often fragile process of coming to see oneself, and to be seen by others, as a leader" (p. 62). Equally important in terms of applying these research findings in constructive ways, the implications for leadership development programming must be more fully understood and tested. Recognizing the need to better understand the factors that contribute to the process of leader identity development, this study was designed with two curiosities in mind: (1) What exactly had contributed to making a relatively short period of time (four days)—that had occurred quite far in the past (three to 13 years)—a "*defining moment*" in the leadership journeys of these participants? And (2) What aspects of that experience had been particularly impactful in shaping their self-perceptions of leadership potential and capacity?

The 108 participants who had attended a WLDI between 2002 and 2012 were invited to participate in the research project *if* they identified themselves as meeting this criterion: Looking back from at least three years after attending, would you describe the influence of the WLDI as having been a "*defining moment*" *on your leadership identity and subsequent leadership journey?* The 23 women who responded to this invitation were mostly white (18); two were African American; two were Asian American; and one was Latina. In terms of the year of participation in the WLDI, we intentionally sought a long-term retrospective; eight had attended the WLDI more than a decade previously (2002 or 2004); six had attended in 2006 or 2008; and nine had participated in 2010 or 2012—so at least three years prior to the period of research.

As contextual information, the WLDI offerings were relatively consistent in length and format. Each cohort involved 18–22 individuals who were selected through an application process. Each of the WLDI offerings was led by a resource leadership team of approximately six cabinet-level leaders, typically all women. Using a combination of presentations, large-group dialogue, and small group interactions, the 15–18 content sessions of each WLDI focused on topics such as introducing the latest leadership literature, presidential expectations of cabinet-level leaders, executive presence, decision making, and budgeting; each participant also received a collection of leadership books in addition to several leadership-related articles. The WLDI setting, a retreat center 2 miles from the Canadian border in Washington state, is intentionally remote; participants are asked to protect the meeting space as a technology-free zone in order to allow participants to focus fully on the content and group interactions.

The participants were each interviewed and asked to describe their feelings and perceptions about themselves as a leader at three points in time (before, during, and after returning from the WLDI). They were also asked: "We are interested to know—in as much detail as you can provide—what made the WLDI a *defining moment* for you?" The interviews were professionally transcribed and analyzed. From the analysis, seven primary themes (awareness, acceptance, affiliation, affirmation, agency, tangible items, and setting) were initially identified.

Approximately six months after the initial round of interviews, each of the participants was asked to identify which two themes best captured the dimensions of the WLDI that had most contributed to that four-day period being a *defining moment* on her leadership journey. Additional information about how and why certain dimensions of the WLDI had been particularly important to them was gathered, which allowed for further refinement of the emerging themes.

Insights Gained

Four primary themes emerged regarding why and how the participants' four-day immersion in the Women's Leadership Development Institute (WLDI) had been self-described as a *defining moment* in their leadership journeys. Identi-fied most frequently as being the strongest resonant theme was the **affirmation** received by participants at the WLDI in relation to their leadership potential, ability, and trajectory. As a close second, many of the participants reported hav-ing left the WLDI with a greater sense of **awareness** of their leadership poten-tial, style, and strengths; a more realistic understanding of their institutional culture; and greater confidence due to familiarity with the leadership literature. Departing the WLDI with a heightened sense of personal **agency** was the next theme, often reflected in self-reports of having greater motivation and confi-dence to step more proactively into leadership roles. Additionally, more than half of the participants expressed a heightened commitment to empower other women and share what they had learned with others. The final theme, **affilia-tion,** assimilated the reflections of many of the participants that the WLDI had provided a network that was rich and life-giving with members of the resource leadership team and other women academics.

Affirmation

> I needed people to really help me identify some of the challenges that women run into. Specifically, so that I could sort my way through some of the lack of affirmation, some of the contextual pieces that I dealt with, some of the wounding in many ways. . . . [The WLDI] strengthened my perception of my ability to lead. It was the first time that one of the presidents who was there pulled me aside and said: "Ultimately, you need to be a college president, and don't let anyone tell you different." That was, in some ways, life changing.
> —Sara, attended the 2006 WLDI as a dean; now a university president

Throughout the interviews, participants described how the WLDI had pro-vided an atmosphere in which they were encouraged to embrace their leader-ship identity and capacity. This embrace reportedly occurred for many of the women through the individual and communal affirmation they experienced from spending time with other women professionals working in higher educa-tion and from the resource leadership team. The transformative power of affir-mation manifested itself in two distinct ways across the participants: through the focused time and space in which the women were encouraged to fully accept and embrace their leadership ability and trajectory and through participants' verbalization of how their self-perceptions had begun to change within that four-day period. Looking back, some described how that realization had been expressed in short declarative outbursts such as "I am a leader!" and "I am enough!" Three primary categories of external affirmation were identified as sources of empowerment and reframed self-perceptions that resonated with them years afterward: (1) the nomination process and identification of being an "emerging leader," as communicated by two leaders from their home institution during the application process; (2) encouragement and modeling from members of the resource leadership team; and (3) peer influence and collegial relationships with other women academics.

Several participants commented on the significance of having been nominated by a key individual (e.g., the provost or president) who may have explicitly articulated the perceived leadership abilities for the first time. As an example, Anne (all names are pseudonyms) described herself as arriving at the WLDI as a "reluctant leader" who was feeling "anxious, tentative, and not ready." However, Anne's supervisor had told her: "I talked to the president; you're going to this WLDI." Anne described her experience prior to that time: "Anything I had ever done in leadership was someone shoulder-tapping me and saying, 'Hey, you need to do X, Y, or Z.'" Targeted encouragement from key leaders on her campus—in this case Anne's supervisor and the president—caused Anne to think about her leadership potential in new ways. Because several of the women interpreted their letters of nomination as signaling proactive recognition of leadership talent, the nomination process itself represented a significant source of affirmation.

The participants also reported ways in which they had powerfully experienced affirmation from members of the resource leadership team. Numerous examples of confirmation—received either publicly or in private—were recounted as having been influential in causing them to reimagine leadership possibilities and trajectories. Mary referenced the more generalized impact of her interaction with a team of experienced women leaders: "I have never had . . . women in leadership roles speak a lot of empowerment into my life to say, 'You can do this.' That was powerful. Very powerful." Danielle similarly referenced the emotional impact of a "galvanizing moment" when a cabinet-level leader counseled her to "stop apologizing for yourself, because you're undercutting your own ability." Danielle described her reaction: "I remember literally gasping, almost getting tears in my eyes."

While the resource leaders played a key role as encouragers and motivators, the participants among themselves offered similar affirmations. Some participants observed that spending time focusing on leadership in the company of other academic women led to conversations that fueled their leadership aspirations and confidence. Specifically, a sense of communal affirmation reportedly emerged as peer participants referenced strengths, perceived talents, and trajectories they observed in one another. Jane, for example, described how being in an environment of mutual support: "really [brought] a confirmation of leadership and leadership styles that you can be a woman and use your own leadership styles; that's good and that's okay."

Awareness

> I think a lot of people, and I did, go in thinking that leadership is much more narrowly defined than it is. I am what I would call an uncommon leader. A lot of people think that leadership is . . . a certain style of personality. It's a certain aggressiveness. It's a certain early desire to go into leadership, and that wasn't me. [I was becoming] much more confident in my "uncommon leadership-ness" and the style that I had, and the way God wired me, and beginning to sense why people were identifying leadership in me when I didn't have what the old-fashioned narrow definition of a leader might be. Finding an "identifying group" . . . and reading some of the newest thinking on women in leadership [led to the healthy realization] that my gender, my faith, [and] my uncommon leadership style was finding a home.
>
> —Beth, attended the 2004 WLDI as director of the school of education; now a vice president for academic affairs

When participants were asked to identify the two most salient themes that represented why and how the WLDI had been a *defining moment* for them, "awareness" emerged as the second-highest resonant theme. Awareness was experienced in three different ways: (1) through awareness of their leadership ability and confidence in their leadership style, (2) through exposure to literature on leadership and gender, and (3) through the commonality of their challenges.

The first area of heightened awareness related to a change that occurred, or began to occur, during the WLDI in their self-perceptions of their own leadership potential and aspirations. Numerous participants referenced leaving the WLDI with heightened awareness of their leadership ability and confidence in their leadership style. Their confidence reportedly came through awareness of individual strengths, talents, and alignment with calling, which were components of the WLDI curriculum. The responses of Anne represented one end of the spectrum:

> I chose "Awareness" first because I really never saw myself as a leader. When I was identified to participate in the WLDI, I thought "Really?" It was definitely through my participation in the program and God's direction that I began to become aware of leadership qualities and potential.

At the other end of the spectrum, Danielle described how she had entered the WLDI with a sense of confidence in her leadership abilities, yet the experience had provided momentum in other ways: "I've always seen myself as a leader in some sort of amorphous way, but greatly appreciated the dialing in on concrete specifics both in myself—through strengths work—and in the new-to-me context of Christian higher education." Contributing to the heightened sense of self-awareness and confidence were sessions and conversations at the WLDI in which the participants identified their talents and dialogued about their sense of calling. Providing a safe space and encouragement for the participants to be self-reflective about these topics opened new ways of thinking about themselves, distinct from the normal categories of gender and organizational hierarchy.

A second dimension of heightened awareness related to the literature that was provided. Through exposure to a broader body of literature related to leadership and gender, the participants described having an increased awareness of the institutional culture on their home campuses. These resources illuminated the challenges of working in male-normed cultures and the well-documented benefits of diversifying senior-level leadership teams. Confirmation from the literature that women's ways of leading can be highly effective, combined with the modeling of women who were successful cabinet-level leaders, reportedly caused several participants to rethink their leadership potential and to move forward with greater confidence. Danielle reported that she had begun "modeling myself more on those women leaders and being . . . more comfortable in my own skin" after attending the WLDI.

The third area of heightened awareness was participants' realization that their challenges were common across other campuses, that the status quo was unacceptable, and that an individual and collective response was needed to bring about needed change. For example, Cindy observed: "WLDI changed my life in terms of figuring what I had always felt [about my leadership ability], how I had not allowed myself to act on it, and why I had not." Previous research has identified that women working in faith-based campus settings often have deep loyalties to a particular institution (Dahlvig, 2011; Longman, Dahlvig, Wikkerink, Cunningham, & O'Connor, 2011) and tend to stay even if the climate is not life-giving. These participants reported that their awareness of the cultural and environmental context for women had been raised, both within and beyond higher education. For many, that broadened awareness created a sense of responsibility to bring about change. Being aware of the common joys and challenges, these women felt strengthened by recognizing that they were not alone; in fact, their experiences were shared by women in other faith-based campuses across the country.

Agency

> After being affirmed in deep relationships, one cannot return to her original leadership roles without an expanded vision and passion. Social psychologists describe agency as "self in action." Returning from [the WLDI], that sense of self being activated to do and to work and to persevere with hope, with determination, with connectedness, is indeed empowering and transformative.
>
> —Amy, attended the 2012 WLDI participant as a department chair; subsequently appointed to a vice presidential role

When asked about their leadership journey after leaving the WLDI experience, participants described having an increased sense of motivation and confidence to step into leadership roles within their institutions, a theme we termed "agency." Additionally, more than half of the participants commented on sensing a heightened commitment to help other women, finding a stronger voice to implement their ideas, and sharing what they had learned with coworkers and staff.

Numerous examples emerged in the data to reflect the willingness, and in some cases eagerness, of the participants to step into broader leadership roles upon their return from the WLDI. Mary's words exemplified this sense of expanded self-confidence and agency: "Even when you don't know all of the parameters, even if you don't know exactly what waits behind that door, it's just, do it!" Similarly, Janelle described how having received a boost in her self-confidence had "inaugurated the process for me of really freeing me to lead out of who I am."

This increased sense of personal agency was also reflected as women began to reframe challenges and discouragements they had encountered at work. As Fiona described, "I didn't go looking for controversy, but I saw controversy and disagreement in a different light. I saw it more as collaborative rather than a threat." For many of the participants, the WLDI rooted their leader identity in a deeper sense of their own efficacy and provided space for them to face and engage hostile situations at their home institutions with a greater confidence.

Building from a stronger sense of courage and agency also offered a context for the women to reimagine their careers and futures. Sara explained that the institute experience allowed her to be ambitious and imagine being a college president. This redefinition of ambition as something positive appeared repeatedly throughout the interviews. Liz's comments illustrated the power of this reframing process:

> There was this light bulb moment that, you know what, ambition is a good thing. It can be a God-given thing, and I actually am ambitious. I'm not content to simply do what I'm doing for the rest of my career. I will get bored. I was already getting bored. I think WLDI helped me figure that out, too. . . . You know what? I'm ambitious, and that's a good thing.

The theme of agency, as reflected in an awakening of openness to—and even aspirations for—greater leadership responsibility, also seemed to contribute to a deeper passion to advocate for and create opportunities for other women (and men) to mature in their own leadership identity. Mary reflected on her increased commitment to this kind of advocacy: "I've become particularly sensitive to and supportive of the career paths of the young women who are in my sphere of influence, the younger female faculty in particular." Meredith confessed that she had not felt a sense of responsibility to develop other women until she had attended the WLDI, but she and others were prompted to initiate opportunities so others on their campus could benefit from similar forms of professional development. Brenda referenced a similar conviction:

> Particularly for women and women at my own institution, there are a number of females in various positions of leadership, but I don't see plans to develop them further to expand skills and knowledge. I think that's very important. At the same time that we are being mentored, we should be seeking out mentoring experiences with other younger or less experienced women. I think that's an important part of our calling to leadership.

This desire to support other women in leadership complemented the heightened sense of personal agency related to their own leadership journeys.

Affiliation

> [The WLDI] provided me with more confidence and such an incredible resource of women to have access to. I felt like it provided just a network for really seeing women who are like me. There's not many role models for women and, particularly at the college that I was at, there were no others like me . . . young women with a Ph.D. It was life-changing for me to be around those women and to see how they moved up, to see how they related in relationships with others.
> —Teresa, attended the 2002 WLDI as associate director of institutional research and effectiveness; subsequently master adjunct faculty of psychology and raising a family

The theme that was ranked fourth by the participants as a reason for the WLDI being impactful to their leadership self-perceptions and identity was labeled "affiliation." Specifically, participants referenced the relational and professional benefits of exploring the intersectionality of gender and leadership with a group of talented academic women. They also described the WLDI as having created a sense of belonging to a larger community and having developed a network and affiliation with a set of people that was deep and rich; several referenced the importance of ongoing conversations over subsequent years. Additionally, the power of being connected to female role models in leadership was frequently emphasized, extending to the participants' sense of responsibility to include others in the "sisterhood."

When asked to articulate in greater detail exactly what had contributed to the transformative impact of this four-day institute, comments related to the uniqueness of being in a women-only environment, the vulnerability and transparency that had quickly developed within the group, and perceptions of finding others who experienced the same struggles yet had a common sense of purpose. Even more than a decade after participating in the WLDI, the participants used words such as "refreshing," "encouraging," "empowering," and "enlightening" to describe their memories of having been embedded into a network of like-minded and like-spirited academic professionals. Teresa described her involvement as a young professional as "life-changing" as she gained confidence from finding other women "who [were] like me." Similarly, Janice reported how she had come to the WLDI feeling isolated and alone as a female faculty member at her institution. Meeting other women helped her to realize that "women have a place at the table in particular, and the leadership styles of women are valid and valuable."

The relational aspects of transparency and vulnerability within the group reportedly allowed WLDI participants to think more seriously about their own potential future leadership roles. Amy, for example, described how she had realized in listening to the stories of others at the institute that she was not alone or "delusional." Similarly, Anne described that having a network of professional colleagues had been affirming to her, making her feel less alone. She commented, "When something happens, you don't think to yourself, this doesn't happen to anyone else."

Many of the participants maintained their networks with individual participants—and particularly members of the resource leadership team—from their institute throughout subsequent years via Facebook group posts and occasional planned or unexpected reconnecting. One participant expressed that regardless of the circumstances, she could always call and receive advice from those who had mentored her at the WLDI. Even when not being directly connected with other participants in her cohort, Janelle described feeling that there was "still this great cloud of witnesses" out there and supporting her. She elaborated:

> Somehow I know that there are other women out there who have the same questions, the same frustrations, the same issues. . . . They are sharp, motivated. Even though I don't talk to, or even see them folks, I know they are there. It's really encouraging just to even remember that experience.

It should be noted that the affiliation theme that emerged in the data likely related in part to the fact that nearly all of the participants were drawn from one subset of U.S. private higher education—the 120 institutions that are aligned with the Council for Christian Colleges & Universities. Although the membership brings together colleges and universities that represent more than 30 Christian denominations, all are historically rooted in the liberal arts and share commonalities in terms of institutional mission. For a variety of historical and theological reasons, the percentage of women in senior-level leadership in these institutions collectively is lower than the national averages (Longman & Anderson, 2016). Accordingly, the participants likely experienced a deeper sense of affiliation than might be common in larger or more diverse groups, given the shared commitment among the participants that all individuals be honored for their gifts, hence a sense of theological urgency to address the underrepresentation of women in senior-level leadership roles.

Much like college alumni 10–20 years after graduation who cannot remember anything about particular courses they took, it may not be surprising that the lasting impact of participation in a four-day Women's Leadership Development Institute, thinking back over a gulf of three to 13 years, largely reflects the relational aspects of that experience. With the press of demanding jobs, parental expectations, and ever-present technology, it is rare that professional women call "time out" to focus on assessing and developing their own skills, gifts, and sense of calling, particularly in the company of other intelligent and committed academics. In the defining moments literature, Shamir and Eilam (2005) outline a process that requires leaders to intentionally return to an event, cognitively "replay" it, "recount" it to others, re-emote the accompanying feelings, "reevaluate" their decisions, and reapply what they learned (p. 410). Based on the level of detail provided by the participants in this study, they had followed those steps in relation to the WLDI having been a *defining moment* on their life's journey.

Discussion and Implications

Educators and professionals from many spheres of influence spend time reflecting on how to change the lives of individuals for the better. In the field of leadership, finding answers to questions regarding how to prepare effective leaders has been hampered by the lack of clarity about even the definition of the words "leader" and "leadership" (Kellerman, 2012; Riggio, 2010); the interplay of relational dynamics among leaders, followers, and context (Kellerman, 2008, 2014); and the growing awareness of the role that intersectionality plays in all aspects of leadership identity development (Egan et al., 2017; Fox-Kirk, Campbell, & Egan, 2017).

Despite the stumbles and failures of local, national, and international leaders that are captured in the news almost daily, progress is being made on several promising fronts. To date, for example, several comprehensive literature reviews have examined the process of leader identity development and the contributors to effective leadership (e.g., Day, 2001; Ely, Ibarra, & Kolb, 2011; Hopkins, O'Neil, Passarelli, & Bilimoria, 2008; Miscenko & Day, 2016; Riggio, 2010). Additionally, evaluations of long-standing leadership development programs are available (e.g., the 50-year history of the American Council on Education's Fellows program [Crandall, Espinosa, Gangone, & Hughes, 2017] and the 40-year history of the Higher Education Resource Services [HERS] program (White, 2014)). At the same time, there have been calls for additional longitudinal research (Riggio & Mumford, 2011) and for deeper explorations into which components of leadership development programs are most impactful in advancing the leader identity process. This chapter concludes by affirming the value of six such contributors discussed here, based on the findings of this study in concert with insights gained from the relevant literature.

The Power of Knowing the Literature

Individuals who are designing leadership development programs typically spend a great deal of time reading leadership literature, attending leadership conferences, and observing effective and ineffective leaders. Yet our conviction is that most participants in such leadership programs have not done the same. Even understanding and embracing the simple concept of leader identity development can be new terrain for attendees, particularly when coupled with the perspective of Ibarra, Ely, and Kolb (2013) that "*the process of coming to see oneself, and to be seen by others, as a leader*" (p. 62, italics added) is fragile, and particularly so for women.

Using creative pedagogical approaches to challenge groups to identify the external factors that influence the experiences of women working in male-normed environments (Ayman & Korabik, 2010; Diehl & Dzubinski, 2016; Ely & Rhode, 2010) can be eye-opening to participants; similarly, offering resources on the internal barriers and the complex work of developing a leader identity (Marchiondo, Myers, & Kopelman, 2015; Miscenko, Guenter, & Day, 2015) can provide helpful understanding and scaffolding. Additional steps that can be taken by aspiring and emerging leaders are laid out in accessible books such as Hewlett's (2014) *Executive* Presence, Ibarra's (2015) *Act Like a Leader, Think Like a Leader*, and Kay and Shipman's (2014) *The Confidence* Code, to name just a few examples.

The Power of Claiming and Granting

Among the promising literature that has emerged related to the leadership identity development process, the contributions of DeRue and Ashford (2010)—particularly regarding the *claiming* and *granting* process—merit further attention in terms of the application of this material in designing leadership development programming. Notably, the dynamic nature of being a leader in a given setting or situation depends in part on the process of what is "claimed" and what is "granted" at three levels of leadership identity: "*individual internalization, relational recognition, and collective endorsement*" (p. 629, italics added). DeRue and Ashford helpfully point out that leadership can be entered into irrespective of having a formal role or position; rather, a leadership relationship "is composed of reciprocal and mutually reinforcing identities as leaders and followers, is endorsed and reinforced within the broader organizational context, and is dynamic over time" (p. 627). Intentional programming around aspects of *claiming* and *granting* in relation to each of the three elements (individual internalization, relational recognition, and collective endorsement), combined with the four dominant themes that emerged from the current findings (i.e., the importance of affirmation, awareness, agency, and affiliation), would offer the basis for a transformative curriculum for women's leadership development programing. Factors related to intersectionality influence both the granting and claiming, opening the potential for engaged conversation among participants in leadership development programs.

The Power of Relationships

Individuals responsible for designing leadership development training likely hope that the content of each presentation and session will prove to be catalytic to the future career success of the participants. Yet the findings of this study, corroborating the work of numerous researchers, suggest that the relationships and networks established through women's leadership development programming potentially carry even more weight and benefit than factual content. Similar to the "affiliation" theme that emerged in the findings of our WLDI research, evaluations of HERS institutes (White, 2014) report similar findings. When queried about what that organization had learned from program evaluations over the years, Judith S. White, HERS executive director, responded: "I find that question ['What was most important to you so far?'] is often most revealing about what impact the experience is having for them. We have come to expect and appreciate that the connections with the other participants is our greatest gift to them" (J. White, personal communication, October 11, 2014). Notably, Kram (1985) and Gibson (2008) have emphasized the importance of women having a "constellation" (Gibson, 2008, p. 653) of developmental relationships, preferably extending beyond the workplace to provide a larger perspective. And recent scholarship by Murphy, Gibson, and Kram (2017) has provided a helpful overview of five types of developmental relationships (mentors, sponsors, peers, executive coaches, and learning partners). Women's leadership development programs offer opportunities to establish interorganizational relationships that contribute to those constellations.

The Power of Women-Only Leadership Opportunities

The benefits of offering programming specifically for women have been documented in the literature (Debebe, 2011; Ely, Ibarra, & Kolb, 2011; Kassotakis, 2017). Debebe (2011) observed that women-only programs provide opportunities to interact with similar others who can provide validation and a safe venue for social comparisons during the leader identity development process. Similarly, a recent summary of the literature by Kassotakis (2017) identified three primary advantages of women-only programming: "(1) participants' sense of safety; (2) structured reflection on identity and factors related to intersectionality; and (3) building social capital via networking safety" (p. 404). For the women in the WLDI research, a sense of empowerment and belonging emerged during the experience of being in an environment that was nonhierarchical and mutually supportive. The relationships did, indeed, create a "sisterhood" that was, for many, the first time of feeling affirmed and connected with other women who had the same passion and commitment for serving students well through higher education.

The Power of Giftedness, Calling, and Purpose

Among the provocative dimensions of the leader identity development work being offered by Ibarra, Ely, and Kolb (2013) is their attention given to the topic of "The Importance of Leadership Purpose" (p. 66). Numerous researchers have identified that the motivators for women to advance into leadership and remain in leadership appear to differ substantially from those of men (Dahlvig & Longman, 2014; Helgesen & Johnson, 2010; Keohane, 2014; Turner, 2012). As Kay and Shipman (2014) noted, one way to expand women's confidence is to change the language from "me" to "we," given that women are more likely to take risks and assume responsibilities if the larger good is at stake. Similarly, Keohane's (2014) research into the leadership aspirations of Ivy League female students found that they were more interested in leading programs related to a cause they believed in rather than for status or power. Research by Dahlvig and Longman (2014) similarly found that women were more inclined to step into leadership in responsiveness to stewarding their talents and calling rather than seeking a higher salary or positional acclaim. Designing women's leadership development programs, therefore, not only needs to introduce women to the barriers (internal and exterior) that hinder women's advancement but also to affirm their talents through assessments such as the Clifton Strengths-Finder and opportunities for reflection around purpose and calling. As Ibarra, Ely, and Kolb note: "Anchoring in purpose enables women to redirect their attention toward shared goals and to consider who they need to be and what they need to do in order to achieve those goals" (p. 66).

The Power of Place

Finally, the remoteness and beauty of the retreat center that has hosted the WLDI programs over the past 20 years was clearly a factor in transformative power of this four-day period. It is undoubtedly more cost-effective to offer leadership development programming to larger groups, in shorter time-periods, and based at hotels with conference facilities close to major airports. In contrast, communications about the WLDI ask participants to "clear the decks" and come ready to focus on their own leadership development. We have found that the charter bus ride of 2½ hours to the Canadian border from Seattle's "SeaTac" Airport (where the group gathers) allows time for decompressing and bonding. The anticipation of time away from the normal pressures of daily life is palpable—laying the groundwork for openness to what Avolio and Luthans (2006) termed a leadership "jolt" (p. 11). Particularly when combined with the intrusiveness of 24/7 access via technology, it is rare for professionals to stop, take stock, and deeply connect with others. Being together with other academic women in a "safe space" and gathering specifically for the purpose of leadership development has been a powerful combination for the WLDI participants, allowing them space to talk freely about their challenges and hopes with an uncommon level of vulnerability and transparency.

Note

1 The contributions of Julie Cowen (Eastern University) and Karen Lindsey (Texas Christian University) during stages of this research project are acknowledged with thanks.

References

Ashford, S. J., & DeRue, A. D. (2012). Developing as a leader: The power of mindful engagement. *Organizational Dynamics, 41*, 146–154.

Avolio, B. J., & Luthans, F. (2006). *The high impact leader: Moments that matter in accelerating authentic leadership development.* New York: McGraw-Hill.

Ayman, R., & Korabik, K. (2010). Leadership: Why gender and culture matter. *American Psychologist, 65*(3), 157–170.

Badaracco, J. L. (1997). *Defining moments: When managers must choose between right and right.* Boston, MA: Harvard Business School Press.

Bennis, W. G., & Thomas, R. J. (2007). *Leading for a lifetime: How defining moments shape the leaders of today and tomorrow.* Boston, MA: Harvard Business School Press.

Catalyst. (2013). *Why diversity matters.* Retrieved from www.catalyst.org/system/files/why_diversity_matters_catalyst_0.pdf

Crandall, J. R., Espinosa, L. L., Gangone, L. M., & Hughes, S. L. (2017). *Looking back and looking forward: A review of the ACE Fellows Program.* Washington, DC: American Council on Education.

Dahlvig, J. E. (2011). *A narrative study of women leading within the Council for Christian Colleges & Universities* (Doctoral dissertation). Retrieved from ProQuest Dissertations & Theses Global. (Accession No. 888186726).

Dahlvig, J. E., & Longman, K. A. (2010). Women's leadership development: A study of defining moments. *Christian Higher Education, 9*(3), 238–258. doi:10.1080/15363750903182177

Dahlvig, J. E., & Longman, K. A. (2014). Contributors to women's leadership development in Christian higher education: A model and emerging theory. *Journal of Research on Christian Education, 23*(1), 5–28. doi:10.1080/10656219.2014.862196

Dahlvig, J. E., & Longman, K. A. (2016). Influences of an evangelical Christian worldview on women's leadership development. *Advances in Developing Human Resources, 18*(2), 243–259.

Day, D. V. (2001). Leadership development: A review in context. *Leadership Quarterly, 11*(4), 581–613.

Day, D. V., & Harrison, M. M. (2007). A multilevel, identity-based approach to leadership development. *Human Resource Management Review, 17*, 360–373. doi:10.1016/j.hrmr.2007.08.007

Day, D. V., Harrison, M. M., & Halpin, S. M. (2009). *An integrative approach to leadership development: Connecting adult identity, development, and expertise.* New York, NY: Psychology Press.

Day, D. V., & Lance, C. E. (2004). Understanding the development of leadership complexity through latent growth modeling. In D. V. Day, S. J. Zaccaro, & S. M. Halpin (Eds.), *Leader development for transforming organizations: Growing leaders for tomorrow* (pp. 41–69). Mahwah, NJ: Erlbaum.

Debebe, G. (2011). Creating a safe environment for women's leadership transformation. *Journal of Management Education, 35*(5), 679–712.

Denzin, N. K. (1989). *Interpretive biography.* Thousand Oaks, CA: Sage Publications.

DeRue, D. S., & Ashford, S. J. (2010). Who will lead and who will follow? A social process of leadership identity construction in organizations. *Academy of Management Review, 35*(4), 627–647. doi:10.5465/AMR.2010.53503267

Diehl, A. B., & Dzubinski, L. M. (2016). Making the invisible visible: A cross-sector analysis of gender-based leadership barriers. *Human Resource Development Quarterly, 27*(2), 181–206.

Eagly, A. H. (2015). Foreword. In S. R. Madsen, F. W. Ngunjiri, K. A. Longman, & C. Cherrey (Eds.), *Women and leadership around the world* (pp. IX-XIII). Charlotte, NC: Information Age Publishing.

Eagly, A. H., & Carli, L. L. (2007). *Through the labyrinth: The truth about how women become leaders.* Boston, MA: Harvard Business School.

Eagly, A. H., & Karau, S. J. (2002). Role congruity theory of prejudice toward female leaders. *Psychological Bulletin, 109*, 573–598.

Egan, C., Shollen, L., Campbell, C., Longman, K. A., Fisher, K., Fox-Kirk, W., & Neilson, B. G. (2017). Capacious model of leadership identities construction. In J. Storberg-Walker & P. Haber-Curran (Eds.), *Theorizing women and leadership: New insights and contributions from multiple perspectives* (pp. 121–140). Charlotte, NC: Information Age Publishing.

Ely, R., Ibarra, H., & Kolb, D. (2011). Taking gender into account: Theory and design for women's leadership development programs. *Academy of Management Learning & Education, 10*(3), 474–493. doi:http://dx.doi.org/10.5465/amle.2010.0046

Ely, R. J., & Rhode, D. (2010). Women and leadership: Defining the challenges. In N. Nohria & R. Khurana (Eds.), *Handbook of leadership theory and practice* (pp. 377–410). Boston, MA: Harvard Business Publishing.

Fox-Kirk, W., Campbell, C., & Egan, C. (2017). Women's leadership identity: Exploring person and context in theory. In S. R. Madsen (Ed.), *Handbook of research on gender and leadership* (pp. 193–206). Northampton, MA: Edward Elgar Publishing.

Gangone, L. M., & Lennon, T. (2014). Benchmarking women's leadership in academia beyond. In K. A. Longman & S. R. Madsen (Eds.), *Women and leadership in higher education* (pp. 3–22). Charlotte, NC: Information Age Publishing.

Gerzema, J., & D'Antonio, M. (2013). *The Athena doctrine: How women (and the men who think like them) will rule the future.* San Francisco, CA: Jossey-Bass.

Gibson, S. K. (2008). The developmental relationships of women leaders in career transition: Implications for leader development. *Advances in Developing Human Resources, 10*(5), 651–670.

Guillén, L., Mayo, M., & Korotov, K. (2015). Is leadership a part of me? A leader identity approach to understanding the motivation to lead. *The Leadership Quarterly, 26,* 802–820.

Helgesen, S., & Johnson, J. (2010). *The female vision: Women's real power at work.* San Francisco, CA: Berrett-Koehler Publishers.

Hewlett, S. A. (2014). *Executive presence: The missing link between merit and success.* New York, NY: HarperCollins Publishers.

Hogg, M. A. (2001). A social identity theory of leadership. *Personality & Social Psychology Review, 5*(3), 184–200.

Hogg, M. A., van Knippenberg, D., & Rast, D. E. (2012). The social identity theory of leadership: Theoretical origins, research findings, and conceptual developments. *European Review of Social Psychology, 23,* 258–304. doi:10.1080/10463283.2012.741134

Hopkins, M. M., O'Neil, D. A., Passarelli, A., & Bilimoria, D. (2008). Women's leadership development: Strategic practices for women and organizations. *Consulting Psychology Journal, 60*(4), 348–365.

Ibarra, H. (1999). Provisional selves: Experimenting with image and identity in professional adaptation. *Administrative Science Quarterly, 44,* 764–791. doi:10.2307/2667055

Ibarra, H. (2015). *Act like a leader, think like a leader.* Boston, MA: Harvard Business Review Press.

Ibarra, H., Ely, R., & Kolb, D. (2013). Women rising: The unseen barriers. *Harvard Business Review, 91*(9), 60–66. Retrieved from http://bit.ly/1bjtvEo

Ibarra, H., Wittman, S., Petriglieri, G., & Day, D. V. (2014). Leadership and identity: An examination of three theories and new research directions. In D. V. Day (Ed.), *The Oxford handbook of leadership and organizations* (pp. 285–300). Oxford, UK: Oxford University Press.

Kark, R., & Van Dijk, D. (2007). Motivation to lead, motivation to follow: The role of the self-regulatory focus in leadership processes. *Academy of Management Review, 32,* 500–528.

Kassotakis, M. E. (2017). Women-only leadership programs: A deeper look. In S. R. Madsen (Ed.), *Handbook of research on gender and leadership* (pp. 395–408). Northampton, MA: Edward Elgar Publishing.

Kay, K., & Shipman, C. (2014). *The confidence code: The science and art of self-assurance—What women should know.* New York: HarperCollins.

Kellerman, B. (2008). *Followership: How followers are creating change and changing leaders.* Boston, MA: Harvard Business School Publishing.

Kellerman, B. (2012). *The end of leadership.* New York, NY: HarperCollins.

Kellerman, B. (2014). *Hard times: Leadership in America.* Stanford, CA: Stanford University Press.

Keohane, N. O. (2014). Leadership out front and behind the scenes: Young women's ambitions for leadership today. In K. A. Longman & S. R. Madsen (Eds.), *Women and leadership in higher education* (pp. 24–39). Charlotte, NC: Information Age Publishing.

Kezar, A. (2014). Women's contributions to higher education leadership and the road ahead. In K. A. Longman & S. R. Madsen (Eds.), *Women and leadership in higher education* (pp. 117–134). Charlotte, NC: Information Age Publishing.

Koenig, A. M., Eagly, A. H., Mitchell, A. A., & Ristikari, T. (2011). Are leader stereotypes masculine? A meta-analysis of three research paradigms. *Psychological Bulletin, 137,* 616–642. doi:10.1037/a0023557

Komives, S. R., Longerbeam, S. D., Mainella, F. C., Owen, J. E., & Osteen, L. (2009). Leadership identity development: Challenges in applying a developmental model. *Journal of Leadership Education*, 8(1), 11–47.

Komives, S. R., Owen, J. E., Longerbeam, S. D., Mainella, F. C., & Osteen, L. (2005). Developing a leadership identity: A grounded theory. *Journal of College Student Development*, 46, 593–561. doi:10.1353/csd.2005.0061

Kram, K. E. (1985). *Mentoring at work: Developmental relationships in organizational life*. Glenview, IL: Scott, Foresman.

Longman, K. A., & Anderson, P. S. (2016). Women in leadership: The future of Christian higher education. *Christian Higher Education*, 15(1–2), 24–37. doi:10.1080/1536 3759.2016.1107339

Longman, K. A., Dahlvig, J. D., Wikkerink, R. J., Cunningham, D., & O'Connor, C. M. (2011). Conceptualizations of calling: A grounded theory exploration of CCCU women leaders. *Christian Higher Education*, 10(3–4), 254–275.

Longman, K. A., & Lafreniere, S. L. (2012). Moving beyond the stained glass ceiling: Preparing women for leadership in faith-based higher education. *Advances in Developing Human Resources*, 14, 45–61. doi:10.1177/1523422311427429

Lord, R. G., & Hall, R. J. (2005). Identity, deep structure and the development of leadership skill. *Leadership Quarterly*, 16(4), 591–615.

Madsen, S. R. (2015). Why do we need more women leaders in higher education? *HERS Research Brief, No. 1*. Retrieved from http://hersnet.org/wp-content/uploads/2015/07/HERS-Research-Brief-No.-1-Susan-Madsen-.pdf

Marchiondo, L. A., Myers, C. G., & Kopelman, S. (2015). The relational nature of leadership identity construction: How and when it influences perceived leadership and decision-making. *The Leadership Quarterly*, 26, 892–908.

Miscenko, D., & Day, D. V. (2016). Identity and identification at work. *Organizational Psychology Review*, 6(3), 215–247.

Miscenko, D., Guenter, H., & Day, D. V. (2017). Am I a leader? Examining leader identity development over time. *The Leadership Quarterly*, 28(5), 605–620.

Murphy, W. M., Gibson, K. R., & Kram, K. E. (2017). Advancing women through developmental relationships. In S. R. Madsen (Ed.), *Handbook of research on gender and leadership* (pp. 361–377). Northampton, MA: Edward Elgar Publishing.

Pallus, C. J., Nasby, W., & Easton, R. D. (1991). *Understanding executive performance: A life-story approach*. Greensboro, NC: Center for Creative Leadership Report #148.

Riggio, R. E. (2010). Leadership development: The current state and future expectations. *Counseling Psychology Journal*, 60(4), 383–392.

Riggio, R. E., & Mumford, M. D. (2011). Longitudinal studies of leadership development: The *Leadership Quarterly*, 22(3), 453–574.

Ritter, B. A., & Yoder, J. D. (2004). Gender differences in leader emergence persist even for dominant women: An updated confirmation of role congruity theory. *Psychology of Women Quarterly*, 28(3), 184–193.

Sandberg, S. (2013). *Lean in: Women, work, and the will to lead*. New York, NY: Alfred A. Knopf.

Shamir, B., & Eilam, G. (2005). "What's your story?" A life-stories approach to authentic leadership development. *Leadership Quarterly*, 16(3), 395–417.

Smith, D. G. (2014). *Diversity and inclusion in higher education: Emerging perspectives on institutional transformation*. Abingdon, UK: Routledge.

Turner, M. C. (2012). *Difference works: Improving retention, productivity, and profitability through inclusion*. Austin, TX: Live Oak Book Company.

Van Manen, M. (1990). *Researching lived experiences: Human science for an action sensitive pedagogy.* New York, NY: State University of New York Press.

Vinkenburg, C. J., van Engen, M. L., Eagly, A. H., & Johannesen-Schmidt, M. C. (2011). An exploration of stereotypical beliefs about leadership styles: Is transformational leadership a route to women's promotion? *The Leadership Quarterly, 22,* 10–21. doi:10.1016/j.leaqua.2010.12.003

White, J. S. (2014). HERS at 50: Curriculum and connections for empowering the next generation of women leaders in higher education. In K. A. Longman & S. R. Madsen (Eds.), *Women and leadership in higher education* (pp. 77–95). Charlotte, NC: IAP Information Age.

Williams, D. A. (2013). *Strategic diversity leadership: Activating change and transformation in higher education.* Sterling, VA: Stylus Publishing.

Woolley, A. W., Chabris, C. F., Pentland, A., Hashmi, N., & Malone, T. (2010). Evidence for a collective intelligence factor in the performance of human groups. *Science, 330,* 686–687.

11

WOMEN'S LEADER IDENTITY DEVELOPMENT

Building a Team for the Journey

S. Lynn Shollen

Women not only undertake journeys related to what they *do* and *experience* in their leadership, but also, and more foundationally, they undertake the journey of identifying themselves and being identified by others as a leader. DeRue and Ashford (2010) term this process *internalizing a leader identity*, the establishment of which is vital for effective leadership. Building an identity seems like a personal and individualized endeavor, so why would one need or even want others—let alone a full team of others—to be involved in the process of her leader identity development? This chapter explains why relationships are not only inherent to the process, but why connecting those relationships to work in tandem as a team is valuable, and particularly so for women leaders. Further, the purpose of the chapter is to help current or aspiring women leaders and those who wish to support them think through relevant team dynamics, identify their needs and corresponding team roles to enhance their leader identity development, and see the idea of constructing a leader identity development team applied in practice.

Leader Identity Development as a Social-Relational Process

Leadership is grounded in relationships and context; thus, internalizing a leader identity occurs through relational and social processes rather than an individual process (DeRue & Ashford, 2010). The complex process of identity work required for one to develop a leader identity necessarily involves other people (Ely, Ibarra, & Kolb, 2011; van Knippenberg, van Knippenberg, De Cremer, & Hogg, 2004). Because leader identity development is a relational and social process, one's social identities can be salient in the process. Tajfel first defined social identity as "the individual's knowledge that he belongs to certain social groups together with some emotional and value significance to him of this group membership" (1972, p. 292). Gender is a significant social identity, especially because its evidence through visual (and other) cues allows it to often be the first characteristic noticed by others and be highly utilized in person perception (Brewer, 1996; Stangor, Lynch, Duan, & Glass, 1992). The social identity of gender is particularly relevant for women seeking to develop and internalize a leader identity because such an aspiration is "fraught at the outset for a woman, who must establish credibility in a culture that is deeply conflicted about her authority" (Ely et al., 2011, p. 9). Indeed, in the context of leadership the gender of the leader affects others' perceptions of and responses to the leader due in part to implicit leadership theories, or people's cognitive models of effective leaders (Lord & Maher, 1993), as well as people's cognitive investigation of social category accessibility and how well the category fits the social context (Hogg & Terry, 2000). Because *leader* is typically cognitively associated with *male* and the social category *male* fits most social contexts of leadership in people's minds (Eagly & Karau, 2002), current or aspiring leaders who socially identify as women may be more likely to question their ability to identify as a leader and may be less likely to be viewed by others as a leader.

The *capacious model of leadership identities construction* contextualizes leader identity development as an ongoing social-relational process affected by various systems and influences acting together over time (Egan et al., 2017). In the model, the leader is considered inextricably linked with relationships and context rather than as an independent entity working through the process of her leader identity development without external influence. The model's capaciousness allows for many possible influences on leader identity, but two of the most pertinent to this discussion are: (1) relationships, largely working in the microsystem context, or the individual's immediate environment; and (2) social identities, largely working in the macrosystem context or larger cultural context (including organizations), where identities are socially constructed and perceived. As the *capacious model* notes, relationships help shape an individual's leader identity through influencing likelihood of leadership success and goal accomplishment and ability to manage group dynamics (Eagly & Carli, 2003; Eagly & Karau, 2002) and by providing the empathy and encouragement necessary to help leaders reach their potential (Murray, Tremaine, & Fountaine, 2012). Relationships can also be influential through mentoring and sponsorship, among other avenues.

Since relationships as well as perceptions and responses to social identity and other leadership-related factors play a role in the development of an individual's leader identity, the identity can be considered as co-constructed among the leader and others involved in the process. DeRue and Ashford (2010) describe leader identity co-construction as a claiming-granting process that occurs through social interactions, shaped through positive and negative spirals. If we take the case of an aspiring woman leader, for example, the process would begin with her attempting leader-like behaviors and having those behaviors affirmed or disaffirmed by others, thereby respectively encouraging or discouraging her future leadership attempts. Consistent affirmation, support, or encouragement from others would create a positive spiral, resulting in the aspiring woman leader feeling more confident and motivated to lead, seeking new opportunities to lead, taking more risks with leadership, and being more likely to be formally recognized as a leader (Ely et al., 2011). In contrast, consistent opposition, resistance, or dissuasion from others regarding her leader-like behaviors would result in the opposite effect. This social-relational, co-construction process of leader identity development, in tandem with the social identity of woman, serves as a main reason why it is essential for current or aspiring women leaders to proactively, purposefully build a team of others to contribute to the positive spiral of her leader identity journey. Levi (2011) notes that utilization of teams is important when complex jobs need to be accomplished, and when "the goal is to improve the way a product is made or a service is provided" (p. 8); building a leader identity can be considered a product, though not in the physical sense, and it is certainly a complex undertaking.

Building a Leader Identity Development Team

An important function and dynamic is overlooked when people who support someone's leader identity development are only considered individually rather than as a team. Per definition, a team is a "special type of group in which people work interdependently to accomplish a goal" (Levi, 2011, p. 2). Some scholars discern that a group becomes a team only when "shared goals have been established and effective methods to accomplish those goals are in place" (Wheelan, 2010, p. 2), which means a group can only be considered a team once it has learned how to be effective. By most definitions of groups or teams, a shared goal and member interdependence are not only required but are the most important characteristics (Levi, 2011; Wheelan, 2010). In the case of surrounding yourself with different people who can support your leader identity development journey, these people do have the shared goal of building your leader identity, and they are working interdependently toward that goal, but they may not realize it. Be sure to be clear with each team member about your goal and that they and others are contributing and combining their specific expertise and abilities toward achieving that goal. You could have your team more explicitly work together to promote obvious interdependence, but it may be impractical to expect various people from different areas of your life to connect via meetings, email, and conference calls to collaborate on your leader identity development. In essence, your team may resemble a cross-functional team such that it combines people from different departments (or in this case, also organizations and areas of your life) whose competencies are necessary for achieving the common goal (Parker, 2003). You can also choose how you refer to your team if the term *team* itself does not sit well with you. For example, the accomplished leader Marie C. Wilson met regularly with her "kitchen cabinet" of people committed to her success, where honest exchanges could be had about her successes and failures (2007, p. 75). One could also consider having her own "board of advisors."

Managing Team Dynamics

Treating the mix of people who contribute to the positive spiral of your leader identity development as a team necessitates that some team dynamics be attended to. Going into elaborate detail is beyond the scope of this chapter, but here are a few elements to consider. The team may not go through the stages of group development together (Tuckman & Jensen, 1977), but be prepared that you may personally go through the stages with each of your team members. When developing a close, goal-oriented professional relationship, you can expect to experience forming, storming, norming, performing, and sometimes even adjourning. Seek the resources that will help you manage those stages well so that a beneficial relationship is not lost out of lack of understanding or frustration. You may need to talk through the stages with your team member(s) so that mutual understanding can be had. Within the group development process, creating the kind of team culture that you desire is foundational (Schein, 2010). Even though team members may not be directly working together, culture as simply "the way we do things around here" (Deal & Kennedy, 1982, p. 4) can be consistent across relationships. For the sake of a leader identity development team that works in a dispersed manner without obvious interdependence, addressing team culture through symbols such as norms, language and jargon, and humor and play may be most relevant (Bolman & Deal, 2013). Consider which norms you would like to establish among all of your relationships to delineate expectations about how members are to behave (Levi, 2011); perhaps dependability, honesty, timeliness, and respect are important. Without establishing positive norms, you may end up with some teammates who withhold information they think would be hard for you to hear, provide you feedback in an unconstructive manner, take weeks to respond to your messages, or routinely cancel meetings when they are too busy, for instance. Developing shared language and jargon that is unique to the team and its purpose can enhance team cohesion and commitment, while humor and play can be utilized to reduce tension and encourage creativity (Bolman & Deal, 2013). Along with mindfully crafting team culture, fostering effective communication is key to dealing with relationship dynamics and promoting team success. Levi (2011) explains the qualities of a supportive communication climate and practical communication strategies among teams. In addition, elucidating specific roles for each team member is particularly essential for the purpose of leader identity development, since you will want to select team members to address specific needs that you have. When you invite someone onto the team, it is important that you and the potential member establish role clarity, or the contribution that person makes to the team and the goal of your leader identity development, in order to reduce conflict and stress that can arise from role ambiguity (Levi, 2011). Further, it will help if each team member knows who else is on the team and the relationship between the various roles people fill (Francis & Young, 1992). The following section will delve into identifying roles in more detail. The literature on cross-functional teams could inform how you approach team dynamics as well (e.g., Parker, 2003), although it is focused largely in the context of product development or other business-oriented projects. It may seem like and actually be more work to get everyone working as a team toward the development of your leader identity development, but functioning as a team toward a shared goal can mean more success for you in the long run and be worth the investment.

Identifying Team Roles

In some situations there is not the luxury of personally selecting team members, but women leaders do have the opportunity to build their own personal leader identity development team. So why not intentionally select the right type and mix of people to support the development of your leader identity rather than leaving it up to serendipity? Why just make do with whoever shows up in your professional or personal orbit at any given time? The journey of leader identity development requires support from various angles, in both professional and personal realms, in order to feed those positive spirals. This is especially true for women leaders, not only because of the social identity issues explained earlier but also because of the multitude of other challenges that women leaders often encounter (e.g., Eagly & Carli, 2007; Fletcher, 2004; Klenke, 2004; Oakely, 2000). Effective teams are created purposefully based on the needs and goal of the group. Members should initially be considered based on their ability to do the task or perform the role (Francis & Young, 1992), but also consider their commitment to supporting your leader identity development, interaction style (i.e., is this someone you can work with, someone who will treat you with respect), and availability and dependability in terms of devoting time to your goal, among other factors.

While selecting your team, it's important to take time to reflect on what you need in order to build your leader identity, which will in turn define the task or role of each member. Each woman leader will have her own particular set of needs at any given time. Having a complementary mix of roles is essential for an effective team; different people will bring different strengths to the team and fill in gaps left by the limitations of others. The literature on mentoring supports the utilization of multiple mentors, especially for women, because one person cannot possibly provide all of the challenge, support, and perspectives needed for professional growth (Higgins & Thomas, 2001; Peluchette & Jean-quart, 2000; Thomas, 2001). The same thinking can be applied to building your team, even if you don't consider each team member a mentor, per se. Consider the qualities, experiences, and positions of people you need on your leader identity development team. It is important to have people who are like you but just as important to have people who differ from you. You will likely need another woman who can understand the generally shared experiences of being a woman leader. Women and leadership can be a sensitive topic (Ibarra, Ely, & Kolb, 2013; Shollen, 2015), and you may need people with whom you can openly have those conversations without fear of judgment. The same can be said about other social identities that you experience as relevant to your leadership and how it is perceived, such as race, ethnicity, sexual orientation, or age. However, social identity is not everything when it comes to leadership. There is plenty that someone who does not identify as a woman can contribute to your leader identity development. (More on this point later.) This need for variety holds for any social identity. It may be helpful to hear another perspective on issues that you think may be occurring due to gender or other social identities. You may need a team member who leads with a similar style as you do or has a similar personality type, so you can process the implications of that style and personality for your leadership. You can also grow by learning about how different styles and personality types are working in practice and having someone offer suggestions about how you may try different approaches or adaptations in certain situations. You may want someone who has had prior experience in the organization that you are working in or in the role that you currently hold or aspire to hold. In contrast, people outside of your organization can offer a more objective perspective since they are not personally involved and are unfamiliar with the political and cultural dynamics. Perhaps having someone who has a similar family structure as yours would be helpful. You will want teammates who you can count on for compassion and comfort and those you can count on to nudge you into discomfort and challenge you to face difficult realities. It will help to have members whose task role it is to play devil's advocate by consistently providing perspectives from other angles or identifying gaps in your thinking or an evaluator/critic who contributes by constructively questioning your ideas and procedures as you think through big decisions (Levi, 2011). You will likely also need members who fill the social role of encourager, as their job is to inspire, embolden, cheer, and reward you (Levi, 2011). Kim Scott (2017) makes a compelling argument for why you want teammates who will be radically candid with you about your leadership, people who will challenge you directly while caring for you personally. Also consider your personal needs, perhaps in terms of having team members whose role it is to make sure you relax and get play time and will not tolerate work-talk during that protected time. Building a team for the purpose of leader identity development is not a one-time task; it requires continual attention as a process that shifts over time, reflecting the *capacious*

model's foundation in "the dynamic building and re-building of leadership identities, rather than assuming that a singular identity is achieved and remains
static" (Egan et al., 2017, p. 126). You will likely revisit the composition of your
team over time and make necessary changes to align with your leader identity
development needs and goals.

Mentors

For leader identity development purposes, essential team members can be generally categorized, at the least, into mentors, sponsors, and friends and family.
However, the first person that you need on your leader identity development
team to feed into those positive spirals is you. Ultimately, it is your responsibility to seek opportunities to practice leadership, take informed risks with
your leadership, seek candid feedback, and interpret the feedback with an open
mind in order to improve. While you need to reflect on your leadership and the
feedback received with accurate self-assessment and look upon yourself through
the same critical eye that you would with other leaders, you also need to engage
in positive self-talk. Self-talk simply defined is inner speech in which a person
talks to oneself about oneself, aloud or within one's own thoughts (Siegrist,
1995). Women can be particularly hard on themselves with negative self-talk,
which could affect self-esteem, self-confidence, and self-efficacy. You cannot
expect your teammates to build you up while you are tearing yourself down.
You are also responsible for taking care of your psychological and physical well-
being. Women tend to give their time and energy to caring for others, per the
traditional gender and social roles (Eagly, Wood, & Diekman, 2000), often at
the expense of taking care of themselves. Many women feel selfish and morally
conflicted if they attend to their own well-being (Henderson & Allen, 1991),
but it's common sense that you can't be your best self or the best leader for others if you are not cultivating yourself at the foundation.

Beyond you, mentors are essential teammates. It is widely accepted that
mentoring is beneficial to women's career progression and leadership development. There are many definitions and varieties of mentoring. Formal mentoring can be defined as a professional, collaborative learning relationship with a
defined purpose that develops over time and is likely arranged or endorsed by
the organization (Bland, Taylor, Shollen, Weber-Main, & Mulcahy, 2009). The
purpose is to facilitate the professional development and success of the mentee.
Formal mentoring is deliberate, structured, and goal-oriented; in contrast, informal mentoring—which can also be beneficial—takes a more casual approach
and is arranged by individuals without organizational support (Bland et al.,
2009). You may benefit from both formal and informal mentors on your team.
The extensive literature on mentoring will explain how to go about forming
those relationships and explain more about what they entail (e.g., Bland et al.,

2009; Johnson, 2015; Kram, 1985; Zachary, 2012). Having at least one formal mentor within the organization—and ideally within the division if applicable—is essential in order to ensure that the mentee is being socialized to the specific structure and culture of the organization (Bland et al., 2009). Although mentoring should at least take the traditional approach of one senior mentor to one junior mentee within the organization, ideally it will be sought in various other forms as well. Other mentoring approaches include peer mentoring, where a pair or small group at similar career stages support one another; group mentoring, where a designated mentor (usually more senior) mentors a group of more junior mentees; or mentoring circles, where a small number of people who differ in career stage, roles, experience, and status learn from one another in order to grow professionally (Bland et al., 2009). The mentoring that occurs in these other approaches could occur within one organization or across two or more organizations. As noted earlier, it is especially important for women to establish multiple mentors and even multiple models of mentoring. Although it is not limited to mentoring, per se, Ibarra and colleagues (2013), among others, encourage as one model the creation of women-only communities in which "similarly positioned women can discuss their feedback, compare notes, and emotionally support one another's learning," as

> identifying common experiences increases women's willingness to talk openly, take risks, and be vulnerable without fearing that others will misunderstand or judge them. These connections are especially important when women are discussing sensitive topics such as gender bias or reflecting on their personal leadership challenges, which can easily threaten identity and prompt them to resist any critical feedback they may receive.
> (pp. 7–8)

However, some women hesitate to engage in formal or informal women-only groups in their professional sphere due to fear of being stigmatized or not wanting to draw attention to gender, among other reasons. In this case, a women-only group may be created in the personal sphere.

Sponsors

While mentors are certainly beneficial, recent evidence indicates that sponsors are key players on your leader identity development team. While comparing mentoring to sponsorship, Ibarra, Carter, and Silva (2010) note studies show that "people derive more satisfaction from mentoring but need sponsorship. Without sponsorship, a person is likely to be overlooked for promotion, regardless of his or her competence and performance" (p. 84). Along with these scholars, Sylvia Ann Hewlett (2013) elaborates on the importance of sponsorship for professionally aspirational women and distinguishes sponsors, or those who get you "real career traction . . . and put you on the path to power and influence" (p. 22), from mentors. Hewlett explains that both mentors and sponsors provide advice and guidance, make introductions, and give feedback, and that mentors are experienced people who help you, support you, build your confidence, provide a sounding board, and offer empathy—all for little in return. In contrast, sponsors are senior people who believe in your potential, advocate for your professional advancement, and encourage you to take risks knowing they will protect you—and they expect your outstanding performance and loyalty in return. According to Hewlett, sponsorship is transactional; a sponsor acknowledges that investment in your career and success is beneficial to his or her own career, the organization, or the vision. Women (and people of color) can benefit the most from sponsorship, because "sponsorship has long been the inside track for Caucasian men. Men are 40% more likely than women, and Caucasians are 63% more likely than professionals of color, to have a sponsor seeing to their success" (Hewlett, 2013, p. 24). Both Ibarra and colleagues (2010) and Hewlett (2013) provide information on how sponsoring works and how to identify potential sponsors. For women working in traditionally male-dominated organizations and sectors, the desirable and available sponsors may be men given that there are few women in top-level positions and white men typically still hold the most authority, power, and influence. This situation provides the vital opportunity, as called for by Barnes (2003), Wilson (2007), and others, to enlist and cultivate men as allies and champions for women's leadership. While there are complexities of mentoring or sponsoring across gender (see Blake-Beard, 2001; Bland et al., 2009; Hewlett, 2013; Johnson, 2015), there is a lot to be gained by both parties from having male mentors or sponsors on a woman's leader identity development team.

Friends and Family

People with whom you have relationships in your personal life can also make valuable contributions to your leader identity development team. Outside of your professional world, friends and family are typically those counted on to provide support in various ways. These teammates are likely the people who know you the best and can provide an empathetic ear during challenging times, be counted on to give you the most candid feedback, non-judgmentally talk through issues related to the social identities that affect your leadership, and hold you accountable for taking time away from work to recharge in the ways that work best for you, for instance. Each woman leader will have unique needs related to the growth of her leader identity; whom you choose to include on your team and what they contribute is not generalizable or prescriptive; rather, it should reflect your individual needs at any phase in time.

Practical Application

What might building a team for the leader identity journey look like in practice? Here's one example, of many possible situations and options. Maya has just started in the position of dean of the business school at a reputable university. Prior to her current position, she successfully held leadership roles in business-related contexts, but never as a dean and never in a higher education setting. Her long-term professional aspirations include working her way to a university presidency. Maya has an 18-year-old daughter who will soon begin her college career at a different university, about four hours away from home. Maya also has a supportive life partner who works full time out of the house and an elderly mother who lives with them.

Maya's change in leadership role and context is significant for her leader identity development because identity is not simply developed and left to remain static; rather, identity changes over time and in response to experiences and circumstances (Oyserman, Elmore, & Smith, 2012). It would be unwise for Maya to assume that her leader identity is solid just because she was successful in the past. Looking through the lens of the *capacious model of leadership identities construction* (Egan et al., 2017), Maya's shift to a new role and different professional and organizational context will alter the effect of many of the systems and influences on her leader identity construction. For example, moving to higher education from the business sector will substantially change factors in the microsystem and macrosystem, and Maya will develop new relationships and perhaps take on a new sense of purpose and a new social identity as "administrator," all of which are influences that can affect her leader identity development. To continue to grow her leadership and leader identity, she needs a team to feed the positive spiral of her leader identity development through consistent affirmation, support, and constructive challenge (DeRue & Ashford, 2010; Ely et al., 2011). It will be beneficial for Maya to reflect on what she needs and purposefully build herself a team to support the development of her leader identity in her current professional phase, and with an eye toward her aspirations.

Maya starts as the center of her own team. She has developed her ability to engage in positive self-talk over the years, become adept at taking informed rather than haphazard risks, and learned to actively solicit and integrate feedback about her leadership. However, she struggles with self-care, especially due to demands on her time from her daughter, mother, and partner. One thing Maya needs to do in her role on the team is to figure out a strategy for improved self-care. Some of her teammates may also have useful ideas and help support her endeavors in this area.

Although certain colleagues and friends may make themselves available early on for support and guidance and Maya may be assigned a mentor by her university, it may not be the right mix or number of people who can give her the variety of support that she needs for growth and success. First, Maya may identify another dean within her university who is well-regarded and has some years of experience to formally mentor her in a traditional, one-on-one, senior-to-junior format (although the dean role itself is equitable, the formal mentor in this case has more experience). Ideally, this mentor would help socialize her to the political and cultural landscape of the organization, provide advice and guidance on dean-level issues and decisions, offer feedback about her leadership, act as a sounding board for matters she needs to discuss, and boost her confidence. She may also identify another more experienced dean or a provost, or a past dean or provost, from another university who can serve as a formal mentor. This mentor may have a more objective view into issues that Maya faces at her university and could provide a place for her to be more forthcoming about her struggles. Since women in particular have to appear exceedingly competent in order to be respected as leaders (Eagly & Carli, 2007), Maya may not be as willing to show any signs of limitations to those who directly judge her ability. She may also seek informal peer mentoring outside of her university. If there is not already an existing group of deans from various institutions gathering for support, she may initiate such a group. It does not have to be a time-intensive undertaking; simply a group of three that meets in person or virtually once a month, or even a few times a year, could be sufficient. A small group may even be more beneficial, as establishing trust among the members is key for a space where people can be honest and vulnerable and the group can be effective (Costa, 2003; Levi, 2011). If Maya is fortunate to have collegial deans who are interested in leadership development at her own university, she may establish a formal or informal peer mentoring group among them as well. These could be good spaces for discussion of the effectiveness of different leadership styles and decision-making processes, among other topics. She would likely benefit from a one-on-one informal peer mentoring relationship with another woman leader in higher education (inside or outside of her university) to share experiences related to the intersecting identities of woman and leader, and potentially of mother-woman-leader or caregiver-woman-leader. Having more than one of these types of teammates or forming a women-only group may be helpful, especially if Maya experiences her social identity of "woman" as particularly salient. She can also draw on the relationships that she has formed over the years in the business sector; she may find formal and informal mentors there who, even though they are not familiar with her current professional context, still have a lot to offer in terms of supporting her leader identity development. There are a variety of factors that play into how many and which types of mentors to seek; the key is for Maya to identify her mentoring needs and be sure they are all getting addressed in some way.

In addition to mentors, Maya would benefit from a sponsor or two as well, to provide opportunities that prepare her for advancement, promote her competencies to others, and connect her with colleagues who could be influential to her career progression and success. The notion of sponsorship could be more complex when applied to a higher education context compared to a business context. A sponsor within her institution could help advance Maya in terms of her success, recognition, and respect within the dean role. However, the path of "upward mobility" within the same higher education organization does not necessarily offer as many opportunities as in a company, or at least a larger company. With only so many positions within the university to advance into beyond dean, peers at the university may be competing for the same positions. Further, colleagues may not want to groom someone for advancement to a different university and lose that person's human capital and the personnel investment made. In Maya's case, she may seek a sponsor (or multiple sponsors) from a different university who can provide the aforementioned functions of sponsorship and also recommend her and connect her to other deans and leaders higher up the hierarchy at various institutions, as well as recommend her to search firms and write letters of support when the time comes. Recall, sponsorship as defined by Hewlett (2013) is a transactional relationship, so the sponsor would need to get something out of the relationship as well. In this case, perhaps the sponsor's reputation is enhanced if he/she recommends Maya and she ends up giving stellar performance in her new role. Maya would be wise to keep an eye out early on for someone who would be a good fit for the sponsor role and establish that relationship well before she's ready to move beyond the deanship.

To supplement and complement the professional relationships that support the positive spirals of her leader identity development, Maya will need to get some friends and family on board as well. Whom she selects will depend on whom she has available in her life and what her needs are. In Maya's case, she has identified four areas for which she needs contributions. First, she has a close woman friend who is a single mother of two children and holds a manager-level position at a bank. This friend provides the space for Maya to talk through the joys and challenges of claiming the social identity of "mother" while also having professional leadership responsibilities and aspirations. She may also have a chance to talk with this teammate about issues related to elder care. Second, Maya has an older brother who relishes in challenging her while he supports her professional endeavors; she could invite him to consistently be her devil's advocate and evaluator/critic when it comes to complex work- or life-related decisions. Her partner, who is quite a rational thinker, may be good in this role as well, so that Maya has more than one perspective. Both of these teammates could also serve as supports and sounding boards for family care matters. Third, despite her overall confidence Maya knows she occasionally needs people who will simply boost her up and tell her she's doing great. She has another friend, a cousin, and her partner whom she can invite to play the encourager role when necessary. Finally, like many hardworking leaders, Maya is not very good at taking time for play and relaxation, but she knows it's essential for her well-being and for the well-being of those around her. She can select a group of friends with whom she has a standing appointment for play time, with the rule that there is no work-talk from anyone during that protected time. Note, Maya will likely have to tell her teammates when she needs their contributions; she cannot expect they will just know when it is time, which circles back to the necessity of effective communication. If Maya has been thoughtful and thorough about identifying her leader identity development needs and crafting a team of people who effectively perform the necessary roles, the outcome should be significant contributions to the positive spiral of her leader identity development from various important angles.

***

The process of internalizing and growing a leader identity may be best served by building a team of people who positively contribute. Having a team is arguably more important for women, considering the implications of their gender identity for leadership. Mindfully crafting a team to meet your personalized needs and attending to team dynamics will help the strategy be more effective, so that in turn the impact on your leader identity development is optimized. While it is important to focus on the work that directly contributes to your own leader identity journey, recognize that your leader identity can also be enhanced by playing a positive role in developing someone else's leader identity. The Roman philosopher Seneca proclaimed that "while we teach, we learn," and a common adage in education is that the best test of whether or not one truly understands a concept is trying to teach it to someone else. It may not be teaching, per se, but guiding or supporting someone else in her leader identity development journey can be a strategy to solidify your own leadership learning. As you serve as a guide in someone else's journey, you are in essence enacting leadership behaviors, further building your view of yourself and people's perceptions of you as a leader, with the bonus of contributing to another woman's positive spiral of leader identity development. Although men tend to resist women's authority and influence more than do women (Eagly & Carli, 2007), women can be tough on each other as well and have been found to reject and penalize successful women (Parks-Stamm, Heilman, & Hearns, 2008). Wilson attributes this phenomenon of women being their own worst enemies to "a function of powerlessness, the view that there's precious little room at the top and the competition is fierce" (2007, p. 74). However, women leaders will continue to lag behind if women hold each other back rather than propel each other forward. Consider that if you—regardless of your gender identity—are not actively doing something to contribute to a woman's positive spiral of leader identity development, then you may by default be contributing to the negative spiral, or at least simply being a bystander. If current or aspiring women leaders you know have not considered creating a team for themselves, take the initiative to suggest that they do so and offer to talk through some options with them. Make yourself available to be a member of other women's leader identity development teams as a mentor, sponsor, or other role. When you reveal, or tell the story of, your leader identity development journey, who will the characters be that have earned your gratitude, and in whose story will you play a significant role?

References

Barnes, T. R. (2003). Strategies for developing white men as change agents for women leaders. In D. L. Rhode (Ed.), *The difference "difference" makes: Women and leadership* (pp. 181–184). Stanford, CA: Stanford University Press.

Blake-Beard, S. D. (2001). Taking a hard look at formal mentoring programs: A consideration of potential challenges facing women. *Journal of Management Development*, 20(4), 331–345.

Bland, C. J., Taylor, A. L., Shollen, S. L., Weber-Main, A. M., & Mulcahy, P. A. (2009). *Faculty success through mentoring: A guide for mentors, mentees, and leaders.* ACE Series on Higher Education. Lanham, MD: Rowman & Littlefield.

Bolman, L. G., & Deal, T. E. (2013). *Reframing organizations: Artistry, choice, and leadership* (5th ed.). San Francisco, CA: Jossey-Bass.

Brewer, M. B. (1996). When stereotypes lead to stereotyping: The use of stereotypes in person perception. In C. N. Macrae, C. Stangor, & M. Hewstone (Eds.), *Stereotypes and stereotyping* (pp. 254–275). New York: Guilford Press.

Costa, A. C. (2003). Work team trust and effectiveness. *Personnel Review*, 32(5), 605–622.

Deal, T. E., & Kennedy, A. A. (1982). *Corporate cultures: The rites and rituals of organizational life.* Reading, MA: Addison-Wesley.

DeRue, D. S., & Ashford, S. J. (2010). Who will lead and who will follow? A social process of leadership identity construction in organizations. *Academy of Management Review*, 35(4), 627–647.

Eagly, A. H., & Carli, L. L. (2003). The female leadership advantage: An evaluation of the evidence. *The Leadership Quarterly*, 13(6), 807–834.

Eagly, A. H., & Carli, L. L. (2007). *Through the labyrinth: The truth about how women become leaders.* Cambridge, MA: Harvard Business Press.

Eagly, A. H., & Karau, S. J. (2002). Role congruity theory of prejudice toward female leaders. *Psychological Review*, 109(3), 573–598.

Eagly, A. H., Wood, W., & Diekman, A. B. (2000). Social role theory of sex differences and similarities: A current appraisal. In T. Eckes & H. M. Trautner (Eds.), *The developmental social psychology of gender* (pp. 123–174). Mahwah, NJ: Lawrence Earlbaum.

Egan, C., Shollen, S. L., Campbell, C., Longman, K., Fisher, K., Fox-Kirk, W., & Neilson, B. G. (2017). Capacious model of leadership identities construction. In J. Storberg-Walker & P. Haber-Curran (Eds.), *Theorizing women & leadership: New insights & contributions from multiple perspectives* (pp. 121–140). International Leadership Association Women and Leadership Book Series. Charlotte, NC: Information Age Publishing.

Ely, R. J., Ibarra, H., & Kolb, D. M. (2011). Taking gender into account: Theory and design for women's leadership development programs. *Academy of Management Learning & Education*, 10(3), 474–493.

Fletcher, J. K. (2004). The paradox of postheroic leadership: An essay on gender, power, and transformational change. *The Leadership Quarterly*, 15, 647–661.

Francis, D., & Young, D. (1992). *Improving work groups: A practical manual for team building*. San Francisco, CA: Jossey-Bass.

Henderson, K. A., & Allen, K. R. (1991). The ethic of care: Leisure possibilities and constraints for women. *Society and Leisure, 14*(1), 97–113.

Hewlett, S. A. (2013). *(Forget a mentor) Find a sponsor: The new way to fast-track your career*. Boston, MA: Harvard Business School Publishing.

Higgins, M., & Thomas, D. (2001). Constellations and careers: Toward understanding the effects of multiple developmental relationships. *Journal of Organizational Behavior, 22*, 223–248.

Hogg, M. A., & Terry, D. J. (2000). Social identity and self-categorization processes in organizational contexts. *Academy of Management Review, 25*(1), 121–140.

Ibarra, H., Carter, N. M., & Silva, C. (2010). Why men still get more promotions that women. *Harvard Business Review, 88*(9), 80–85.

Ibarra, H., Ely, R., & Kolb, D. (2013). Women rising: The unseen barriers. *Harvard Business Review, 91*(9), 60–66.

Johnson, W. B. (2015). *On being a mentor: Guide for higher education faculty* (2nd ed.). New York, NY: Routledge.

Klenke, K. (2004). *Women and leadership: A contextual perspective*. New York, NY: Springer.

Kram, K. E. (1985). *Mentoring at work: Developmental relationships in organizational life*. Glenview, IL: Scott Foresman.

Levi, D. (2011). *Group dynamics for teams* (3rd ed.). Thousand Oaks, CA: Sage Publications.

Lord, R. G., & Maher, K. J. (1993). *Leadership and information processing: Linking perceptions and performance*. New York, NY: Routledge.

Murray, N., Tremaine, M., & Fountaine, S. (2012). Breaking through the glass ceiling in the ivory tower: Using a case study to gain new understandings of old gender issues. *Advances in Developing Human Resources, 14*(2), 221–236.

Oyserman, D., Elmore, K., & Smith, G. (2003). Self, self-concept, and identity. In M. R. Leary & J. P. Tangney (Eds.), *Handbook of self and identity* (pp. 69–104). New York, NY: Guilford Press.

Parker, G. M. (2003). *Cross-functional teams: Working with allies, enemies, and other strangers*. (2nd ed.). San Francisco, CA: Jossey-Bass.

Parks-Stamm, E. J., Heilman, M. A., & Hearns, K. E. (2008). Motivated to penalize: Women's strategic rejection of successful women. *Personality and Social Psychology Bulletin, 34*(2), 237–247.

Peluchette, J., & Jeanquart, S. (2000). Professionals' use of different mentor sources at various career stages: Implications for career success. *The Journal of Social Psychology, 140*(5), 549–564. doi:10.1080/00224540009600495

Schein, E. (2010). *Organizational culture and leadership* (4th ed.). San Francisco, CA: Jossey-Bass.

Scott, K. (2017). *Radical candor: Be a kick-ass boss without losing your humanity*. New York, NY: St. Martin's Press.

Shollen, S. L. (2015). Teaching and learning about women and leadership: Students' expectations and experiences. *Journal of Leadership Education, 14*(3), 35–52.

Siegrist, M. (1995). Inner speech as a cognitive process mediating self-consciousness and inhibiting self-deception. *Psychological Reports, 76*(1), 259–265.

Stangor, C., Lynch, L., Duan, C., & Glass, B. (1992). Categorization of individuals on the basis of multiple social features. *Journal of Personality and Social Psychology, 62*(2), 207–218.

Tajfel, H. (1972). Social categorization. English manuscript of 'La catégorisation sociale.' In S. Moscovici (Ed.), *Introduction à la psychologie sociale* (Vol. 1) (pp. 272–302). Paris, France: Larousse.

Thomas, D. (2001). The truth about mentoring minorities: Race matters. *Harvard Business Review, 79*(4), 98–107.

Tuckman, B. W., & Jensen, M. A. C. (1977). Stages of small group development revisited. *Group & Organization Management, 2*(4), 419–427.

Van Knippenberg, D., Van Knippenberg, B., De Cremer, D., & Hogg, M. A. (2004). Leadership, self, and identity: A review and research agenda. *The Leadership Quarterly, 15*(6), 825–856.

Wheelan, S. A. (2010). *Creating effective teams: A guide for members and leaders* (3rd ed.). Thousand Oaks, CA: Sage Publications.

Wilson, M. C. (2007). *Closing the leadership gap: Add women, change everything.* New York, NY: Penguin Group.

Zachary, L. J. (2012). *The mentor's guide: Facilitating effective learning relationships* (2nd ed.). San Francisco, CA: Jossey-Bass.

12

EFFICACY AND GROWTH MINDSETS BUFFER AGAINST IDENTITY THREAT FOR WOMEN IN LEADERSHIP POSITIONS

Crystal L. Hoyt and Jeni L. Burnette

Women can be at a distinct disadvantage in leadership positions, especially considering legitimacy begins with "the process of being perceived by others as a leader." Women are often keenly aware of the pervasive stereotypes surrounding their gender and are cognizant that others may perceive and treat them accordingly—termed identity threat. These stereotype-based expectations of inferiority can be threatening and psychologically taxing. In this chapter, we discuss the powerful role of belief systems in shaping the meaning of those threats. Specifically, we focus on leadership efficacy and growth mindsets for understanding responses to identity threat and the effectiveness of leader role models. We conclude with how the cognitive approach taken in this chapter can be assimilated with interpersonal processes—namely the importance of role models. This integrated intrapersonal and interpersonal perspective can inform interventions designed to encourage belief systems that attenuate deleterious threat effects.

Identity Threat for Females in Leadership

Elite leadership has long been, and largely remains, the purview of white men. For example, in the United States, over the 228 years of democracy and across 44 individual presidents, 43 of them were white—all were male. More diversity can be seen in Congress's membership, but it remains dominated with this one demographic. In 1968, when Shirley Chisholm became the first black woman elected to Congress, she noted "That I am a national figure because I was the first person in 192 years to be at once a congressman, black, and a woman proves, I think, that our society is not yet either just or free." Social identities, and intersecting identities including race and gender, play an important role in leadership. Identities impact who is seen as and chosen to be a leader, how leaders are evaluated, and how individuals perceive themselves in terms of their leadership capabilities and their experiences in leadership positions.

Social identities are critical for understanding leadership, in large part, because leadership is a social influence process involving the conferral of legitimacy that begins with "being perceived by others as a leader" (Lord & Maher, 1991, p. 11). Determinations of who makes for a legitimate leader are informed by many factors, including whom people see as "fitting" the preconceived notion of a leader. Abundant research demonstrates that people evaluate their leaders and potential leaders in reference to their intuitive notion of an ideal leader or their implicit leadership theories (ILTs; Forsyth & Nye, 2008; Hogg, 2001; Lord & Maher, 1991; Kenney, Schwartz-Kenney, & Blascovich, 1996). These ILTs often reflect both white and male standards (Koenig, Eagly, Mitchell, & Ristikari, 2011; Rosette, Leonardelli, & Phillips, 2008). In this chapter, we narrow our focus to understanding how the culturally masculine intuitive notions of leadership can undermine women in leadership positions.

Historically, women's occupation of lower status positions relative to men gave rise to both gender roles and gender stereotypes (Eagly, 1987). The gender-based stereotypes that are most relevant to the perception and evaluation of leaders are those that associate women with taking care and being communal and men with taking charge and being agentic (Deaux & Kite, 1993; Dodge, Gilroy, & Fenzel, 1995; Eagly, Wood, & Diekman, 2000; Heilman, 2001; Hoyt, 2010; Williams & Best, 1990). According to role congruity theory, these stereotypic beliefs about women as a social group give rise to biases against women in leadership because the expectations associated with the female gender role are incongruent with those associated with the leader role (Eagly, 2004; Eagly & Karau, 2002; Heilman, 2001). The biases that are manifest from the incongruent role include people demonstrating less favorable attitudes toward female than male leaders, and women experience a greater difficulty than men in attaining and being viewed as effective in top leadership roles (Eagly & Karau, 2002). Importantly, these stereotyped-based expectancies not only influence how women are perceived and treated, but they also shape the way women behave and think about themselves.

People are often acutely aware of identity-based stereotypes that impugn their competence and that others may be judging them by these expectations. Take United States Supreme Court Justice Sonia Sotomayor, for example. As a Latina, Justice Sotomayor has described her experiences confronting negative stereotypes associated with being an "affirmative action admittee," an "emotional Latina," and a "poor Latina from New York." When individuals feel that they might be judged by or that they might do something that would inadvertently confirm a negative stereotype, scholars refer to this as stereotype threat (Steele & Aronson, 1995). Stereotype threat is one of the most widely researched topics in the field of social psychology (Steele, 1997;

Steele, Spencer, & Aronson, 2002). This threat can be psychologically burdensome and can result in deleterious vulnerability responses including under-
performance and decreased engagement from the domain where the threat
is present (Hoyt & Murphy, 2016). Other people, however, are impervious
to threats or even show positive, reactance responses by actively engaging in
counter-stereotypical behavior. Justice Sotomayor appears to be in the latter
category; she has admitted to getting satisfaction out of proving her doubters
wrong.

What predicts when women are more or less vulnerable to stereotype threat
in leadership domains? In trying to answer this question, a recent review highlights cues to stereotype threat, consequences of stereotype threat, and moderators of stereotype threat appraisals and responses (Hoyt & Murphy, 2016). In
the current chapter, we home in on moderators. Namely, whether women meet
potential threats to their identity with susceptibility or reactance depends on a
number of factors including a host of individual differences. Critically, factors
that influence the extent to which women see themselves as having, or being
able to develop, leadership abilities moderate responses to threat. Although
identity threat is a pervasive "threat in the air," how people respond to these
threats can be driven in large part by their belief systems or what such threats
mean to the person experiencing them. More specifically, belief systems that
serve to bolster women's confidence in their ability to be a successful leader,
including leadership self-efficacy and mindsets about the nature of leadership,
can help buffer women from deleterious threat effects. That is, these beliefs
systems can play a powerful role in shaping the meaning of stereotype threat.

Belief Systems and Leadership: Self-Efficacy and Mindsets

Belief systems influence how we perceive and act toward leaders, but they also
shape the way we as leaders think about ourselves and the way we behave.
Whether people endorse or reject traditional implicit leadership theories and
whether and how these expectations affect us in our own leadership roles is
largely dependent on individual differences in belief systems. Beginning with
the influential early writings of William James, the field of psychology has
endorsed the notion that personal beliefs are paramount in shaping people's
behavior and ultimately their reality. For example, James noted, "Whilst part of
what we perceive comes through our senses from the objects around us, another
part (and it may be the larger part) always comes out of our own head" (James,
1890, p. 103). Scholars such as Piaget (Piaget & Garcia, 1991) have maintained
that meaning systems are as important as logical thinking in shaping people's
behavior. Kelly (1955) suggested that belief systems can be thought of as transparent templates people wear to perceive and interpret the world around them.

Powerful beliefs systems that can shape the meaning assigned to stereotype-based expectations of inferiority are those relevant to evaluations of one's abilities; in this chapter, we focus on self-efficacy and mindsets.

Self-Efficacy

Self-efficacy is critical in buffering deleterious responses to stereotype threat. As a critical component of Bandura's social-cognitive theory (1986), self-efficacy refers to "beliefs in one's capabilities to organize and execute the courses of action required to produce given attainments" (Bandura, 1997, p. 3). Empirical studies consistently reveal that self-efficacy influences goals, effort, persistence in the face of adversity, thought patterns, stress reactions, and performance (Bandura, 1997). Thus, it is not surprising that a strong sense of efficacy is vital to personal agency and ultimately human accomplishment (Bandura, 1997). It is also perhaps not that unexpected that how women respond to stereotype threat depends in large part on their beliefs regarding the extent to which they see themselves as having the requisite leadership abilities. For example, research has shown that only women who rated themselves low on those traits that are stereotypically associated with leadership demonstrated deleterious threat responses (Bergeron, Block, & Echtenkamp, 2006).

Researchers have explored how women who have high versus low levels of self-efficacy for leadership respond when put in a position to disconfirm the gender-leadership stereotype that associates men more strongly than women with leadership (Hoyt & Blascovich, 2007). In this research, they prescreened undergraduate women for their levels of self-efficacy, and those in the upper and lower 25% of scores were invited to participate in the research. When the women arrived at the study, they were informed that they were randomly selected to serve as the leader of an ostensible three-person group. The women were randomly assigned to be explicitly primed with the gender leader stereotype or not. To prime the stereotype, participants were given a folder to look through that presented images of male leaders and were given information regarding the gender gap in top leadership roles. They were also told that one reason for the gender gap in top leadership roles is that men are more effective leaders and that this research is looking at these gender differences. Participants in the control condition were asked to look through a binder comprised of images of and information regarding the virtual reality lab. These participants were told that the research is designed to better understand leadership; thus, this condition likely implicitly activated gender leader stereotypes.

After this stereotype threat manipulation, all participants engaged in a task requiring them to advise and motivate "employees" on a simulated hiring committee. Fashioned off virtual workplaces, the participants held this meeting within an immersive virtual conference room with what they believed were two other participants all networked together into one meeting room; the meeting allowed for one-way communication from the leader, and this communication was recorded. After the virtual meeting, participants completed self-report measures including their perceptions of how well they performed, how much they identified with the leadership domain, and psychological well-being, including self-esteem and depressed affect. Additionally, leadership performance was assessed by having two independent and trained raters, who were blind to conditions, code audiotapes of the meetings. Results showed that under stereotype activation, women with high, versus low, levels of leadership self-efficacy performed better, identified more with the domain of leadership, and reported greater levels of psychological well-being.

Using a similar paradigm, Hoyt and Blascovich (2010) further investigated the cardiovascular responses of high and low efficacy women confronted with stereotype activation in the domain of leadership. According to the biopsychosocial model of challenge and threat, individuals exhibit physiological patterns of threat when they are placed in self-relevant motivated performance situations where the demands and uncertainty of the situation outweigh perceived personal resources. They predicted that women with high levels of efficacy, for whom leadership is highly self-relevant, would show cardiovascular patterns of threat when performing a leadership task with the gender-based stereotype activated either explicitly or implicitly; however, those with low efficacy were not predicted to demonstrate threat patterns because the leadership domain is less self-relevant. Results supported these predictions. Moreover, the stereotype threat experienced by the high efficacy women was accompanied with behavioral and self-report responses consistent with stereotype resilience or reactance, as opposed to stereotype vulnerability, in line with the previous research (Hoyt & Blascovich, 2007). In the explicit, versus implicit, stereotype activation condition, high efficacy women demonstrated increased leadership performance and similarly positive levels of perceived performance, identification with leadership, and well-being. Low efficacy leaders did not show cardiovascular patterns of threat, and they showed patterns of assimilating to the negative stereotype, even more so when the stereotype was explicit, on the self-report and behavioral measures.

In sum, this research points to the powerful role of self-efficacy in moderating responses to stereotype activation, and it indicates that resilience and reactance stem from physiological experiences of threat, whereas the harmful stereotype vulnerability responses can occur without physiological threat reactions. Thus, the relationship between negative group stereotypes, belief systems, and individual responses is far from simple. Nonetheless, the research reviewed here points to the key finding that women who see themselves as having leadership abilities are protected from deleterious consequences of the gender-based stereotype that impugns their leadership capabilities.

Mindsets

In addition to the important role of efficacy in buffering against threat, even if one does not yet have the ability, believing one can develop it is also a critical component of understanding vulnerabilities to threat. Mindsets, or what many scholars refer to as implicit theories, refer to the lay, intuitive beliefs people have regarding the changeable vs. fixed nature of human abilities. People vary in their mindsets from believing attributes are relatively static entities (fixed theorists) to believing they can be developed (growth theorists). These belief systems play an important role in determining affect, behavior, and cognition across a range of domains (e.g., Burnette, 2010; Hong, Chiu, Dweck, Lin, & Wan, 1999; Martocchio, 1994; Wood & Bandura, 1989). Mindsets are an integral part of people's motivational systems and influence both self-regulatory processes and goal achievement (e.g. Burnette, O'Boyle, VanEpps, Pollack & Finkel, 2013). Individuals with growth mindsets set goals focused on learning and development; they strive for those goals using effortful strategies; and, when facing setbacks, they maintain positive expectations about the potential for future success. These mastery-oriented approaches, in turn, predict better performance. In contrast, individuals with fixed mindsets focus on proving their abilities, usually relative to others; they view effort as an indication of a lack of ability; and, when facing setbacks, they feel anxious and disengage. These helpless-oriented strategies correlate negatively with goal achievement.

Additionally, most of the links between mindsets and self-regulation are strongest under ego-threat, or when there is a threat to one's self-image. Considering this, mindsets can be particularly important meaning systems for stigmatized individuals. More specifically, mindsets have great potential to buffer from stereotype threat. Stereotypes are essentially fixed-mind-set labels; they imply that the trait or ability in question is fixed and that people from some identity groups have the ability and others do not. Indeed, much of the harm that stereotypes do comes from the fixed-mindset message they send. The growth mindset depicts abilities as acquirable and sends an encouraging message to those who have been negatively stereotyped—one that can promote renewed motivation and engagement.

There is a growing literature showing that growth mindsets can work to counter the nefarious effects of identity threat (e.g., Aronson, Fried, & Good, 2002; Blackwell, Trzesniewski, & Dweck, 2007; Good, Aronson, & Inzlicht, 2003). For example, researchers have shown that interventions designed to encourage underrepresented students to believe that abilities within academic domains can be developed have been effective at increasing positive academic outcomes including a sense of belonging and interest in the academic field. The benefit of growth mindsets for off-setting identity threat extends beyond academics and include leadership-relevant tasks such as negotiating. For example, Kray and colleagues (Kray, Locke, & Haselhuhn, 2010) showed that only when women believe that negotiating skills can be developed are they able to successfully react against the blatant stereotype that women are inferior negotiators.

Similarly, in the context of entrepreneurial leadership, growth mindsets predict important outcomes related to successful leadership (Pollack, Burnette, & Hoyt, 2012). More specifically, in this work, in the first study, participants were induced to endorse either a fixed or a growth mindset about the nature of entrepreneurial ability after reading one of two *Psychology Today*-type of articles that presented compelling evidence for the respective mindset. All participants were then told that entrepreneurial ability is primarily driven by masculine traits, to provoke stereotype threat for the female participants. As predicted, women in the *growth mindset* condition reported greater self-efficacy regarding future entrepreneurial endeavors than those in the fixed-mindset condition. In the second study, they endeavored to generalize their findings to both women and men; thus, they changed the threat from one situated in stereotyped-based expectations to a threat to business success due to the economic recession. Results demonstrated that those with growth mindsets of entrepreneurial ability reported greater self-efficacy than those with more fixed beliefs. This second study shows that the palliative effect of growth mindsets extends to threats beyond those stemming from stereotype-based expectations.

In summary, we have demonstrated how self-efficacy and mindsets can serve as moderators of the link between identity threat and deleterious outcomes, with higher efficacy and stronger growth mindsets helping to buffer against potential nefarious effects. Interestingly, in addition to the direct link between these two beliefs systems and responses to threat, they can also operate together (Burnette, Pollack, & Hoyt, 2010). For example, in a sample of 50 undergraduate women following the introduction of a high-stakes stereotype threat environment, mindsets mattered most for those reporting low self-efficacy. That is, women with low efficacy and fixed mindsets reported classic stereotype threat vulnerability responses including lower self-esteem and significantly reduced post threat self-efficacy (Burnette et al., 2010). This study highlights how mindsets generate a network of allied cognitions. Overall, greater efficacy and a growth mindset can work independently and together to foster resilience in the face of identity-based leadership threats for females.

Integration of Cognition and Interpersonal Processes

Contrary to a common American narrative, individual achievement does not happen in a vacuum. Rather, a powerful factor influencing people's pursuit and attainment of goals are interpersonal processes. For example, people often look to others for motivation and inspiration. Role models can inspire achievement by suggesting that one could reach that level of success and demonstrating how to achieve one's goals. Thus, beyond belief systems, role models can serve as important interpersonal resources that help buffer women from deleterious responses to negative stereotypes (Latu, Schmid Mast, Lammers, & Bombari, 2013).

However, role models can have opposing effects. Although they hold the potential to inspire and offer hope, they also have the potential of highlighting how deficient one is in comparison (Collins, 1996, 2000; Lockwood & Kunda, 1999; Suls, Martin, & Wheeler, 2002; Wood, 1989). For example, although research has shown that female role models can protect women from vulnerability responses to threats to their identity in leadership roles (Latu et al., 2013), other research has shown that elite female leader role models can have self-deflating effects (Hoyt & Simon, 2011). Across two studies, Hoyt and Simon presented women with role models (or not) before undertaking a leadership task. In the first study, women exposed to elite leader female role models, relative to those exposed to elite male models or a control condition, reported lower levels of perceived performance, greater task difficulty, and greater feelings of inferiority. In the second study, in addition to corroborating the negative impact of elite female leaders on participants' self-perceptions, it also showed that this in turn adversely affected their leadership aspirations. Furthermore, this study showed more positive responses to nonelite female leader role models who disconfirm the negative stereotype. These studies illuminate the potential dark side of elite female leader role models in the stereotype-relevant domain of leadership.

One factor that can help delineate when female leader role models will be injurious and when they will be inspiring to women are the two fundamental belief systems outlined earlier—namely efficacy and mindsets. First, abundant research into self-efficacy shows that high levels of self-efficacy are associated with anticipating success in the relevant domain; thus, having high efficacy can promote viewing the success of superstar role models as attainable. Hoyt (2013) investigated the role of leadership self-efficacy in moderating the influence of top-level leader role models on how much women identify with leadership and aspire to be leaders and their leadership performance. Using an experimental methodology, female participants were told that the study was focused on examining college students' transition to the workplace and was examining both perceptions of role models and the performance of organizational tasks. The participant was told she was randomly selected to be a member of an upcoming three-person group that would be meeting virtually. After completing a leadership self-efficacy questionnaire, participants were presented with either elite, nonelite, or no (control) role models before serving as the leader of an ostensible three-person group.

Although in their original research they showed that exposure to outstanding female leader role models can adversely affect women's leadership-related self-perceptions and behaviors (Hoyt & Simon, 2011), this follow-up research suggests that these deleterious effects only hold for those without high levels of efficacy. Indeed, exceptional role models were shown to be less beneficial for those with low levels of efficacy. Specifically, women with low, relative to high, efficacy were less inspired by the superstar role models and subsequently showed lowered identification with leadership, leadership aspirations, and performance. Self-efficacy did not moderate responses to the nonelite role models who were equally inspiring to participants regardless of their level of leadership self-efficacy. In sum, extremely successful female leader role models have the potential to be inspiring or self-deflating to women, and a key factor that helps distinguish which response ensues is women's leadership self-efficacy.

Second, like self-efficacy, mindsets can influence the effectiveness of role models. Believing that abilities can be cultivated should enable people to respond positively to high-achieving role models and remain hopeful and confident in their abilities. More specifically, when comparing oneself to the role model, growth theorists are likely to have positive expectations for their potential future success, and they are more likely to identify and connect with the role model. However, those with fixed mindsets are likely to compare their fixed ability to that of the successful role model and lose self-confidence. For example, in a marketing context, growth theorists were equally motivated by both moderately and highly challenging role models (i.e., models portraying behavior that is relatively easy or more difficult to imitate), whereas only moderately, not highly, challenging role models influenced fixed theorists (Wentzel, Henkel, & Tomczak, 2010). And, within an academic context, high-level superstar role models have a positive impact on those who believe intelligence can be developed but fail to inspire those who think intelligence is fixed (Lockwood & Kunda, 1997).

In two studies, Hoyt, Burnette, and Innella (2012) examined how mindsets about leadership might influence the effect of role models on leadership-relevant self-perceptions and performance. In the first study, they assessed women's mindsets of leadership before either presenting them with role models or not and then engaging in a leadership task. In the second study, they investigated the causal role of mindsets by manipulating them, and they extended their investigation to examine effects on both women and men. Across both studies, those with growth mindsets showed more positive responses to the leadership role models than those with fixed mindsets. Specifically, growth theorists reported greater confidence in their leadership abilities and more positive affect after completing the leadership task, and they performed better on the task than fixed theorists. Additionally, they showed that identifying with the role model was the psychological process that linked people's mindsets and their self-evaluations of leadership competence as well as their affect following the task.

***

The research reviewed in this chapter shows that understanding how gender-based leader expectations impact us depends largely on important belief systems including self-efficacy and growth mindsets. Moreover, how much we benefit from role models also depends on these belief systems. This understanding can contribute to designing interventions to attenuate harmful threat effects for females in leadership contexts. For example, scholars have demonstrated the efficacy of scalable psychological interventions, including those designed to promote growth mindsets, to thwart identity threat (Paunesku et al., 2015; Walton, 2014).

Building on these empirical approaches, leadership practitioners might look to the expanding psychological literature into wise psychological interventions as they seek to foster growth mindsets of leadership and/or people (Walton, 2014; Yeager & Walton, 2011). Such interventions "are psychologically precise, often brief, and often aim to alter self-reinforcing processes that unfold over time and, thus, to improve people's outcomes in diverse circumstances and long into the future" (Walton, 2014, p. 74). Drawing upon the precise, well-developed theoretical work into implicit theories, wise growth mindset interventions provide people with evidence of the malleable nature of the targeted attribute—for example, evidence that with hard work and the right strategies, leadership ability can grow like a muscle. Often such interventions include a "saying is believing exercise," such as writing a note to someone, which encourages people to elaborate on the growth mindset message in their own words. Women and practitioners seeking to navigate potential leadership challenges can draw on the tools used in interventions to encourage growth mindsets. For example, three tips for fostering one's own growth mindset are to focus on the process of becoming a leader, view challenges as opportunities to grow, and remind yourself of times a growth mindset has or can be beneficial.

Similarly, practitioners can consult the well-developed social-cognitive theory (Bandura, 1986) to gain an understanding of how they might promote self-efficacy. According to Bandura (1997), there are four sources of efficacy information: mastery experiences, vicarious learning, verbal persuasion, and physiological and affective states. Interventions designed to promote self-efficacy can home in on these sources. For example, we can work to bolster leadership self-efficacy by providing opportunities for success on increasingly complex leadership challenges (mastery experiences), opportunities to observe the leadership strategies of peers and mentors (vicarious learning), or by making people aware of their leadership potential and nominating them for leadership programs (verbal persuasion; Murphy & Johnson, 2016). Furthermore, by identifying the critical role of efficacy and mindsets in buffering against identity threat, this research helps to identify those who may benefit most from interventions designed to promote more positive responses to stereotype threat.

Overall, growth mindsets and efficacy hold great potential as leverages for increasing the number of underrepresented voices among the leaders in society. One of the most powerful weapons to fight gender-based biases is being aware of them and the important psychological processes involved. We sought in this chapter to illuminate two of these key processes by reviewing the literature related to how growth mindsets and efficacy can buffer against the potential deleterious effects of identity threat. We hope this review is the first of many that will investigate the potential for growth mindsets and efficacy to foster greater interest and involvement of underrepresented groups in leadership positions.

References

Aronson, J., Fried, C. B., & Good, C. (2002). Reducing the effects of stereotype threat on African American college students by shaping theories of intelligence. *Journal of Experimental Social Psychology, 38*(2), 113–125. doi:10.1006/jesp.2001.1491

Bandura, A. (1986). The explanatory and predictive scope of self-efficacy theory. *Journal of Social and Clinical Psychology, 4*(3), 359–373. doi:10.1521/jscp.1986.4.3.359

Bandura, A. (1997). *Self-efficacy the exercise of control.* New York, NY: Maxmillan.

Bergeron, D. M., Block, C. J., & Echtenkamp, A. (2006). Disabling the able: Stereotype threat and women's work performance. *Human Performance, 19*(2), 133–158. doi:10.1207/s15327043hup1902_3

Blackwell, L. S., Trzesniewski, K. H., & Dweck, C. S. (2007). Implicit theories of intelligence predict achievement across an adolescent transition: A longitudinal study and an intervention. *Child Development, 78*(1), 246–263. doi:10.1111/j.1467–8624.2007.00995.x

Burnette, J. L. (2010). Implicit theories of body weight: Entity beliefs can weigh you down. *Personality and Social Psychology Bulletin, 36*(3), 410–422. doi:10.1177/0146167209359768

Burnette, J. L., O'Boyle, E. H., VanEpps, E. M., Pollack, J. M., & Finkel, E. J. (2013). Mind-sets matter: A meta-analytic review of implicit theories and self-regulation. *Psychological Bulletin, 139*(3), 655–701. doi:10.1037/a0029531

Burnette, J. L., Pollack, J. M., & Hoyt, C. L. (2010). Individual differences in implicit theories of leadership ability and self-efficacy: Predicting responses to stereotype threat. *Journal of Leadership Studies, 3*(4), 46–56. doi:10.1002/jls.20138

Collins, R. L. (1996). For better or worse: The impact of upward social comparison on self-evaluations. *Psychological Bulletin, 119,* 51–69. doi:http://dx.doi.org/10.1037/0033-2909.119.1.51

Collins, R. L. (2000). Among the better ones: Upward assimilation in social comparison. In J. Suls & L. Wheeler (Eds.), *Handbook of social comparison: Theory and research* (pp. 159–172). New York, NY: Kluwer Academic/Plenum.

Deaux, K., & Kite, M. (1993). Gender stereotypes. In *Psychology of women: A handbook of issues and theories* (pp. 107–139). Westport, CT: Greenwood Press.

Dodge, K. A., Gilroy, F. D., & Fenzel, L. M. (1995). Requisite management characteristics revisited: Two decades later. *Journal of Social Behavior and Personality, 10*(6), 253–264.

Eagly, A. H. (1987). *Sex differences in social behavior: A social-role interpretation.* Hillsdale, NJ: Erlbaum.

Eagly, A. H. (2004). Few women at the top: How role incongruity produces prejudice and the glass ceiling. In D. V. Knippenberg & M. A. Hogg (Eds.), *Leadership and power: Identity processes in groups and organizations* (pp. 79–93). London: Sage Publications.

Eagly, A. H., & Karau, S. J. (2002). Role congruity theory of prejudice toward female leaders. *Psychological Review, 109*(3), 573–598. doi:10.1037/0033–295x.109.3.573

Eagly, A. H., Wood, W., & Diekman, A. B. (2000). Social role theory of sex differences and similarities: A current appraisal. In T. Eckes & H. M. Trautner (Eds.),

The developmental social psychology of gender (pp. 123–147). Mahwah, NJ: Lawrence Erlbaum Associates.

Forsyth, D. R., & Nye, J. L. (2008). Seeing and being a leader: The perceptual, cognitive, and interpersonal roots of conferred influence. In *Leadership at the crossroads* (Vol. 1) (pp. 116–131). Westport, CT: Praeger.

Good, C., Aronson, J., & Inzlicht, M. (2003). Improving adolescents' standardized test performance: An intervention to reduce the effects of stereotype threat. *Journal of Applied Developmental Psychology*, 24(6), 645–662. doi:10.1016/j.appdev.2003.09.002

Heilman, M. E. (2001). Description and prescription: How gender stereotypes prevent women's ascent up the organizational ladder. *Journal of Social Issues*, 57(4), 657–674. doi:10.1111/0022-4537.00234

Hogg, M. A. (2001). A social identity theory of leadership. *Personality and Social Psychology Review*, 5(3), 184–200. doi:10.1207/s15327957pspr0503_1

Hong, Y., Chiu, C., Dweck, C. S., Lin, D. M., & Wan, W. (1999). Implicit theories, attributions, and coping: A meaning system approach. *Journal of Personality and Social Psychology*, 77(3), 588–599. doi:https://doi.org/10.1037/0022-3514.77.3.588

Hoyt, C. L. (2010). Women, men, and leadership: Exploring the gender gap at the top. *Social and Personality Psychology Compass*, 4(7), 484–498. doi:10.1111/j.1751-9004.2010.00274.x

Hoyt, C. L. (2013). Inspirational or self-deflating: The role of self-efficacy in elite role model effectiveness. *Social Psychological and Personality Science*, 4(3), 290–298. doi:10.1177/1948550612455066

Hoyt, C. L., & Blascovich, J. (2007). Leadership efficacy and women leaders' responses to stereotype activation. *Group Processes & Intergroup Relations*, 10(4), 595–616. doi:10.1177/1368430207084718

Hoyt, C. L., & Blascovich, J. (2010). The role of leadership self-efficacy and stereotype activation on cardiovascular, behavioral and self-report responses in the leadership domain. *The Leadership Quarterly*, 21(1), 89–103. doi:10.1016/j.leaqua.2009.10.007

Hoyt, C. L., Burnette, J. L., & Innella, A. N. (2012). I can do that: The impact of implicit theories on leadership role model effectiveness. *Personality and Social Psychology Bulletin*, 38(2), 257–268. doi:10.1177/0146167211427922

Hoyt, C. L., & Murphy, S. E. (2016). Managing to clear the air: Stereotype threat, women, and leadership. *The Leadership Quarterly*, 27(3), 387–399. doi:10.1016/j.leaqua.2015.11.002

Hoyt, C. L., & Simon, S. (2011). Female leaders: Injurious or inspiring role models for women. *Psychology of Women Quarterly*, 35(1), 143–157. doi:10.1177/036168 4310385216

James, W. (1890). *The principles of psychology* (Vol. 1). New York, NY: H. Holt.

Kelly, G. A. (1955). *The psychology of personal constructs*. New York, NY: W. W. Norton.

Kenney, R. A., Schwartz-Kenney, B. M., & Blascovich, J. (1996). Implicit leadership theories: Defining leaders described as worthy of influence. *Personality and Social Psychology Bulletin*, 22(11), 1128–1143. doi:10.1177/01461672962211004

Koenig, A. M., Eagly, A. H., Mitchell, A. A., & Ristikari, T. (2011). Are leader stereotypes masculine? A meta-analysis of three research paradigms. *Psychological Bulletin*, 137(4), 616–642. doi:10.1037/a0023557

Kray, L. J., Locke, C., & Haselhuhn, M. (2010). In the words of Larry Summers: Gender stereotypes and implicit beliefs in negotiations. In A. A. Stanton, M. Day, & I. Welpe (Eds.), *Neuroeconomics and the firm* (pp. 101–115). Northampton, MA: Edward Elgar Publishing.

Latu, I. M., Schmid Mast, M., Lammers, J., & Bombari, D. (2013). Successful female leaders empower women's behavior in leadership tasks. *Journal of Experimental Social Psychology, 49*(3), 444–448. doi:10.1016/j.jesp.2013.01.003

Lockwood, P., & Kunda, Z. (1997). Superstars and me: Predicting the impact of role models on the self. *Journal of Personality and Social Psychology, 73*(1), 91–103. doi:10.1037/0022–3514.73.1.91

Lockwood, P., & Kunda, Z. (1999). Increasing the salience of one's best selves can undermine inspiration by outstanding role models. *Journal of Personality and Social Psychology, 76*(2), 214–228. doi:10.1037/0022–3514.76.2.214

Lord, R. G., & Maher, K. J. (1991). *Leadership and information processing: Linking perceptions and performance.* Cambridge, MA: Unwin Hyman.

Martocchio, J. J. (1994). Effects of conceptions of ability on anxiety, self-efficacy, and learning in training. *Journal of Applied Psychology, 79*(6), 819–825. doi:10.1037/0021–9010.79.6.819

Murphy, S. E., & Johnson, S. K. (2016). Leadership and leader developmental self-efficacy: Their role in enhancing leader development efforts. *New Directions for Student Leadership, 149*, 73–84. doi:10.1002/yd.20163

Paunesku, D., Walton, G. M., Romero, C., Smith, E. N., Yeager, D. S., & Dweck, C. S. (2015). Mind-set interventions are a scalable treatment for academic underachievement. *Psychological Science, 26*(6), 784–793. doi:10.1177/0956797615571017

Piaget, J., & Garcia, R. (1991). *Toward a logic of meanings* (P. Davidson & J. A. Easley, Jr. (Eds.)). Hillsdale, NJ: Erlbaum.

Pollack, J. M., Burnette, J. L., & Hoyt, C. L. (2012). Self-efficacy in the face of threats to entrepreneurial success: Mind-sets matter. *Basic and Applied Social Psychology, 34*(3), 287–294. doi:10.1080/01973533.2012.674452

Rosette, A. S., Leonardelli, G. J., & Phillips, K. W. (2008). The White standard: Racial bias in leader categorization. *Journal of Applied Psychology, 93*(4), 758–777. doi:10.1037/0021–9010.93.4.758.

Steele, C. M. (1997). A threat in the air: How stereotypes shape intellectual identity and performance. *American Psychologist, 52*(6), 613–629. doi:10.1037/0003–066x.52.6.613

Steele, C. M., & Aronson, J. (1995). Stereotype threat and the intellectual test performance of African Americans. *Journal of Personality and Social Psychology, 69*(5), 797–811. doi:10.1037/0022–3514.69.5.797

Steele, C. M., Spencer, S. J., & Aronson, J. (2002). Contending with group image: The psychology of stereotype and social identity threat. *Advances in Experimental Social Psychology Advances in Experimental Social Psychology, 34*, 379–440. doi:10.1016/s0065–2601(02)80009–0

Suls, J., Martin, R., & Wheeler, L. (2002). Social comparison: Why, with whom, and with what effect? *Current Directions in Psychological Science, 11*(5), 159–163. doi:10.1111/1467–8721.00191

Walton, G. M. (2014). The new science of wise psychological interventions. *Current Directions in Psychological Science, 23*(1), 73–82. doi:10.1177/0963721413512856

Wentzel, D., Henkel, S., & Tomczak, T. (2010). Can I live up to that ad? Impact of implicit theories of ability on service employees' responses to advertising. *Journal of Service Research, 13*(2), 137–152. doi:10.1177/1094670510363304

Williams, J. E., & Best, D. L. (1990). *Sex and psyche: Gender and self viewed cross-culturally* (Vol. 13, Cross Cultural Research and Methodology). Newbury Park, CA: Sage Publications.

Wood, J. V. (1989). Theory and research concerning social comparisons of personal attributes. *Psychological Bulletin, 106*, 231–248. doi:10.1037/0033–2909.106.2.231

Wood, R., & Bandura, A. (1989). Impact of conceptions of ability on self-regulatory mechanisms and complex decision making. *Journal of Personality and Social Psychology, 56*(3), 407–415. doi:10.1037/0022–3514.56.3.407

Yeager, D. S., & Walton, G. M. (2011). Social-psychological interventions in education: They're not magic. *Review of Educational Research, 81*, 267–301. doi:10.3102/0034654311405999

PART III

Looking at Women's Leadership Journeys Ahead

Cutting-Edge Perspectives

13

THE LEADER-FOLLOWER CYCLE

Using Followership as a Means to Empower Women

Lisa DeFrank-Cole and Brent Bishop

In 2017, women held 5.2% of CEO positions in S&P 500 companies (Catalyst, 2017). We know women are underrepresented as senior leaders in nearly every sector, not just in business (DeFrank-Cole & Tan, 2017). If women find themselves represented as followers in much of their careers, traversing a circuitous route to leadership (if they ever get there at all), how can we teach them to be effective followers and to be seen as leadership prospects in the future? We posit that by harnessing their influence, even if they do not yet have authority, they will have more opportunity to transition from an "exemplary follower" role to a leadership role, with the help of mentors and sponsors.

This chapter serves as a think piece regarding the manner in which a woman may use followership to help her in two ways: (1) To increase her awareness of and education about followership to enable her to become an exemplary follower, and (2) To use her exemplary followership skills as a pathway to a leadership position. The authors introduce a model entitled "the leader-follower cycle" and hypothesize that it will aid women in moving from followership roles to leadership roles. If influence without authority is familiar terrain for many women, how can being an "exemplary follower" (Kelley, 1992) help women move ahead? Advocating to see more women in leadership roles, the authors assert that one possible way forward is to teach women the partnering skills necessary to use their influence to effect change in their roles as followers and transition to leadership positions.

Followers are not "sheep," or people who just do what they are told to do, but willing participants in the goal accomplishment of an organization. This is where women can flourish. Women are said to be communal, warm, and gentle (Eagly, 2007) and generally more democratic in their leadership style (Eagly & Johnson, 1990). How can we use these strengths to better understand problems and to reach goals? By using followership skills that build a collaborative environment—not one with competition at its core.

First, we need to acknowledge that 80–90% of work that gets done in an organization is completed by followers (Kelley, 1992). Let's recognize that fact and encourage organizations to value and appreciate followers and to change the culture from the ground up. If women utilize the influence they already have as followers to accomplish goals, they will not only feel more empowered but perhaps may be seen as more adept at stepping into leadership roles by those above them in rank.

Defining Followership

Knowing that a leader is someone who influences a group of people to achieve a common goal (Northouse, 2017), how do we define followers? Kellerman (2012) states that "followers are subordinates who have less power, authority, and influence than do their superiors" (p. xx). There are, however, other variables at play. For example, two common measures of a follower are (1) the degree to which he or she may be engaged with an organization, and (2) whether or not a follower uses dependent or independent thinking skills (Kelley, 1992). Followers contribute ideas to the decision-making process and preferably are fully engaged in assisting leaders in accomplishing the goals of an organization.

Followership has been researched since the mid-1950s, and discussion of followers in the social science literature was present decades earlier (Baker, 2007). Unfortunately, leadership has received the majority of the research attention, and followership was relegated to the back seat. As organizations began to flatten and the global economy developed in the 1980s and 1990s, more responsibility was shared with followers, despite them not having any training or support for such roles. Here again, rather than research being conducted on followers as the primary subject, scholarship in the area of leadership gained more momentum. "Instead, the focus was recentered on leadership: developing new leadership skills and even developing those leadership skills in followers. There was no focus on the leader-follower relationship or on the demands placed on each role" (Baker, 2007, p. 52). Even though we intuitively know that it takes both leaders and followers to effectively accomplish goals, research and development on only one of these elements has dominated the academic landscape. If we learn about the unique components that define both leaders and followers and understand how they work together, we will be more productive.

In dance (think *Dancing with the Stars* or *World of Dance*), we see one partner as the leader and the other as a follower; however, we would not think to train them separately (Hurwitz & Hurwitz, 2017). Yet that is exactly what we do with leaders on a routine basis. We often talk of developing leadership skills but rarely speak of the skills needed to be an effective follower. We need to think of them collectively. In this chapter, we explain how the two entities work together to create an integrated and effective partnership. By expanding our collective leadership AND followership skills, we give opportunity to many people to be engaged in problem solving and goal accomplishment.

We need to rethink our connotations about the term "follower" and reclaim it with a positive association, not unlike we associate the term with Twitter. We are all followers, and sometimes, we are leaders. The relationship between the two is fungible in that sometimes we are leaders and other times we are followers. The role of followers is not to be disparaged but rather recognized and lauded for the contributions that they make.

The Followership Crisis

Our world is a leader-centric one. Our history books are filled with the acts of great leaders and how they altered the courses of ancient and modern history. In the science community, we stare in awe at the achievements of great scientists who have brought us into the modern technological era. Religious leaders are also heralded as beacons of virtue, and we look at them as role models for our own lives. Our society puts an immense amount of trust in our leaders because that is exactly who the spotlight is always directed toward. Individuals and companies together have invested billions of dollars in what Barbara Kellerman calls the "leadership industry." But why? Even with the amount of information our field has gathered, the amount of leadership trainings that have been administered, and the number of best-selling leadership books that have been published, there is a leadership crisis.

According to Gallup, approval ratings of the U.S. Congress have been below 50% since June of 2003 and currently sit at an abysmal 13% (Gallup, 2017a). President Donald Trump's approval rating has remained below 50% for his first 300 days in office and has gradually decreased over that period of time (Gallup, 2017b). And recently many male leaders in government, film, and news industries are being exposed for sexually harassing and/or assaulting young women. Even though our faith in leaders has continued to diminish, we still invest in the leadership industry as we always have, waiting for some great savior to appear before us. As Kellerman (2008) states: especially in times of crisis "followers need(ed) nothing so much as a leader to whom they could turn for comfort and guidance" (p. 55).

The power of followers has grown particularly in recent history in the form of different movements that have slowly chipped away at the power, authority, and influence of leaders. With the advent of social media, any one person has the capability to have his or her ideas instantly shared worldwide and become influential overnight. For example, the 2017 Women's March mobilized an estimated 5 million people in the United States (Chenoweth & Pressman, 2017) less than three months after the election of Donald Trump. This modern technological era has given followers more influence over their leaders than ever before, yet the money and attention are still invested primarily in leaders. Our leadership crisis may very well be a followership crisis in disguise, and our society simply has put little effort into researching followership.

A study was conducted where 300 C-suite executives were asked questions pertaining to followership (Agho, 2009). The study found that 95.7% of the executives surveyed believe people do not know how to follow and 96.1% said that effective followership is more than simply doing what one is told to do. Through work conducted by Marc and Samantha Hurwitz, they have found that followership is "one of the most important determinants of career success" (Hurwitz & Hurwitz, 2017, p. 14). This demonstrates a few things: (1) followership is a more active and crucial role than society (in the U.S. context) would like us to believe; (2) our society currently lacks effective followership, and this may be the source of many "leadership" problems; and (3) effective followership has untapped potential that could help fix the leadership crisis and create better leaders for our future.

Followership Education

Developing effective followership skills can help in the advancement of women by increasing the pool of exemplary followers. An individual's followership has been found to be one of the top determinants of career success, and it is the very thing that executives seem to think is missing in the workplace (Agho, 2009). It is the spark that gets the fire started. Therefore, one must start by educating herself about followership.

When we use the term "followership education," we are first referring to the process of removing the bias against being a follower. There is no point in trying to teach someone how to be an effective follower if he or she does not see the benefits of developing effective followership skills. Years of being exposed to phrases like "don't be a follower, be a leader" and "the youth are the leaders of tomorrow" has the effect of embedding leader-centric thinking into our culture. Because of this, some people can be very resistant to the idea, especially people who feel like they are natural-born leaders. They can feel threatened by the idea that leadership is not actually an ivory tower for looking down upon the unfortunate followers.

A good followership foundation for women may be built by exploring the works of Robert Kelley, Ira Chaleff, and Barbara Kellerman. These three authors formed the bedrock of the followership literature as a field in its own right. Robert Kelley began the movement in 1988 with his *Harvard Business Review* article titled "In Praise of Followers." Later in 1992, the publication of his book, *The Power of Followership*, demonstrated the benefits that could come with studying followership as its own entity. Ira Chaleff then provided the momentum for the movement when *The Courageous Follower* was published. The book built off of what Robert Kelley had started by also considering situations where a follower must have the courage to stand up against a leader. And in 2008, Barbara Kellerman published *Followership*, which provided a new perspective on the followership theory that already existed. This helped to create more debate within the followership community and helped to continue its growth. Also in 2008, *The Art of Followership*, edited by Ronald Riggio, Ira Chaleff, and Jean Lipman-Bluman, provided an anthology by leading scholars and practitioners about the nascent field. This volume contained a rich collection of chapters about the interactions between leaders and followers and contained the works of two of the three authors mentioned earlier, plus many others. (As an aside, *The Art of Followership* emanated from the Kravis-de-Roulet Conference at Claremont McKenna College in 2006, the same event from which this book, *Women's Leadership Journeys*, was conceived in more recent years.) These publications, along with the more contemporary work of Marc and Samantha Hurwitz, are examples of major attempts by the followership community to address the followership crisis.

Robert Kelley described our misguided societal view of leadership as "the myth of leadership." Kelley (1992) argues "the myth defines leadership in such a narrow way that we mere mortals can never hope to fit the bill, even though we are spurred on to try" (pp. 16–17). Our society has such impossibly high expectations for our leaders that they will almost certainly fail. This shows the importance of developing a cadre of what Robert Kelley calls "exemplary followers." Exemplary followers possess the ability to think independently and are actively engaged in the group. From Kelley's point of view, this is the gold standard that all followers should strive to be one day. A dependent-thinking follower (such as a passive follower or a conformist follower) does not possess the necessary ability to speak up when what the leader is doing is wrong, a concept that is explored in more depth by Ira Chaleff. And a passively engaged follower (such as the passive follower or an alienated follower) does not possess the shared desire to achieve the common goal of the group (Kelley, 1992). This is why independent-thinking and active followers are the most beneficial to the leader and stand out among the rest.

Ira Chaleff (2009) similarly identified two variables in his book *The Courageous Follower*: (1) the follower's desire to support the leader and (2) the ability to challenge the leader. These two elements are analogous to Kelley's active engagement and independent thinking, respectively. Although Chaleff provides similar findings when it comes to defining follower typology, he also adds three key ideas to the followership canon: (1) All follower types are important/useful, not just exemplary ones; (2) Followers adhere to the "common purpose" before they follow the leader; and (3) There are seven examples of courage that "courageous followers" utilize.

The first point can be seen by simply looking at the terminology used by each of them. Where Kelley (1992) has the *passive, alienated, conformist*, and *exemplary followers*, Chaleff has *resources, individualists, implementers*, and *partners*.

The connotation of Chaleff's (2009) typology suggests that all follower types are useful in different ways. For example, the term *conformist follower* suggests that this type of follower mindlessly or blindly follows, but an *implementer* sounds like someone who can take a straightforward task and complete it quickly and effectively.

Chaleff also identifies the concept of the "common purpose" as the sort of driving force for courageous followership. Both the leader and the followers are working in service to the common purpose. That is why when a leader does something that goes against achieving the common purpose, a courageous follower will intervene. A great depiction of this concept is Eugene Delacroix's 1830 painting, *Liberty Leading the People*, which depicts the figure of a woman leading the French people during the French Revolution. Yes, the French revolutionaries had leaders, but both the leaders and followers were working together to achieve the common purpose (liberty, as represented by the figure of a woman) for all citizens.

Finally, Chaleff (2009) provides a list of the ways courageous followers act in service to the common purpose. Some examples include the courage to take responsibility and the courage to take moral action. The courage to take responsibility is simply the idea that if one, as a follower, is the cause for failing to achieve the common purpose, then she should admit it. This can be a hard pill to swallow, but it makes sense. Imagine a hypothetical scenario where a group has a leader who is very passionate for the common purpose of the group and is very effective in this role. If a follower does something that sets the group back drastically and stays quiet about it, then most likely it will be the leader who will be ousted. This would be detrimental to achieving the common purpose because that leader was working hard toward achieving it and is now gone.

Another example of courage, the courage to take moral action, is also very difficult to achieve when the time comes for it. If a follower is asked by a leader to do something immoral, she must take action if it is a feasible option. There is a plethora of examples in human history where someone followed an order because she felt the pressure from authority, maybe because a job was on the line or even lives. The problem is, the excuse of "I was just following orders" is not sufficient in the end. Chaleff (2009) has further elaborated the need for followers to take action in the form of intelligent disobedience.

Intelligent disobedience is a type of training developed for guide dogs to ensure they always obey unless obeying a command that endangers the dog and/ or the human it is guiding. Ira Chaleff (2015) describes how this idea can and should be developed for humans in his book *Intelligent Disobedience: Doing Right When What You're Told to Do Is Wrong*. In the book, he describes a scenario where a young female nurse disagrees with a male doctor on what medication should be given to a cardiac patient who just came into the emergency room in the 1960s. She informs the doctor that her training has taught her that the medication he prescribed can lead to death in cardiac patients, but the doctor tells her to "just do it!" In the face of differing levels of experience, differences in levels of formal training, and facing the gender dynamic in the 1960s, did the nurse obey or disobey? The answer is she obeyed, but not entirely. She grabbed the medication, hooked the patient up to the IV, and then told the doctor everything was set up but that he needed to turn the valve because her training forbade it. Suddenly when the risk was in the doctor's hands, he decided to change to a different medication, and the patient fully recovered (Chaleff, 2015, p. 9).

This anecdote from Chaleff demonstrates the importance of learning intelligent disobedience and how it can empower women in the face of an authority trying to suppress their followership. Intelligent disobedience is the first step to changing the organization's culture. That is exactly what the women of Hollywood are doing for the film industry right now. Their exceptional acts of intelligent disobedience are now causing many people inside and outside of the film industry to crack down on the sexual assault cases that plague their organizations. These women are shifting to the role of exemplary followers, which allows for the shift to different leadership roles in the film industry. Finally, these women film leaders will promote that same type of followership, thus creating a positive feedback loop, effectively changing the organizational culture.

In 2008, Barbara Kellerman provided a different view of followership typology. Kellerman argues that active engagement is the primary determinant of one's follower type. This is a product of how she defines a follower. Kellerman is not saying that independent thinking is not important but simply that at the core of what makes one follower different from another follower is his or her degree of engagement.

This causes Kellerman's (2008) follower types to lie on a continuum defined by the level of active engagement. First is the *isolate*, a follower so removed from the process that she is unaware she is a part of it. Next is the *bystander*, who is still removed from the process, not because of ignorance, but because she chooses not to be a part of it. The first follower type that actually engaged as part of the process is the *participant*. She follows the orders of the leader but is most likely to jump ship at the first sign of an oncoming iceberg. The *activist* follower actually has a passion for the leader's message and will do her best to make it a reality. And, lastly, the *diehard* follower is so passionate for the leader or cause that she would be willing to literally give up her life.

One of the interesting contributions that Kellerman made to followership was stirring the pot of debate in the group of people who study it. She demonstrated that the followership community was still very young and legitimate debates were needed to prevent walking down a narrow road of thought. Her differing angle to followership from Kelley's and Chaleff's serves as inspiration for continued followership research and theory building.

Many people who are now advocates for followership have said it came to them as an epiphany. Once anyone spends enough time educating themselves on followership, she also realizes the power it has to making an organization better. Not everyone is in a leadership role, but everyone is a follower in some way. Yet companies invest billions of dollars into leadership training every year. Kelley (1992) found that the overall impact a leader has on her organization is only 10–20%. Yet 95.7% of C-suite executives believe that people do not know how to follow (Agho, 2009). There is so much untapped potential that could positively affect our organizations through bettering our own followership skills and the capabilities of those followers around us. Contemporary followership works have begun to focus on how to improve one's followership and leadership skills in order to make the sum of the parts greater than the whole.

Partnerships

The most recent attempt to address the followership crisis has been made by Marc and Samantha Hurwitz in their 2017 book, *Leadership is Half the Story*, where they established the generative partnership model. The term "generative partnerships" describes the beneficial, respectful, and positive relationships between leaders and followers and was coined by the Hurwitz couple. Their philosophy is driven by a set of five guiding principles:

1. Partnerships need leadership AND followership: they are equal, dynamic, and different;
2. Leadership is setting the frame, followership is creating within it;
3. Lean in to build connection;
4. Value the positive, and build on it;
5. Have deeply shared goals.

(p. 40)

The first guiding principle establishes the idea that leaders and followers are equal, dynamic, and different. That is to say, both roles are necessary in the leadership process, occasionally the roles get swapped, and the skills and duties for each role are different. This guiding principle represents a philosophy where leaders and exemplary followers are only separated by the name of their respective roles, not by their abilities or importance.

One of the duties of a leader is to provide a "frame." Leaders provide frames for relationships, decision making, and most communication, whereas the followers are responsible for building within the frames (Hurwitz & Hurwitz, 2017, pp. 55–66). For example, a leader may clarify what is acceptable in their working relationship, how one refers to the other (first name, by title, etc.), and time frames in which it is appropriate to meet (outside of work, for example). And once the leader establishes that relationship frame, it is now on the followers to build that relationship with their leader, while staying within the constraints of the frame.

Although the remaining three principles do not explicitly mention leaders and followers by name, they apply equally to both. The philosophy of leaning in to build connection, for leaders, has to do with leaning in rather than taking a hands-off management approach. Likewise, for a follower, she should lean in rather than hide from the leader or ride on the leader's coattails. There exists a "generative point" for each partnership that properly balances all of these aspects.

Both the leader and follower should focus on positivity, in their language and attitudes, and more importantly should build off of it. Tearing others down to bring them back up still leaves them at the level they started at rather than in a better place. It is more beneficial to identify what made the partnership work effectively and ask how to make it even better in the future rather than simply identifying the shortcomings.

Lastly, the leader and follower should have deeply shared goals. This is synonymous to Chaleff's common purpose. The focus of the partnership is not to impose some power dynamic from one person onto another but to succeed at fulfilling a set of shared goals.

These examples provide information on the ways others have defined followership and give suggestions for how leaders and followers may work together. We provided this primer on followership as a way to educate the reader on the main concepts before proposing a model on the leader-follower cycle. The model will demonstrate the current followership environment in organizations and specifically how it affects women.

The Leader-Follower Cycle

In our attempts to better understand the current situation as it relates to followership and to address how women may use followership as a pathway to leadership, we created a flow chart titled the leader-follower cycle. Its aim is to help us understand how exemplary followership is so crucial to the success of the entire organization. The model provides a visualization that depicts women continuing on the followership circle and, at a point of intervention, how they can change course to reach senior leadership roles.

By providing formal training on the topics of followership education, intelligent disobedience, and generative partnerships, individuals may go from being a typical follower to a heightened state sometimes called "exemplary followers" (Kelley 1992). These exemplary followers "possess a repertoire of skills and values that are both learnable and doable . . . they are simply able to carry out their jobs and to work with others in a way that adds considerable value to the enterprise" (p. 129). These individuals help to move an organization forward and accomplish its goals.

At this point, "leader" and "follower" are merely names for the roles of the two individuals, not necessary implying importance of one over another. This makes the transition to leadership for the exemplary followers seamless as they differ only by titles, not by level of importance. Women continue in followership roles and may not have an opportunity to take a leadership position due to societal norms and biases currently existing, so the idea of a pathway to leadership through exemplary followership may have promising possibilities. We are quick to point out, however, that we do not disparage the role of followers but recognize that some women do wish to hold leadership positions, and we want them to reach their potential.

We learn from Sally Helgesen (1995) that hierarchical structures are not the organizational configurations in which women thrive. Women work better when they are in the middle of things—in webs of influence.

> Since web structures are circular rather than pyramidical, those who emerge in them as leaders tend to be people who feel comfortable being in the center of things rather than at the top, who prefer building consensus to issuing orders, and who place a low value on the kind of symbolic perks and marks of distinction that define success in the hierarchy. This preference on the part of web-style leaders infused their organizations with a collegial atmosphere, which in turn enables people to focus upon *what* needs to be done rather than *who* has the authority to do it.
>
> (Helgesen, 2005, pp. 20–21)

Thus, the leader-follower cycle uses joining circles to demonstrate where women may do their best work.

In thinking about the circular model, we wanted to visually represent how and why some women move into leadership positions rather than continuing in followership roles. We were reminded by the literature about the importance of mentors and sponsors to women's upward mobility into leadership roles (and as mentioned by other authors in this book, Scott; Pace; Longman, et al.; Shollen; Tyson; and Madsen & Dahlvig). The place in which a woman would transition out of an exemplary follower role and move into a leadership role needs a catalyst for this action to occur. This spark that changes a person's direction from followership to leadership requires sponsorship. The term sponsor, as we are using it, is derived from Sylvia Ann Hewlett's (2013) work. We believe mentorship is extremely important, and we also know that sponsorship does produce a catalyst event that enables women to move into leadership roles.

Mentors listen, offer advice, and share their time (Hewlett, 2013). A sponsor, however, "sees furthering your career as an important investment in his or her own career, organization, or vision. Sponsors may advise or steer you, but their chief role is to develop you as a leader" (p. 20). While someone may look to another person as a mentor or sponsor who may be a catalyst on a micro (individual) level, the authors acknowledge that public policy and organizational governance may also provide a stimulus on a macro level. Regardless of micro or macro, having an impetus to move in a different direction is what will put women on the path to leadership. In this chapter, we most often think of women having another person (micro level) as a mentor or sponsor. Having such a sponsor is a catalyst for the transition to take an exemplary follower on the pathway to leadership.

Figure 13.1 is a visual representation of how the leader-follower cycle works for women currently on a micro level (meaning at the individual level rather than the organizational level). In the left circle is the followership cycle, where there exist two potential pathways. Women can either continue to stay as traditional followers (thick line and smaller circle) or make the move to exemplary followership (thin line and larger circle) through followership education or by other means. Exemplary followers then provide followership mentoring to other followers to help produce more exemplary followers. The majority of people, regardless of gender, take the path of *regular followers* because it is the more accessible path. This "more accessible path" is represented by the thicker line, whereas the less accessible paths are represented by thinner lines.

The size of the circles represents the amount of effort needed to take that path. The path to exemplary followership and the path to leadership are longer journeys (require more effort or energy) than the one to remain a regular follower. For women, the route society has offered them is to move along as *regular* followers. Therefore, steps need to be taken in order to open up the routes to exemplary followership. With more women becoming exemplary followers, this will create a larger pool of women who can provide mentoring to other women and perpetuate a positive followership cycle.

These exemplary female followers, with the help of sponsors, can then transition to a leadership role in the circle on the right side. The catalyst of a sponsor, as represented by the jagged rectangle shape, serves as a catapult for women

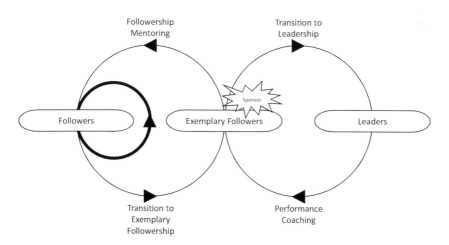

FIGURE 13.1   Leader-follower cycle (female)

to attain a leadership role. They assist in providing the energy required to make the journey around the leadership circle. Once in the circle on the right side of the model, it is expected that these women will coach other exemplary followers and potentially be their sponsors.

Regarding context, even though the model does not explicitly use words to depict it, context is inherently present. Not only does the thinness or thickness of the lines represent accessibility, the lines are elements of context. It shows the reader how accessible the organization has made certain pathways. For example, the organizational culture may have made the leadership cycle's line *thin* for women but *thicker* for men. The contextual element of gender bias may be seen in the model this way.

Another example of how context is represented in the model may be seen when looking at how the roles are defined within it. Exemplary followers would adapt their followership style to fit the context they are in and the leader with whom they are collaborating. This means that some elements of context, although not seen, manifest in how the term "exemplary follower" is defined for a given case. For example, an "exemplary follower" in a U.S. Army infantry unit (where obeying orders quickly and effectively can mean life or death) would be very different from an "exemplary follower" in academe (where taking time to share thoughts and ideas is more valued). Context does not change the structure of the model, it simply changes how we define the roles of exemplary follower or even the leader.

Leadership, followership, and context are all represented in the model. These three elements are most relevant not only when analyzing organizations and their current situations, but also when thinking about how to improve performance. Specifically regarding women, we recognize that all three elements are a necessary part of the discussion when thinking about how they may take on greater leadership roles in society. To apply this model in a realistic situation, we looked for a current case that would demonstrate how it works.

Hollywood Case Study

A current case that demonstrates the leader-follower cycle in action is women in Hollywood. While it is perhaps not the first place that one would look to identify concepts of leadership and followership, we believe there are some interesting elements to explore. Women have not held leadership roles as producers or directors, for example, in the same percentages as men. In Hollywood women made up only 2.7% of the directors, 11.2% of writers, and only 20.5% of the producers in the film industry in 2007 (Smith, 2010). This disparity in the numbers of women in top leadership roles has caused the films themselves to be affected. With men primarily in the leadership roles, female characters are written from the point of view of a man, not by an actual woman, leading to inaccurate representations of real women in film.

This makes Hollywood a good case for studying how the leader-follower cycle can be applied.

The sexual assault/harassment allegations that began with Hollywood producer Harvey Weinstein now include several members of the Hollywood elite. It is really the first time that people who are bringing the claims are publicly seeing justice. While women may have been paid-off by hush money in the past (perhaps not the best type of justice), many cases were not public due to nondisclosure agreements.

On October 5th, 2017, a *New York Times* article written by Jodi Kantor and Megan Twohey was published detailing several accounts from actresses, assistants, and women interested in starting their careers about how Weinstein sexually harassed and/or assaulted them in return for favors/career advancement. The article explains how Weinstein and his company's executives paid settlements to multiple women to ensure silence about his activities. He also had his company release a documentary on campus sexual assault; funded the 2016 Clinton campaign; and took part in women's marches in Park City, Utah, as ways to be seen in the public eye as a champion of women's rights, in an attempt to preemptively weaken any potential accuser's case. This is a case where a leader used his position to suppress any chance at effective followership. According to Lauren O'Connor, a former Weinstein employee, "I am a 28 year old woman trying to make a living and a career. Harvey Weinstein is a 64 year old, world famous man and this is his company. The balance of power is me: 0, Harvey Weinstein: 10" (Kantor & Twohey, 2017, para. 9). But once these two women reporters gave a platform for these courageous followers to speak up, they inspired so many women to do the same.

This phenomenon is an example of when the pathway to exemplary followership is made more accessible. The women interviewed in the New York Times article made their move to exemplary followership by having "the courage to take moral action" against Harvey Weinstein. By doing this, they also became role models to other women he had abused, a form of followership mentoring. Now, there is a constant flow of more and more women moving to exemplary followership roles since the path has been made more accessible. This would be represented on the model as the followership cycle's line becoming thicker.

Even though the story is not a pleasant one, it represents elements in our model as a case in point. With more women in Hollywood now perpetuating the exemplary followership cycle, steps need to be taken to get the leadership cycle of the model more accessible. As discussed earlier, the catalyst needed is a sponsor. Producer and actress Reese Witherspoon is an example of someone who has made the move to a top leadership role and is a sponsor for future inclusion of women as writers, directors, and producers.

Witherspoon has often played the role of a woman who get things done (Blasberg, 2017), which is a reflection of her real-life character. She believes that the reason women continue to be offered boring, one-dimensional roles is

due to the leadership. That is why Witherspoon started her own film production company with the assistance of investors, to fund films with better roles for
women, women directors, writers, etc. While we do not know who sponsored
Reese Witherspoon to create her company, we hypothesize that there were one
or more investors in her life who motivated her to pursue leadership roles, such
as being a producer/director, and financially assisting with the creation of her
films.

This is an example of sponsorship and shows the important role it plays in
the leader-follower cycle. These sponsors (in the form of her initial investors)
have put Witherspoon in a position where she can now provide sponsorships
and mentoring to other women who want to become leaders in Hollywood.
This will inevitably create a pool of sponsors who can continue to advocate
for women, thus thickening the line of the leadership circle (the path has
become more accessible) and hopefully creating a better organizational culture
in Hollywood.

The leader-follower cycle demonstrates how women at all levels—followers,
exemplary followers, and leaders—can collaborate with each other to advance
their cause. It shows how acts of exemplary followership can bring about
change and affect the culture of an organization. And it shows why sponsors
are so important for women to make the move from exemplary followership to
leadership. We predict that more women will be moving into top roles in the
film industry over the next few years as the followership and leadership cycles
become more accessible.

Utilizing the Model: A Higher Education Example

Imagine a leader-follower partnership between an assistant professor and a full
professor at a university. If the assistant professor wants to get promoted, be an
active member on campus, and become a future leader in the academic community, then she could focus on navigating her way around the leader-follower
cycle. The first step for the assistant professor would be to leave the regular
follower loop and practice exemplary followership skills. The junior professor
would need to be an active member in the campus community, keeping in mind
her contractual obligations to her department. It is unlikely that a senior-level
professor would get to know a junior-level assistant professor if she was not participating in activities that would get her noticed.

At the core, an exemplary follower takes on a followership style that comple-
ments the leader's style. For example, if the senior-level professor is willing to
serve as a coauthor on a research/writing project, then the assistant professor
would learn how to interact in an effective and efficient manner to complement
the style of the senior-level professor. She needs to meet the timelines set forth
by the senior-level professor and not be seen as using their occasions together
inefficiently.

In time, the senior-level professor would invest in, advocate for and develop the assistant professor as a leader. We theorize that because of this sponsorship, the junior-level assistant professor would get promoted to associate and presumably full professor and take on a more position-based leadership role if she wanted one, at the university or in a professional association. It can take a period of time to practice these skills, but eventually if they are done well, the assistant professor would move into that exemplary follower role and then into a leadership role.

Surrounding this cycle is the context of the department, the university, and the academic discipline in which these two women reside. Elements might include the kinds of journals in which the duo publishes, culture of department, and who gets promoted, as well as the climate for women on this particular campus. While simplistic in nature, this example provides a more common paradigm for women to follow than perhaps the case study about Hollywood. Though the industries are different, we posit that the leader-follower cycle would be used in the same manner in both contexts.

***

We no longer need rigid hierarchies for leadership to manifest itself but rather web-like patterns and networks. The model we developed, the leader-follower cycle, identifies pathways for women to use exemplary followership as a transition to leadership. The design of the model, in circular fashion, puts women—and exemplary followers—directly in the middle. As discussed earlier in this chapter, women are comfortable in the middle of things rather than being in stuck in systems that point upward, with only one heroic leader at the top.

The partnerships between leaders and followers provides a new road ahead—one filled with collaboration and appreciation for everyone's contributions. Allies and exemplary followers will provide a support structure to produce stronger women leaders. And that provides a hopeful future in a changing world.

Lastly, we invite people to test our model in their own organizations, using their own case studies, and report what they find. As with any new theory, we want it to be pushed, pulled, and stretched to see if it represents what we have hoped it would.

References

Agho, A. (2009). Perspectives of senior-level executives on effective followership and leadership. *Journal of leadership and Organizational Studies, 16*(2), 159–166.

Baker, S. D. (2007). Followership: The theoretical foundation of a contemporary construct. *Journal of Leadership & Organizational Studies, 14*(1), 50–60.

Blasberg, D. (2017, November 1). How Reese Witherspoon is changing Hollywood for women; with projects ranging from her HBO series "Big Little Lies" to her production franchise to her growing lifestyle brand, Witherspoon has become a force in female storytelling. *The Wall Street Journal Magazine*. Retrieved from https://search.proquest. com/docview/1958271653?accountid=2837

Catalyst. (2017). *Women CEOs of the S&P 500*. New York: Catalyst. Retrieved from www.catalyst.org/knowledge/women-ceos-sp-500

Chaleff, I. (2009). *The courageous follower: Standing up to & for our leaders* (3rd ed.). Oakland, CA: Berrett-Koehler Publishers.

Chaleff, I. (2015). *Intelligent disobedience: Doing right when what you're told to do is wrong*. Oakland, CA: Berrett-Koehler Publishers.

Chenoweth, E., & Pressman, J. (2017, February 7). This is what we learned by counting the women's marches. *The Washington Post*. Retrieved from www.washingtonpost. com/news/monkey-cage/wp/2017/02/07/this-is-what-we-learned-by-counting-the-womens-marches/?utm_term=.b74a402824bb

DeFrank-Cole, L., & Tan, S. (2017). Reimagining leadership for millennial women: Perspectives across generations. *Journal of Leadership Studies*, 10(4), 43–45.

Eagly, A. (2007). Female leadership advantage and disadvantage: Resolving the contradictions. *Psychology of Women Quarterly*, 31, 1–12.

Eagly, A. H., & Johnson, B. T. (1990). Gender and leadership style: A meta-analysis. *Psychological Bulletin*, 108(2), 233–256.

Gallup. (2017a). Congress and the public. Retrieved from http://news.gallup.com/ poll/1600/congress-public.aspx

Gallup. (2017b). Gallup daily: Trump job approval. Retrieved from http://news.gallup. com/poll/201617/gallup-daily-trump-job-approval.aspx

Helgesen, S. (2005). *The web of inclusion: Architecture for building great organizations*. Washington, DC: Beard Books.

Hewlett, S. A. (2013). *Forget a mentor, find a sponsor: The new way to fast-track your career*. Boston, MA: Harvard Business Review Press.

Hurwitz, M., & Hurwitz, S. (2017). *Leadership is half the story: A fresh look at followership, leadership and collaboration*. Toronto: University of Toronto Press.

Kantor, J., & Twohey, M. (2017, October 5). Harvey Weinstein paid off sexual harassment accusers for decades. *The New York Times*. Retrieved from www.nytimes. com/2017/10/05/us/harvey-weinstein-harassment-allegations.html

Kellerman, B. (2008). *Followership: How followers are creating change and changing leaders*. Boston: Harvard Business Press.

Kellerman, B. (2012). *The end of leadership*. New York: Harper Collins.

Kellerman, B. (2015). *Hard times: Leadership in America*. Stanford, CA: Stanford University Press.

Kelley, R. (1988). In praise of followers. *Harvard Business Review*, 66, 142–148.

Kelley, R. (1992). *The power of followership: How to create leaders people want to follow and followers who lead themselves*. New York: Doubleday.

Oc, B., & Bashshur, M. R. (2013). Followership, leadership and social influence. *The Leadership Quarterly*, 24, 919–934.

Riggio, R., Chaleff, I., & Lipman-Bluman, J. (2008). *The art of followership: How great followers create great leaders and organizations*. San Francisco, CA: Jossey-Bass.

Smith, S. L. (2010). *Gender oppression in cinematic content? A look at females on-screen & behind the camera in top-grossing 2007 films*. Report, Annenberg School for Communication and Journalism, University of Southern California. Retrieved November 30, 2017 from https://seejane.org/wp-content/uploads/2007Films_GenderReport.pdf

14

LEADERSHIP AND LACTATION

Barbara Kellerman

For the last quarter century, facts and figures pertaining to women and leadership in America have remained almost immutable. Despite some changing attitudes, and some changing structures, and some changing policies, the numbers of women in top positions of political and corporate leadership specifically—and group and organizational leadership generally—have stayed stubbornly the same. To take perhaps the most obvious examples, in 2017 women held approximately 4% of CEO positions at America's 500 largest companies (Merelli, 2017). And, in 2017 women held approximately 20% of seats in the U.S. Congress (Center for American Women in Politics, 2017). There has been no notable increase in either of these numbers for decades. Moreover, the numbers per se can be misleading. Though as of this writing 21 members of the U.S. Senate are women, of these only five are Republicans. Since Republicans currently control the Congress, this necessarily means that between January 2017 and January 2019 women are significantly underrepresented in the legislative power hierarchy.

Nor do the figures at slightly lower levels give us reason to rejoice. While we know that the highest positions of leadership are the most difficult to attain, for women especially, and that somewhat lower on the organizational hierarchy is more equity, even here the numbers are not heartening. For example, at international banks women make up less than 25% of senior staff (Jaekel & St-Onge, 2016). This notwithstanding the fact that, as the *Financial Times* put it:

> global financial institutions have thrown the kitchen sink at improving
> gender diversity, rolling out everything from the standard—women's networks, better maternity leave, and subsidized child care—to the extreme,

in one case shipping breast milk across the globe to make working and caring for a newborn easier.

(Jenkins, Marriage, & Noonan, 2017)

No wonder there is anger, frustration, and cynicism. For while there has been some progress toward gender equity and diversity, and while on the surface being family friendly is now no less than politically correct, the pace of change for women at high levels remains frustratingly and, increasingly, inexplicably slow. In fact, some of the frustrations triggered by the sluggish rate of change, experienced by women and men alike, are precisely in consequence of well-intentioned efforts that continue nevertheless to fall far short.

Given that gender equity in positions of leadership and management remains still so elusive a goal, the question increasingly must be why. Why, despite at least two decades of numerous and various efforts to achieve greater gender diversity at and near the top, are women still so far from the goal that ostensibly they want to reach? This chapter will address this question, though given where it ends up, the answers might be less than fully satisfying.

On Being a Parent

Whereas 10, 20 years ago the reasons for gender inequities in the workplace, especially at the top, were primarily thought to be external—for example, socialization, the so-called male leadership model, 24/7 workplace demands, patriarchal hierarchies, gender stereotyping, women's lack of mentors, sponsors, and role models—increasingly the reasons are thought to be internal, innate. Though some of these could be in consequence of nurture rather than nature, it could also be argued that innate differences between women and men include women's proclivity to feel less confident than men, at least in certain circumstances; women's proclivity to hold back rather than to lean in, at least in certain circumstances; and women's proclivity to being overly congenial at the expense of being appropriately assertive, at least in certain circumstances. Innate differences could also be said to include those between being a mother and being a father.

Turns out that nothing has a greater impact on women's professional trajectories than being a mother. For example, we now know that motherhood explains to a considerable extent the gender pay gap. When men and women finish school and start working, they are paid roughly equally. But, when women are in their late 20s and early 30s, that is, when they start to have children, this begins to change. They begin to earn less than men. Moreover, the effect of this change is especially strong on women who are college educated and who are in high earning occupations. Having children is "particularly damaging to their careers" (Miller, 2017a, para. 3).

On the surface, the reason is obvious; it is external. It is the unequal division of labor at home, even when both spouses are working full time. More specifically, women who are ambitious to rise to higher levels of leadership and management tend to find that, however well-organized they are, "it is hard to combine family responsibilities with the ultra-long working hours and the 'anytime, anywhere' culture of senior corporate jobs" (Schumpeter, 2012, para. 4). This obviously raises the question of why women should be so much more strongly affected by being a parent than men—about which more later. Suffice to say at this point that being a mother—partly but not only because women do more than their share (more than half) of domestic work—has a far greater negative impact both on wages and on attaining a position of senior leadership than does being a father. Small wonder a 2007 study by McKinsey found that 54% of senior women executives surveyed were childless, compared with 29% of men (McKinsey & Company, 2007). And small wonder that of these women, fully one-third were single, nearly double the proportion of men without partners (Schumpeter, 2012). Even in 2017, unmarried women without children continue to earn closer to what men do (Miller, 2017a).

As is well known by now, public policy in America is particularly unsupportive of parents who prefer to stay in the workplace—not to speak of those ambitious to get to the top. Whereas in other developed countries the average length of paid parental leave has increased from 17 weeks in 1970 to just over a year today, in the United States it was zero in 1970, and it remains zero to this day (Organization for Economic Co-operation and Development, 2017). Only 13% of U.S. employees have access to formal paid family leave, and the rate is much lower for low-income employees (Bureau of Labor Statistics, 2014). Shulevitz (2016) states that one consequence of this is that women wait longer to have a child. First-time mothers have aged nearly five years since 1970. Of course, the impact of public policies so antiquated are far greater on women than on men, for women are far more likely than men to take time out from work to care for young children. One study showed that fully 44% of baby boomer women had at some point taken a break of more than six months to care for their offspring; for men, in contrast, the figure was just 2% (Ely, Stone, & Ammerman, 2014). This yawning gap is explained in part—though not in whole—by the failure of both government and businesses to replace services provided by what once was, for some, the stay-at-home wife.

This failure does not, however, of itself, explain why only 2% of men take more than six months off to care for children—in contrast to 44% of women (Ely, Stone, & Ammerman, 2014). It is a disparity that, it must be emphasized, is by no means only an American phenomenon. Though the Scandinavian countries are frequently held up as paragons of virtue when it comes to gender equity, even in Scandinavia the differences are striking. Women in Sweden, for example, constitute only about a quarter of managers in the private sector. Moreover, to the point of this chapter, they take fully 75% of all parental leave, and they work part-time more than three times as often as do men (Hegedus, 2012).

One of the ironies of all this is that attitudes toward gender equity both at home and in the workplace may be changing—but not in ways that we might anticipate. Instead of being more supportive of gender equity, millennials, men particularly, seem to be less supportive. Surveys suggest that men aged 18 to 25 are more traditional in their attitudes toward egalitarian divisions of labor than their elders. While the reasons for this slippage of support for women in the workplace are not completely clear, the early evidence is that "the decline in support for 'nontraditional' domestic arrangements stems from young people witnessing the difficulties experienced by parents in two-earner families" (Coontz, 2017, para. 8). The numbers do not, in any case, lie. At best, Americans remain ambivalent about whether adult women working, in particular if they are mothers, is a good thing. In fact, over half believe that children are better off with a mother who is at home full time and does not hold an outside job. To boot, as Jill Filipovic recently reported, "only 8 percent say the same thing about fathers" (Filipovic, 2017, para. 13).

Again, cause and effect relationships are not easy to delineate. But there is little doubt that for women certainly there are negative correlations between being a parent and being a high wage earner and between being a parent and being a high-level leader or manager. Clearly one of the reasons for this disparity is that though men do more work in the home than they used to, women continue to carry much the heavier domestic load. "They're still expected to take on the bulk of the chores, like laundry, cooking, cleaning, and child care that allow households to function" (Berman, 2017, para. 3). Of itself, responsibility for taking on tasks like these goes a long way toward explaining why more women than men pass up certain career opportunities—such as, for example, those involving travel—that are likely to result in higher pay and better opportunities for professional advancement. But, as the title of this chapter implies, it does not fully explain a phenomenon that has proven stubbornly resistant even to remediation that is well-intentioned.

On Being a Woman

We know by now that women and men experience their work lives differently. Around the office men are more likely than women to feel professionally confident, to believe they are on track to an executive role, and to be well rewarded. As a 2016 article in the *Wall Street Journal* put it:

> Women perceive a steeper trek to the top. Less than half feel that promotions are awarded fairly or that the best opportunities go to the most deserving employees. A significant share of women say that gender has been a factor in missed raises and promotions. Even more believe that their gender will make it harder for them to advance in the future—a sentiment most strongly felt by women at senior levels.
>
> *(Waller, 2016, para. 4)*

Hard to know, though, which is the chicken and which the egg. What is cause and what effect? For example, do women "perceive a steeper trek to the top" because their trek to the top is steeper? Or is their trek to the top steeper because they perceive it to be steeper?

There is, however, a new area of research that contributes to our understanding of why, even now, still so few women are in positions of leadership. It suggests that there is a difference between women and men in the level of their ambition. Put directly, women view professional advancement as "less desirable" than do men. In other words, for whatever reason, females are less eager to rise to positions of senior leadership and management than males. This disparity is in evidence not only among adults but among adolescents as well. Among college students, men are significantly more likely to play leadership roles on campus (Princeton University Reports, 2011). And they are twice as likely as women to see themselves as someday running for office (Miller, 2016).

Once again, the explanations for the disparity tend toward the external, not internal. So, for example, when we ask why so few women seek political office in comparison with men, the answers tend to include (1) women are less likely than men to be encouraged by others to run; (2) women are less likely than men to raise the requisite money; and (3) women are less likely than men to be able to access important personal, professional, and political networks. Less frequently cited are answers that I call internal—such as, for example, women more than men want to, or at least they think they should, stay close to home to take care of children; and women more than men want to, or at least they think they should, be caregivers, including of their parents. (Note: As stated by Family Caregiver Alliance (2003), in 2015, fully 66% of caregivers were female.)

More than a decade ago, I first speculated that among the differences between women and men might be the level of their ambition to lead and that this difference might be dictated not only by external circumstances but also by internal preferences. I further speculated that these sorts of differences might be hard wired. In a book that appeared in 2003, I wrote:

> Work at the top of the greasy pole takes time, saps energy, and is usually all-consuming. Maybe women's values are different from men's values. Maybe the trade-offs high positions entail are ones that many women do not want to make. Maybe when deciding what matters most, gender matters. . . . The difference may be that more women than men have children whom they badly want, and often need, to spend time with. The difference may be that women are less motivated than men to limit the number of family tasks they undertake and the interests they pursue. In short, the difference may be that women are less willing than men to incur the costs of leadership, particularly if the benefits, such as money and power, are less valued.

> (Kellerman, 2003, p. 55)

I want to be clear here: this is not either or. Women are less likely than men to be in positions of leadership not *only* because of external constraints or *only* because of internal ones. What I am arguing is that among those of us who continue to try to explain why the number of women leaders is still so low, it will no longer suffice to focus only on explanations that are external. We must expand our understanding to include explanations that are internal—specifically innate differences between women and men. Yes, women do have disproportionately heavy family responsibilities, and yes, frequently workplaces are reluctant or even unwilling to treat women and men equally. But, it is also true that in a recent study of 30,000 workers, 54% of men but only 43% of women wanted to be a top executive. And, it is also true that in a 2015 poll taken by *Time*, only 38% of women, compared with 51% of men, described themselves as very or extremely ambitious (Rhode, 2016). In other words, the explanations for the disparity in distribution of leadership roles are more various and more complex than we have assumed up to now.

Tellingly, before they become parents, women are not measurably less ambitious than men. But, after they become parents, gender differences in the levels of ambition become apparent. It is possible, therefore, and perhaps even probable, that being pregnant in and of itself and breastfeeding in and of itself affect women in ways that relate to the riddle of women and leadership—that they change women in ways that, among other things, make them not only willing but eager to stay close to their children. And make them, in consequence, at least for a time, less ambitious to lead. (Note: Fully 80% of American mothers try to breastfeed. Moreover, more than half of all American mothers are still breastfeeding babies at the age of six months (Fox, 2016).)

We know by now that pregnancy affects women—literally. Some effects are temporary, such as, for example, physical transformations and surging hormones, including estrogen and progesterone, which help prepare women's bodies for carrying a child. Additionally, there is growing evidence that pregnancy causes some enduring changes in a woman's brain, especially in areas such as social cognition (Caruso, 2016). While the exact, total impact of pregnancy on women's minds and bodies is not yet known, so far the evidence suggests that it "renders substantial changes in brain structure," changes that are not transient but that last for at least two years (Hoekzema et al., 2017). As one evolutionary psychologist puts it, we now have the "longest-term evidence" yet of "changes in the brain after pregnancy." This suggests that

as a parent, you're now going to be solving slightly different adaptive problems, slightly different cognitive problems than you did before you had children. You have different priorities, you have different tasks you're going to be doing, and so your brain changes.

(Mel Rutherford, as cited in Caruso, 2016)

The concluding sections of this chapter will focus on this single explanation of why women view professional advancement to leadership roles as less desirable than do men—motherhood. Of course, there are several lenses through which to view this phenomenon, such as women being simply less interested than men in the accumulation of power. Moreover, compared to men, women associate more negative outcomes with high power positions, such as conflicts and constraints, including on their time. But, whatever the causes, the effect is the same; according to Gino, Wilmuth, and Brooks (2015), "Compared to men, women view professional advancement as equally attainable but less desirable" (p. 12354). Therefore, women do not hold as many high-level positions as men in part at least because their priorities are different—especially though not exclusively after they become mothers.

On Being a Primate

I am a political scientist. I am not a biologist or a sociobiologist or an evolutionary psychologist or a geneticist or an ethologist or a zoologist. I am, however, a student of women and leadership, and, as suggested, I have long been interested in the lack of adequate explanations for why, despite the political and ideological changes that have taken place since the inception of the modern women's movement a half century ago, still so few women are in positions of leadership, especially at the highest levels. Moreover, the reasons given for the persistence of this gender disparity increasingly have struck me as inadequate. To be sure, they are factually and, also, politically correct, grounded as they are in contemporaneous conventional wisdoms such as unconscious biases, rigid workplace structures, and inadequately supportive public policies. They are, in other words, necessary to understanding what has happened or, more pointedly, to understanding what has not happened. But are they sufficient? Do we know as much as we might about the persistence of women in the middle but not at the top? This chapter seeks to answer this question. It turns to sociobiology to expand our understanding of women and leadership.

I grant that human beings are different from other animals. But, for the purposes of this discussion, from this point on I am going to assume that human beings are human *animals* and that, as such, they are governed by the laws of biology. More specifically, the remainder of this chapter will be grounded in sociobiology: the scientific study of the biological basis of social behaviors in organisms, including human beings. The assumption is that by comparing ourselves to other, similar, species, we have something to learn about our own, particularly as it relates to women and leadership. Harvard professor Edward O. Wilson, who did more than anyone else to insert sociobiology into the mainstream of modern scientific thought, describes the discipline as attempting to "place humankind in its proper place in a catalog of the social species on Earth." His assertion was that this "macroscopic view has certain advantages over the traditional anthropocentrism of the social sciences. In fact, no intellectual vice is more crippling than defiantly self-indulgent anthropocentrism" (Wilson, 2004, p. 17).

Wilson emphasized what on some level we already know: that human history goes back much further than we generally remember. So, if we really want to understand human nature, we cannot simply go back six millennia, we must go back hundreds of millennia, to precivilizations, to evolution as a conception. What we discover then is that when humans became meat eaters, they found that the most reliable way to get meat was to have a division of labor. For a group to harvest a high-energy, widely dispersed source of food, such as a large animal, roaming about as a loosely organized pack of children and adults was inefficient. It was much more efficient for women and their children to remain, in effect, at home, at their campsites, while men went out to hunt for meat, later to share with those left behind. This increased the likelihood that not only would the men survive but their women and, especially, their children as well—children who had to survive to ensure that the group, the species, did the same. In other words, toward the beginning of human history was a gender division: a division of labor between men and women, in which the women stayed at home to do the domestic work, child care particularly, while the men left home to bring back the bacon.

This origin story is important because it explains in part why, in "most non-human primate species and in virtually all human societies, mothers are the primary caregivers of infants" (Smith, 2005, p. 35). The eminent biologist Robert Sapolsky (2017) put it this way: "Everybody needs a mother. Even rodents; separate rat pups from Mom a few hours daily and, as adults, they have elevated glucocorticoid levels and poor cognitive skills, are anxious, and, if male, are more aggressive. Mothers are crucial" (p. 188). Naturally, there are several reasons why mothers are primary caregivers, not just one, including brawnier fathers who historically certainly have been better equipped to secure food than feebler mothers; and, of course, mammal mothers who have breasts that lactate. As Harriet Smith (2005) pointed out, in nonhuman primates, mothers are always there. They are there *with* their infants and young children, and *for* their infants and young children.

> As a baby grows up, it uses its mother as a safe base from which to explore the world. At first, it moves a short distance away from her and then returns. . . . The infant happily embarks on its independence as long as it is neither hurt nor frightened and its mother remains close by. The baby uses its mother's body to regulate its level of arousal; when it is scared or hurt it clings, and when it is secure and comfortable, it lets go and scampers off to explore.

> (p. 46)

Obviously, certainly contemporaneously, among human mothers the range of parenting behaviors varies widely. It is affected by, shaped by, factors ranging from the ecology to the economy. Variations are especially apparent in the amount of time that mothers spend in direct contact with their babies, in patterns and preferences pertaining to nursing and in levels of responsiveness to offspring. However, what I want particularly to point out, because it so obviously bears on women and leadership, is that until recently the behavior of human mothers varied little from the basic primate patterns of parenting. Only since women, and men as well, became heavily influenced by interventions such as by the medical establishment, and only since more women began to work away from home, did human patterns of parenting begin to deviate significantly from patterns of parenting that characterize other primates. Until relatively recently, human mothers and their babies were in constant contact. Until relatively recently, human mothers nursed their babies pretty much on demand. And until relatively recently, since human mothers and their babies slept together, the former were available to respond to the latter at the first sign of their distress.

On Being a Primate Parent

Obviously not all primate parenting is alike. Different primates parent differently. But there are some commonalities, a few to which I already alluded, that seem particularly germane. Among them is the level of attachment between mother and child (Sapolsky, 2017). Invariably, if only because of the female's capacity to feed her child, this level is comparatively high. In some primates, it is extremely high. For example, bonobos, when compared to chimpanzees, have a slow rate of development, which explains why bonobo mothers are more attentive to their offspring for a longer time than chimpanzee mothers. Before three months of age bonobo babies never leave their mothers, and even at six months, they are rarely seen more than a meter apart from their female parent. This does not of course mean that chimpanzee mothers are slackers. Most parental care among chimpanzees is the responsibility of the mother, and is critical to the survival and well-being of their offspring. This persists until 6 to 9 years of age, when chimpanzees become increasingly independent, though they remain close to their mothers. (Note: Humans share 99% of their genes with chimpanzees (Wong, 2014).) Somewhat similarly, female baboons are especially vigilant during the first four months of their offspring's lives and more vigilant overall when lactating than when nonlactating. In other words, though there are differences in patterns of primate parenting, these should not detract from the overarching point: among all or at least most new primate mothers there is a strong tendency, born for eons out of necessity, to stay close to their children.

Increasingly scientists—now generally free from the constraints of having, for religious reasons, to artificially separate human animals from other animals—are studying similarities between human and nonhuman primates. For example, an article in the journal *Neuroscience and Biobehavioral Reviews* titled "The Biology of Human Parenting: Insights from Nonhuman Primates," suggested that *all* primate parenting is sensitive not only to experience and to social and cognitive processes but also to neuroendocrine mechanisms. In fact, it is precisely because "many psychological and social mechanisms underlying parenting are likely to be very similar in humans and other primates" that we can presume that "primates represent excellent animal modes to investigate the potential role played by neuroendocrine mechanisms in regulating human parenting and in how these mechanisms interact with psychological and social processes" (Maestripieri, 1999, p. 411).

Similarly, an article in *Science* notes that it became possible in recent years to explore the biological correlates of human parenting through technologies such as brain imaging, endocrine studies, and gene association studies. What such studies show is that "similar mechanisms support animal and human parenting, with a shift to greater involvement of cortical systems in humans" (Rilling & Young, 2014, p. 771). In other words, while human animals and other animals are not the same, there are powerful similarities, especially between humans and other mammals. Moreover, future studies are likely to find "even more parallels in the regulation of parenting and its consequences" between, for example, rodents and humans (Rilling & Young, 2014, p. 776).

In 2017, a pioneering study published in the journal *Nature* identified a genetic basis for monogamous behavior in mice. While the finding that genes play a role in the social and sexual behaviors of mice was, of itself, interesting, it was the possible if not probable parallels between humans and mice that gained the most attention. As the *New York Times* put it, "The finding may one day help scientists make sense of how human couples bond and care for their children. Mammals share many of the genes governing the production of hormones and neurotransmitters in the brain" (Zimmer, 2017, para. 6). All this is, of course, not only of theoretical interest but of possible practical consequence. Seems the more we understand about the power of the mother-child bond, especially, the more we understand about why women and leadership was, until very recently, tantamount almost to being an oxymoron.

Which brings us to fathers. What part does Daddy play in bringing up baby? Here's the good news, sort of. In about 90% of bird species, the males stay around to help. They share the duties of nest-building. They incubate eggs. They feed brooding females and the chicks. They even train their young to lead independent lives. But, depending on your point of view, here is the bad news: Among mammals the figures are very different. "Males provide direct care of their young in less than 5% of mammal species. . . . Most mammal fathers are deadbeats with a 'love 'em and leave 'em' approach, sticking around only to mate" (Ackerman, 2016, para. 1). I hasten to add that the paternal behavior of adult male primates with infants varies widely. It "runs the gamut from co-primary caregiver to disinterested onlooker" (Smith, 2005, p. 76), with human primate fathers coming out rather well, particularly in comparison with their nonhuman primate brethren.

Human fathers can and sometimes do provide three types of paternal care. They protect against infanticide. They give sustenance. And they bestow resources. But the role of devoted caregiver is not one that male primates generally embrace, either human or nonhuman. In fact, "there appear to be no human societies in which fathers *typically* act as co-primary caregivers" (Smith, 2005, p. 82). In a study of 80 preindustrial human cultures, mothers were primarily if not exclusively the caretakers of infants (Smith, 2005). Importantly, those societies in which fathers are most involved with babies and young children and in which they spend most of their time in the approximate vicinities of their families are those in which monogamy is the rule. This means, among other things, that these are the circumstances in which fathers can be reasonably sure of their paternity (Smith, 2005). This issue—the issue of paternity—is in fact key to more fully understanding how primate parenting evolved. Why should a male invest in parenting unless he is reasonably certain that he is parenting his own child? With women, in contrast, no problem. There is certainty: mothers tote the embryo in utero and then deliver their child for, in effect, the world to see. Thereafter they visibly lactate, testifying yet again to their status as a parent and to their critical role in ensuring the survival of the species.

In the main, then, human fathers do not have primary responsibility for routine child care. In this sense, the behavior of fathers with their infants in both preindustrial and industrial societies "is more similar to that of nonhuman primate fathers than it is to that of primate mothers" (Smith, 2005, p. 87). This is not to say that fathers are uninvolved. They do commonly enjoy playful and enduring relationships with their children. However, the role of fathers is clearly different from and historically far less central and critical than the role of mothers. Of course, no one can write about this subject in the first quarter of the twenty-first century without acknowledging that we are living in changing times and that fathering behaviors are plastic. While father as pinch-hitter "is still the most common role played by both human and nonhuman primate fathers," it is impossible not to acknowledge that as fathers become more involved in parenting, the differences between mothers and fathers diminish. As Smith put it, "When Dad is cooking dinner and bathing the kids on a regular basis, play will no longer be his primary specialty" (Smith, 2005, p. 107).

As we move, finally, to consider the implications of the connections between human animals and other animals for women and leadership, I will state the obvious: raising a child alone is difficult. Which explains why cooperative care of young is found in all human societies, especially when the father is formally or informally polygynous and, in consequence, often or even largely absent.

Women without men around to help raise their children depend on others—other members of their families or groups—to provide additional support. It requires no great leap of imagination to speculate that when a woman with a young child has to leave her child behind even briefly, the question of who, during her absence, will care for her child becomes crucial. Small wonder recent studies indicate that policies providing assistance to families caring for young children have the biggest positive effect on women's employment and pay. One key reason: such policies help women work, while other policies help them take breaks from work. Given that "there is a higher premium for careers from *staying* in the market" (Miller, 2017b, para. 16), the relationship between child care and women and leadership seems obvious (italics mine).

Women and Leadership

I am arguing that a genuine understanding of human behavior—here the persistent paucity of women in positions of leadership—requires attention not only to proximate context but to distal cause, here the evolutionary origins of gender divisions. I am not, in other words, denying the importance of explanations other than evolution, such as those that are psychological or sociological or organizational or economic. All I am saying is that questions about complex human phenomena—why even now, well into the twenty-first century, only approximately 4.2% of *Fortune* 500 CEOs are women—demand answers that are complete and completely objective (Merelli, 2017).

The thesis that the evolutionary origins of gender divisions explain to a considerable extent the meager numbers of women leaders has one overweening policy implication. Again, this is not to say that other policies, or for that matter other personal and professional strategies, are unimportant. They are not. They are important at the individual level—such as those that pertain to competence and style and interpersonal relationships. And they are important at the institutional level—such as those that pertain to commitment and training and sponsoring and behavioral design. Rather it is to say that those measures, public and private, that *support women in their roles as mothers* are likely to have the greatest impact, both short and long term. Among their other benefits, they are likely to contribute the most consistently and significantly to increasing the number of women in leadership roles.

Given the growing recognition that most women struggle when they return to work within weeks or months after having had a baby—we are, after all, primates—as earlier mentioned, at least some organizations are acknowledging the challenge. In consequence, they are offering benefits (especially to women they really want to retain) such as, for instance, a slow transition back to work and breast-milk shipping services. There is, moreover, apt advice all over the place, for example, in a recent book tellingly titled *Back to Work After Baby: How to Plan and Navigate a Mindful Return From Maternity Leave*, which, however, as its title suggests, puts the onus for "navigating a mindful return from maternity leave" on the woman, not on the system within which she is embedded (Mihalich-Levin, 2017). But this is so important an issue that to in effect privatize it, to leave it up to individuals and individual groups and organizations to chart their own course, is to surrender it to the vagaries of the marketplace. The hard truth is that if we want more women to be leaders, what we need above all are *public policies designed to support mothers*.

To be sure, as we have seen in the Scandinavian example, family-friendly public policies are not any sort of panacea. It appears that mothers' impulse to be near their infants and young children transcend in importance even the most well-intentioned and well-designed public policies. Still, from everything we now know about the human animal, good, affordable child care especially is critical to enabling women to ascend the professional ladder. "Of any policy aimed to help struggling families, aid for high-quality child care has the biggest economic payoff for parents and their children—and even their grandchildren" (Miller, 2017b, para. 2). Among its other benefits, such child care enables women to stay at work, to remain at their jobs without suffering the deleterious professional effects of significant interruption in their professional trajectories.

Again, it seems clear that not all women, especially if they are new mothers, want to "stay in the market." Many, for reasons we now better understand, prefer to stay at home if they can with their babies, certainly during the first year, even if they think, or know, that it will hurt their careers—even if they think, or know, that it will make it less likely that they will in time be a "leader." After all, from what we can now tell, women tend to be less ambitious in the conventional sense than men. Nevertheless, we can certainly surmise that more women would opt to remain in the workplace even after motherhood if they could be assured that their babies and young children were receiving top flight child care.

Which raises this question—why are they not? Why are American children particularly disadvantaged in this regard? The fault, dear reader, is not in the stars, but in ourselves. As I earlier indicated, Americans remain ambivalent about whether mothers of young children should even be working outside the home—not to speak of working exceedingly hard, as senior leaders and managers are apt to do. Additionally, Americans lack a robust feminist movement or any sort of critical political mass that is consciously and carefully organized to push for and, in time, pass legislation that would make it measurably easier for women to reach leadership roles at the highest levels. The bottom line is this: the distance that separates us from other mammals and, for that matter, from our earlier selves, is not great. Among other similarities, while males and females make babies, it is the female of the species that carries babies, delivers babies, and subsequently feeds babies. Inevitably, then, ineluctably, the primal connection between leadership and lactation persists—which is why good, affordable child care should not be an individual issue, but an institutional one.

References

Ackerman, J. (2016, June 16). Why bird dads are superior. *Wall Street Journal*. Retrieved from www.wsj.com/articles/why-bird-fathers-are-superior-1466086239

Berman, J. (2017, April 4). Equal pay day: This is how much more unpaid work women do than men. *Marketwatch*. Retrieved from www.marketwatch.com/story/this-is-how-much-more-unpaid-work-women-do-than-men-2017-03-07

Bureau of Labor Statistics. (2014). Leave benefits: Access. *Employee Benefits Survey*. Retrieved from www.bls.gov/ncs/ebs/benefits/2014/ownership/civilian/table32a.htm

Caruso, C. (2016, December 19). Pregnancy causes lasting changes in a woman's brain. *Scientific American*. Retrieved from www.scientificamerican.com/article/pregnancy-causes-lasting-changes-in-a-womans-brain/

Center for American Women and Politics. (2017). *Women in the U.S. Congress 2017*. Retrieved from www.cawp.rutgers.edu/women-us-congress-2017

Coontz, S. (2017, March 31). Do millennial men want stay-at-home wives? *New York Times*. Retrieved from www.nytimes.com/2017/03/31/opinion/sunday/do-millennial-men-want-stay-at-home-wives.html

Ely, R. J., Stone, P., & Ammerman, C. (2014). Rethink what you 'know' about high-achieving women. *Harvard Business Review*, 92(12), 100–109.

Family Caregiver Alliance. (2003). *Women and caregiving: facts and figures*. San Francisco, CA: National Center on Caregiving at Family Caregiver Alliance.

Filipovic, J. (2017, April 28). Are women allowed to love their jobs? *New York Times*. Retrieved from www.nytimes.com/2017/04/28/opinion/sunday/are-women-allowed-to-love-their-jobs.html

Fox, M. (2016, August 22). More moms breastfeed but not for long enough, experts say. *NBC News*. Retrieved from www.nbcnews.com/health/health-news/more-moms-are-breastfeeding-their-babies-not-long-enough-experts-n636216

Gino, F., Wilmuth, C. A., & Brooks, A. W. (2015). Compared to men, women view professional advancement as equally attainable, but less desirable. *Proceedings of the National Academy of Sciences*, 112(40), 12354–12359.

Hegedus, N. (2012, December 17). In Sweden, women make up 45% of parliament but only 13% of corporate leadership. *Quartz*. Retrieved from https://qz.com/37036/in-sweden-women-make-up-45-of-parliament-but-only-13-of-corporate-leadership/

Hoekzema, E., Barba-Müller, E., Pozzobon, C., Picado, M., Lucco, F., García-García, D., . . . Vilarroya, O. (2017). Pregnancy leads to long-lasting changes in human brain structure. *Nature neuroscience*, 20(2), 287–296.

Jaekel, A., & St-Onge, E. (2016, October 25). Why women aren't making it to the top of financial services firms. *Harvard Business Review*. Retrieved from https://hbr.org/2016/10/why-women-arent-making-it-to-the-top-of-financial-services-firms

Jenkins, P., Marriage M., & Noonan, L. (2017). Diversity delay sparks anger and frustration. *Financial Times*, 13.

Kellerman, B. (2003). You've come a long way, baby—and you've got a long way to go. In D. Rhode (Ed.), *The difference 'difference' makes* (pp. 54–55). Stanford, CA: Stanford University Press.

Maestripieri, D. (1999). The biology of human parenting: Insights from nonhuman primates. *Neuroscience & Biobehavioral Reviews*, 23(3), 411–422.

McKinsey & Company. (2007). *Women matter: Gender diversity, a corporate performance driver*. Retrieved from www.raeng.org.uk/publications/other/women-matter-oct-2007

Merelli, A. (2017, March 7). Only 4.2% of Fortune 500 companies are run by women. *Quartz*. Retrieved from https://qz.com/925821/how-rare-are-female-ceos-only-4-2-of-fortune-500-companies-are-run-by-women/

Mihalich-Levin, L. (2017). *Back to work after baby: How to plan and navigate a mindful return from maternity leave*. Washington, DC: Mindful Return.

Miller, C. C. (2016, October 25). Winning? A women's problem is actually deciding to run. *New York Times*. Retrieved from www.nytimes.com/2016/10/25/upshot/the-problem-for-women-is-not-winning-its-deciding-to-run.html

Miller, C. C. (2017a, May 13). Motherhood has role in the gender pay gap. *New York Times*. Retrieved from www.nytimes.com/2017/05/13/upshot/the-gender-pay-gap-is-largely-because-of-motherhood.html

Miller, C. C. (2017b, April 20). The power of day care. *New York Times*. Retrieved from www.nytimes.com/2017/04/20/upshot/how-child-care-enriches-mothers-and-especially-the-sons-they-raise.html

Organization for Economic Co-operation and Development. (2017, March 16). *Trends in parental leave policies since 1970*. Retrieved from https://www.oecd.org/els/family/PF2_5_Trends_in_leave_entitlements_around_childbirth.pdf

Princeton University Reports. (2011). *Report of the steering committee on undergraduate women's leadership*. Princeton, NJ: Princeton University.

Rhode, D. (2016). *Women and leadership*. New York, NY: Oxford University Press.

Rilling, J. K., & Young, L. J. (2014). The biology of mammalian parenting and its effect on offspring social development. *Science, 345*(6198), 771–776.

Sapolsky, R. M. (2017). *Behave: The biology of humans at our best and worst*. New York, NY: Penguin Press.

Schumpeter. (2012, August 25). The mommy track. *The Economist*. Retrieved from http:/www.economist.com/node/21560856/print

Shulevitz, J. (2016, June 12). How to fix feminism. *New York Times*. Retrieved from www.nytimes.com/2016/06/12/opinion/sunday/how-to-fix-feminism.html

Smith, H. (2005). *Parenting for primates*. Cambridge, MA: Harvard University Press.

Waller, N. (2016, September 27). How men and women see the workplace differently. *Wall Street Journal*. Retrieved from http://graphics.wsj.com/how-men-and-women-see-the-workplace-differently/

Wilson, E. O. (2004). *On human nature*. Cambridge, MA: Harvard University Press.

Wong, K. (2014, September 1). Tiny genetic differences between humans and other primates pervade the genome. *Scientific American*. Retrieved from www.scientificamerican.com/article/tiny-genetic-differences-between-humans-and-other-primates-pervade-the-genome/

Zimmer, C. (2017, April 20). Why are some mice (and people) monogamous? A study points to genes. *New York Times*. Retrieved from www.nytimes.com/2017/04/19/science/parenting-genes-study.html

15

DO COMPETITIVE ENVIRONMENTS PUSH GOOD FEMALE LEADERS AWAY? COMPETITION AND THE LEADERSHIP GENDER GAP

Jeffrey A. Flory

Unequal representation by women in key areas of leadership persists throughout society and the economy, despite recent advances and heavy resources invested in correcting imbalances. In the private sector, for example, the managerial landscape in much of the industrialized world is heavily tilted toward men. The relative absence of women is particularly striking at the top—almost 95% of *Fortune* 500 CEOs in the U.S., for example, are male (Bellstrom, 2015; Leahey, Fairchild, & Zarya, 2016; Murray, 2016; Zweigenhaft, 2015). This gender imbalance persists among lower levels of corporate leadership as well, and extends far beyond the large and well-known companies. For example, among all U.S. businesses with at least 100 employees, the proportion of women in management has remained mostly flat since 2000 at around 30% (Dobbin & Kalev, 2016; see Figure 15.1). These levels of female representation in leadership are remarkably low, given significant advances in educational achievements by women in the last couple of decades—for example, the proportion of MBA graduates in the U.S. accounted for by women has more than doubled since 1980 to nearly equal that of men, rising from 22% to almost 50% in 2014 (National Center for Education Statistics, 2015). While important for many reasons, this leadership gender gap has gone hand-in-hand with key economic inequalities, such as women being significantly behind men in wages, income, and career advancement (e.g., Altonji & Blank, 1999; Azmat, Guell, & Manning, 2006; Bertrand & Hallock, 2001; Blau & Kahn, 2000; Goldin, 1990).[1]

Sharp gender imbalances in leadership are also pervasive in the public sector. While this is perhaps most striking in the percentage of U.S. presidents and vice presidents that have been women (zero, for anyone not keeping track), female representation among presidential cabinets also remains low (17% in 2017), and female representation in U.S. Congress remains below 20% in 2017. At

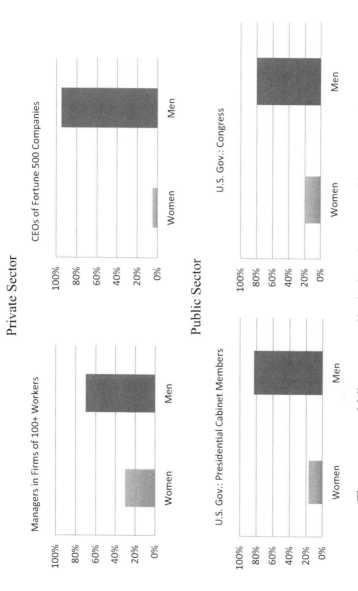

FIGURE 15.1 The percentage of different types of leadership roles comprised by women and men

the state level, the percentage of governors accounted for by women has stayed below 25% over the last decade, and female representation in state legislatures has hovered around 20%–24% for the last quarter of a century.[2]

While discrimination, stereotypes, and human capital differences are all likely to play a role (Blau & Kahn, 2000; Goldin & Rouse, 2000; Reuben, Sapienza, & Zingales, 2010; Spencer, Steele, & Quinn, 1999), a prominent new line of research in economics has uncovered another critical factor that may be driving these gender imbalances: men and women can react very differently to competition incentives and competitive environments. A rich and growing literature in the field of experimental economics has shown that, even among men and women of the same skill level, men have a tendency to be attracted to situations in which they compete, while women often avoid these situations. Indeed, a consistent pattern of behavior replicated across a wide variety of settings suggests women often shy away from competitive environments, whereas men covet them and often thrive in them (Gneezy, Niederle, & Rustichini, 2003; Niederle & Vesterlund, 2007). This may help explain the relative dearth of women in top positions and high-profile careers in private or government sectors, since such positions are typically achieved through competition against others.

This evidence first emerged based on insights from lab experiments that explore the different environments in which men and women prefer to work for short periods on specific tasks. More recent work has also unearthed provocative and insightful findings from experiments conducted with actual employees in real workplaces, which confirm these behavior patterns do in fact affect decisions about genuine jobs and employment. The origins of this gender difference in reaction to competition are still a matter of debate (current evidence suggests that both nature and nurture play important roles).[3] However, its existence across a multitude of settings and its impacts on career and job choices by men and women are by now well established. The question is what to do about it. This chapter discusses major findings emanating from the latest work in this area and explores some of the practical policies and approaches to correcting gender imbalances suggested by this research.

What Do We Mean by Differences in Competitiveness Between Men and Women?

It is helpful to clarify a few important concepts and terminology to provide some more complete context for the discussion in this chapter. First, the word "competitive" can have a variety of meanings. In this chapter, I use the word to mean something very specific: willingness to compete against other individuals for a reward (e.g., a monetary prize, a job, a promotion, elected office, etc.). This discussion is not meant to imply that this trait is bad or good per se. While much of modern culture and society would seem to extol the virtues of being competitive, for this narrow definition of competitiveness as willingness to enter competitions, it is not clear that it is necessarily "good" to be competitive.[4]

The value of entering a competition depends on the costs incurred by choosing to invest the time, energy, personal or emotional commitment, and other resources into competing, and possibly losing all those investments, against the potential benefits of winning (and possible enjoyment from the act of competing itself). Whether the benefits of competing outweigh the costs will differ from person to person. However, the fact that competitions are such a widely used tool to select individuals for various roles in society, the economy, and public life (entrance into a high-profile career track, a job promotion within a firm, a coveted role in public office, etc.) means that differences in willingness to compete that fall along lines of gender or identity, rather than skill, can create unequal representation in different sectors of the economy and in positions of power, wealth, and leadership that are not based on ability. That is, if certain segments of the population are systematically more drawn toward competitions (regardless of their ability to win them) while other segments are systematically pushed away from them (even if they are skilled enough to win), this can create important imbalances in representation that are troubling not only from a perspective of equity but also from efficiency—i.e., maximizing economic and social benefits.

Second, it is important to bear in mind that when we speak of sex-based behavioral differences, we are talking about characteristics of the *entire population* of women as compared to the *entire population* of men—not specific individuals. The strength of any given behavioral trait (generosity, risk-taking, competitiveness, etc.) varies from individual to individual, such that individual people lie along a distribution from the very low end to the very high end—think of a simple bell curve, for example. There is absolutely no question that there are extremely competitive women and extremely competitive men—these would be taken from the right tail of the distribution for men and women. Rather, the question is whether the distribution for all male individuals looks different than that for all female individuals. Another way to think of it is whether women *on average* are more or less willing to compete than men *on average*. Figure 15.2 helps illustrate this point. It shows two hypothetical distributions of competitiveness—one for men and one for women. The horizontal axis represents willingness to compete, and the vertical axis represents the percentage of all individuals (the percentage of all women in one curve, the percentage of all men in the other). The figure depicts the population of males as being further to the right than that for females—i.e., more competitive in general—but note that there are still some women just as there are some men in the far right tail that are extremely competitive. It is just that there are more men than women in the far right tail. The question from a social scientific and policy perspective is whether this hypothetical figure depicts the truth.

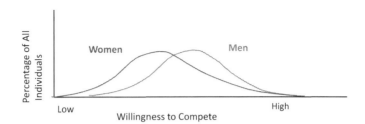

FIGURE 15.2   Hypothetical distribution of competitiveness across the entire population of men and women

Finally, note that ability, talent, intelligence, creativity, people and management skills, etc., may not necessarily go along with a high degree of competitiveness. This can be a major problem if we want highly talented and skilled
individuals as leaders and yet we are using selection mechanisms that involve
competition. Some highly skilled individuals who might be great leaders may
never throw their hat in the ring simply because they do not enjoy competing.
This can become an even bigger problem if we are interested in greater gender
equity in leadership and if there is a male-female difference in willingness to
compete. It therefore behooves us to better understand whether there might be
a gender gap in willingness to compete, and if so, how large it is, what causes it,
how it manifests, and whether its dissuasive impacts on women's participation
in certain activities can be mitigated.

Do Competitive Environments Deter Entry by Women?

As it turns out, there is very strong evidence that such a difference between
men and women in willingness to compete does in fact exist. One of the first,
most rigorous, and certainly the most well-known study on this comes from
a lab experiment by Niederle and Vesterlund (2007), who show a very sharp
difference between men and women in willingness to enter competitions and
provide insights into some of the possible explanations for why. Their findings
have been widely replicated over the last decade. As a brief background, these
lab experiments typically proceed as follows. First, the experimenter recruits
a group of undergraduate students to participate in an experiment in which
they can earn money for their performance of a given task. Once situated, the
experimenter introduces the task—calculating simple math problems, solving
mazes, verbal puzzles or games, throwing a ball in a bucket, etc. Subjects are
paid based on how well they do at the task and are often given the chance to
first experience two different compensation regimes before they are then asked
to choose their preferred compensation regime of the two. Subjects typically
have a choice between a noncompetitive piece-rate incentive scheme and a

tournament incentive scheme. For example, under the piece-rate, the subject might be paid $1 per successful attempt over a five minute period (e.g. $1 for each addition problem correctly solved, or each ball successfully thrown into a bucket, or each maze solved, etc.). Under the tournament pay regime, the subject might be paid $3 per successful attempt if she outperforms one or more anonymous competitors and $0 per success if she is not the winner.

A result that has consistently emerged from these experiments is that men tend to prefer the competitive environment over the noncompetitive environment, whereas women tend to prefer the noncompetitive environment. Moreover, this is true even in tasks where women are more skilled and even for high-ability women who likely would have won the competition had they entered it. In their pioneering study with 80 undergraduate students from the University of Pittsburgh, Niederle and Vesterlund (2007) found that 73% of men choose the competition regime, while only 35% of women do, in a simple addition task in which there is no difference between men and women in performing the task. (They use a math task, and men and women both correctly solve about 10.5 addition problems on average under the piece-rate and 12 problems in the tournament.) That is, even though they are not any worse at the task, the women in their subject pool are less than half as likely as the men to choose to compete. The similar performances between men and women mean that there is no gender difference in the probability of winning when everyone is forced to compete—men and women both have about a 25% chance of winning.

So, when given the chance of choosing whether or not to compete, why do more than twice as many men enter the competition than women, even if they are not more skilled at the task? The authors advance two main explanations. The first is that men are far more overconfident than women. They found that among their subjects, both men and women tend to believe they have a higher chance of winning than they actually do—that is, they believe their own performance puts them at a higher rank compared to their peers than it actually does. However, this over-assessment of own ability compared to others is much higher among men than among women. For men, the belief that they are better than their would-be competitors causes even low-performing men to enter the competition, despite the fact that they will likely lose (and therefore earn $0). For women, their mild overconfidence in their own ability still is not enough to push them into competing—something continues to hold them back

The second explanation the authors advance as a main driver is a difference between men and women in *preference* for competition. They hypothesize that men may derive joy from the act of competing itself and that women may experience the opposite—a type of "psychic cost" rather than the "psychic benefit" that men get out of competing. They note there are plausible origins for a gender-based pleasure or displeasure from competition that are biological (e.g., evolution) as well as others that are cultural (e.g., socialization). Whatever the original cause, they found that even after eliminating the effects from differences between men and women in confidence, as well as any possible effects from differences between men and women in risk-appetites, there remains a significant difference between men and women in their willingness to enter tournaments. The authors concluded that over 40% of the gap between men and women in willingness to enter competitive environments is driven by this pure taste (or distaste) for operating under the pressure of competition.

The result of these two factors (a gender difference in confidence and in competition preference) is an enormous gap between men and women in the willingness to enter into competitions. They also lead to large proportions of men and women making the wrong choice—at least in terms of what would give them the highest reward from working on the task. A substantial proportion of low-performing male subjects select into the competitive environment, which makes the overall monetary reward for these men *lower* than it would be if they chose piece-rate, since they are likely to lose the competition (they simply are not good enough to win). They also found a large proportion of high-performing female subjects avoid the competitive environment and select the piece-rate, which makes *their* overall monetary payoff from working on the task lower than it would be. Had these women chosen the competition, they would likely have won and made far more money.

From the perspective of using competition mechanisms to select the highest-skilled individuals to fill certain positions, the fact that competitions seem able to attract many low-ability men along with the high-ability ones poses a relatively moderate problem. Since the lower ability of these men inhibits their ability to win competitions, they are likely to be eliminated from the candidate pool anyway and thus not be selected. However, the fact that high-ability women are pushed away is far more serious. If they do not enter the competition, they clearly cannot be selected even if they are the most skilled. This would mean competition-based selection mechanisms are pushing away high talent—and pushing away highly skilled women in particular. Beyond the possibility that this pushes high-ability women away from top positions, we also see a clear negative material consequence to women who eschew competitive environments. At least in the well-defined environment of tasks done in a lab, the authors found this tendency causes women to make choices that lead to lower monetary outcomes for themselves.

This gender difference, by now quite thoroughly documented across several laboratory experiments, has also been recently shown to have substantial impact on career choices and willingness to enter into certain jobs or work environments. For example, Buser, Niederle, and Oosterbeek (2014) show in one study that choices over willingness to enter competitions in the lab strongly predict what type of academic field high school boys and girls go into, in an environment in the Netherlands where this choice has a significant effect on future career outcomes. The authors found that, even among students with the same academic ability, willingness to enter competitions strongly correlated with entrance into the more prestigious fields of math and science.

Expanding this research in a different direction, Flory, Leibbrandt, and List (2015) conducted the first experimental study to directly test whether the findings that come from the lab also manifest in choices of men and women in their daily lives. By running an experiment in the field that included over 9,000 job-seekers from all across the U.S., they examined whether competitive environments can push women away and whether they create a gender gap in willingness to work in a given position. Using job ads and variation in wage contracts for a real job that hired people into 30 different open positions, they were able to examine *directly* whether the persisting gap in employment outcomes between men and women can be attributed to responses to competition and whether women disproportionately shy away from competitive work settings.

More specifically, in order to test whether men and women respond differently to competitive work environments, they posted employment advertisements to an internet job board in 16 major U.S. cities and randomized interested job-seekers into different compensation regimes for the same type of position. That is, if a given individual expressed interest in the open position, the compensation structure they were offered was then randomly determined (i.e. by chance, through a random number generator—the digital equivalent of a roll of a die).[5] So if two different individuals in a given city were interested in the job, they could end up with different compensation structures. There were five different basic pay regimes that a job-seeker could be offered: (1) fixed-wage compensation, (2) compensation depending mildly on individual relative performance, (3) compensation depending heavily on individual relative performance, (4) team relative performance, or (5) on elements of uncertainty. Each job-seeker was only ever made aware of the pay regime he or she was offered and did not know that other job-seekers could have been offered different pay regimes. After being told the pay regime, each job-seeker then decided whether to formally apply for the position or instead not apply.

This is the first known attempt to analyze whether competition incentives affect men's and women's labor choices differently using a controlled natural economic setting where subjects are unaware they are part of an experiment.[6] In some ways, the findings confirmed many of the results from the lab-based literature, but there were also some intriguing and instructive differences. Similar to the robust findings from the lab that even highly skilled women have a far greater tendency than men to avoid environments where rewards are based on competition with others, Flory et al. (2015) found that competitive workplaces create a gender disparity in job interest. In particular, they found that when switching from the fixed wage to pay that depends on relative performance, the probability that men apply rose by as much as 15 percentage points compared to the probability that women apply. This can be seen in

Figure 15.3a. While there was already somewhat of a gender gap in application rates even in the fixed-wage regime, this 15 percentage-point jump in likelihood of men applying compared to women due to the introduction of competition-based compensation causes the gap between men and women in interest for the job to increase by 125%. Figure 15.3b shows that this 15 percentage-point jump in the gender gap induced by the competitive work environment is due almost entirely to women becoming less interested in the job. Compared to the fixed-wage pay structure, where 45% of initially interested women applied, under the relative-performance-based pay regime, only 30% of initially interested women followed through and completed the application after learning the pay structure.

Importantly, however, they also found several features of the work environment that can reduce this effect. For example, if competition in the workplace is team-based rather than individual, such that pay is affected by the relative performance of one's team with respect to another team, the competition-based pay regime no longer induces a gap in interest between men and women. Also, when the stakes of the competition are decreased, so that a smaller proportion of the employee's compensation depends on whether she performs better or worse than her coworker, the gender gap caused by the competition-based pay

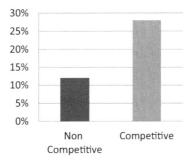

FIGURE 15.3a   How much more likely men are to apply compared to women

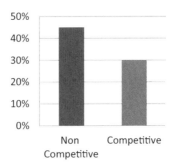

FIGURE 15.3b   Percent of women applying

regime shrinks to the point of disappearing. The type of job task and nature of the work also appears to play an important role: when switching from a version of the job that has more stereotypical male associations to a version that has more stereotypical female associations, the impact of the competition-based pay regime drops considerably.

The Impact of Age on the Gender Gap in Desire to Compete

As the number of studies exploring the gender difference in competitiveness has continued to expand and the pattern of a sharp difference between men and women in willingness to enter competitions becomes increasingly clear, several new insights have emerged that help us better understand some of the limits of this difference and its potential causes. For example, several studies have found compelling evidence that age can play an important role in the manifestation of sex-based differences in willingness to compete. This is important, since the standard population used for most lab experiments is comprised by university students. If a person's age affects competitiveness, for men or women (or both), this will not be detected if all studies focus on adults age 18–22 (the most common ages for undergrads).

Since students are an easily accessible population for participants in lab experiments, it is perhaps not surprising that discussion of the impacts of age initially focused on what happens when moving to populations younger than university students. Dreber, Essen, and Ranehill (2011) tested for evidence of sex-based differences in willingness to compete among 7- to 10-year-olds using a variety of tasks, including running races, jumping rope, and dancing, and found no evidence of any difference in willingness to compete between boys and girls. Andersen, Ertac, Gneezy, List, and Maximiano (2013) also found no gender gap in willingness to compete among preadolescent children but evidence that girls become less competitive right around the age of puberty.

More recently, a handful of studies are expanding the age range of subjects upward and beginning to discover evidence that the gap may also disappear as adults grow older. For example, Flory, Gneezy, Leonard, and List (in press) conducted lab experiments with over 800 adults ranging in age from 18 to 90 years old and found the gender difference in willingness to compete completely disappeared right around age 50. Following the experimental protocol created by Niederle and Vesterlund (2007), they replicated the main findings of the earlier study among student-aged adults, showing a sharp difference between men and women in preference for entering competitions, causing men to be 15–25 percentage points more likely to enter competitions, regardless of ability. However, when moving to older-age adults they found the gap completely vanishes, and that this is driven mostly by a sharp rise in women's willingness to compete right around age 50. While the men in their study showed no evidence of any change in competitiveness across age, women 50 and older are far more willing to compete than women under 50. In fact, the difference between younger women and more mature women in competitiveness is as large as the gap between younger men and younger women (if not larger).

These findings are illustrated in Figures 15.4a and 15.4b, which show the percentage of men and women in different age categories that select to perform a task under the competitive compensation regime in round three of the experiment after having experienced working on the task under the noncompetitive regime in round one and the competitive regime in round two. The results shown are from a sample of adults in the U.S. between the ages of 18 and 75. In Figure 15.4a, we see in the first two columns that among individuals below the age of 50, men are far more likely to enter the competitive work environment: while about 40% of women choose to enter competition, nearly 70% of men do. However, in the last two columns, the gap between men and women completely disappears and even slightly reverses: while about 70% of men 50 and older choose competition, 75% of women do. Figure 15.4b presents the same data, but slightly rearranged to underscore the source of this dramatic change in the gender gap in competitiveness around age 50. In the first two columns, we see quite clearly that younger men are no more nor less willing to compete than more mature men—about 70% from each age group compete. The last two

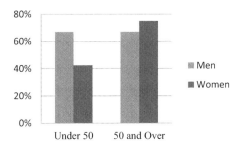

FIGURE 15.4a Gender difference in competition entry U.S. sample

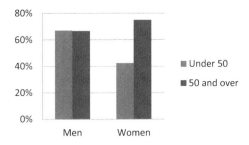

FIGURE 15.4b Age difference in competition entry U.S. sample

columns show a dramatic spike in willingness of women to compete when moving above age 50—a jump from about 40% in the younger age group to 75% in the more mature age group. Thus the probability that older women choose to compete is nearly twice that of younger women.

It is worth noting that this simple first-cut analysis of the data does not take into consideration potential differences in skill level between men and women at the task. However, more careful analysis of the data by the authors shows that the same underlying pattern—a sharp difference between men and women at younger ages, a large spike in competition entry among women after age 50, and no change in competition entry by men as age increases—remains even after accounting for the influence of ability to perform the task. Thus they found that older women have just as strong a preference for competition as men of all ages, independent of skill level, causing the gender gap in competitiveness to vanish among older adults.

The experiment was conducted not only in the U.S. but also in an extremely different setting—rural villages in the sub-Saharan country of Malawi. Intriguingly, while overall rates of competition entry were somewhat lower in Malawi, the gender pattern was exactly the same: a large gap between younger women and all men which completely vanished when moving across the age 50 threshold due to a jump in competitiveness among women after this age. The authors interpret the fact that age 50 is the focal point of this result in such widely differing cultures as suggestive that menopause may play a role in the change in competitive disposition of women. They note this could be due to hormonal shifts and the neuroendocrinological evidence linking hormones and behavior (particularly a handful of studies showing links between competition choices among women and estrogen, progesterone, and cortisol levels), or to possible changes in social roles and expectations that may accompany a woman's transition to nonchildbearing years, or both. Whatever the underlying reason, the empirical results are sharp and have strong implications: while many had taken the robust evidence of a gender difference in early adulthood as indicative of how adults at all ages behave, this study is the first to suggest this may be far from the truth and that such a perspective may be severely underestimating the competitiveness of more mature women.

Two other studies (Charness & Villeval, 2009; Buser, Geijtenbeek, & Plug, 2015) used lab experiments to examine competition preferences among adults of a broad age range. Both studies had relatively few adults in the student age range compared to many more subjects of older ages, and neither study found a measurable difference between men and women in their preference for competition. This is precisely what we would expect if younger adult women shy away from competition while more mature women are just as competitive as (or slightly more competitive than) all men, since the competitiveness of the latter would push the average competitiveness of all women in the sample up, closing the gender gap. In their field experiment study of job-entry decisions of adult men and women in actual labor markets, Flory et al. (2015) also found evidence that the gender gap in willingness to enter a competitive environment shrinks with age such that it disappears among older adults. Their finding also appears to be driven by an increase in women's willingness to enter competitive environments relative to that of men as women age.

Finally, there is one other study whose results stand somewhat apart from those already mentioned. Mayr, Wozniak, Davidson, Kuhns, and Harbaugh (2012) reported that men are more willing to compete than women at all ages. Since their design makes it possible they are detecting differences in appetites for risk rather than interest in competing and the task they use in their experiment may deemphasize interpersonal aspects of competition, it is unclear whether their findings support or challenge those discussed earlier. This suggests more work and replication around age effects is needed before firmly concluding that women become more competitive with age.

However, if the gender gap does in fact disappear at some age because older women are more competitive, this has important practical implications for women in leadership. For example, it may imply that workplaces and other environments with high levels of competitiveness disproportionately deter women compared to men only within certain age ranges and not in others. It also implies that selection mechanisms based on competition may indeed systematically disadvantage women, but perhaps not at all ages. If women with almost half their professional lives in front of them are no less competitive than men, incentives should take this into account in order to more effectively achieve their ends. It may also affect how to best design processes used to select skilled leaders—managers, executives, elected officials, and other leadership roles—with possible differences in the use of competition-based selection methods based at least partly on age. Since the impact of age on competitive disposition of men and women remains a relatively new area, patience is warranted before moving too swiftly on policy implications. But the practical importance is clear.

How Universal Is This Greater Competitiveness in Men Than Women?

Exploring the question of universality of the male-female competitiveness gap in a different direction, several studies examined the extent to which culture and socialization may play a role in the genesis of this gender gap, which may in turn shed light on possible policy approaches to shrink or eliminate the gap or prevent it from appearing in the first place. First, while the original findings by Niederle and Vesterlund (2007) of a large difference between men and women in willingness to compete was based on a sample of students from the University of Pittsburgh, many of the replications of their findings since that time come from other Western modern industrialized countries—predominantly European. So there is little evidence that it is purely a U.S. phenomenon.

Second, several studies have found very similar results in nonindustrialized developing countries. For example, the Flory et al. (2017a) study discussed earlier, which found a very similar size in the gender gap among student-aged adults when using the same protocol, involved subjects from villages in rural Malawi (a sub-Saharan country in Africa among the poorest countries in the world) in its main experiment. Moreover, in a smaller follow-up experiment that involved adults from the U.S. and which used the exact same experimental protocol, they found the exact same pattern as among the adults from rural Malawi: a large gender gap among student-age adults, no change in willingness of men to compete as age increases, and a sharp increase in willingness of women to compete right around age 50, causing more mature women to be just as competitive as all men so that the gender gap disappears. So there is also little evidence that this is a behavioral phenomenon limited to the modern Western world.

There is, however, some very intriguing evidence on the role of culture that comes from a different source of cultural variation—institutions and practices of matrilineal societies. The first and most well known of these is a study by Gneezy, Leonard, and List (2009), which compared preferences for competition among men and women from a matrilineal society to those among men and women from a patriarchal society, using the same experiment. Among the subjects from the patriarchal society (men and women from the Maasai tribe in Tanzania), they found the standard result seen in many other studies throughout the world that younger men are far more competitive than younger women.[7] However, among the subjects from the matrilineal society (men and women from the Khasi tribe in the Meghalya region of northeast India), not only is there no evidence that men are more competitive than women, but in fact the *reverse* appears to be true. While the Maasai men are nearly twice as likely as Maasai women to enter competitions (50% of males compete versus 26% of females), the Khasi women are nearly 40% (14 percentage points) more likely to compete than Khasi men (54% of Khasi females competing versus 39% of Khasi men).

Two additional studies expand subject pools both along the dimension of culture as well as the dimension of age, to shed further light on the role of culture on the gender difference in competitiveness. The Andersen et al. (2013) study mentioned earlier included children from both matrilineal and patriarchal societies. Participants in the experiment were children aged 7–15 from the matrilineal Khasi of northeast India and the nearby patriarchal Kharbi society, also in northeast India. The pattern they found of no gender gap before puberty, with a gender gap that emerges around puberty due to a sharp drop in willingness to compete by girls after the onset of puberty, exists only in the patriarchal society. Among the children from the matrilineal society, there is no gender gap at any age. Flory, Leonard, Tsaneva, and Vasilaky (2017b) looked at the full spectrum of ages spanning childhood through advanced adulthood in neighboring matrilineal and patrilineal cultures in Malawi, enabling them to examine the impact of culture on both age effects that have surfaced in the literature—the onset of decreased willingness among females to compete as well as its disappearance. Among the individuals from patrilineal tribes, they found a significant gender difference in willingness to compete emerges around puberty due to a sharp decline in competitiveness among girls and that the gender difference disappears around age 50 due to a sharp increase in competitiveness among women past this age. Among individuals from matrilineal tribes living in the same general area, there is no evidence of a gender gap at any age.

Closing the Gap: Are There Ways to Increase Willingness to Compete Among Women?

Having established a strong and persistent gender gap across most societies and at least half the professionally active years of most adults (18–50), a steadily growing branch of this research has shifted its focus to testing various methods of eliminating the difference by encouraging women to compete. Findings from the lab so far are encouraging. For example, Balafoutas and Sutter (2012) identify four different techniques that work to varying degrees to encourage women to enter competitions at the same rate as men. In a lab experiment with 360 university students, they found that they can shrink the gender gap in willingness to compete by stipulating a replay of the competition if no women are among the winners the first time and that they can erase it completely by introducing quotas (so that at least one of two winners must be a woman) or by giving preferential treatment to women in saying that ties go to female contestants (in case of equal performance). Finally, they found they can even slightly reverse the gender gap when giving a stronger preferential treatment to women by stipulating that a woman performing slightly worse than a man (1 point below) beats the man. Importantly, they report that these interventions create large increases in willingness to compete by strong female performers, without dissuading competition entry from strong male performers. That is, these methods worked in the lab to induce the high-ability women to throw their hat in the ring instead of settling for the noncompetitive option, without pushing away the high-ability men. So this increased the overall number of high-quality competitors from both genders. Moreover, they showed that the four interventions did not cause any efficiency losses, a common criticism of policy tools that might pass over better-performing men for the sake of promoting women. Rather, the average ability of the winner does not change. They interpret their results on the four interventions they test in the lab as suggestive that similar types of affirmative action policies in business, politics, and academia may work to attract significantly more high-ability women into these sectors without the negative impacts on performance that some critics of affirmative action fear.

Niederle, Segal, and Vesterlund (2013) also examined an environment in which high-performing women fail to enter competitions they can win and similarly found that introducing a form of affirmative action in the lab increases female entry. In particular, they found that by guaranteeing women equal representation among winners, they are able to substantially increase the number of high-performing women in the applicant pool and help close the male-female difference in willingness to compete. Brandts, Groenert, and Rott (2014) took a different approach to addressing the gender gap and encouraging high-skilled women to throw their hat in the ring. They found that receiving advice from a more experienced and better-informed person can increase competition entry in the lab by strong-performing women and reduce it by weak-performing men. The expected gender of competitors may also have an influence: Gneezy et al. (2003) suggests women perform better in contests against women than against both women and men, and Niederle et al. (2013) suggest women may be more likely to enter contests when more of their competitors are women than men.

Finally, a few studies have found that the nature of the job task and stereotypes around that task may also matter. For example, Shurchkov (2012) replicated the standard sharp gender difference first found in Niederle and Vesterlund (2007) with a simple math task and then showed that when switching to a very different task based on verbal skills, men are no longer more willing to compete than women. She posits gender-task associations as an explanation for this finding (some have argued that stereotypes suggest men are better at simple math tasks while women are better at verbal tasks). Grosse and Riener (2010) found similar results in a lab experiment that uses a verbal task, and Niederle and Vesterlund (2011) note that while the jury is still out, it is possible the size and existence of the gender gap in competitiveness may depend partly on the task domain or type of work. This is consistent with the field experiment done in actual workplaces discussed earlier (Flory et al., 2015). There, the authors found the competition-based wage contract creates the largest gender gap in a version of the job that has stereotypically "male" associations, compared to an identical job with the male associations stripped.

***

The stubborn persistence of large gender inequalities in employment outcomes and positions of leadership is disturbing on multiple fronts—not only from an equity perspective but also for its potential negative impacts on economic growth and overall social well-being. This is particularly true when these imbalances are not the result of differences in innate ability, since it prevents the allocation of talent and labor to its most productive uses in the economy and impedes the free flow of individuals to positions and roles in society that maximize social benefits. Researchers have offered several explanations for why such gender inequities persist in labor markets, employment, and positions of power. Until recently, economists had focused most attention on the roles of gender differences in skills (Blau & Kahn, 2000), discrimination and stereotypes against women (Goldin & Rouse, 2000, Reuben, Sapienza, & Zingales., 2010; Spencer, Steele, & Quinn, 1999), and differences between men and women in time taken out of the labor force (Hotchkiss & Pitts, 2007; Phipps, Burton, & Lethbridge, 2001). This chapter highlighted a different factor believed to play a powerful role—a systematic tendency for men to be attracted to competitions and for women to avoid them, regardless of skill level.

There is a rich and dynamic literature in support of these findings, the research is still very much ongoing, and it continues to grow. As we have seen, there are some important limits to the gender difference in willingness to compete, such as the fact that it disappears in some cultures where society is more centrally organized around women, that it may depend on gender stereotypes about the work or job tasks, and that it may disappear with age as women develop an increasing proclivity for entering contests. However, since the teens and twenties are a critical period in determining life paths and career trajectories, the consistent results across most societies of a sharp male-female difference in willingness to compete during these ages is concerning. They may have large consequences on early career choices that influence later options and opportunities. If aversion to competition as a young adult closes off certain pathways to high-profile opportunities and leadership positions in later life, the findings based on young adults suggests this will contribute to substantial gender imbalances at all ages.

Nevertheless, the limits to the general pattern, coupled with the evidence that it is driven by different tastes for (or against) entering contests rather than differences in skills between men and women, suggest opportunities to help break the pattern, close the gap between men and women in willingness to throw their hat in the ring, and reduce gender imbalances in leadership roles. Breaking or minimizing gender-task associations represents just one possibility of leveraging these limits to the general pattern to try to "undo" this tendency toward competition-aversion among women. The field experiment with actual employment positions discussed earlier provides one example of how the framing of a job and its duties may either diminish or exacerbate gender differences in willingness to apply in a competitive work environment, depending on the language used. The private sector is beginning to leverage some of the findings emerging from this research—for example, through innovation in recruiting methods by major corporations and other "diversity and inclusion" initiatives that seek to raise representation of women in high-profile positions. For example, in Flory, Leibbrandt, Rott, and Stoddard (2017c), the researchers partner with recruiting activities of a *Fortune* 500 company to test the effects of messaging meant to break stereotypes in an industry typically perceived as male dominated and competitive by introducing more female associations. But there is much further room to bring practice and research together to fuel progress toward greater representation of women in top leadership roles.

Moreover, the expanding evidence that the competitiveness gap changes with age and may not exist at all for the latter half of a woman's professional life suggests that policies and approaches aimed at enhancing representation of women in leadership may benefit from accounting for this possibility. The findings around age are relatively new, and there is one study suggesting the gap may persist, so further replication is needed before drawing definitive conclusions. However, if further study confirms that the main locus of the gender difference in competitiveness is indeed among younger adults and disappears when women still have nearly half their professional lives ahead of them, this may offer policy opportunities to enhance female representation at upper levels of leadership. Examples might include targeting outreach efforts toward more mature women (if leadership positions involve working in competitive environments or passing through candidate-selection processes with a high degree of explicit competition) or de-emphasizing the role of competition, particularly at the earlier stages (i.e., younger ages) of selection funnels that ultimately lead to high-profile positions later on in one's professional life.

The set of results showing that the gender difference can depend on culture is also instructive. It suggests the observed differences may not be inherently physiological—or at the very least that culture can have a substantial mitigating impact on behaviors that may have a partly physiological origin. Behavior is often understood as jointly determined by nature and nurture. The findings on changes across matriliny and patriliny also raise the possibility that some of these behaviors may be learned through socialization, or at the very least that they are responses to institutions and social and economic arrangements that we have the ability to alter. If it is believed that it is valuable to encourage women to compete or eliminate gaps between men and women in their willingness to enter contests or work in competitive environments, these findings may help open the way for an approach through socialization or encouraging social arrangements that foster stronger inclinations toward competing among women.

Notes

1 Blau and Kahn (2000) report that according to one index of occupational segregation by sex, 54% of all women in the workforce in 1997 would have to change jobs to equalize the occupational distribution of men and women. They note that in 1999, women were still much more concentrated than men in administrative support and service occupations (accounted for by 41% of the female labor force vs. 15% that of men). They also report that weekly earnings of female full-time workers, though they rose from 61% of men's comparable earnings to 76.5% over 1978 to 1999, appear to have reached a maximum in the mid-1990s at around three-quarters the amount of male earnings. Bertrand and Hallock (2001) report that among the five highest-paid positions at each of a large sample of U.S. firms, only 2.5% are women, and they earn 45% less than the men.

2 Figures on female representation in government come from the Center for American Women and Politics. For additional information, see www.cawp.rutgers.edu/facts/levels_of_office.

3 See for example Flory et al. (2017b) for a discussion of how the logic of evolution can interact with different societal types to yield specific gender-dependent patterns in competitive behaviors.

4 Indeed, some studies suggest links between competitiveness and competition on the one hand and unethical behavior such as lying and cheating on the other. See, for example, Charness et al. (2013), and Flory et al. (2016).

5 Using randomization to assign individuals to different treatment groups (i.e. different experiences) is the cornerstone of experimental economics. This approach, sometimes referred to as a randomized control trial (RCT), is generally considered the "gold standard" in determining causality. That is, it allows us to know whether action A truly causes effect B and obtain a fairly precise measure on how large or small the impact is. For example, in this setting, using randomization to determine which compensation structure the job-seeker was offered helped ensure the control group (those offered the fixed wage) was statistically identical to each of the different treatment groups, so the post-treatment differences in behavior could be attributed to the treatment.

6 In the nomenclature of economics, this is generally referred to as a "natural field experiment"—a definition articulated in Harrison and List (2004) as an experiment with a nonstandard subject pool (i.e., not students), with field context in the task and information set, and where the subjects are naturally undertaking the tasks as part of their normal economic goings-on without knowing they are in an experiment.

7 Nearly all of their subjects were in their 20s and 30s.

References

Altonji, J. G., & Blank, R. (1999). Race and gender in the labor market. In O. Ashenfelter & D. Card (Eds.), *Handbook of Labor Economics* (Vol. 3C) (pp. 3144–3259). Amsterdam: Elsevier Science.

Andersen, S., Ertac, S., Gneezy, U., List, J. A., & Maximiano, S. (2013). Gender, competitiveness, and socialization at a young age: Evidence from a matrilineal and a patriarchal society. *Review of Economics and Statistics, 95*(4), 1438–1443.

Azmat, G., Guell, M., & Manning, A. (2006). Gender gaps in unemployment rates in OECD countries. *Journal of Labor Economics, 24,* 1–37.

Balafoutas, L., & Sutter, M. (2012). Affirmative action policies promote women and do not harm efficiency in the laboratory. *Science, 335*(6068), 579–582.

Bellstrom, K. (2015). Why 2015 was a terrible year to be a female fortune 500 CEO. *Fortune.* Retrieved from http://fortune.com/2015/12/23/2015-women-fortune-500-ceos/

Bertrand, M., & Hallock, K. F. (2001). The gender gap in top corporate jobs. *Industrial and Labor Relations Review, 55,* 3–21.

Blau, F., & Kahn, L. M. (2000). Gender differences in pay. *Journal of Economic Perspectives, 14,* 75–99.

Brandts, J., Groenert, V., & Rott, C. (2014). The impact of advice on women's and men's selection into competition. *Management Science, 61*(5), 1018–1035.

Buser, T., Geijtenbeek, L., & Plug, E. (2015). *Do gays shy away from competition? Do lesbians compete too much?* Working Paper.

Buser, T., Niederle, M., & Oosterbeek, H. (2014). Gender, competitiveness, and career choices. *The Quarterly Journal of Economics, 129*(3), 1409–1447.

Charness, G., Masclet, D., & Villeval, M. (2013). The dark side of competition for status. *Management Science, 60*(1), 38–55.

Charness, G., & Villeval, M. (2009). Cooperation and competition in intergenerational experiments in the field and the laboratory. *American Economic Review, 99*(3), 956–978.

Dobbin, F., & Kalev, A. (2016). Why diversity programs fail. *Harvard Business Review.* Retrieved from https://hbr.org/2016/07/why-diversity-programs-fail

Dreber, A., von Essen, E., & Ranehill, E. (2011). Outrunning the gender gap—boys and girls compete equally. *Experimental Economics, 14*(4), 567–582.

Flory, J. A., Gneezy, U., Leonard, K. L., & List, J. A. (in press). Gender, age, and competition: The disappearing gap. *Journal of Economic Behavior and Organization.*

Flory, J. A., Leibbrandt, A., & List, J. A. (2015). Do competitive workplaces deter female workers? A large-scale natural field experiment on gender differences in job-entry decisions. *Review of Economic Studies, 82*(1), 122–155.

Flory, J. A., Leibbrandt, A., Rott, C., & Stoddard, O. (2017c). *Increasing workplace diversity: Evidence from a recruiting experiment at a fortune 500 company.* Working paper.

Flory, J. A., Leonard, K. L., Tsaneva, M., & Vasilaky, K. (2017b). *Towards a deeper understanding of female competitiveness and the gender gap: Evidence from patrilocal and matrilocal cultures.* Working paper.

Gneezy, U., Leonard, K. L., & List, J. A. (2009). Gender differences in competition: Evidence from a matrilineal and a patriarchal society. *Econometrica, 77*(5), 1637–1664.

Gneezy, U., Niederle, M., & Rustichini, A. (2003). Performance in competitive environments: Gender differences. *Quarterly Journal of Economics, 118*, 1049–1074.

Goldin, C. (1990). *Understanding the gender gap: An economic history of American women.* New York, NY: Oxford University Press.

Goldin, C., & Rouse, C. (2000). Orchestrating impartiality: The impact of "blind" auditions on female musicians. *American Economic Review, 90*, 715–741.

Grosse, N. D., & Riener, G. (2010). *Explaining gender differences in competitiveness: Gender-task stereotypes.* Jena Economic Research Papers. No. 2010, 017.

Harrison, G., & List, J. A. (2004). Field experiments. *Journal of Economic Literature, 42*, 1009–1055.

Hotchkiss, J. L., & Pitts, M. M. (2007). The role of labor market intermittency in explaining gender wage differentials. *American Economic Review, 97*(2), 417–421.

Leahey, C., Fairchild, C., & Zarya, V. (2016). Women CEOs in the Fortune 500. *Fortune.* Retrieved from http://fortune.com/2013/05/09/women-ceos-in-the-fortune-500/

Mayr, U., Wozniak, D., Davidson, C., Kuhns, D., & Harbaugh, W. T. (2012). Competitiveness across the life span: The feisty fifties. *Psychology and Aging, 27*(2), 278–285.

Murray, A. (2016). Guess what? Fortune 500 companies are hiring! *Fortune.* Retrieved from http://fortune.com/2016/06/06/lessons-fortune-500/

National Center for Education Statistics. (2015). *Digest of Education Statistics: 2015.* Retrieved from https://nces.ed.gov/programs/digest/d15/

Niederle, M., Segal, C., & Vesterlund, L. (2013). How costly is diversity? Affirmative action in light of gender differences in competitiveness. *Management Science, 59*(1), 1–16.

Niederle, M., & Vesterlund, L. (2007). Do women shy away from competition? Do men compete too much? *Quarterly Journal of Economics, 122*, 1067–1101.

Niederle, M., & Vesterlund, L. (2011). Gender and competition. *Annual Review of Economics, 3*(1), 601–630.

Phipps, S., Burton, P., & Lethbridge, L. (2001). In and out of the labour market: Long-term income consequences of child-related interruptions to women's paid work. *Canadian Journal of Economics/Revue canadienne d'économique, 34*(2), 411–429.

Reuben, E., Sapienza, P., & Zingales, L. (2010). *The glass ceiling in experimental markets.* Working paper.

Shurchkov, O. (2012). Under pressure: Gender differences in output quality and quantity under competition and time constraints. *Journal of the European Economic Association, 10*(5), 1189–1213.

Spencer, S. J., Steele, C. M., & Quinn, D. M. (1999). Stereotype threat and women's math performance. *Journal of Experimental Social Psychology, 35*, 4–28.

Zweigenhaft, R. L. (2015). The rise and fall of diversity at the top: The appointments of Fortune 500 CEOs from 2005 through 2015. *Who Rules America?* Retrieved from http://www2.ucsc.edu/whorulesamerica/power/rise_and_fall_of_diversity.html

16

LOOKING FORWARD

The Contours of Women's Representation in U.S. Politics

Vanessa C. Tyson

Political representation for women in the United States remains both a controversial and complicated topic, in part because women as a social group are nowhere near monolithic in both their personal interests and their policy preferences but also because of the varying issue positions of women who hold elected office. Some agreement exists, however, on *how* women should be represented, through descriptive, substantive, and symbolic means. That is, must women be represented by women, and if so does the quality of that representation necessarily vary from men? Moreover, does that representation substantively vary along the lines of a gender gap, or are partisan affiliations more important? Finally, which women, in light of the existence of more and less privileged subgroups, reap the benefits of political advocacy in the U.S. arena?

What rarely comes into question, however, is the extent that women as representatives and equal participants have largely been excluded from the political process throughout American history and continuing through contemporary times. The "Founding Fathers" of this country universally omitted fair and equal representation for women at a categorical level, fully marginalizing the interests and preferences of women as a collective group, negating their voices, and subsuming their needs. White women achieved suffrage in 1920, but seldom could women of color share in that achievement. Not until the passage and enforcement of the Voting Rights Act of 1965 could most women of color participate in the franchise, but even then, many women who happened to be language minorities were subject to various language barriers that would subsequently be addressed.

While advocates overcame legal barriers to voting throughout the twentieth century, women of all ethnicities still faced social norms and societal pressures discouraging their full participation. Gender roles suggested that any ambition, political or otherwise, remained a distinct characteristic of masculinity. Femininity, in contrast, required both submissive behavior and the prioritization of the needs and wants of others. Though women increasingly achieved in educational settings in the latter decades of the century and broke down barriers by attaining graduate degrees in fields like law, medicine, and business, they continually faced opposition and social pressure to not assume leadership roles in these industries (Rhode, 2014). Moreover, women faced tremendous discrimination in employment processes and practices broadly—from salary disparities, unequal responsibilities, and less prominent roles to overt sex discrimination and sexual harassment during interviews and on the job (Rhode, 2014).

In more recent years, we witnessed demonstrable gains made by women in electoral politics, though nowhere near the parity many would hope for. At the federal level, women now comprise nearly 20% of the United States Congress. Still, American voters, via the Electoral College, have yet to elect a woman to the presidency or the vice presidency, and only four women have been nominated and confirmed to serve on the Supreme Court in the entirety of U.S. history. At state and city levels, vast disparities also emerge: women comprise only 12% of current state governors and less than 25% of state legislators. Meanwhile, women serve as mayors in roughly 20% of cities with populations at or above 30,000 people, as well as 20% of the 100 most populated cities in the U.S. (Center for American Women and Politics, 2017).

In this chapter, I offer contextual analysis regarding political representation by and for women in the United States, with specific attention paid to the 2016 U.S. presidential election and the defeat of former Secretary of State Hillary Clinton. From there, I focus on two dynamics that directly impact the contours of women's representation. First, utilizing contemporary events and historical knowledge, I identify social and political cleavages that impede feminist consciousness among women as a collective. Second, I offer suggestions and alternatives for successfully bolstering a greater sense of feminist consciousness.

Hillary Clinton and the Motherless State

Both the 2008 and 2016 presidential elections brought significant attention to the realities of and potential for increasing women's political leadership in the United States, particularly in an executive role. The prominent candidacy of former first lady-turned-Senator (and later Secretary of State) Hillary Rodham Clinton heightened awareness among the electorate of the severe lack of women holding elected office. A longtime member of the Democratic Party, Clinton would have been the first woman to hold the highest office in the land. In a country that recently ranked 83rd in the number of women holding federal elected office, this possibility was no small feat (McDonagh, 2009).

No stranger to unprecedented achievements, Clinton was the first woman to reach a major-party ticket as the presidential nominee in 2016. Her loss to Donald Trump, however, largely signified a profound defeat for those who championed gender equality and inclusive politics. Trump generated a campaign based on nationalistic, Islamophobic, and misogynistic rhetoric, which highlighted the extreme, though oft-unspoken, realities of sexism in the U.S. political arena. In a venue long known for being a "boys' club," Trump utilized overt sexist and nationalist appeals in his movement to "Make America Great Again." In so doing, he triggered both conscious and subconscious misogynistic beliefs about women's ability to serve as trustworthy, competent leaders possessing both stamina and resolve. His hostile sexism as a candidate surfaced as early as the first Republican presidential debate, when he admonished Fox News journalist Megyn Kelly for posing a challenging question about his past sexist remarks about both women and their body types.

The election of Donald Trump signified more than the defeat of the first woman on a major-party ticket. It reflected the realities of gatekeeping, opportunity-hoarding, and a biased electorate that continually impede female candidates as they seek public office. These dynamics should neither be ignored in electoral politics, nor should they be dismissed in the subsequent process of policy formulation in legislatures and executive branches. In an industry structured to reward ambition and competition (two traits largely deemed masculine) (Rudman & Glick, 2008), women often face resentment for their desire to participate in U.S. politics. Moreover, women seldom receive the necessary camaraderie and mentorship that their male counterparts benefit from in the legislative process.

The lack of support for women as capable executives remains an extremely troubling dynamic in political spaces. That is, while women have made significant gains in getting elected to legislative offices, a problematic underlying narrative surfaces suggesting that women cannot competently and independently lead the nation—nowhere did this dynamic more greatly manifest than the 2016 U.S. presidential race, which culminated with audio recordings referencing incidents of sexual assault made by the future president, Donald Trump. Clinton's defeat, in ways both large and small, quickly added to the evidence that even the most highly-qualified female candidates would be denied the presidency and all the power that accompanies holding the Oval Office.

More generally, it seems that the structures of American political institutions do not lend to the rise of and support for female candidates. To the contrary, with the utilization of winner-take-all electoral politics, women's strength through cooperative efforts are rarely rewarded—those strengths become weaknesses in electoral politics, where the electorate seemingly gravitates toward dominant behavior and extreme points of view. In essence, the current system remains unconducive to a collaborative environment that often encourages consensus building and mutual respect, which female candidates and elected officials are more commonly known for (Swers, 2001, 2002).

Meanwhile double standards repeatedly plague women who pursue their leadership dreams. The necessary ambition required to run for office seems largely antithetical to the traditional gender roles assigned to women in everyday American spaces. Partially due to what Eileen McDonagh (2009) refers to as the "Motherless State," this dynamic roots itself in the founding period of American history. In their quest to build a society without a monarch—rejecting the political structures of the United Kingdom and other nations—the "Founding Fathers" of this country precluded one particular avenue to the rise of a female leader, that of heredity. Not only did men exclude women from leadership during the inception of the United States, they prevented their participation in public life through multiple means, effectively relegating women to the domestic sphere and little else (Baker, 2008). Such relegation further lent itself to consequent double standards we witness in present-day society, where women who opt to engage in public life remain subject to greater scrutiny and harsher assessments.

These double standards exist for women not only for possessing lofty dreams but for daring to fully participate in political institutions dominated by men and founded within a larger context of patriarchy. Subject to intense scrutiny over their physical appearance and wardrobe choices, female candidates and elected officials face tremendous backlash when and where they do not conform to societal norms regarding both behavior and presentation (McDonagh, 2009). The simple act of running for office as a woman serves as a rejection of traditional gender roles where women were expected to stay out of the public sphere of influence and remain in private homes providing care for children and family members, cooking, cleaning, and handling all matters of the home.

Another point merits attention in this case—while most American voters claim they would support a female candidate, and indeed Hillary Clinton won the popular vote in November 2016, 48% of those who cast a vote in the 2016 general election opted for a candidate whose well-documented misogyny and repeated disrespect toward women remained at the forefront of his political campaign. This trend repeats itself throughout U.S. history—the political behavior of everyday Americans (and their leaders) is often at odds with the principles of fairness and justice for groups that have long been marginalized and excluded from leadership roles. For example, in the years preceding the defeat of the Equal Rights Amendment in 1982, the country witnessed very contradictory behavior—when threatened with the potential implications of women's equality, state legislators balked at supporting the cause, effectively quashing constitutional protections for women (Mansbridge, 1986).

What are the policy implications of this "Motherless State" that severely lacks female representation? Social policy continues to be the most prominent answer. Women who legislate disproportionately provide more support for reproductive rights, welfare policies, and the politics of care—elderly care, child care, health care—than the men they work with (McDonagh, 2009; Swers,

2002). Moreover, they tend to be more liberal when it comes to crime (rehabilitation vs. punishment), education and afterschool programs, food stamp programs, and community-based activities (Swers, 2002). Demographically speaking, single mothers and their children remain disproportionately over-represented in poverty statistics. According to the U.S. Census Bureau, more than 26% of single mother households exist at or below the poverty threshold (Semega, Fontenot, & Kollar, 2017), more than double the rate for single father and married-couple households below the poverty line and comprising more than half of all households at or below the current poverty threshold.

The continued dearth of women in elected office, particularly in legislative and executive positions where they are able to exercise greater decision-making autonomy, results in lower support for public education, a strong safety net, and access to resources for economically disadvantaged families who struggle to make ends meet amid limited opportunities and crippling poverty. Meanwhile, women across the country remain disproportionately poor despite both electoral gains and increased participation in social, cultural, and economic leadership (Bullock, 2013).

Partisan Differences, Identity Politics, and the Quality of Women's Representation

Women's political leadership varies tremendously along partisan lines, though most scholars agree that women's participation in the policy formulation process improves the quality of deliberation in legislative bodies, particularly in debates where issue positions have yet to crystallize (Mansbridge, 1999). Although unilateral support for reproductive freedoms does not exist among women elected to office, nor does support for comprehensive poverty policies and support for children, we see international evidence of increased support for the politics of care (child care, health care, elderly care, and the like) when both the absolute number and percentage of women increase in national governments (McDonagh, 2009). Moreover, regardless of partisan differences in the United States, we see that Republican women in Congress offer stronger support for women's health issues (broadly defined) and the provision of health care for the U.S. population than do their male counterparts (Swers, 2002).

All that said, historically feminism and feminists have not dealt well with difference, particularly along the lines of race and class. For much of the twentieth century, the "women's movement" consisted of white, wealthy women, and consequent advocacy reflected a lack of racial and class understanding that impeded the potential solidarity of the movement. Research suggests that the actual quality of representation often varies within marginalized social groups, with advocates opting to reflect the interests and preferences of only the more privileged subgroups within the group (Strolovitch, 2006; Strolovitch, 2007). For instance, some advocates indicate that they represent *all* women, when in truth they articulate and lobby for the preferences of wealthy women, who happen to be overwhelmingly white.

The movement for women's equality over the last century begs the question: which women? Substantial doubts arise when female candidates not only marginalize other social groups through implicit and explicit bias but also when they appear to capitalize upon that social bias to further their political careers. To better explain through example, when wealthy, white female candidates expect women of color and poor women to automatically and unequivocally support their candidacies, they inadvertently dismiss all other identities, expecting one's womanhood to dominate and subsume powerful experiences that have shaped the lives and life chances of women of color and poor women. This faulty logic can and often does imperil female candidates in their quest to encourage solidarity and voter participation.

Diversity within and among women as a social group surfaces through both overlapping and intersecting identities. While white women of privilege and means have largely dominated the women's movement, the realities of poor women, women of color, and female members of the lesbian, gay, bisexual, transgender, and queer community often remain hanging in the balance—will the privileged subgroup that more likely has the social capital (as well as financial resources) necessary to gain office fervently advocate for the very real substantive needs of more disadvantaged subgroups? Are those privileged women even aware of the needs of more disadvantaged women and the communities in which they take part?

American society, with its long history of white supremacy coupled with patriarchy and capitalism, has stigmatized women of color and poor women through the oppressive means of cultural imperialism, where certain groups are deemed inferior by dominant groups (Young, 1990). Societal attitudes and system-instilled norms characterize privileged individuals and communities as more inherently deserving and repeatedly seek to justify the privileges they benefit from, thus perpetuating systemic inequality (Jost, Banaji, & Nosek, 2004). Poorer communities and individuals that routinely suffer from resource deprivation remain sedimented at the bottom of an economic hierarchy and blamed for their lack of social mobility (Bullock, 2013).

In order to better solidify support among female voters for female candidates in U.S. politics, those candidates need to not only embrace women from all races, ethnic groups, socioeconomic statuses, sexual orientations, and the like, but they must go far beyond optics to comprehend the lived experiences of those with fewer privileges. Furthermore, female candidates must consciously and emphatically reject the stigmatization of disadvantaged subgroups if they expect political support in return. In essence, solidarity is a two-way street. Meanwhile, significant disparities exist in policy attitudes between racial and ethnic groups with respect to social policy, crime and incarceration policies, and health policy (Kinder & Sanders, 1996). Women who opt to run for office as leaders of and advocates for other women cannot champion themselves as icons of inclusion while simultaneously failing to address the needs and preferences of women who disproportionately fall into the category of "other" and whose overlapping and intersecting identities are muted by those with greater privilege.

Silent Identities and Salient Issues

> If it's a legitimate rape, the female body has ways to try to shut that whole thing down.
> —Former Missouri U.S. Rep. Todd Akin (R-02), August 2012

In the 2012 election cycle, Missouri U.S. Senate candidate Todd Akin made national headlines with his controversial quote about "legitimate rape" pertaining to reproductive rights and sexual violence. In essence, without any scientific evidence to base his claim, then-Rep. Akin made clear that only specific instances of rape, in his opinion, could lead to a pregnancy, because women's bodies could defensively prevent pregnancy. In making such a claim, he not only justified his decision to deny rape victims the right to terminate a pregnancy but also implied that rape victims make false claims about consequent pregnancies resulting from their sexually violent trauma.

In using the statement "legitimate rape," Akin unknowingly tapped into a *silent identity* held by many Americans, yet rarely discussed—that of sexual assault survivors. While survivors of sexual violence rarely publicize the trauma they previously experienced, that unique trauma remains a profoundly upsetting memory, one that commonly serves as a life-altering event. To promote policies that would outright deny rape survivors autonomy over their bodies essentially wrongs a rape survivor for a second time. Both in the case of rape and in the case of a consequent pregnancy, the survivor is denied control over her body—first by an assailant, then again by her government.

By silent identity, I explicitly mean the emergence of a defining identification not immediately apparent to anyone other than the identifying individual, but whose decisions, choices, and worldviews are substantively changed by specific life-altering experiences such as sexual assault. While certain identities form in response to and in dialogue with public actions and occurrences or within familial and community settings, a silent identity emerges from uniquely private life events, unrecognized by the outside world but triggered by it nonetheless. These silent identities also have a uniqueness—an additional factor of stigma that requires victims to remain silent, dealing with the aftermath of pain and trauma largely in isolation for fear of public rebuke and castigation.

Surviving sexual assault often remains a silent identity due to many factors, both personal and societal. Shame and stigma, combined with the perception that victims will not be believed, let alone supported, by their communities and loved ones, remain critical factors in the continued silence that takes place. The puritan legacy of the United States, along with the patriarchy embedded within it, relegates sex and sexuality to sinful behavior, one that should not be discussed in "polite" company. For sexual assault survivors, not only have they suffered serious injury both physically and psychologically, but those injuries occur in a sexual context, one deeply private and problematically characterized as immoral.

A penchant for blaming victims for the crimes committed against them repeatedly surfaces in U.S. politics, a dynamic very common when addressing sexual assault. Assumptions about the clothing a victim wore, the prior relationship the victim had with the perpetrator, and the sexual history of the victim seemingly become public domain in shaming women and shifting blame from the assaulting party to the assaulted. Such tactics were frequently employed when (white) women began entering the workplace in the early 1900s (Baker, 2008). Any sexual harassment or assault they experienced on the job was deemed their own fault because they should have remained in the home (Baker, 2008).

In the 2016 U.S. presidential election, sexual assault and harassment rose to the forefront of American politics. Although these issues also surfaced during the 1990s when Bill Clinton served as president, greater awareness seemed to characterize the energy of 2016. The day after the inauguration of newly elected President Trump, demonstrations and protests of women's rights occurred worldwide, with an estimated 5 million participants. In Washington, DC, alone, roughly half a million people took part in the Women's March—the largest single-day protest in United States history (Chenoweth & Pressman, 2017).

True political leadership requires individuals to get out in front of the public with agendas that meet the needs of those they wish to lead. To bolster feminist consciousness, women who want to lead would do well to acknowledge the overwhelming but often unspoken threat of sexual violence in commonplace interactions. They need to reject patriarchal structures of power that leave women (and children) vulnerable to abuse and assault. Certain female leaders, notably U.S. Senator Kirsten Gillibrand (D-NY), have publicly advocated for sexual violence survivors through proposing policy changes that would more effectively address the structural reasons that sexual assault and rape go vastly underreported in the military. Through continued and unrelenting advocacy, a stronger sense of sisterhood and solidarity can be bolstered and maintained.

***

The potential contributions by and for women in American politics and policy are infinite, provided numerous individuals and structures adjust from patriarchal norms to truly support legitimate expectations of inclusion and respect. Moreover, the experiences and realities of women's lives cannot be dismissed in the course of political expedience, regardless of partisan politics. The repeated utilization of misogynistic stereotypes about women as candidates, the continued dismissal of issues that disproportionately affect women, the myriad endeavors to limit women's bodily autonomy, and the triggering of silent identities all illustrate the dynamics women face as they attempt to navigate the U.S. political arena.

Meanwhile, ample evidence suggests that the participation of women in national politics improves the quality of discourse (Mansbridge, 1999) and in certain cases has shortened government shutdowns. In the budget impasse of 2013, led primarily by U.S. Senator Ted Cruz (R-TX), it was the 20 female members of the Senate who achieved a bipartisan compromise that concluded the standoff that closed national parks and required all nonessential federal employees to stay home from work without pay (Weisman & Steinhauer, 2013). Women's leadership through compromise and the willingness to find common ground despite the partisan rancor of 2013 certainly suggests a departure from the highly polarized status quo on Capitol Hill, as well as their ability to effectively govern.

For women, the personal is political, but the political is also deeply personal due to the influence politics and policy have in our everyday lives. Current political leaders must practice real inclusion, particularly if they expect solidarity in return. Optics alone are insufficient proof of racial, ethnic, and socioeconomic diversity. Furthermore, cleavages of nationality, gender identity, sexual orientation, immigrant status, and disability must also reach the forefront of political agendas nationwide.

Feminists and their allies must consistently identify and challenge social norms and stigmas that prohibit strong, vibrant coalitions posed as catalysts for change. Those coalitions, both at the grassroots level and within the upper echelons of policy making, remain crucial to the ultimate goal of equality and societal equity. The achievement of this goal requires those in power to actively embrace difference, not simply speaking to difference when it is convenient or when it serves a specific purpose. And women in positions of power must be willing to share the spotlight with those who have been traditionally marginalized within the women's movement writ large. Those in power must actively seek out the opinions and needs of disadvantaged subgroups to improve the quality of advocacy for *all* women during every step of the policy process.

References

Baker, C. (2008). *The women's movement against sexual harassment.* Cambridge, MA: Cambridge University Press.

Bullock, H. E. (2013). *Women and poverty: Psychology, public policy, and social justice.* Malden, MA: Wiley Blackwell.

Center for American Women and Politics. (2017). *Fact sheet: Women in elective office 2017.* Retrieved from www.cawp.rutgers.edu/women-elective-office-2017

Chenoweth, E., & Pressman, J. (2017, February 7). This is what we learned by counting the women's marches. *The Washington Post.* Retrieved from www.washingtonpost. com/news/monkey-cage/wp/2017/02/07/this-is-what-we-learned-by-counting-the-womens-marches/?utm_term=.eef77a283096.

Dodson, D. L. (2006). *The impact of women in Congress.* Oxford, UK: Oxford University Press.

Fels, A. (2004). *Necessary dreams: Ambition in women's changing lives.* New York, NY: Pantheon.

Heim, P., Murphy, S., & Golant, S. (2001). *In the company of women: Turning workplace conflict into powerful alliances.* New York, NY: Putnam.

Jost, J. T., Banaji, M., & Nosek, B. (2004). A decade of system justification theory: Accumulated evidence of conscious and unconscious bolstering of the status quo. *Political Psychology,* 55(6), 881–919.

Kahn, K. F. (1996). *The political consequences of being a woman: How stereotypes influence the conduct and consequences of political campaigns.* New York, NY: Columbia University Press.

Karpowitz, C. F., & Mendelberg, T. (2014). *The silent sex: Gender, deliberation and institutions.* Princeton, NJ: Princeton University Press.

Kinder, D. R., & Sanders, L. M. (1996). *Divided by color: Racial politics and democratic ideals.* Chicago, IL: University of Chicago Press.

Lawless, J. L., & Fox, R. L. (2010). *It still takes a candidate: Why women don't run for office.* Cambridge, MA: Cambridge University Press.

Lawless, J. L., & Fox, R. L. (2017). *Women, men & US politics: Ten big questions.* New York, NY: Norton.

Mansbridge, J. (1986). *Why we lost the ERA.* Chicago, IL: University of Chicago Press.

Mansbridge, J. (1999). Should Blacks represent blacks and women represent women? A contingent "yes". *Journal of Politics,* 61(3), 628–657.

McDonagh, E. (2009). *The motherless state: Women's political leadership and American democracy.* Chicago, IL: University of Chicago Press.

Rhode, D. L. (2003). *The difference "difference" makes: Women and leadership.* Stanford, CA: Stanford University Press.

Rhode, D. L. (2017). *Women and leadership.* Oxford, UK: Oxford University Press.

Rudman, L. A., & Glick, P. (2008). *The social psychology of gender: How power and intimacy shape gender relations.* New York, NY: Guilford.

Semega, J. L., Fontenot, K. R., & Kollar, M. A. (2017). *U.S. Census Bureau, current population reports, p60–259, income and poverty in the United States: 2016.* Washington, DC: U.S. Government Printing Office. Retrieved from www.census.gov/data/tables/2017/demo/income-poverty/p60-259.html

Swers, M. L. (2001). Understanding the policy impact of electing women: Evidence on research on Congress and State Legislatures. *PS: Political Science and Politics,* 34(2), 217–220.

Swers, M. L. (2002). *The difference women make: The policy impact of women in Congress.* Chicago, IL: University of Chicago Press.

Valian, V. (1998). *Why so slow? The advancement of women.* Cambridge, MA: Massachusetts Institute of Technology Press.

Weisman, J., & Steinhauer, J. (2013, October 13). Senate women leaders in effort to find accord. *New York Times.* Retrieved from www.nytimes.com/2013/10/15/us/senate-women-lead-in-effort-to-find-accord.html

Wolbrecht, C., Beckwith, K., & Baldez, L. (2008). *Political women and American democracy*. Cambridge, MA: Cambridge University Press.

Young, I. M. (1990). *Justice and the politics of difference*. Princeton, NJ: Princeton University Press.

Young, I. M. (1994). Gender as seriality: Thinking about women as a social collective. *Signs 19*(3), 713–738.

17

WHAT IS NEXT FOR WOMEN AND LEADERSHIP RESEARCH AND THEORY? MAKING A CRITICAL IMPACT FOR THE FUTURE

Susan R. Madsen and Jolyn Dahlvig

After nearly two decades of studying ways to strengthen the impact of women in the world, we still get questions from time to time about why it is so important to continue exploring women and leadership in all its complexity, multidimensionality, and intersectionality. Our simple response is this: evidence continues to show that refining, clarifying, and creating theory (i.e., theorizing)—as well as exploring and investigating new questions and hypotheses through rigorous quantitative and qualitative research methodologies—can change and improve practice (Madsen, 2017a; Storberg-Walker & Haber-Curran, 2017). The blending of theory and practice is the bottom line. Practice, at the individual, group, organization, community, and country levels, needs to improve and expand to (1) prepare more girls and women to lead and to (2) change existing policies, processes, and structures that do not provide enriching environments for them to do so.

There are many compelling reasons why continuing our exploration of women and leadership is imperative, but we will highlight only two. First, there is no question that we still do not have enough women leaders in politics, business, government, education, nonprofits, and other settings and sectors in any country (Adler, 2015; Goryunova, Scribner, & Madsen, 2017). Although some progress has been made, Joshi, Neely, Emrich, Griffiths, and George (2015) have called this progress "both promising and problematic" (p. 1459), as there continue to be ongoing, persistent challenges with efforts to strengthen women's impact around the world. In 2015, Joshi et al. reported that "gender equality appears to be at the forefront of the global humanitarian agenda" (p. 1459), and because of complex global, political, economic, cultural, technological, and social dynamics, the gender element of this agenda appears to be strengthening, not subsiding.

Second, hundreds of peer-reviewed studies have documented the benefits of having women in top management and leadership positions in any type of organization and in society as well (Madsen, 2015). For example, a host of studies has found that when women are in leadership teams or on boards, in many cases there is improved financial performance for the company or organization. Research has found that when women are included, there may be increased profitability, better economic growth, faster debt reduction, lower risk of insolvency, better business deals, less risky bids, and much more (e.g., Committee for Economic Development, 2012; Lillenfeld, 2014). Studies have also shown that organizational climates are strengthened, corporate social responsibility (CSR) and organizational reputations are increased, talent is better leveraged, and innovation and collective intelligence is also enhanced (Catalyst, 2013; Woolley, Chabris, Pentland, Hashmi, & Malone, 2010). More specifically, when women are on boards and in leadership roles, organizations tend to have greater employee satisfaction, a smaller gender pay gap, lower corporate fraud, more corporate social responsibility initiatives, greater creativity and problem-solving capabilities, stronger team decision making, and reduced groupthink (Madsen, 2015). These are only a few benefits of having women in key positions, but it is clear that gender and other types of diversity are vital in today's world for groups and organizations to thrive. Hence, developing leadership skills and abilities in girls and women is a critical imperative for current and future local, national, and global success.

This Book

The 17 chapters in this edited volume add to the existing literature base in broadening the understanding of women's leadership and how women develop leadership throughout their lives. Understanding women's leadership journeys, how successful women have navigated these journeys, and how to move forward to make a critical impact for the future are important contributions toward leading change through theory, research, and practice. Madsen's research through the years (e.g., Madsen, 2008, 2009) has produced some of the first publications exploring the lifetime leadership development journeys of high-profile women leaders in higher education, government, and business; this kind of research makes a valuable contribution to the field of women and leadership. Research that explores the backgrounds, experiences, challenges, opportunities, and perspectives of women in various contexts and cultures helps provide beneficial insight into how best to develop and train women so they can effectively influence on a larger scale (Madsen, 2007, 2010).

To summarize what readers have learned as they have read and reflected on the contents of this book, we will briefly highlight what has been offered. First, Part I explored women's leadership journeys through highlighting five stories. These included chapters that investigated the community service leadership of three women (a mother, daughter, and granddaughter) and compared it across the generations; highlighted the experiences of one woman who spent her life leading in high-profile roles in sectors such as government, foreign service, business, and higher education; offered findings from a study that focused on the leadership journeys of female trustee board chairs at private colleges and universities; followed a college president's journey to leadership; and explored one woman's career journey in business and social entrepreneurship. The book editors, Drs. Tan and DeFrank-Cole, have successfully argued that, because of their journeys, women have distinct attributes that are conducive to strong leadership and are uniquely situated to lead and influence in a host of ways.

Part II of this book focused on how women navigate their journeys toward leading and provided readers with examples of ways they can navigate their own journeys to impactful leadership. These chapters illustrated the role of relationships and motivation to lead in women's career transitions into entrepreneurship and explored how diverse women progress to achieve their leadership aspirations. They highlighted an array of leadership qualities, including the role of courage in pushing through comfort zones and taking risks that lead to greater confidence and learning. The chapters also described the importance of defining moments in women's leadership self-perceptions and identity development. Furthermore, chapters focused on a variety of strategies women can use, such as building a team to support the development of leader identity and utilizing leadership efficacy and growth mindsets to buffer against identity threat. Role transitions, aspirations, courage, defining moments, identity development, and efficacy and growth mindsets have all been shown to be key elements in developing and strengthening leadership in girls and women (Madsen, 2017a). These chapters add depth and breadth to the scholarly conversation regarding specific practices.

Finally, looking to the future is central to any discussion about strengthening girls and women through leadership development. Chapters on leading through followership; the role of biology in leadership; the role of gender in competitiveness; insights from women in politics and government; and next steps for impact-centered women and leadership research and theory make important contributions to the women's leadership field. Often the mental models held by theorists, researchers, and scholars are not flexible and do not allow them to see and understand what is needed to strengthen current practice for women's leadership development. Shaking up these mental models is key to research that fills needed gaps through innovative, creative, and thoughtful questions. This section helps readers do just that.

Next Steps

The work of understanding women's leadership needs to continue if we want to see more women join the leadership ranks in all sectors, especially government, business, and education. There continue to be ongoing, persisting challenges with efforts to strengthen women's impact around the world, and there continue to be unequal opportunities and treatment of women in nearly all countries, contexts, and sectors (Longman & Madsen, 2014; Madsen, Ngunjiri, Longman, & Cherrey, 2015; Ngunjiri & Madsen, 2015). In fact, one McKinsey Global Institute (2015) report stated that "gender inequality is a pressing global issue with huge ramifications not just for the lives and livelihoods of girls and women, but more generally, for human development, labor markets, productivity, GDP growth, and inequality" (p. II). Hence, even with some progress, the path toward gender parity still remains elusive in many respects (Goryunova et al., 2017).

In looking to the future, it is important to consider what lies on the many horizons of women and leadership research and theory and how we can move forward to make a critical impact. To be honest, research on gender and leadership has increased dramatically over the past decade. In fact, as is articulated recently in the first author's latest book (Madsen, 2017b), "thousands of research- and theory-based books and articles have been published on various elements of women and leadership within different sectors, industries, cultures, countries, and contexts" (p. XXV). And, as most readers will agree, "newspaper, magazine, blog, and other social media articles (for example, stories, editorials, personal perspectives, summaries of research) are released daily within communities, states and provinces, nations, and across the globe" (p. xxv). Yet, there remain countless gaps in our understanding of women, leadership, and development.

One critical element of moving the women and leadership agenda forward is to ensure that theorists and researchers stay abreast of both the most current literature and the most current needs and gaps in practice (see next sections for more details)—identifying how theory and research can best be utilized for developing leadership in girls and women. For example, Anderson, Baur, Griffith, and Buckley (2017) identified potential gaps by examining how leadership theory applies and possibly does not apply to the emerging generation of workers. Does a generation known for prioritizing personal lives over professional accomplishments respond to a transformational leader's vision in the same way as previous generations? And, how does this play out within organizations specifically related to women's aspirations, ambitions, and career development plans? Anderson et al. posed questions pushing researchers to examine existing leadership theory and continue developing new understandings, and we encourage scholars to add the gender construct into any of these inquiries. Another example relates to the empirical evidence suggesting that the "think manager, think male" (Schein, 1975) stereotype might be changing in Western society (Braun, Stegmann, Haernandex Bark, Junker, & van Dick, 2016; Lemoine, Aggarwal, & Bujold Steed, 2016). Building on current literature, researchers might ask to what extent do the younger generations embrace androgynous descriptions of leadership, and how does this change impact our practice and women's leadership development? As society changes, established assumptions need to be questioned and explored anew.

In addition to understanding generational shifts that inform research and practice, Emerson and Murphy (2015) applied current psychological theory to explore the impact of an organizational mindset (tacit/fixed or incremental/growth) on women's leadership. Applying stereotype threat and mindset theory to organizational culture revealed insight into women's willingness to approach leadership opportunities within particular contexts. The interdisciplinary nature of women's leadership necessitates testing multiple frameworks to expand our collective understanding. Anderson et al. (2017) and Emerson and Murphy (2015) are examples of current research that influences both theory building and practice.

Future research and theory will not impact individuals, organizations, and societies in meaningful ways and lead to change that is so desperately needed in all contexts and cultures unless we take the research paths less traveled—we must explore and investigate new questions. An example of a research road less traveled is the work by Hammond, Clapp-Smith, and Palanski (2017) that moved beyond workplace boundaries to understand "cross-domain processes for leader development" (p. 481). Based in sense making and identity work, Hammond et al. extend our exploration of leadership to include all aspects of life, which is a complicated theory-building task with implications for leader formation programs. We do not need to retrace the well-traveled research paths that others have explored but need to embrace the challenge of forging new ground.

Forging new ground should mean rigorous attention to the theoretical assumptions of the researchers and theorist. In fact, Storberg-Walker and Natt och Dag (2017) proposed that scholars challenge themselves regarding the paradigms or lenses they use to guide their work. They offer Burrell and Morgan's (1979) four-quadrant sociological framework (functionalist, radical humanist, interpretive, and radical structuralism) to assist scholars and others in clarifying their goals and purposes. Reminiscent of Hassard and Wolfram Cox (2013), Storberg-Walker and Natt och Dag suggest being clear about the theoretical underpinnings of research to enhance theory building and foster the methodological rigor and inventiveness necessary for developing new knowledge. It is not our goal to provide depth regarding one specific framework here but just to state that attention to understanding one's own assumptions and lenses are key to strategic and intentional scholarship moving forward.

In addition to the studies previously mentioned, we now highlight some sources and topics that may be helpful in identifying new research terrain. First, the conclusion of *The Asilomar Declaration and Call to Action on Women and Leadership* (Women and Leadership Affinity Group, 2017) identified four valuable and up-to-date areas for critical future research. The original source includes potential research questions under each of the subcategories listed; here we will include two samples for each category:

1. *Increasing Equality in Power and Decision-Making*: types of power, language of power, attitudes toward power and influence, demographic distortions, discrimination and second-generation gender bias, handling leadership conflicts, generational shifts, and male and female decision-making processes. Questions: How does context influence effective use of power for women? How does context influence perceptions of power and influence?
2. *Helping Girls and Young Women Become Leaders*: finding the female voice, leadership identity, setting and achieving goals, lifelong passion for leadership, leadership success programs, adolescent girls' advocacy and leadership initiatives, obstacles in transitioning from girlhood. Questions: What can be learned about the development of leadership aspirations and abilities in young girls? Building upon research that individuals become leaders by internalizing a leadership identity, what factors help girls and young women have confidence in their emerging leadership identity?
3. *Expanding Leadership Education and Development Worldwide*: expanded perspectives on leadership, leadership for social change, counteracting belief in the "natural order," adjustments in life span, addressing victimization, alternative models for leadership, women-only leadership programs. Questions: How can research more effectively focus attention on sustaining solutions that encourage attention to policies on safety, equality, education, and peace? What kinds of research could shift the focus of leadership effectiveness to addressing the basic needs and rights of the community, such as the right to an education that manifests in social change?
4. *Advancing Women in Leadership*: leadership aspirations, going beyond gender, cross-cultural research and social justice, organizational ecosystems, ethics, shaping a leadership mindset, sponsors and bullies, broadening the dialogue, and the influence of media. Questions: What factors contribute to the "learning cycle" that is at the heart of becoming a leader for women? How can leadership research be nuanced in ways that address the influence of different cultural perspectives on women's leadership aspirations and possibilities (e.g., regional and religious perspectives on women leaders)?

The Asilomar Declaration challenges future researchers to advance gender-related dimensions of leadership studies. As this document outlines, "such research will enhance our understanding of individual, organizational, and societal dynamics and advance both inclusive and effective leadership practice" (Women and Leadership Affinity Group, 2017, p. 42). It highlights the need for research to be interdisciplinary, to address the complexities of the social construction of gender, to be multi-paradigm, and to encompass and honor the multiple ways of knowing and understanding what it means to be human. The documents suggest that research methods for such inquiry need to be diverse and to offer a compelling alternative to the male-normed, reductionist, objectivist, and rationalist scientific method. This section of *The Asilomar Declaration* concluded by asking scholars to thoughtfully navigate the "space between scholarship and advocacy, between research and practice, and between thinking and doing" (p. 42).

Second, eight recent books on women and leadership have or will be published in the Women and Leadership Book Series through a partnership with the International Leadership Association and Information Age Publishing. Faith Wambura Ngunjiri, Karen A. Longman, and Susan R. Madsen have been the series editors and ensured that the latest in theory and research has been summarized and shared in these volumes. If readers are planning to do theorizing or research on women and leadership in higher education (Longman & Madsen, 2014), global leadership (Ngunjiri & Madsen, 2015), international perspectives (Madsen, Ngunjiri, Longman, & Cherrey, 2015), media (Elliott, Stead, Mavin & Williams, 2016), communication (Cunningham, Crandall, & Dare, 2017), theory development (Storberg-Walker & Haber-Curran, 2017), board leadership (Devnew, Burke, Le Ber, & Torchia, forthcoming), or politics (Rosser-Mims, McNellis, Johnson Bailey & McIlmoyl, forthcoming), we recommend the books referenced here and listed in the references as guides for what is known and what questions are still not answered. In addition to these books, other publications have been released that can guide the work of thoughtful and responsive scholars (for example, Storberg-Walker & Madsen, 2017).

Third, based on decades of research and application, we believe that scholarship needs to be strengthened in four core areas. First, advancing women and leadership theory remains an area that is just recently beginning to emerge in great force. Yet there are still few leadership theories that help explain women's leadership in ways that are helpful for the design of leadership development programs. Current literature has begun to unleash possibilities, focusing on various approaches to women and leadership theory (e.g., social psychological, sociological, sociolinguistic, organizational and management sciences, and critical leadership theory) (Madsen, 2017a), as well as work on new concepts and theories, new models and methods, and new insights and ideas (Storberg-Walker & Haber-Curran, 2017). Previously highlighted as an exemplar, Emerson and Murphy's (2015) application of empirically substantive psychological constructs (mindset and stereotype threat) to women's leadership could translate well into leadership development interventions. Within education, brief mindset interventions have been linked to positive long-term benefits (Dweck, 2006). Beyond mindset, Luthans, Avolio, and Youseff (2015) offer empirically tested strategies for building the positive human capacities of hope, resilience, optimism, and self-efficacy. By definition, psychological capital must be theoretically robust and open to development (not a trait); therefore, these constructs have a great deal to offer leadership development initiatives. While mindset and psychological capital have been applied to various settings, testing mindset and/or psychological capital-based interventions' effectiveness in developing women leaders is needed.

The second core area in which scholarship needs to be strengthened is that, although more scholarship has been published in recent years, there still remain few theories and studies focused on individual motivators to lead. These include such constructs as women's leadership aspirations, ambitions, and/or identity; the role of purpose, calling, and/or power in women's leadership experiences; how women and men define leadership, success, and/or choice; and the neuroscience that explores similarities and differences between genders and how they can impact leadership and leadership development. Exploring women's leadership across multiple domains may inform the complexities around women's motivation to lead. As previously referenced, Hammond et al. (2017) offers a framework for thinking about women's holistic development incorporating multiple contexts, leadership theories, and intrapersonal dimensions. This type of sophisticated analysis is needed when considering the complexities of motivators to lead. Third, although we believe there is more to explore in the areas of gender-based leadership challenges and barriers, we caution scholars to thoroughly explore the vast amount of literature already published (Diehl & Dzubinski, 2016), as many of the challenges are already clearly defined and much of the focus going forward needs to be exploring and investigating interventions that can remove those barriers. Madsen and Scribner (2017) conducted an in-depth study on cross-cultural gender research in 15 management journals. In addition to other constructs, they investigated the tone and topics of hundreds of scholarly journal articles and found that challenges and obstacles were a popular focus of studies. The fourth area in which scholarship needs to be strengthened is around developing leadership in girls and women for both informal and formal roles of influence. There is, however, some clarity around specific elements of women's leadership development in terms of advancing women through developmental relationships, gender differences in developmental experiences, the value of women-only leadership programs, and future strategies for developing women as leaders (Madsen, 2017a). Gender-specific theory is now beginning to emerge, but research focused on evaluating existing and new programs and tools is still scarce. Even more scarce is longitudinal research that tracks the impact of interventions across years and decades.

In addition, we would be remiss if we did not mention the need for more theory and research that guides women and leadership work in diverse countries and regions, cultures, races/ethnicities, industries and sectors, generations, socioeconomic situations, and many other areas that could influence women's opportunities, challenges, and overall experiences (Madsen & Scribner, 2017). While excellent work continues to be published globally (Kark, Preser, Zion-Waldoks, 2016; Kuzhabekova & Almukhambetova, 2017; Samier, 2015), understanding the nuanced implications of culture and context on women's leadership development could be insightful across cultural and geographic boundaries. We would encourage, however, scholars to carefully articulate the similarities between groups (as there are many) and then highlight the unique elements that are also important in designing and developing interventions.

Finally, it is important for emerging and established scholars to be responsive to the current events of the day and to respond quickly—which does not happen often in academia—with findings and recommendations. For example, Hillary Clinton's surprising loss in the 2016 U.S. presidential election has resulted in extensive public and private dialogue. Individuals, groups, and organizations are searching for answers based on evidence—not just emotion. We argue that women and leadership scholars should rise up in a timely fashion to provide evidence that can be used for leading social change. Responding to critical and timely questions requires new mental models for scholars who have been taught in doctoral programs that studies must take years to complete and must only be published in peer-reviewed journals. Also, to have the most broad and immediate impact on actual practice, scholars need not confine research findings to academic venues. Contemporary technologies—blogs, podcasts, TED talks, and other social media platforms—allow scholars to distill researched ideas and offer best practices quickly to millions more people. Expanding platforms outside the ivory tower can drive social change and empower more women across the globe.

***

We began this chapter by articulating reasons why it is still important to continue exploring and investigating women and leadership. Next, we summarized the chapters from this book and discussed why they are important in moving forward to make a critical impact for the future. We then laid out directions for future research by discussing several existing agendas and proposing a few new areas of great import and urgency. We argued that we need to shake up our existing mental models and be more thoughtful in theory and research to practice, and we discussed the need for scholars to be more reflective and conscious in terms of the research questions we are asking for future studies. We also offered a challenge for us to be more responsive to pressing needs of the day in our field and specific areas of focus and to embrace technologies that allow for broad and rapid dissemination of research and best practices.

More than ever in the history of the world, we believe that we need more women and leadership theorists, researchers, scholars, and practitioners who will use their heads, hearts, and hands in the important work of creating, refining, exploring, and investigating women's leadership and leadership development. Moving forward, our work needs to focus on research questions that are linked to practice. When we move women's leadership from inquiry into actionable knowledge, we can make a more substantial difference. We know many scholars in other fields who argue that theorists and researchers do not need to link to practice—that this is not their job, that scholars should spend years creating theory and conducting research for the sake of general inquiry. However, we disagree, particularly for the field of women and leadership.

We are trying to change the world. We need to bring more women to the global table. If we truly care about making a critical impact for the future, we do not have the luxury to follow lines of inquiry that are not linked to direct practices that strengthen the impact of girls and women today and in future generations. There remain too many unanswered questions linked to guiding, influencing, and affecting practice and policy. The bottom line is that we need to provide evidence that helps change public policy now. We need to inform people who are asking questions in business, nonprofit organizations, government, and educational settings now. We need more research that addresses pressing questions in society now. We need to evaluate more change interventions based on rigorously tested women and leadership theory and research now. We need new findings that get us all thinking outside the box for solutions now. We need to make a larger difference by moving theory and research to practice now. In sum, we need answers now that challenge us to shake things up as theorists, scholars, researchers, and practitioners so we can help change the status of women globally. *Now.*

Overall, we are turning a corner in terms of women's leadership, but one corner leads to another, and another. We need to feel and create greater urgency for the work we are doing. There is a momentum that moves women's leadership forward in ways we have not seen in past generations. We agree that it is sometimes two steps forward and one step back, and we must admit that there are still times when we are taking one step forward and two steps back. Yet, the numbers of women leaders around the world are at least moving slowly forward. Although work remains to be done, as we do our part, life will change for one girl at a time, for one woman at a time, for one family or group at a time, for one entity at a time, for one community at a time, and even for one country at a time. Each of our contributions may be different—such as researching, publishing, speaking, mentoring, coaching, teaching, educating, motivating, inspiring—but they are all in the realm of leading change. And we believe that leading change through this work will change the world!

References

Adler, N. J. (2015). Women leaders: Shaping history in the 21st century. In F. W. Ngunjiri & S. R. Madsen (Eds.), *Women as global leaders* (pp. 21–50). Charlotte, NC: Information Age Publishing.

Anderson, H. J., Baur, J. E., Griffith, J. A., & Buckley, M. R. (2017). What works for you may not work for (Gen)Me: Limitations of present leadership theories for the new generation. *The Leadership Quarterly, 28,* 245–260.

Braun, S., Stegmann, S., Haernandex Bark, A. S., Junker, N. M., & van Dick, R. (2016). Think manager-think male, think follower-think female: Gender bias in implicit follower theories. *Journal of Applied Social Psychology*, 47, 344–388.

Burrell, G., & Morgan, G. (1979). *Sociological paradigms and organizational analysis*. London: Heinemann.

Catalyst. (2013, January 23). Why diversity matters. Retrieved from www.catalyst.org/knowledge/why-diversity-matters

Committee for Economic Development. (2012). *Fulfilling the promise: How more women on corporate boards would make America and American companies more competitive.* Retrieved from www.fwa.org/pdf/CED_WomenAdvancementonCorporateBoards.pdf

Cunningham, C. M., Crandall, H. M., & Dare, A. (Eds.). (2017). *Gender, communication, and the leadership gap.* Charlotte, NC: Information Age Publishing.

Devnew, L. E., Burke, R. J., Le Ber, M. J., & Torchia, M. (Eds.). (forthcoming). *More women on boards of directors: An international perspective.* Charlotte, NC: Information Age Publishing.

Diehl, A. B., & Dzubinski, L. M. (2016). Making the invisible visible: A cross-sector analysis of gender-based leadership barriers. *Human Resource Development Quarterly*, 27(2), 181–206.

Dweck, C. S. (2006). *Mindset: How you can fulfil your potential.* New York, NY: Random House.

Elliott, C., Stead, V., Mavin, S., & Williams, J. (Eds.). (2016). *Gender, media, and organization: Challenging mis(s)representations of women leaders and managers.* Charlotte, NC: Information Age Publishing.

Emerson, K. T. U., & Murphy, M. C. (2015). A company I can trust? Organizational lay theories moderate stereotype threat for women. *Personality and Social Psychology Bulletin, 41*(2), 295–307.

Goryunova, E., Scribner, R. T., & Madsen, S. R. (2017). The current status of women leaders worldwide. In S. R. Madsen (Ed.), *Handbook of research on gender and leadership* (pp. 3–23). Cheltenham, UK: Edward Elgar Publishing.

Hammond, M., & Clapp-Smith, R., & Palanski, M. (2017). Beyond (just) the workplace: A theory of leader development across multiple domains. *Academy of Management Review, 42*(3), 481–498.

Hassard, J., & Wolfram Cox, J. (2013). Can sociological paradigms still inform organizational analysis? A paradigm model for post-paradigm times. *Organization Studies*, 34(11), 1701–1728.

Joshi, A., Neely, B., Emrich, C., Griffiths, D., & George, G. (2015). Gender research in AMJ: An overview of five decades of empirical research and calls to action. *Academy of Management Journal*, 58(5), 1459–1475. doi:10.5465/amj.2015.4011

Kark, R., Preser, R., & Zion-Waldoks, T. (2016). From a politics of dilemmas to a politics of paradoxes: Feminism, pedagogy, and women's leadership for social change. *Journal of Management Education, 40*(3), 293–320.

Kuzhabekova, A., & Almukhambertova, A. (2017). Female academic leadership in the post-Soviet context. *European Educational Research Journal*, 16(2–3), 183–199.

Lemoine, G. J., Aggarwal, I., & Bujold Steed, L. (2016). When women emerge as leaders: Effects of extraversion and gender composition in groups. *The Leadership Quarterly, 27*, 470–486.

Lillenfeld, D. E. (2014, January 7). Measures to increase gender diversity on corporate boards gain traction. *New York Law Journal, 251*(4), 1–2.

Longman, K. A., & Madsen, S. R. (Eds.). (2014). *Women and leadership in higher education.* Charlotte, NC: Information Age Publishing.

Luthans, F., Youssef, C. M., & Avoilio, B. J. (2015). *Psychological capital and beyond.* New York, NY: Oxford University Press.

Madsen, S. R. (2007). Developing leadership: Exploring childhoods of women university presidents. *Journal of Educational Administration, 45*(1), 99–118.

Madsen, S. R. (2008). *On becoming a woman leader: Learning from the experiences of university presidents.* San Francisco, CA: Jossey-Bass.

Madsen, S. R. (2009). *Developing leadership: Learning from the experiences of women governors.* Lanham, MD: University Press of America.

Madsen, S. R. (2010). Leadership development in the United Arab Emirates: The transformational learning experiences of women. *Journal of Leadership and Organizational Studies, 17*(1), 100–110. doi:10.1177/1548051809345254

Madsen, S. R. (2015). Why do we need more women leaders in Utah? *Research & Policy Brief, Utah Women & Leadership Project.* Retrieved from www.uvu.edu/uwlp/docs/uwlpbrief2015no5.pdf

Madsen, S. R. (Ed.). (2017a). *Handbook of research on gender and leadership.* Cheltenham, UK: Edward Elgar Publishing.

Madsen, S. R. (2017b). Introduction. In S. R. Madsen (Ed.), *Handbook of research on gender and leadership* (pp. XXV-XXXVII). Cheltenham, UK: Edward Elgar Publishing.

Madsen, S. R., Ngunjiri, F. W., Longman, K. A., & Cherrey, C. (Eds.). (2015). *Women and leadership around the world.* Charlotte, NC: Information Age Publishing.

Madsen, S. R., & Scribner, R. T. (2017). A perspective on gender in management: The need for strategic cross-cultural scholarship on women in management and leadership. *Cross Cultural & Strategic Management, 24*(2), 231–250.

McKinsey Global Institute. (2015, September). The power of parity: How advancing women's equality can add $12 trillion to global growth. *McKinsey & Company.* Retrieved from www.mckinsey.com/global-themes/employment-and-growth/how-advancing-womens-equality-can-add-12-trillion-to-global-growth

Ngunjiri, F. W., & Madsen, S. R. (Eds.). (2015). *Women as global leaders.* Charlotte, NC: Information Age Publishing.

Rosser-Mims, D., McNellis, J., Johnson-Bailey, J., & McIlmoyl, M. (Eds.). (forthcoming). *Advancing women in leadership: Shaping pathways in the political arena.* Charlotte, NC: Information Age Publishing.

Samier, E. (2015). Emirati women's higher educational leadership formation under globalization: Culture, religion, politics, and the dialectics or modernization. *Gender and Education, 27*(3), 239–254.

Schein, V. E. (1975). Relationships between sex role stereotypes and requisite management characteristics among female managers. *Journal of Applied Psychology, 60*(3), 340.

Storberg-Walker, J., & Haber-Curran, P. (Eds.). (2017). *Theorizing women & leadership: New insights & contributions from multiple perspectives.* Charlotte, NC: Information Age Publishing.

Storberg-Walker, J., & Madsen, S. R. (2017). *The women and leadership theory think tank report 2015.* Retrieved from www.uvu.edu/uwlp/docs/wlthinktankreport2015.pdf

Storberg-Walker, J., & Natt och Dag, K. (2017). Creativity in theorizing for women and leadership: A multi-paradigm perspective. In S. R. Madsen (Ed.), *Handbook of research on gender and leadership* (pp. 65–84). Cheltenham, UK: Edward Elgar Publishing.

Women and Leadership Affinity Group. (2017). The Asilomar declaration and call to action on women and leadership. In S. R. Madsen (Ed.), *Handbook of research on gender and leadership* (pp. 24–48). Cheltenham, UK: Edward Elgar Publishing.

Woolley, A. W., Chabris, C. F., Pentland, A., Hashmi, N., & Malone, T. W. (2010, October 2). Collective intelligence: Number of women in group linked to effectiveness in solving difficult problems. *Science Daily*. Retrieved from www.sciencedaily.com/releases/2010/09/100930143339.htm

INDEX